THE GLOBAL CHANCELLOR

The Global Chancellor

*Helmut Schmidt and the Reshaping of the
International Order*

KRISTINA SPOHR

OXFORD
UNIVERSITY PRESS

OXFORD

UNIVERSITY PRESS

Great Clarendon Street, Oxford, OX2 6DP,
United Kingdom

Oxford University Press is a department of the University of Oxford.
It furthers the University's objective of excellence in research, scholarship,
and education by publishing worldwide. Oxford is a registered trade mark of
Oxford University Press in the UK and in certain other countries

© Kristina Spohr 2016

The moral rights of the author have been asserted

First Edition published in 2016

Impression: 1

Published in the United States of America by Oxford University Press
198 Madison Avenue, New York, NY 10016, United States of America

British Library Cataloguing in Publication Data
Data available

Library of Congress Control Number: 2015956793

ISBN 978–0–19–874779–6

Printed in Great Britain by
Clays Ltd, St Ives plc

Vaarille

For Zara and George Steiner

He is convinced most of the time that
he's the only real leader in the western world.
He is also probably right.
The problem is he's German.

One of Schmidt's party colleagues in Hamburg
21 September 1980

Perfektionistisch,
launisch,
stets auf der Suche,
fordernd,
inspirierend,
immer zuverlässig.

Henry Kissinger
23 November 2015

Contents

List of Illustrations

List of Abbreviations

AAPD	*Akten zur Auswärtigen Politik der Bundesrepublik Deutschland*
AdsD	Archiv der sozialen Demokratie, Koblenz, Bonn
BA	German Federal Archives (*Bundesarchiv*)
BSR	Federal Security Council (*Bundessicherheitsrat*)
CDU	Christian Democratic Union of Germany (*Christlich Demokratische Union Deutschlands*)
CSCE	Conference on Security and Cooperation in Europe
CSU	Christian Social Union (*Christlich-Soziale Union*)
DEB	Depositum Egon Bahr
DKP	German Communist Party (*Deutsche Kommunistische Partei*)
DPC	Defence Planning Committee (NATO)
DzD	*Dokumente zur Deutschlandpolitik*
EA	Eigene Arbeiten
EC	European Community
ERW	enhanced radiation warhead ('neutron bomb')
EU	European Union
FAZ	*Frankfurter Allgemeine Zeitung*
FBS	forward-based systems
FDP	Free Democratic Party (*Freie Demokratische Partei*)
FRG	Federal Republic of Germany (West Germany)
G5	Group of Five
G6	Group of Six
G7	Group of Seven
GDR	German Democratic Republic (East Germany)
GLCMs	ground-launched cruise missiles
GWU	George Washington University
HLG	High Level Group (NATO)
HSA	Helmut Schmidt Archiv
HSPA	Helmut Schmidt Privatarchiv, Hamburg
IISS	International Institute for Strategic Studies, London
INF	intermediate-range nuclear forces
IRBMs	intermediate-range ballistic missiles
JCL	Jimmy Carter Presidential Library, Atlanta
LRTNFs	long-range theatre nuclear forces
LTDP	long-term defence programme
MBFR	mutual and balanced force-reduction (talks)
MIRV	multiple independently targetable re-entry vehicles
NARA	National Archives and Records, College Park
NATO	North Atlantic Treaty Organization
NPG	Nuclear Planning Group (NATO)
NSA	National Security Archive, Washington, DC
OPEC	Organization of Petroleum Exporting Countries
PAAA	Politisches Archiv des Auswärtigen Amts, Berlin

PII	Pershing II missiles
RB	reduced blast (warhead)
RW	radiological warfare
SALT	Strategic Arms Limitation Talks
SCC	Special Coordinating Committee (USA)
SG	Special Working Group (NATO)
SLCMs	submarine-launched cruise missiles
SPD	Social Democratic Party of Gemany (*Sozialdemokratische Partei Deutschlands*)
TNA	The National Archives, Kew, London
TNFs	theatre nuclear forces
US DDRS	US Declassified Documents Reference System
ZA	Zwischenarchiv

Acknowledgements

One of the great pleasures of completing a book is the chance it affords to express my gratitude to all the individuals who facilitated the process of researching and writing it. I would like to thank first the numerous helpful archivists and staff of the Bundesarchiv, Politisches Archiv des Auswärtigen Amts, Friedrich-Ebert-Stiftung, Jimmy Carter Presidential Library, Gerald R. Ford Presidential Library, Ronald Reagan Presidential Library, US National Archives, Georgetown University Library Special Collections, Library of Congress, National Security Archive, Wilson Center, UK National Archives, and the Margaret Thatcher Foundation, as well as of AP images, Bundesbildstelle, DPA, Stern, and Sven Simon Fotoagentur. I am especially grateful to Helge Danielsson who helped me gain access to Norwegian Defence Ministry papers, Jonathan Hunt and Margit W. Gaarmann for their assistance at the Reagan Library and Staatsbibliothek zu Berlin, and Horst Haitzinger for his cartoon.

This work, however, only became what it is thanks to my time at the Helmut Schmidt Privatarchiv in Hamburg with the indefatigable assistance of Frau Heike Lemke. Over the course of two years I spent more than a dozen weeks with her, scouring documents, speeches, notes, book manuscripts, and photos. I also owe it to Frau Lemke that I was able to have my second, long conversation with Helmut Schmidt on 15 October 2015 at his home. Barely a month later he would be dead. It is here that I wish to express my deep gratitude to the late chancellor for granting me access to his papers in spring 2013 and also for the first, very lengthy interview in October 2013 at his office, which Frau Andrea Bazzato of *Die Zeit* so kindly organized then.

In exploring global Cold War politics and the German predicament therein through Helmut Schmidt's eyes, I have accumulated many intellectual debts. Over many years I have greatly enjoyed the congenial atmosphere of Christ's College, Cambridge. I learned a lot from doctoral students—my own at LSE and those of other scholars, especially Elizabeth Benning, Eirini Karamouzi, Rui Lopes, Zhong Zhong Chen, and Rita Augestad Knudsen, as well as Martin Albers, Bernhard Blumenau, Mathias Häussler, Andreas Lutsch, and Ilaria Parisi. Conversations with Markku Anttila, Frederic Bozo, William Burr, Stefan Forss, Tim Geiger, Jussi Hanhimäki, Beatrice Heuser, Mark Kramer, Chai Lieven, Piers Ludlow, Vojtech Mastny, Emmanuel Mourlon-Druol, Gottfried Niedhart, Leopoldo Nuti, Kathryn Rix, Patrick Salmon, Daniel Sargent, Mary Elise Sarotte, Benedikt Schoenborn, Brendan Simms, Georges-Henri Soutou, Jyrki Vesikansa, Richard Vinen, Jakob von Weizsäcker, Arne Westad, and Benjamin Ziemann helped me sharpen my arguments and look at the 1970s from many different perspectives.

Then there are the inspiring historians and friends who so generously gave up their time to read this work, whatever the state of completion. It is thanks to them that in spite of the lack of any leave and my being Deputy Head of Department this book got written. My first debt is to Steve Casey. Not only did he introduce me to the wonderful haven of the Library of Congress and the bizarre inner workings of the NARA; he read all drafts, and, above all, kept reminding me that life and 'Schmidt' surely mattered more than the daily excesses of LSE admin troubles. During the most intense writing phase, it was David Reynolds who ventured to enter into conversation with me over 'Helmut the First'. I cannot possibly repay the huge intellectual debt for all those stimulating hours of discussion and sometimes fierce debate, but I take solace in the fact that talking history was really fun for both of us.

I am also very grateful to Richard Evans, Jon Parry, and James Mackenzie who offered thoughtful feedback and instant reactions to my introduction; and to Sönke Neitzel, Andreas Rödder, and Jonathan Steinberg: all three provided immensely insightful comments on the final draft, and Jonathan pushed me to think about the title.

Last, but not least, I thank Christopher Clark for reading at the end every word so critically—with so much care and fondness.

In all of this, my adorable god-children (Anna Lisa, Daniel, James, and Clio) put everything to do with world politics into proportion, drawing me into that happiness beyond history. But thanks are also due for the many sparkling conversations with certain non-history friends—Sanna, Lizzie, Gavin, Nick, Uli, Alexia, Kolfinna, Torsten, Peter, Ariel, Dorle—in recent times often in the purposely chosen remoteness of Tortola, Arrowsic, and Grindavík.

I was fortunate that my editor at OUP, Robert Faber, his assistant editor, Cathryn Steele, and the production manager, Manikandan Chandrasekaran, bore with me over the book's changing nature and timetable, epitomized in the title debate and then the sudden media pressures after Schmidt's death. I appreciate their support in these matters and all their work in facilitating a very speedy production. I also benefited from my copy editor Henry MacKeith's super-precise work in seeking out any inconsistencies and wading through my multilingual footnotes, and I am glad he remained good-humoured when I forcefully stuck to my choice of words.

My parents, Marjatta and Edmund, have always been there in thought and offered their unwavering support, even if I have not been much of a physical presence in their lives in Germany. This is a book for them to look back at a time and place when they were young and I was only taking my first steps, literally.

Finally, there is my Finnish grandfather Toivo Anttila who, at 104, is—like Schmidt was—a man of the century and also someone who knew and fought war. He used to be a farmer, not a chancellor. I am indebted to him for many things that are much more important than this book but which made writing the book and understanding Schmidt, the man, possible. One generation down are Zara and George Steiner, whom I deeply admire 'als Intellektuelle und Menschen' and to whom I express my gratitude for their friendship and love over many years in Cambridge. *The Global Chancellor* is dedicated to them.

ARKS, 6.xii.2015

Introduction

In 1982, near the end of Helmut Schmidt's chancellorship, *Der Spiegel* delivered a damning verdict on his eight and a half years in power. Schmidt was dismissed as a 'good chancellor with a bad record, because few things stood out or endured as proof of success'. By contrast, the West German weekly described his predecessor Willy Brandt as 'a bad head of government with a good record in power', praising the achievements of his *Ostpolitik* in revolutionizing Bonn's relations with East Germany and the Soviet Union.

This has also been the verdict of historians. For instance, in Archie Brown's study of political leadership, Konrad Adenauer, Willy Brandt, and Helmut Kohl figure as West German chancellors who redefined the politically possible and introduced radical changes of policy, whereas Schmidt merits one paragraph with the observation that he 'hardly matched' the 'historical significance' of Brandt.[1] Similarly, historian Ronald J. Granieri, describing recent impressions of German chancellors, features Adenauer and Kohl in what he dubs the 'Christian Democrat Hall of Fame'. For the 'Social Democratic Hall of Fame' he links Brandt—'the great titan of the post war SPD'—with Gerhard Schröder who brought the party back to power in 1998 after 'sixteen years in the wilderness' due to what was widely perceived as the divisive effects of Schmidt's 'neo-Cold Warrior' policies that split the party and in turn destroyed his coalition.[2]

When Schmidt died on 10 November 2015—aged 96—the cascade of obituaries offered in one short moment multiple perspectives on him as a man of the century, a '*Jahrhundertmann*'. After thirty years as an elder statesman, Schmidt, they pointed out, had won the respect and even the affection of most Germans, as what the *Badische Zeitung* called 'the omniscient counsellor (*Universalratgeber*) of the German people'. But the judgement on his chancellorship remained lukewarm. Indeed, the elder statesman image never entirely superseded the original slightly patronizing appraisal of Schmidt as essentially a sober 'pragmatist' and 'competent' manager in the face of crises such as Baader Meinhof terrorism who made little progress on the big issue of the 'German question'. In the same vein, the *Frankfurter Allgemeine Zeitung* praised Schmidt for his 'power and elegance', but concluded that the 'achievements of his political life [his *politische Lebensleistung*] did not reach the heights attained by Konrad Adenauer and Helmut Kohl'; nor was he 'idolized' like Brandt. In other words, compared with those regarded as the 'best' leaders of the Federal Republic, Schmidt's chancellorship was found lacking.

This book takes a different view of Helmut Schmidt's place in history, by setting his chancellorship in a wider, global context. From this perspective, he emerges as a pivotal figure, shaping international affairs in a crisis-ridden decade.[3] During the 1970s the Western world experienced global turmoil—economic, social, and political. In the wake of the financial and energy crises, capitalism seemed to be faltering. And as détente between the superpowers came under pressure, the prospect of a more peaceful era in world politics was fading. Deep anxieties over political and socio-economic stability plagued not just Western political elites but also ordinary people, generating acute political tensions. Global and local issues became increasingly intertwined. Nowhere was the perception and reality of crisis more intense than on the front line of Europe's Cold War divide, in the Federal Republic of Germany (FRG).

In what follows, I examine how Schmidt tackled these problems in West Germany, Europe, and the wider world. He was ahead of his time in discerning the dynamics of what would become known as 'globalization'. As chancellor he developed diplomatic mechanisms, notably informal summitry, and created institutions such as the G7 (Group of Seven) that were needed to facilitate cooperation in an ever more interdependent world. At a time when East–West tensions were on the rise, he worked to maintain and expand dialogue between the two superpowers—building on Adenauer's policy of *Westbindung* and Brandt's *Neue Ostpolitik*, both of which had concentrated on rehabilitating Germany in the heart of Europe. He also anticipated the emergence of China as the world's third power and inserted himself into the diplomacy of triangularity. Schmidt was distinctive in being a leader as comfortable with questions of economics as of security, and in combining both in a skilfully crafted policy of peace and stability that transformed West Germany into a protagonist on the global stage.

Schmidt's unusual versatility in security and economics had deep personal and intellectual roots. His interest in military affairs grew out of his experience in the wartime *Wehrmacht* and post-war *Bundeswehr* (West German armed forces), on which he drew as defence minister under Brandt from 1969 to 1972. He also had a degree in economics and served as Brandt's finance minister in 1972–4 before suddenly being appointed chancellor in May 1974 when Brandt's government collapsed amid scandal. But what Schmidt brought to the top job was not merely rich and diverse experience but also an unusual depth of thought and reflection. Ever since the 1950s, he had written regularly on politics and international affairs for his local Hamburg newspaper *Bergedorfer Zeitung* and for the Social Democratic Party. In the 1960s he authored two best-selling books on strategy and defence, which were translated into English—giving him a reputation as a defence intellectual on both sides of the Atlantic. Similarly his theoretical analyses of the global economic crisis and his conceptual thinking about the centrality of global economic governance in foreign policy earned him the nickname 'the world economist' (*Der Weltökonom*). This was the intellectual capital on which he drew for the new global order that he would help to design.[4]

No other statesman of the 1970s was both a doer and thinker on this scale.[5] Schmidt's close friend and ally, the French President Valéry Giscard d'Estaing, had even greater experience in financial affairs, but he was a technocrat who lacked Schmidt's background in defence. Nor was Giscard a writer or conceptual thinker.

Henry Kissinger, the American national security adviser and later secretary of state, had immense experience of diplomacy and security and he could utilize his scholarly hinterland as a historian and political scientist at Harvard.[6] At the end of Richard Nixon's presidency, after Watergate took hold, and under Nixon's successor Gerald Ford, Kissinger was effectively the maker of American foreign policy. But he was not at home in economics and, however influential, he never held political office. Schmidt, by contrast, was a head of government and thus held ultimate responsibility as a democratic leader. This obliged him to conduct foreign policy all the time in the electoral arena. The task proved particularly difficult because of his shaky political base—leading a coalition government with the Free Democrats, who became increasingly fractious and, without ever being party chief, trying to manage a Social Democratic Party whose left wing was deeply sceptical about his diplomatic priorities. Schmidt therefore provides an intriguing example of what political scientist Robert Putnam has called 'playing games at two levels': the international and the domestic.[7]

Schmidt deserves attention, then, as a remarkable practitioner in global affairs who had to juggle policy and politics. He did so with sufficient success to win two elections and hold on to office against the political odds from May 1974 to October 1982—much longer than any of his predecessors (Ludwig Erhard, Kurt Georg Kiesinger, and Brandt) except Adenauer. His long tenure as chancellor also compares favourably with that of his major Western counterparts: Schmidt interacted with four US presidents (Nixon, Ford, Carter, and Reagan), three British prime ministers (Wilson, Callaghan, and Thatcher) and two French presidents (Giscard and Mitterrand).

Moreover, this book will argue that through his skill and longevity he also left legacies that have outlived him and still endure as marks of real statesmanship. At a time when the Bretton Woods system of international financial management had broken down, Schmidt, together with Giscard, was the key architect of the G7 forum of political leaders who took charge of global economic management in the 1970s. Despite its faults and subsequent changes, this institution survives to the present day. On the European plane, Schmidt—again with Giscard—created the European Monetary System, which proved a stepping stone to the euro and complete European economic and monetary union. On the security front, Schmidt was the principal inspiration for NATO's 1979 'dual-track' strategy of re-establishing a nuclear balance in Europe by negotiating arms reductions under the threat of deploying new missiles. The Alliance's implementation of this strategy helped maintain NATO cohesion and credibility, and allowed it to negotiate from a position of strength. This firmness in part paved the way for the Soviet–American treaty of 1987 to eliminate intermediate-range nuclear forces (INFs)—the first time the two superpowers agreed to scrap a whole category of nuclear weapons. Although the missile deployment in the FRG was pushed through by Schmidt's successor, Helmut Kohl, and the INF treaty was concluded by the superpowers, Schmidt's dual-track policy can be said to have helped defuse the Cold War.

Schmidt's major initiatives in the domains of economics and security also enhanced West Germany's global influence and status, to lasting effect. By the early 1970s, Bonn had already established itself as a leading player in the global economy, but Schmidt's achievement, by means of the G7, was to convert this economic weight into political power and to secure a place at the top table of global economic governance. Furthermore, he raised West Germany's geopolitical salience to the level of a 'world power' through his participation as an equal in top-level summit discussions about nuclear policy and European defence. Over the dual track in 1979 the key strategic decisions were taken by the FRG together with America, Britain, and France—the three Western victor powers of World War Two and also members of the nuclear club. This 1 + 3 position of quasi-equality was gained in spite of the fact that Germany remained divided and still lacked full sovereignty. In 1980–2, as the 'New Cold War' set in, Schmidt went on to act as intermediary, or what he preferred to call 'double interpreter', between Moscow and Washington, thereby enhancing West Germany's diplomatic role. The 1 + 3 format, together with Schmidt's adroitness as double interpreter, showed that the Bonn republic was now overcoming its wartime past and moving into a position of equality, as well as gaining respect and credibility, among the world's great powers. None of his four predecessors, not even Adenauer or Brandt, had achieved such purchase in world affairs. Helmut Schmidt was indeed the global chancellor.

Schmidt did not, of course, resolve the German question. Brandt had already made the big leap of normalizing relations with the GDR and the Soviet bloc, and in the Schmidt era the next step—German unification—was simply not conceivable or possible because of renewed Cold War gridlock. By the late 1980s, the situation was much more fluid and then the sudden and surprising fall of the Wall opened up a fortuitous historic opportunity for his successor, Helmut Kohl. Nevertheless, if Schmidt had not so skilfully turned West Germany into a major diplomatic actor in the 1970s, Kohl would have found it much harder in 1990 to secure the agreement of the four victor powers (America, Russia, Britain, and France) for the unification of the two Germanies. In other words, 1 + 3 and double interpretation proved to be important precursors of 2 + 4.

* * * * *

This is a novel perspective. Over the past decade a few lengthy biographical works on Helmut Schmidt have appeared in German, together with several monographs on aspects of his foreign policy.[8] There have also been useful studies on Schmidt's economic diplomacy, including his role in the making of the G7.[9] But none within the compass of a single volume has tackled the chancellor's handling of both economic and security issues, while keeping an eye on how all this interacted with his domestic concerns. Another distinctive feature of *The Global Chancellor* is that the book takes Schmidt seriously as a sophisticated conceptual thinker, exploring the roots of his ideas and his evolution into a 'published expert' with unique authority. By delineating Schmidt's intellectual hinterland before he assumed the chancellorship, we are able to appreciate his actions as political leader in new ways. As a result Schmidt—often considered as merely a pragmatic crisis-manager and viewed predominantly through the looking glass of German domestic politics—is revealed here as a statesman-intellectual with the ideas and experience, the vision and determination, to shape the course of world events. Because I locate his foreign policy in the broad international context, this study can contribute to the growing literature on the 1970s as an era of emerging global interdependence. It is striking, however, that key works in this field scarcely mention Schmidt: Niall Ferguson's major edited collection *The Shock of the Global: The 1970s in Perspective*, for example, gives him only three brief mentions in over 430 pages.[10]

What follows is not an exhaustive account of Schmidt's chancellorship. I do not seek to cover every single aspect of his foreign policy. Some issues are not addressed in detail, for instance the specifics of Franco-German relations or developments in European integration.[11] Nor do I dwell on terrorism, either domestic or international, which was at times an urgent and politically sensitive threat to the FRG in the 1970s; or on the growing contemporary debate about the 'North–South divide'.[12] My focus is on peace and security at a higher level, namely what Schmidt saw as two truly existential threats to West Germany and the West as a whole: the potential collapse of capitalism and the possible outbreak of a third world war that would bring with it nuclear Armageddon. The book therefore stands out by straddling international history, intellectual biography, and domestic politics.

It also raises some larger theoretical implications for thinking on international relations (IR). First, by providing a case study of the role of human agency in politics and foreign policy; weighing up the relative importance of personality and intentions in shaping events, as opposed to the structural forces of time, place, and system. This has been a long-standing preoccupation of IR theorists, evident in classic works such as those by Kenneth Waltz and John Spanier.[13] To a remarkable extent, given the constraints within which Schmidt operated, he was often able to get his way on big issues. Much of this was due to the priority he gave to direct political communication with foreign leaders—a second general theme running through this book. He reflected on it theoretically and acted on it in practice, especially through intense and informal summit diplomacy.[14] Third, and closely related to communication, was Schmidt's concept of political friendship.[15] With some leaders he felt an instinctive personal rapport as well as discerning a genuine alignment of national interests, notably with Giscard. Even where interests were largely opposed, as in the case of the Soviet bloc, cultivating good personal relationships could ease tensions or at least reduce unpredictability, as he believed was possible with Brezhnev. Yet, despite Schmidt's pre-occupation with effective communication and political friendship, he completely botched relations with Jimmy Carter, leader of the FRG's most important international ally. Carter constantly got under his skin and Schmidt often found it difficult to keep his temper with the American president. It is striking that this accomplished theoretician and practitioner of personal diplomacy could sometimes lose control of his own personality, endangering the goals he was trying to achieve.

The novelty of *The Global Chancellor* lies not only in its approach to the subject and the underlying themes but also in the substantial array of sources on which it rests. I made extensive use of printed sources in German, French, and English—memoirs, newspaper articles, and opinion polls, as well as electoral and economic data. These helped to situate the man in his larger national and international context. The main base, however, is the government archives of Germany, the United

States, Great Britain, and Norway. Additionally, in Germany I worked extensively in collections at the Friedrich-Ebert-Stiftung (the SPD party's foundation), and was allowed to consult Schmidt's voluminous personal papers at his private archive in Hamburg, including drafts of his publications and speeches, plus notes, off-the-record briefings and interviews—all of which are invaluable in revealing how his thinking developed and his political career evolved. Helmut Schmidt also graciously granted me two lengthy interviews, in 2013 and 2015, which added colour and atmosphere to the documents—bringing history alive. The first, at his *Die Zeit* office, was a formal meeting with the elder statesman; the second, in his home three weeks before his death, was a more personal encounter with Schmidt the man.

The book proceeds broadly along chronological lines but there is some shifting back and forward in time to set up particular themes. It is therefore worth briefly prefiguring the structure and argument here. The opening chapter, on Schmidt and the management of the global economic crisis of the mid 1970s, begins by laying out the political circumstances—international and domestic—that were his inheritance in May 1974, when he was unexpectedly catapulted into power after the Guillaume spy affair brought down his predecessor, Willy Brandt. The global capitalist economy was reeling from a series of major international crises during 1973–5, which had shattered the West's sense of stability and security: the collapse of the Bretton Woods monetary system, the explosion of oil prices, the worldwide recession, and the ensuing malaise of inflation and stagnation ('stagflation'). Schmidt was immediately thrust into being a 'crisis-manager'. But he approached that task with considerable experience as a finance minister, and with a clear conceptual perspective based on a recognition that global economics had moved to the centre of foreign policy and that economic stabilization was essential for the survival of Western democracy in the Cold War. The chapter traces the evolution of the G7 into a new form of global economic governance through four summits, from Rambouillet in 1975 to Bonn in 1978. While external pressures may have pushed Western leaders into cooperation, Schmidt's catalytic role was crucial. As a way to broker compromise, he cleverly exploited the FRG's leverage as a world economic power and the strength of the West German stabilization model (reducing inflation before promoting growth), capitalizing on his commitment to direct personal engagement among leaders.

Chapter 2, on security issues, runs in parallel to the first, again exploring the experience and ideas he brought to bear when he entered the Chancellery. This traces Schmidt's evolution into a defence intellectual of transatlantic renown during the 1950s and 1960s and also draws attention to his role as a crisis-manager when a massive tidal wave hit Hamburg in February 1962, winning him the sobriquet 'Lord of the Flood' and national recognition as an effective leader. He assumed office as chancellor at a time when superpower détente was on the wane and *Ostpolitik*, the hallmark of the Brandt government, had lost its momentum. Schmidt had been one of the architects of that policy—a point that is often overlooked—but, unlike Brandt and his aide Egon Bahr, he deemed relations with the

Soviet bloc to be a question of security as much as diplomacy. In other words, they had to be understood in the context of the East–West balance of power (which, in Schmidt's mind, encompassed China, the world's emerging third power). This approach, which he had developed in his writings over the previous decade, had come into particularly sharp focus in 1966 during a car journey that he made with his family across Eastern Europe and Western Russia, all the way to Moscow. The trip left him with a profound sense of both the geo-political power and also the economic vulnerability of the Soviet Union. Around this apparent paradox he built his belief that it was only possible to negotiate meaningfully with Moscow from a position of military equilibrium. Unlike Bahr, whom he considered a utopian idealist, he did not advocate pan-European solutions to East–West problems. Unlike the White House, as détente cooled he was determined to maintain dialogue between East and West in order to advance arms control in Europe and progress on the German question. These strategic ideas would guide West German foreign policy throughout Schmidt's chancellorship. By the time he won re-election in 1976 *Ostpolitik* had become an aspect of defence policy: his mantra now was deterrence first, détente second.

This leads us into the theme of the third chapter; the so-called 'neutron bomb affair' in 1977–8 that generated a fundamental crisis of confidence between Bonn and Washington. The arguments over strategy were exacerbated at the human level by the friction between the chancellor and new American president Jimmy Carter, whom Schmidt considered unfit for the job from the outset. The Carter administration proposed to develop enhanced radiation warheads (ERWs), popularly known as neutron bombs, as a way to offset Soviet conventional superiority in Europe. Despite his personal antipathy to the ERWs (and all nuclear weapons), Schmidt was willing to support the deterrent value of the neutron bomb in order to shore up the European balance of power. But the West German media focused on what would happen if deterrence failed and the weapons were used in so-called 'limited nuclear warfare' in Central Europe, with Germany as the principal battlefield. This issue was played up by Bahr and the SPD left, leaving Schmidt teetering uneasily between his own political party, on one hand, and America as the FRG's military protector (*Schutzmacht*), on the other. His balancing act was made even harder by the Soviets who, on top of their conventional build-up, had started to deploy new SS-20 intermediate-range missiles, targeted on Western Europe, while also exploiting West German opposition to the ERWs through a public relations 'peace campaign'. The neutron bomb affair rumbled on for nine months. Gradually the chancellor worked his way towards a compromise position, first expressed in a major speech in London in October 1977 and painstakingly elaborated in a package deal with key NATO allies. But then Carter got cold feet about the ERWs and pulled out suddenly over the Easter weekend in 1978. Schmidt was furious at this U-turn, feeling it as a personal humiliation having put himself on the line for the president, and also as an ignominious snub to the Federal Republic. And because he had worked so hard to keep in step with the Americans against much of his party, he found SPD Schadenfreude even harder to bear.

Even after ERWs disappeared from the diplomatic agenda, the underlying problem of European nuclear security remained unresolved. This was what Schmidt called the 'grey area': imbalances in the European theatre that were not addressed in either strategic arms limitation talks (SALT) between the superpowers or the discussion on reduction of conventional forces between the two blocs (the so-called mutual and balanced force-reduction (MBFR) talks). Chapter 4 examines how NATO addressed this Euro-strategic security gap through the momentous dual-track decision of December 1979. The decision's seeds had been sown in internal Alliance discussions in 1977–8, but it was Schmidt who, as in the international economic sphere with the G7, instigated the crucial deliberations, at Guadeloupe in January 1979, bringing together the leaders of West Germany, France, Britain, and America. This 1 + 3 summit reflected Schmidt's basic diplomatic precepts: a meeting of a few key statesmen away from the media spotlight and conducted in an atmosphere of privacy and candour. Moreover, the Western Alliance's final decision on the dual track eleven months later embodied Schmidt's fundamental strategic concept of attaining an equilibrium of military forces in Europe—in this case by either negotiating mutual arms reductions or, if that failed, redressing the nuclear imbalance through new deployments. Both in diplomatic practice and strategic thought, therefore, Schmidt had decisively shaped NATO's decision. His success was all the sweeter considering his humiliation over the neutron bomb the previous year. And in the process he created a space for the Federal Republic at the nuclear top table—treated as an equal partner by the three Western countries that had defeated and occupied Germany in 1945. In the evolution of the G7, Schmidt had translated his country's position as an economic world power into commensurate influence in global economic governance. But in security matters, his achievement was more remarkable, given the FRG's low standing as a divided and semi-sovereign state excluded from the nuclear club. Through serious expertise and skilful diplomacy, Schmidt had leveraged power out of a position of impotence.

Yet success came at a price at home and abroad, as the final chapter makes clear. Although the SPD grudgingly backed the dual-track decision, Schmidt was denounced as a hawk by the pacifist left of his party. (Their mounting disaffection, as well as the fraying of the coalition, would pave the way for his downfall in October 1982.) Moscow immediately attacked NATO's decision, rejecting any talks on nuclear arms control, and its invasion of Afghanistan a few days later caused a total rift with Carter and the United States. Now superpower relations entered a state of deep freeze. Schmidt, in deep gloom about the international situation, talked of being on the brink of World War Three. He feared it would only need a small spark somewhere around the globe to ignite catastrophe in Europe—which made the situation analogous to 1914 when, as he saw it, the world had suddenly slithered into war over a crisis in the Balkans. In these circumstances, Schmidt was convinced that dialogue must be maintained at all costs between the superpowers, and he saw himself as the only leader who could bring this about. While loyally if grudgingly sticking with Carter over the American boycott of the Moscow Olympics, he was also the only Western leader in 1980–1 to travel to the Kremlin and to host Brezhnev in return. Schmidt believed that if the Soviets were driven into complete isolation, they might strike out belligerently. It was only in late 1981 that the chancellor coined the term 'double interpreter' but he was inter-acting in this way with Moscow and Washington throughout the New Cold War of the early 1980s. This was what he called *Weltpolitik*, a term that, of course, had sinister connotations from the era of the pre-1914 *Kaiserreich* but which Schmidt used unapologetically and in new ways. For him, engaging in *Weltpolitik* was inescapable if one wanted to address West Germany's political predicament in an era of global Cold War, and also essential if one wished to advance the country's prosperity in an era of interdependence.

This book is the story of how, under the leadership of Helmut Schmidt, West Germany came of age on the global stage.

1

The World Economist

It was an unlikely end and an improbable beginning. The finale of Willy Brandt's chancellorship came out of the blue, when Günter Guillaume, his close personal aide, was arrested on 24 April 1974 as an agent of the East German secret service. Brandt initially tried to bluff things out but his reputation was already tarnished by stories about his philandering and by his declining popularity within the Social Democratic Party (SPD) and in the country at large. On 6 May Brandt offered his resignation to Federal President Gustav Heinemann. And thus, improbably, Helmut Schmidt was catapulted into the chancellorship, which he would hold for eight and a half years.[1]

Schmidt had been Brandt's finance minister since 1972, having previously served as defence minister from the start of Brandt's government in 1969. The SPD turned to him as a rising star with extensive experience and Heinemann formally offered him the chancellorship on 16 May, which the Bundestag then confirmed by a vote of 267 to 225. At fifty-five, Schmidt was the youngest leader in the twenty-five-year history of the Federal Republic. He brought to the job real expertise in economics, as we shall see in this chapter; and also in defence policy, the subject of the next. Indeed this combination of skills in economics *and* defence made Schmidt a distinctive figure, both in West Germany and across the Western world.

The press was certainly intrigued by his first days in power; vivid stories abounded. One British journalist noted that Brandt had taken his desk with him, leaving Schmidt with 'only the portentous old piece of furniture' used by Konrad Adenauer, in an old-fashioned 'baroque' style. Schmidt regarded this as tasteless and crass; it was flung out unceremoniously and in its place he installed the 'nice modern desk' from his office in the Finance Ministry.[2]

Style also conveyed substance. Schmidt's working habits were organized and direct. He did not want to lose any time, forming his coalition cabinet of the Social Democrats and Free Democrats within a record-breaking ten days (see Figure 1.1), which the *New York Times* saw also as a sign of his skill as a deft political negotiator.[3] He brought to the chancellorship a business-like attitude—one paper likened him to a company director[4]—and imposed discipline on his colleagues in a way that the easy-going Brandt had rarely done.[5] The modern desk from the Finance Ministry also signified his priorities as chancellor in 1974, a year marked by deepening global economic crisis.[6] Moreover, his background as an economist as well as finance minister emboldened him to take a lead on these issues in a way that no West German chancellor had done since Ludwig Erhard. His inaugural speech as

Figure 1.1 Schmidt and his Cabinet, 16 May 1974.
Source: DPA.

chancellor insisted that economic stability could not be separated from military security: together these would be the foundations of peace. Schmidt told the Bundestag that his government's motto would be 'continuity and concentration'. He wanted to sustain Brandt's achievements in improving East–West relations but, for the moment, he would focus on pulling Germany and its allies out of the unprecedented economic crisis of soaring inflation, stagnant production, and high unemployment that had engulfed the West after two decades of steady growth and prosperity. His approach was avowedly pragmatic—'no government can work miracles', he proclaimed. Schmidt wanted to 'concentrate on what is essential and seek to achieve what is possible now'.[7]

THE POLITICIAN AS ECONOMIST

Schmidt had already set out the essential features of the world economic crisis in a memorandum he wrote as finance minister in April 1974, just one month before becoming chancellor. This 'Ökonomisches Papier' presented the crisis in the guise of a theatrical drama. Its prologue, he suggested, was the collapse in 1971 of the Bretton Woods monetary system which had been based on the convertibility of dollars into gold at a fixed rate. By 1973 all the world's major currencies were floating: in other words, their exchange rates were set not by governments but by the ebb and flow of international currency markets. This fundamental monetary insecurity both exacerbated and was exacerbated by domestic inflation. Act one, for Schmidt, was the explosion of oil prices following the Arab–Israeli war of October 1973, when the OPEC oil cartel drove up prices fourfold by the end of the year and also restricted supplies to noted backers of Israel, such as the United States and the Netherlands. OPEC's use of oil as a diplomatic weapon undermined another foundation of the West's post-war economic growth and stability—namely cheap, secure supplies of energy. Schmidt feared that OPEC would herald other raw material cartels. Act two was marked by the emerging trend, in response to infla-tion and the oil crisis, towards protectionist trade arrangements on a bilateral basis and a deepening global depression—reminiscent of how the world economy had disintegrated in the early 1930s. Schmidt was sure that cooperation and inter-dependence had been vital for Western economic growth since 1945. If stagnation persisted and autarchic tendencies developed, he foresaw a third and perhaps final act in which economics undermined politics, when the 'democratic structures within the industrial societies would break up', especially in countries such as Japan and those of the European Community that were heavily reliant on overseas exports and imported energy. The dire scenario set out in his paper, Schmidt insisted, was 'not an apocalyptic vision but a real possibility for the world economy'.[8]

The world economic crisis represented a shipwreck of all the ideas and institu-tions that had guided the West since 1945. Three major challenges presented themselves. A new system of international monetary management was needed to replace Bretton Woods. Equally important was a rethinking of economic philoso-phy now that the expansionary assumptions of Keynesianism were no longer axio-matic. The other great novelty was the sudden and basic challenge to Western prosperity from the cartel of Middle Eastern oil producers—previously ignored in the global power balance. When Schmidt assumed the chancellorship, the Western response to these three challenges had been hesitant, ineffective, and highly nation-alist—a case of *sauve qui peut* by each country, without clear grip and direction from political leaders. Brandt was no exception, being preoccupied with *Ostpolitik* relations with the Soviet bloc. Coming at the problem from his experience as finance minister, Schmidt made economics central to his foreign policy in the first years of his chancellorship. He was equally clear that answers had to be found cooperatively through discussion with fellow Western leaders: no narrowly national response to the crisis would work. Here Schmidt was drawing on his own experi-ence and memory of interwar Germany, ravaged first by hyperinflation and then severe depression in the decade 1923–33, the consequence of which, no German leader could forget, was the collapse of democracy and the triumph of dictatorship.[9]

Economics was inseparable from security. Two months after becoming chancel-lor, Schmidt made this point bluntly to the NATO Council. Although admitting that such a meeting 'might not be considered by everybody to be the appropriate audience', Schmidt had no compunction about lecturing NATO leaders at length on the problems of inflation, increased oil prices, and 'enormous, unheard-of' balance-of-payments deficits in many member states. The fact that these 'very, very grave dangers' in the world economic situation had not, in his opinion, been prop-erly understood gave him far more concern than the problems of East–West talks on arms control and 'all the rest of the fields which are so properly dealt with by foreign secretaries and defence secretaries'. This was the first time that Schmidt attended a NATO Council meeting as chancellor, making his economic interpretation of security even more striking. Schmidt was consciously offering a radical redefinition of strategy and foreign policy: these words, he argued, must not be confined to their classic fields but should encompass nothing less than the whole world economy. He spoke at a time when the détente agreements of the early 1970s signalled a new equality between the superpowers. Schmidt was concerned that, if the West was undermined by economic crisis, not only would its economic model lose credibility but democracy itself might collapse and with it the whole NATO alliance. The crisis of capitalism was, in short, a crunch point of the Cold War. He saw his role as rallying fellow statesmen to 'stabilise national economies and stabilise the world economy by international action'—a task he deemed second only to that of securing 'world peace', by which he meant avoiding nuclear annihilation.[10]

In this critical situation, political leadership was vital and Schmidt had no doubt that he was the man to provide it. This was partly because of his experience as finance minister, which had given him deep and detailed awareness of the economic crisis in a way Brandt never had or wished to have. It is noteworthy that many of the foreign political leaders with whom he would later shape a new regime of international economic governance had also been schooled as ministers of economics or finance.[11] Yet Schmidt's expertise in this area also had deeper roots. He had done an economics degree at university in his native Hamburg. One of his professors was Karl Schiller, later a ministerial colleague when serving as economics minister in 1966–72. Schmidt's student dissertation in 1949 examined the German and Japanese currency reforms after the Second World War. The Deutschmark (DM), introduced in 1948, proved vital not only for West Germany's economic recovery but also to restore national pride. And the DM would become a hallmark of the Bonn Republic's identity. Schmidt also highlighted the centrality of West Germany's financial rehabilitation for the post-war prosperity and political stability of Europe and the Western world. The whole story stood in marked contrast to the consequences of the economic black hole of the interwar period. These were lessons that Schmidt applied to the 1970s when thinking about what the FRG could do to help resolve the world economic crisis.[12]

On the face of it, West Germany had been less damaged than other allies by the collapse of Bretton Woods and the oil shock. To be sure, its own economy was more stable than the rest of Western Europe: in Germany the annual inflation rate in 1973 ran at 6.9 per cent and 7.2 per cent in 1974. The equivalent figures for United States were 4.7 and 10.2 per cent, and for France 6.4 per cent and 12.0 per cent. In terms of price stability, Bonn in fact outperformed everybody else. Moreover, the DM, alone among major currencies except for the Swiss franc, appreciated in value during this period. Nevertheless, Schmidt kept insisting, West Germany was not an island. If inflation deepened and real incomes declined, this would aggravate tensions between employers and employees, causing social unrest, and raise fundamental questions about the future of capitalism. His answer was a balanced policy, avoiding 'austerity' and seeking to stimulate investment, but eschewing Keynesian remedies that, he believed, would only fuel inflation.[13]

Schmidt was also conscious that West Germany had barely recovered from the violent social and political upheavals of 1968 and this posed particular problems for his own party. The SPD was in transition. No longer a hardline workers party, it attracted new and radical members who were students, academics, and white-collar staff. By the end of the 1970s two-thirds of the membership would be formed by these new recruits, often anti-capitalist and anti-American in outlook. His party political problems were exacerbated by Brandt's continued popularity with the left. Schmidt decided to retain Brandt as party chairman to ensure continuity and rebut any accusations that he had undermined his predecessor. This worked in the short term to ensure SPD unity and also saved him from the hassles of party management but over the long run it detached him from the grass roots. Holding his disparate and polarized party together (and keeping alive his friendship with Brandt across their ideological differences) would prove a growing problem for Schmidt as his chancellorship progressed; yet all this was essential for a conducting a stable foreign policy that commanded confidence abroad.[14]

Within the framework of international cooperation that Schmidt considered so important, two pillars stood out. In security issues, NATO was central, especially West Germany's alliance with the United States—Bonn's 'protector power' (*Schutzmacht*) since the Berlin Airlift of 1948 and the North Atlantic Treaty of 1949. The presence of US troops on West German soil, under the overall umbrella of America's nuclear arsenal, was critical for Bonn, which had been denied access to atomic, biological, and chemical weapons as a condition for joining NATO in 1955. Schmidt himself was deeply committed to the transatlantic partnership. He spoke fluent English—eliminating the need for interpreters—and had been a regular visitor to the United States since 1950, when he spent six weeks in Chicago, clocking up some forty visits by the time he became chancellor. On his own admission Schmidt 'marvelled' at America with its 'incredible vitality and dynamism', its 'optimistic disposition', and the 'moving spontaneity' of its people. His political contacts had been strengthened during his time as finance minister: he worked closely with George Shultz, US Treasury Secretary in 1972–4, who valued his grasp of both economic and security problems. 'When he arrived at my office, I saw immediately that we could communicate directly and easily', Shultz recalled in his memoirs. 'His penetrating intellect and great warmth and humor impressed me as those of a leader with an unusual breadth of vision. He was, I saw, both creative and energetic, deeply conscious of Germany's history and his place in history.' The respect he commanded in Washington would stand Schmidt in good stead after he became chancellor.[15]

The FRG's bond with the United States remained axiomatic for Schmidt but, by 1974, he had become worried about America's reliability as a partner. More than the 1973–4 oil crisis, he blamed America's deficit funding of the Vietnam War for fuelling world inflation. And the weakening of the American economy and the humiliating failure in Indochina, eventually overrun by the communists in 1975, raised questions about US power, while the Soviet Union appeared to be on the rise. Worse still, there were doubts about American leadership itself because of the power vacuum in Washington. President Richard Nixon had been destroyed by the Watergate scandal: forced to resign in August 1974, he was succeeded by his vice president Gerald Ford, a long-time Republican congressman with limited ability and no executive experience. Man to man, Schmidt and Ford got on very well: they were soon on first-name terms, shared jokes, and, as Ford put it, saw 'eye to eye on almost everything'. Indeed the president would later cite their relationship to underscore 'a point overlooked in discussions of foreign policy—the importance of personality'. That said, Ford was essentially a caretaker president (the first president never to have been on a national ticket). Admittedly the veteran Henry Kissinger remained in charge of foreign policy, having served as Nixon's national security advisor since 1969 and then from 1973 as secretary of state to Nixon and Ford. But the general undermining of American power in 1973–5 at a time of global economic crisis caused real concern in Bonn about the solidity of its transatlantic bond.[16]

The German–American relationship will be a major theme of later chapters. Equally important for Schmidt was the European Community, which had brought the Federal Republic, after the trauma of the *Hitlerzeit*, into a new era of peace and prosperity. For Schmidt, the Atlantic and European pillars were mutually reinforcing. As he put it in his inaugural speech, Bonn was fundamentally committed to 'the political unity of Europe in partnership with the United States'.[17]

At the heart of the European Community was the Franco-German tandem, forged by Konrad Adenauer and Charles de Gaulle in the Elysée Treaty of 1963. During the Brandt era relations had sometimes become strained, but a new chapter opened in May 1974, when Schmidt's elevation to the chancellorship on 16 May was followed three days later by the election of Valéry Giscard d'Estaing as president of France. The two men had much in common. Both were economists by background and had been finance ministers before taking on the role of national leaders. Even more important, they had already become good friends, regularly dining incognito at a favourite restaurant, *Au Boeuf*, at Blaesheim in Alsace, and talking animatedly in English—the foreign language they were both most comfortable in—allowing them to talk *à deux*. And by May 1974 they had developed a real relationship of trust, based on their commitment to the European project and on the need to combat inflation and protectionism. This bond transcended ideological and party allegiances, because Giscard's Gaullist background was a far cry from Schmidt's roots in social democracy. Not surprisingly, given this strong political friendship, Schmidt's first foreign trip as chancellor was to Paris at the end of May, only two weeks after taking office, and this was followed by a formal Franco-German summit on 8–9 July. These two meetings were the prelude to an intensely close relationship between the two leaders. Between 1974 and 1981 they met fourteen times as part of the biannual process of summits stipulated in the Elysée Treaty, and a further ten times officially. They also had countless weekly telephone conversations, as well as many meetings on the margins of multilateral summits (Figure 1.2 shows them in animated discussion at Schloβ Gymnich in Bonn).[18]

Figure 1.2 Schmidt and Giscard, 8 July 1974.
Source: AP.

But there were limits to the cooperation between Bonn and Paris. One example was France's flip-flops on monetary policy. In an attempt to achieve some convergence of European currencies in an era of floating exchange rates, the two governments had supported the idea of a currency 'snake'—a loose banding of exchange rates. Although this was intended as a first step towards eventual monetary union, in January 1974 France pulled out of the snake, despite the offer of a massive loan from Bonn. By the summer, however, French policies were again moving somewhat closer to the thinking in Bonn: Schmidt was pleased that Giscard, as president, now seemed to be adopting his tough line on inflation. For Schmidt, price stability was what he called an 'existential question' (*Lebensfrage*) for all of Europe, and it could only be achieved by coordinated international action because the world economy was so interdependent.[19] Transatlantic relations were an even more important area of divergence between the two governments. Giscard, in line with the Gaullist tradition, tried to keep some distance from the United States, whereas Schmidt's instincts were always more Atlanticist. On the oil crisis, for instance, Henry Kissinger wanted consumer solidarity to confront OPEC and force down its prices, whereas Giscard favoured the more consensual approach of an international conference of consumers and producers. France, unlike the FRG, refused to join Kissinger's International Energy Agency, leaving Kissinger fuming about 'French sabotage'. It was not until the end of 1974 that the Americans and French patched up their differences: Washington agreed to participate in Giscard's consumer–producer conference, while Paris said it would cooperate 'on parallel paths' with the IEA to cut energy use and develop alternative fuels. But the Ford administration's energy conservation plans were blocked by Congress and France's grand conference, which finally opened in December 1975, made little progress because of the huge divergence between the interests of the industrial states, the OPEC cartel, and the less-developed countries.[20]

For Schmidt, the consumer–producer impasse was symptomatic of a deeper problem. As he wrote in *Foreign Affairs* in April 1974, despite the 'fantastic boom' in the world economy since 1945, international economic institutions had failed to keep up with changing conditions to ensure 'an undistorted exchange of goods and services' among all nations. In his view, therefore, the world economic crisis was 'not so much one of production as a crisis of its institutions in structural respects'.[21] Although a new framework for global governance would be difficult to attain, Schmidt at least hoped to foster informal cooperation across the North–South divide to avoid protectionism. But by 1975 his top priority was to create a forum for economic cooperation among the developed industrial states. NATO was purely a security organization and the European Community did not include the United States or Japan. So Schmidt looked to create something new that brought together the United States, Japan, and the leading states of Western Europe—Britain, France, and West Germany.

He saw these countries as bearing special responsibility because of their dominance in the world economy. His thinking on this issue sharpened from Christmas 1974, when he finally had time for reflection after seven months of frenzied activity since becoming chancellor. On 21 December he gave a long interview to *Der Spiegel* about West Germany's place in the world, which the magazine published on 6 January 1975 in an issue entitled 'Germany: World Power against Its Will' (*Deutschland: Weltmacht wider Willen*). Schmidt admitted that the FRG was still a 'middle power' in military matters but when it came to sustaining 'the monetary system of the free world economy', he said, it was a 'world power' (*Weltmacht*) of the same rank as America, Japan, France, and Britain, acting as what he called their 'first-class partner'. Schmidt acknowledged that the term *Weltmacht* aroused images of Kaiser Wilhelm II and memories of the Hitler era, so the FRG needed to avoid being portrayed once again as 'the ugly German'. Whereas the United States could get away with seeming imperial, West Germany could not. As Schmidt's press spokesman Klaus Bölling put it: 'We must not march around abroad with plumage on our helmets'. But the chancellor also urged West Germans to avoid 'carrying around inferiority complexes' that would hamper their ability to fulfil the world role that the circumstances of the 1970s now demanded. Schmidt's comments on West Germany's global role were widely noted by the foreign media.[22]

This understanding of the ongoing economic crisis prompted Schmidt to redefine the agenda of international relations. On 17 January 1975, presenting to the SPD his 'Guiding Thoughts on Our Foreign Policy', the chancellor stressed the need to think in radically new ways, with an emphasis on the global:

> Foreign policy today is... for us not just the specialist discipline of well-dressed, white-bearded, well-behaved diplomats, it is equally world economic policy, world raw materials policy, world agrarian policy, world monetary policy, world development policy and world security policy... We live today... in a universal system of mutually

dependent nations, marked by total interdependence of political and economic developments. This has so far not been understood by many foreign policymakers. I mean not only in Germany but across the world.[23]

This new understanding had to come from the very top. It would not emerge from specialist bureaucrats—'economic nerds' (*Fachidioten der Ökonomie*) as Schmidt also described them—or from traditional diplomats who 'can barely differentiate between exchange rates and share indexes'. In his view, only national statesmen could appreciate the complex global political interconnections and act upon them.[24] Hence the special role of the leaders of the world economic powers. By June 1975, in fact, Schmidt was talking privately about the concept of 'global economic governance' (*Weltwirtschaftsregierung*).[25]

Schmidt's concerns had a clear historical dimension. He saw the current economic crisis as the worst to face the West since the 1930s. It was not just the collapse of production and the high levels of unemployment that seemed analogous but also the total lack of understanding among economists about what was going on and the complete failure of governments to act cooperatively. In such circumstances, he kept insisting, economic collapse bred political extremism: in the 1930s, fascism was the main beneficiary; in the mid 1970s he feared the rise of Eurocommunism in Portugal and especially Italy, where the communists picked up a third of the vote in the 1975 elections. Schmidt also believed that the Americans did not properly appreciate this critical nexus of economics and politics. Even Kissinger, he said, approached the world economic crisis 'from the traditional viewpoint of power politics'. Not being an economist by training, the US secretary of state—Schmidt believed—looked at international affairs in terms of the triangular relationship between America, Russia, and China. Kissinger's priorities for the West were dictated by geopolitics and ideology, whereas Schmidt was sure that the salient issue in the mid 1970s was the potential unravelling of global capitalism and, with it, Western democracy. This had to be addressed cooperatively before any Cold War problems could be resolved.[26]

CONFRONTING THE WORLD ECONOMIC CRISIS: THE RAMBOUILLET SUMMIT, 1975

Schmidt's ideas about collaboration and governance took firmer shape in conversation with Giscard in June 1975. They drew on their own experience of the so-called 'Library Group' meetings—informal gatherings of the finance ministers of America, Germany, France, Britain, and Japan to discuss international monetary problems. The Group's nickname was derived from the venue for its opening meeting in 1973, the White House Library. Schmidt and Giscard now discerned its potential, when translated to the higher level of political leaders, for handling general economic problems. Nothing definite was agreed at their June 1975 summit, but unexpectedly, on 9 July, Giscard spoke out in a press interview about holding an 'international economic summit' later in the year.

This was a striking démarche, applying for the first time to economic affairs the practice of high-level summitry that in the 1970s was becoming a familiar tool of international politics. It reflected Schmidt's precept that economics was now the big issue of foreign policy. But turning this idea into practice required tackling several major questions. Who would be the participants? This issue was much less clear than over, say, arms control. Which country should be allowed the advantage of acting as host? What mattered in such an unprecedented crisis: concrete policies or the appearance of leadership? And should the economic summit be a one-off crisis measure, or a regular feature of international relations?

Schmidt was surprised and somewhat irritated that Giscard had gone public, but he went along with the proposal, turning it to his own ends. The French president, critical of American policy, wanted the summit to promote a return to fixed exchange rates, whereas the chancellor wished to address the larger macro-economic problems of rising unemployment and declining international trade. The two men did not resolve these differences when they met again on 26 July. So Schmidt decided to thrash out a common concept the following day with Ford and Kissinger who were then in Europe. To them Schmidt stressed his agreement with the French president on the urgent need to confront global economic problems, adding 'Giscard says what I have been saying since a year ago [in] May'. The chancellor again emphasized the larger implications of the worldwide recession: 'The West is undergoing the greatest political crisis since World War Two. The functioning of the democratic industrial nations is at stake. By comparison, the Soviet Union's policy, the conflict in the Middle East, the situation in the Eastern Mediterranean, or the problems of Portugal are of lesser rank.' If this were a political or military crisis, Schmidt went on, 'the leaders would get together and act. Since it is economic, we leave it to our finance ministers.' But, he warned, 'if we leave it this way for five years, there will be a political disaster'. Not only was it therefore vital for the statesmen to address these economic issues now, Schmidt also made clear that special responsibility lay with America. 'Let me speak a few frank words', he told Ford. 'The leadership here should be by the United States.'[27]

'That is difficult', replied Ford rather lamely. His administration was divided on how to handle the economic crisis. Neo-liberals in and around the US Treasury, especially William Simon and Arthur Burns, opposed Giscard's desire to re-establish fixed exchange rates. While the president was not willing to contradict them, Schmidt's wider agenda for the summit offered Ford a way out and this was endorsed by the State Department. Earlier in July 1975 Ford had announced his intention to run for the presidency in his own right the following year, so an international summit with a broad remit addressing inflation and unemployment would be good publicity to help boost his image as a world statesman. Ford was persuaded. 'My immediate reaction is favourable to a meeting', he declared. Schmidt also stressed the psychological value of such a gathering. 'If an economic conference should take place this year', he told Ford, 'we shouldn't expect too many results. If we could create the impression we intend to work together and coordinate our policies, that will be enough.' His main concern was that they were

Figure 1.3 Helsinki, 'The Big Four', 1 August 1975.
Source: Bundesbildstelle.

seen to be doing something soon: the summit must take place 'before the real winter comes'.[28]

A few days later, on 31 July 1975, Ford, Schmidt, and Giscard, together with British Prime Minister Harold Wilson, met during the Helsinki Conference on Security and Cooperation in Europe (CSCE) (see Figure 1.3). This was another example of 1970s top-level summitry, but on a massive scale: it involved thirty-five nations from across the Cold War divide, coming together in a media spectacle to sign an agreement produced by three years of bureaucratic negotiations. This was not summitry of the sort that Schmidt advocated and the Library Group had pioneered—small-scale, intimate talks among leaders. Yet the Helsinki pageant did provide convenient cover for the Big Four to meet on the margins and clarify their thinking on economic summitry, guided by a memo from Schmidt. They agreed to hold an economic summit conference in the autumn, including the Japanese prime minister, Takeo Miki, but no concrete details about the agenda were as yet confirmed.[29]

Their discussion took place during an informal walk in the gardens of the British Embassy but it was presented to the media as something more substantive. The *New York Times* editorialized it as nothing less than a summit in itself—an encouraging sign that 'the top leaders of the principal countries' had decided to 'take counsel together instead of relying entirely on separate measures, applied domestically'.

The editorial saw this as 'a first step in the direction of periodic meetings' and urged 'the progressive construction of institutional machinery to make joint decision-making at the summit a fact'. If this method succeeded in managing global economic crisis and growing Western interdependence, the *Times* predicted, it would 'dwarf in importance the so-called European "security" conference' that had 'made it possible'. Schmidt could not have wished for a more ringing endorsement of his claim that in the mid 1970s stabilizing the world economy was more important for peace than shoring up European détente.[30]

A few days after his return to Washington, Ford decided to send George Shultz to Europe to plan the summit in more detail. The choice of emissary was quite deliberate. In Bonn on 27 July Schmidt had made clear his confidence in Shultz, with whom he had worked well in the Library Group in 1973–4, even though the latter no longer held any government office. 'My obsession', Schmidt exclaimed, 'is with the fact that the economic leaders in the US—Simon, Greenspan, and regrettably even Burns—look too much to domestic problems and not to world effects', whereas Shultz, he felt, could see the big picture. Ford and Kissinger agreed, and Shultz was duly despatched to Bonn. On 17 September he reported back on ten hours of talks on the proposed summit with Schmidt and Giscard. 'It is interesting how much time they spent with George', Kissinger remarked. 'It shows how seriously they take it.'[31]

There was also debate about who should act as host and who should participate. On the first point, Giscard refused to come to the United States and Schmidt was reluctant. So they eventually agreed that the summit would take place in France, on the grounds that Giscard had publicly initiated the idea and that it would boost his prestige at home. As host, the French president now exerted an effective veto over the invitation list, much to Ford's irritation. Giscard and Schmidt favoured a meeting of just the Big Five, but both Italy and Canada pressed for inclusion. The Americans were keen on Canada—Shultz noted that it was 'our biggest trading partner'—whereas Italy, as he put it, 'would just clutter the landscape'. By early October all the G5 members consented to Italy's inclusion, not least because of the country's sensitive political situation, but Giscard resisted all Ford's pleas to invite the Canadians. He argued that it would open the door to many other requests and undermine the aim of a small, informal gathering; and, as host, he carried the day. The summit would be a G6 meeting, including Italy and excluding Canada. Despite these various transatlantic tensions, Washington was now fully behind the summit as Schmidt conceived of it. In a major speech in Pittsburgh just beforehand, Kissinger stressed that, although the 'immediate task of the summit is to deal with economic questions', more fundamentally 'it is a step to confirm and consolidate allied cooperation in every sphere at a crucial moment in history'—to address 'the erosion of people's confidence in their society's future and the resulting loss of faith in democratic means'. He quoted a version of Benjamin Franklin's famous aphorism from 1776, when the American colonies declared independence: 'we must hang together, or we shall surely hang separately'.[32]

Two centuries after Franklin's maxim on the necessity of working together, the mood across the West in the autumn of 1975 was indeed panicky. The economic indicators had worsened in the eighteen months since Schmidt assumed office, and economists as much as politicians were befuddled by the emerging combination of deepening recession and rampant inflation—or 'stagflation', as this bizarre phenomenon became known. More than 15 million people were unemployed in the six leading industrial countries. In the United States the jobless rate was over 8 per cent, and the German figure was 5 per cent, roughly the same as Britain and France; but in all these countries unemployment had reached levels not previously known in the post-war period. The total number of West Germans out of work had almost doubled in just one year, to over one million. As for inflation, Germany's rate was around 6 per cent per annum, but America's figure was 9 per cent and France's 10 per cent, while in Italy and Britain inflation was out of control at over 20 per cent. Such levels were catastrophic for the West. More than two years after the initial oil shock, Western publics could see little sign of recovery and feared that the gains in living standards since 1945 might now be in jeopardy. Before the summit Clyde Farnsworth, a correspondent for the *New York Times*, tried to capture the mood with some vox pop quotations. 'You sense that people are more afraid now', said one French female worker. 'No one wants to take a false step for fear of being thrown out of a job.' A farmer in the Franconia region of West Germany warned that politicians had 'better do something about it pretty soon'. The challenge for Western leaders, said Farnsworth, was to show that 'man and reason' and not 'the blind forces of nature are still in control of events'.[33]

The summit took place at the Château de Rambouillet, some thirty miles southwest of Paris, on 15–17 November 1975. A medieval hunting lodge that had become a royal palace and eventually a summer residence for French presidents, Rambouillet evoked what Jim Callaghan, Britain's foreign secretary, called 'the country house atmosphere that Giscard had intended and in which he felt so much at home'. The accommodation was cramped—Jean Sauvagnargues, the French foreign minister, had to deal with urgent telegrams on a table placed in a corridor, while senior British officials perched on gold chairs in Napoleon's bathroom and their juniors worked from a caravan in the muddy grounds. Only three people from each country were allowed in the marble conference room: the political leader, finance minister, and foreign minister. Nevertheless, the cosy setting helped warm up the diplomatic atmosphere over a rainy weekend, assisted by log fires and relaxed dinners in the evenings. It was particularly important that all the heads of government, except Aldo Moro of Italy, spoke English: as Callaghan noted, 'this common language resulted in a quick-fire exchange of views, while the round table around which we sat was small enough to enable interjections to be made easily without interrupting the general flow of argument, and clarifications could be instantaneous'. As Schmidt had hoped, this was an informal occasion and a genuine discussion, because the leaders knew that nothing they said would be made public.[34]

At the opening session on 15 November, Schmidt was tasked with setting the scene—a role that suited his taste for the sweeping overview. 'It is necessary to stimulate consumption, promote expansion and keep interest rates from rising' he told his fellow leaders. 'And since the depth of the recession has been partly due to psychological uncertainty, it is important to send a message of confidence from Rambouillet.' The benefits of the meeting were indeed primarily on that psychological level. Some commentators were sceptical—the London *Spectator* dismissed the summit as 'more hot air than hot news'—but *Die Zeit* saw at least 'a weak ray of hope for the world economy', picking up on Ford's statement about 'a new spirit—a spirit of cooperation and confidence stemming from a deeper understanding of our common destiny and our joint conviction that free peoples can master their future'.[35]

In fact there was more going on behind the scenes than met the public eye.[36] The summit brought to a conclusion protracted talks between France and America over monetary policy. Certainly, as Callaghan suggested, 'the knowledge that the summit was to take place spurred the negotiators of both sides to settle'. Just hours before the summit opened the French finally accepted the principle of floating exchange rates, while the Americans conceded that the G6 should intervene in the foreign exchange markets to check 'disorderly fluctuations'. The Rambouillet summit endorsed this all-important deal, ending an argument that had rumbled on since the collapse of the Bretton Woods system. Eventually codified in an amendment to the International Monetary Fund's Articles of Agreement during 1976, the agreement moved the Western world away from fixed institutionalized rules to more fluid international management—what one scholar has called a regime of 'surveillance'.[37]

Rambouillet also suggested that the international managers of the future might no longer be the IMF or the World Bank but the leaders of the G6. And their final 'Declaration' covered not just monetary issues but, as Schmidt had always intended, the global economic crisis as a whole, particularly issues of unemployment, inflation, and energy. 'The purpose of our meeting', the G6 declared, was 'to review our progress, identify more clearly the problems that we must overcome in the future, and to set a course that we will follow in the period ahead.' Yet nothing precise was said about policies, targets, or timing. The declaration ended vaguely: 'We intend to intensify our cooperation on all these problems in the framework of existing institutions as well as in all the relevant organizations.' At the end of 1975 it remained to be seen whether Rambouillet was merely a one-off event.[38]

CONSOLIDATING THE G7: TOWARDS 'WORLD ECONOMIC GOVERNANCE'

For Schmidt, like Giscard, the value of Rambouillet lay in its informal discussion, free from the heavy hand of bureaucracy and the intrusive eyes of the media. They favoured further summits, but only if firm policy decisions were likely. On the American side, Kissinger had already specified before Rambouillet that he wanted the summit to be the start of a permanent and more formal process that would incorporate the government bureaucracies. He stated publicly: 'The United States will propose that Ministers of our countries responsible for economic policy meet periodically to follow up on policy directions set at the summit and to review what further decisions may be needed.' Prime Minister Miki of Japan, coming from a political culture that favoured planned consensus rather than informal spontaneity, endorsed the idea of regular economic summits supported by bureaucratic machinery. On the plane home from Rambouillet, Kissinger went out of his way to tell journalists that another summit would be held in a year's time, possibly earlier, setting up the United States as the likely host.[39]

By April 1976 Washington as whole was serious about what Kissinger and Alan Greenspan, chairman of the Council of Economic Advisors, called 'a second Rambouillet-type meeting'. Despite some signs of Western recovery, there were grave worries about Italy and Britain, whose governments were running serious spending deficits and borrowing heavily, thereby fuelling inflation and straining their currencies. Greenspan, who had been against the device of an economic summit a year before, now favoured it as a disciplinary measure against profligate governments. Ford was also attracted by the prospect of another summit, in order to bolster his election campaign ahead of the vote in November. When the president approached Schmidt about this idea in mid April, the chancellor replied that he was 'very much in favour' but added that 'before we definitely decide for another conference to be held, it should, however, be made sure, as was done last time, that there is sufficient substance to warrant a successful outcome of the conference. I would be glad to go into these questions with my old friend George Shultz.' After talking with Shultz on 9 May, Schmidt was not sure that the conference would be very productive. Like Giscard and Callaghan (now Britain's prime minister), he was reluctant to do something simply to boost Ford's electoral chances. But eventually all three concluded that, despite their various reservations, it was imperative to hold another summit soon in order to reinforce the public image of Western cooperation.[40]

The agenda for the meeting underlined the importance that this forum had already attained for handling vital international issues, showing the constant linkages between specific economic questions and the larger political context. These included sustained but non-inflationary growth, promotion of global trade, and strengthening of the European Community, as well as North–South relations and aid to Africa. Not mentioned publicly, but, as Ford said privately, a 'central focal point of a summit discussion would necessarily be the problem of Italy'—whose economy was in chaos and where Eurocommunism was on the rise. Because the president was this time the initiator, he could ensure Canada's presence at the table, thereby turning the G6 into the G7. Ford's agreement not to hold the summit in Washington but in America's Caribbean territory of Puerto Rico mitigated any impression that the summit was intended to help Ford's electioneering, and holding the event in late June would precede the formal announcement of his candidacy. Here was another feature of international summitry: the potential publicity benefits for domestic politics. Schmidt, too, played that game with his own election campaign. To the SPD party conference, he portrayed the summit as a chance for him to consolidate the German and international recovery that had been underway since Rambouillet. Taken together, he said, the two meetings showed the importance of establishing 'international management' of the interdependent national economies (*Internationalökonomie*) of the Western world and

Figure 1.4 'The World Economist' en route to the Puerto Rico G7, 27 June 1976.
Source: Bundesbildstelle.

the leading role that the Federal Republic ought to play in this process (see Figure 1.4).[41]

The summit took place near San Juan, the capital of Puerto Rico, at the El Dorado Beach Hotel on 27–8 June and lasted barely twenty-four hours. One participant said that whereas Rambouillet was like 'an elegant house party, the atmosphere this time was more like a holiday weekend'. The actual business did not detain the leaders for long. Despite concerns earlier in the year, by the time the summit convened, recovery had taken hold. World trade had picked up, unemployment was in rapid decline, and communist gains in the Italian elections proved less alarming than feared.[42] The final communiqué spoke of 'a broad and productive exchange of views on a wide range of issues' and 'a welcome opportunity to improve our mutual understanding and to intensify our cooperation in a number of areas'. To many observers this sounded like nothing more than a PR exercise. To quote the caustic words of the German daily *Handelsblatt*: 'in at least one point, the Puerto Rico economic summit has fulfilled all expectations: it was largely superfluous'.[43]

Once again, however, more had actually happened away from the limelight. Much of the main business was sorted out in a secret lunch meeting of the four leading powers—America, Britain, France, and West Germany—before the formal G7 sessions began. This lunch addressed the ultra-sensitive issue of Italian near-bankruptcy. Schmidt, representing Italy's largest creditor, was determined not to provide any further credits for Italy and the other three agreed. He went on to leak the existence of the meeting and the decision on Italy to the press a few weeks later. This caused an international outcry against what French socialist Pierre Mauroy called German 'neo-colonialism' and the Italian paper *Il Messaggero* dubbed the 'Diktat di Schmidt'. But the chancellor was unrepentant about his calculated indiscretion. It showed how he had imposed Germany's financial and political discipline on its most erratic EC partner. And the leak about the lunch also served to highlight the place of the FRG at the West's top table—pre-figured by the walk-in-the-park *à quatre* at Helsinki in 1975. As *Der Spiegel* noted sarcastically, all this gave new resonance to the SPD's 1976 election slogan—*Modell Deutschland*.[44]

And, in a larger sense, Rambouillet and Puerto Rico had demonstrated the value for global politics of this new kind of international summitry, involving a group of key powers discussing a range of politico-economic issues along similar lines to the more traditional bilateral encounters between the superpowers, focused on arms control. 'Not since the early '50s', Kissinger remarked to Ford's Cabinet the following day, 'has there been such a spirit of cooperation among the allies. All this talk about the Soviet bloc being on the offensive and the democracies on the decline just isn't true. These leaders are dynamic and the West under this sort of coordinated action can handle all the problems before us easily.' The intensity and intellectual quality of debate among the G7 leaders were also a far cry from standard, pre-packaged diplomatic meetings: even former critics of the idea of an economic summit were impressed, including Treasury Secretary William Simon and Alan Greenspan. For Simon 'the key aspect was the informality of the meeting and the frankness and honesty of the dialogue', while Greenspan called Puerto Rico 'an extraordinary meeting…There was a real intellectual grappling with major philosophical issues.'[45]

Puerto Rico established the G7 as an institution. In December 1976, Giscard and Giulio Andreotti, the new Italian premier, called publicly for another meeting in mid 1977. Schmidt, Callaghan, and Prime Minister Takeo Fukuda of Japan all agreed, each bidding for his own country as host. This time the British won out, mainly because the NATO summit was already scheduled for London in May 1977 and it would be convenient to hold the two events in sequence. The G7 date was set for 6–8 May. By now the character of this summitry was becoming more formalized and bureaucratic. In advance of Puerto Rico only one brief preparatory meeting had been held,[46] just two weeks before. For London, however, there were two, starting a couple of months before, and each lasting two days—conducted by an advance guard of close advisers to the summiteers, aptly dubbed 'sherpas'. This moved the process away from the informal, intimate style that Schmidt strongly preferred.[47]

In the event, London accomplished little of lasting value despite fine words and ambitious pledges. The Germans inserted into the final declaration the words: 'Inflation does not reduce unemployment. On the contrary it is one of its major causes.' And this endorsement of the *Modell Deutschland* was regarded at the time in Bonn as a major achievement of German diplomacy. By the end of 1977, however, unemployment was still at a post-war peak, and inflation remained disconcertingly high in some countries (the annual rates for Britain and Italy ran at 17 or 18 per cent a year, compared with Germany's rate of 3.5). Moreover, national governments resorted to more intensive protectionist measures during the winter of 1977–8. By mid 1978 *The Times* was calling the London summit a fiasco. Yet this only made another meeting seem more necessary. Schmidt and Callaghan had no doubt that 'each summit meeting had reinforced our confidence in one another, despite the fact that we could obviously not expect to wipe all the world's problems off the face of the earth in two days'. The process of collaboration was more important than the results of individual meetings.[48]

In preparing for the next summit, there was a real difference of priorities. Callaghan, together with the new US President Jimmy Carter, wanted the strongest economies with low inflation and big export surpluses—especially Germany and Japan—to pursue a coordinated Keynesian stimulus policy and thus act as the 'locomotive' of global growth. Carter was taking a different line from his predecessor: Ford, like Schmidt, had been more concerned about the dangers of inflation. Fukuda endorsed Carter's stimulus package, speaking movingly about his participation in the World Economic Conference in London in 1933 when the leading countries failed to coordinate their responses to the depression, encouraging the slide to protectionism and fascism. 'In the 1930s in London', he said, 'we witnessed the world moving into war. We cannot afford that mistake again.' But Schmidt remained much more fearful about inflation—for him, as usual, the 'existential question' (*Lebensfrage*) of global economic policy.[49]

The 'locomotive' debate rumbled on in 1978. Schmidt was very keen that the next summit should take place in Germany and the White House was sympathetic but intended to use its consent as leverage. Carter wanted 'further stimulus measures by the Federal Republic' on the grounds that 'higher German growth is needed to reduce the problems we face in foreign exchange markets, while contributing to the economic well-being of the entire industrial world'. In return he would give the chancellor what he desired: as the Americans put it, 'a mid-July Summit in Bonn, with a presidential visit to Germany thrown in'. Schmidt was now becoming more receptive to American pressure for reflation because the FRG's economy was not growing as fast as expected. It had failed to reach its 1977 growth target of 5 per cent and by April 1978 the prognosis for that year was down to 2.5 per cent. In the spring Schmidt and Carter reached a private consensus on what each of them needed to do: a German stimulus package in return for effective American anti-inflationary action to strengthen the dollar and reduce oil imports. But the chancellor still faced serious opposition at home. Although the *Bundesbank* reluctantly adopted his new position on economic expansion, there remained considerable political opposition from the SPD to the necessary tax cuts and to higher budget deficits from the banking community. So the German debate about expansion still remained in the balance when the G7 convened in Bonn on 16–18 July.[50]

Economic summitry had now become a big-time spectacle. The leaders met at the elegant Palais Schaumburg, a neoclassical building which had until recently been the Federal Chancellery. 'Regardless of whether the conference solves any of

the world's economic problems', wrote one American journalist, 'it already quali-
fies as a full-fledged media event. Some 2,500 reporters are accredited here'—five
times the number covering Rambouillet. The leaders sat around a huge table in a
salon overlooking the Rhine. 'Black notebooks, pencil trays and water pitchers
were set at each place, along with mineral water for the Europeans and Coca-Cola
for the Americans.' Schmidt clearly relished his chance to play host. Welcoming
his visitors at the opening session, he told them about Bonn's equivalent of Rome's
seven hills—the Siebengebirge, across the Rhine. 'We are seven delegations',
he said in a line widely reported in the press, 'and we must avoid having each
one climb his own summit, but stay together and climb the peak which confronts
us all'.[51]

Pleasant surroundings and fine words could not, however, conceal the challenge
facing the summiteers. All had to juggle international and domestic pressures but
Schmidt faced particular problems as the leader of a coalition government in which
the FDP (also known as Free Democrats or Liberal Democrats) occupied 42 of the
coalition's 284 seats in the Bundestag—critical for a clear working majority over
the CDU/CSU. The Liberal Democrats were in favour of tax cuts but many Social
Democrats were opposed. Although Schmidt had agreed in principle in the spring
to boost the West German economy, he held out right to the end of the summit on
the precise scale of the stimulus package. 'Make them [the Americans and their
allies] force me to do it', he said privately, 'so that in the end I can'. By appearing
to cave in to overwhelming foreign pressure for growth, while extracting concessions from America over controlling inflation and oil imports, he managed to sell
the summit package to his SPD colleagues.[52]

The Bonn summit ended with the declaration of 'a comprehensive strategy' to
'create more jobs and fight inflation, strengthen international trading, reduce payments imbalances, and achieve greater stability in exchange markets'. The G7
stressed that they were 'dealing with long-term problems, which will only yield to
sustained efforts' and that their strategy was 'a coherent whole, whose parts are
interdependent'. Although the core of the deal was between America, Germany,
and Japan, each of the seven countries made specific commitments: to borrow
Schmidt's simile, they had deliberately roped themselves together at the summit to
reach their common goal of global economic recovery. In the words of journalist
Flora Lewis, 'the acceptance that no single country or group of countries could be
expected to bear the brunt of an overall effort was the source of the intense satisfaction among leaders'. Or, as Schmidt put it more pithily, 'the world economy is
our fate. It can only be directed through collaboration.'[53]

Reflecting on the evolution of the G7 between 1975 and 1978, Schmidt had no
doubt that 'if there hadn't been these four summits in the last four years, the world
economy would most likely have tumbled into an equally deep depression to that
of the 1930s'. Even if later G7 meetings became routine, highly public and
intensely bureaucratic, Callaghan, for his part, was convinced that 'economic summits of the kind that took place at Bonn foster a sense of political and economic
direction in handling the world's problems'. And looking back systematically in
2014 at G7 summitry, veteran observer Nicholas Bayne rated Bonn as the only

'Straight A' summit in the period 1975–83. (By contrast he awarded Puerto Rico a D and London a B-.) Bayne even judged the 1978 Bonn summit to be 'a supreme example of collective decision-making at leader level'.[54]

Observers at the time also saw Bonn as a historic moment. The German political commentator Theo Sommer asked whether these annual economic meetings heralded the dawn of a 'new political reality'. Henry Owen, Carter's Sherpa, was sure this was now the case, calling them 'a law of life'—with the summits recognized as a modest but vital means to coordinate national growth, employment, monetary policies, and investment strategies. Bonn was also significant because the world media widely hailed it as '*ein Schmidt-Gipfel*'—'Schmidt's summit'. Peter Jenkins in the *Guardian* said that Schmidt was the decisive actor because 'his view of the economic world'—more 'monetarist' than 'neo-Keynesian'—'is going to prevail' and because 'there has been a significant shift of power... in the industrial world'. This 'Schmidt summit' showed him 'standing higher than ever before on the international stage, more nearly shoulder-to-shoulder with an American President than any post-war German leader'. This was not only a European perspective. For the *New York Times*, the Bonn summit marked 'the full emergence' of West Germany 'from the shadow of the United States in international economic councils', while the *Wall Street Journal* stated that under Schmidt the Federal Republic had 'developed into a world power... economically and also increasingly politically'. The use of the sensitive term 'world power'—redolent of the *Kaiserreich*—was significant. American journalist Paul Lewis saw Bonn as 'another sign that, 30 years after losing World War II, West Germany is finally acquiring the diplomatic muscle to match its economic strength'. He said that Schmidt had chosen in a judicious way to act as 'Europe's paymaster'; spending 'Germany's trade surplus—the fruit of its economic strength—on financing the further unification of Europe and increasing his country's diplomatic authority within Europe and abroad'.[55]

The phrase about financing further European unification was an allusion to the concurrent EC decision at Bremen in July 1978 to float their currencies as a bloc against the dollar. The idea of a 'European currency fund' had been touted since the collapse of Bretton Woods and the oil shock in 1972–3. Schmidt was originally sceptical because monetary management would only be successful if all the members were committed to coordinated stability policies. By the spring of 1978, however, he had changed his mind because of the persistent weakness of the dollar, evident in his fencing with Carter ahead of the Bonn summit. He believed that floating exchange rates hampered growth in the FRG and Western Europe as a whole. Half of the EC's trade was within the Community and 25 per cent of the EC's GDP was accounted for by world trade, compared with only 7 per cent for the United States. Harmonizing exchange rates was, in Schmidt's view, essential for Western European recovery, especially given America's 'benign neglect' of exchange rate stability. And, so he hoped, successful European monetary cooperation would have a disciplining influence on American balance of payments policy. The Bremen meeting agreed to consider an outline scheme produced by Schmidt, with the support of Giscard. The White House was dismissive and so were many commentators—the West German trade journal *Handelsblatt* scoffed that 'an old, worn-out dress has been ironed again'—but Schmidt's initiative laid the basis for the European Monetary System (EMS), established in March 1979. It was a further sign of his significance as an economic statesman and of the shifting transatlantic balance of power.[56]

Close observers at the time saw the Bonn summit of July 1978, together with the Bremen scheme, as a personal triumph for Schmidt. *Der Spiegel* depicted him at the 'zenith' of his career, with opinion polls showing him to be as popular as Adenauer and Erhard at their peaks in 1959 and 1965. The main Bonn paper, *General-Anzeiger*, called him 'Helmut the Great', while the US Senate majority leader Robert Byrd likened his dynamic leadership to that of Napoleon. Byrd, of course, was a Democrat, and his remark could be read as an implicit critique of his own president.[57] For the shift in the balance of power was not just a matter of national weight, but also a personal issue. The struggle between Schmidt and Carter over inflation versus growth, which had dogged the London and Bonn summits, involved not merely policy issues but a rivalry for influence and leadership. This would prove a fundamental problem for much of Schmidt's chancellorship, and it deserves closer attention.

Carter arrived in Washington as a political outsider. He had never sat in Congress and his only executive experience was as a one-term Governor of Georgia. His 1976 election campaign had tried to make a virtue of his greenness, claiming that he had not been corrupted by life inside 'the Beltway', and this appealed to an American public disillusioned by Watergate. But to Europeans the peanut farmer from Georgia seemed an implausible president. Schmidt was a notable sceptic. Speaking to Callaghan in May 1976 he aired his 'uncertainty' about the world situation and how America would cope in superpower relations if 'a very much unknown farmer governor' took over the White House. By contrast he had developed a close rapport with Ford, in the course of eight meetings over two years (see Figure 1.5), and they agreed on many policy issues. The chancellor spoke openly about their relationship to *Newsweek* in October 1976, three weeks before the US presidential election. Because this interview became notorious, it is worth quoting at length. Asked about German–American relations, Schmidt commented in English: 'I think the very good relations between the two countries are now so well established and so well founded that I don't think that a change in either Washington or in Bonn could endanger that'. But, he went on, 'personal relationships do play a role'—noting that 'a great amount of confidence' had been built up between himself and President Ford. 'I have a great personal feeling' for him, Schmidt added, 'and I think on his side he has some sympathy as well for myself'. The chancellor then dug himself in deeper with rather mangled phrasing: 'I have to abstain from any interference in your campaign, but what I have said about my personal relationships with the President, this can be stressed. I really like your President, and I think he has done quite a bit of help in these past two years. I have been taking advice from him. This has been a two-way affair. But on the other hand, I am not going to say anything about Mr Carter, neither positive nor negative; I have met him for one hour only.'[58]

Figure 1.5 Schmidts, Fords, and Kissingers with Melvin Laird, July 1976.
Source: Bundesbildstelle.

That last sentence was a belated attempt by Schmidt to cover himself against accusations of meddling in American electoral politics, but his comments were a fundamental breach of diplomatic etiquette and also an astonishing political gaffe. Headlines such as 'I like Ford' went around the world, and one of his staff was obliged to send apologies to the Carter team blaming the faux pas on an interview given very early in the morning, when the chancellor was not particularly careful about his words. Embarrassment increased after Carter won the election, and the new president never forgave Schmidt's snub.[59]

On the surface, a Social Democratic chancellor should have found a Democratic president to be a closer ideological bedfellow than the Republican Ford. But after this disastrous start, the Schmidt–Carter relationship only went from bad to worse during 1977 and 1978. Schmidt was irritated by Carter's obsession with reflationary economic policies, especially after seeing eye to eye with Ford on the pitfalls of Keynesianism.[60] And whereas Ford was malleable, Carter became increasingly dogmatic about his positions once he had made up his mind. Another area of conflict was Carter's Baptist passion for an idealist foreign policy, privileging human rights, at odds with Schmidt's focus on realpolitik and the balance of power. Foreign Minister Hans-Dietrich Genscher publicly dismissed Carter as 'a religious visionary', while *Der Spiegel* stated bluntly that Schmidt 'considers him an unpredictable dilettante who tries to convert his private morality into world politics but is in reality incapable of fulfilling the role of leader of the West'.[61]

But this was not all. These public outbursts, remarkable in the context of normal diplomatic protocol, came at a moment of particular German–American tension in April 1978 over the so-called neutron bomb—an episode to be discussed more fully in chapter 3. The neutron bomb crisis accentuated the personal friction between the two leaders and enhanced Schmidt's conviction that Carter was simply not up to the job, even though in public they were keen to present a united front, often with gushing mutual praise.[62]

Overall, however, his falling out with Carter was an aberration from Schmidt's philosophical commitment to 'political friendships', and, on a practical level, it stood in marked contrast with his close and productive rapport with Giscard, through which he had been able to initiate the EMS and the G7 process. Schmidt could look back with satisfaction on having provided direction and cohesion for the West in the face of an economic crisis that had threatened, like the Great Depression of the 1930s, to undermine the democratic political order. In doing so he had even earned himself a media nickname—the 'world economist' (*Weltökonom*).[63]

* * * * *

Although the world economic crisis was Helmut Schmidt's top priority in the first years of his chancellorship, neither he nor his colleagues could separate it from the larger context of the Cold War, in which capitalism vied with communism in a global struggle. And the challenge of the Cold War was, at root, to find security and stability in the nuclear age when weapons of mass destruction presaged potential annihilation. Nowhere was this concern more acute than in Germany, because the Cold War border between East and West split the country in two and constituted the front line between the two great nuclear antagonists. Moreover, as the defeated power of the Second World War—indeed the nation that had caused that horror—Germany had been deprived of its own capacity for self-defence after 1945. Even though the Federal Republic had become a world power in economic terms by the 1970s, bestowing real diplomatic clout on Bonn, in issues of hard security the country could never escape the shadow of dependence on the United States as West Germany's protector power. This was the perennial conundrum facing Schmidt and it would become more acute as East–West relations worsened during the course of his chancellorship. His basic approach to the dilemmas of German security is the subject of the next chapter.

2

The Strategist of Balance

For Schmidt, Germany's security had two essential dimensions. In the early years of his chancellorship, as we have seen, the economic stability of the West was top of the agenda, but the underlying issue for him was always to sustain the Cold War military balance in the interests of peace. He believed that West Germany's position and very existence depended on close ties with the United States. As expressed in his inaugural address in May 1974, the Atlantic Alliance constituted 'the fundamental basis of our security and it remains the necessary political framework for our efforts to promote global détente'.[1] Without this partnership with America, there could be no progress in East–West relations or on the German question. Schmidt was willing to continue the process of relaxing tensions (*Entspannungsbereitschaft*) but he insisted that all this had to go hand in hand with the ability to defend (*Verteidigungsfähigkeit*). For him, further détente required a 'balance of forces to secure peace'.[2]

It is significant that Schmidt never once referred to '*Ostpolitik*' in his first policy statements as chancellor, even though he endorsed his predecessor Willy Brandt's efforts in this direction and had every intention to continue German–German *rapprochement* and dialogue with the East. Indeed, when Schmidt spoke in his inaugural about 'continuity', he meant the goals and methods of *Ostpolitik* in general rather than any specific agenda inherited from Brandt. Schmidt felt that he operated within constraints that Brandt had simply not faced a few years earlier, so one had to act more pragmatically.[3] And he was consciously driven by strategic thinking on *Realpolitik* lines, based on his conceptions of the East–West balance of power. These ideas were independent from yet parallel to the more idealistic visions of international relations espoused by Brandt and his close aide Egon Bahr in their approach to *Ost-* and *Deutschlandpolitik*, which included a more utopian, pan-European security architecture. Schmidt liked to concentrate on what was feasible and therefore pursued the stabilization of existing structures amid an increasingly unstable world.[4]

Yet Schmidt was not merely a reactive pragmatist. His approach to German and global security in the 1970s was rooted in concepts that he had been working out for more than a decade. Economic management had been a matter of necessity—and he had done it with skill and a broad vision—but Schmidt's true passion lay in military strategy. To understand his ideas and actions as chancellor we must therefore reflect on his speeches and writings from the 1960s, and in particular his two notable books, *Verteidigung oder Vergeltung* (1961) and *Strategie des Gleichgewichts* (1969).[5] In short, we must look back to Schmidt the defence intellectual.

THE DEFENCE INTELLECTUAL

As a thinker on defence, Schmidt was second to none in West Germany. With the exception perhaps of Franz Josef Strauß from the opposition CDU/CSU, who had been defence minister in 1956–62 and had overseen West Germany's rearmament and integration into NATO, nobody was as well versed as Schmidt on NATO deterrence strategy, both overall doctrine and force planning. Having spent some fifteen years before he entered the chancellery specializing in nuclear weapons and security issues, three of these (1969–72) as Brandt's defence minister, it can even be argued that none of his predecessors in the Chancellery had been able to debate defence and Cold War nuclear politics with the same skill and on such equal terms with US policymakers as did Helmut Schmidt.

Schmidt was also a defence intellectual of global rank. Among his international contemporaries, Kissinger was his closest counterpart as a strategic thinker. What is more, after an initial chance encounter at Harvard in 1958,[6] they would become life-long friends. This relationship went so deep that Kissinger, at the state funeral for Schmidt on 23 November 2015, would speak of him as a 'special friend' and a 'pillar in my life'[7] (see Figure 2.1). As intellectuals, both men thought deeply, carefully, and systematically about the global Cold War, and they also sought to educate the general public with their books, media commentaries, and other publications, well before reaching the peaks of their political careers during which they sought to shape international affairs. This process of thinking, writing, and debating within academic and

Figure 2.1 Schmidt and Kissinger, February 1974.
Source: Sven Simon.

policy circles prepared them for their roles at the highest level of government. But Kissinger's heyday in power was the early 1970s—the era of superpower détente, shuttle diplomacy, and East–West summitry that he created as Nixon's national security adviser. 'Super-K' was less effective as secretary of state under Ford, and, after Democrat Jimmy Carter entered the White House in 1977, he came to be seen as a 'flawed architect'. His edifice crumbled almost as soon as he left office, partly because it lacked domestic electoral support and partly because his highly personal diplomacy never got to grips with the intricacies and effects of the Cold War at the regional level or with the systemic transformations in the world economy.

Schmidt was different. Most importantly, he was a politician, not merely an adviser. And, after 1974, as a head of government (and thus with the backing of the German electorate), he occupied a platform from which to turn ideas into action—something that Kissinger, as an adviser or Cabinet member, never had. In further contrast with Kissinger, Schmidt had deep knowledge of finance and economics as well as military strategy. In the 1970s, this was an unusual combination of assets, which endowed Schmidt with unique authority in international affairs. For him it was axiomatic that Western security had to be based on the two elements of economic stability and military balance. Whether his efforts would give rise to durable international structures remained to be seen.[8]

What were the roots of Schmidt's outlook on security policy? Born in 1918, he was of the generation that had come of age in the Nazi era. He had been exposed to the full force of National Socialist ideology without possessing the experience of previous political epochs to have some perspective on what he was being told. Nevertheless, his awareness of having a Jewish grandfather made him more dubious about Nazism, and daily life in the Third Reich instilled him with a profound scepticism about any grand ideological schemes. Schmidt experienced combat as a young officer on the Eastern front in 1941 and later, after the creation of the West German *Bundeswehr* in 1955, he served as a captain in the reserve (see Figure 2.2). These experiences—he was the only West German chancellor to have fought at the front—coloured his views of the post-war world and of how the Federal Republic ought to navigate the East–West conflict as it became increasingly entrenched.[9] Defence was also a feature of his early political career. Having won a seat in 1953 as one of Hamburg's representatives in the *Bundestag*, Schmidt shot to prominence as a brilliant debater—a parliamentarian who dared to speak his mind and did so eloquently in big, controversial debates. His know-all, confrontational manner earned him the nickname—almost a brand name—'Schmidt-*Schnauze*' ('Schmidt the Lip'; see Figure 2.3).[10] In the Bundestag he quickly made a name for himself on issues of defence and international security.

Schmidt blended military experience and a Euro-Atlantic outlook in a way that won him credibility within the defence establishment but which was unusual among the SPD elite. Both Willy Brandt and Herbert Wehner (leader of the SPD parliamentary party, 1969–83) had spent the Second World War in exile in Scandinavia. Kurt Schumacher, the party's first post-war leader, was incarcerated in concentrations camps for almost the entire Nazi period. After the Federal Republic was created in 1949, he opposed Adenauer's policy of *Westbindung*, focusing on

Figure 2.2 The reserve officer, 23 October 1958.
Source: DPA.

national unification based on neutrality. Indeed, it might appear a paradox that Schmidt tried to make his career in a Social Democratic Party that was so fixated on the German question, inclined to pacificism, and dominated by an anti-military wing. Yet this paradox also accounted for Schmidt's rise. He was one of the few Social Democrats[11] who could shield the party from allegations of unrealism in foreign and defence policy during the intense debate about national security that raged in the 1950s and 1960s.

Figure 2.3 'Schmidt the Lip': Bundestag, 24 April 1958, with Adenauer and Erhard looking on.
Source: AP, Horst Faas.

The central questions in this debate were West German rearmament, the deployment of American nuclear weapons on German soil, and NATO's overall nuclear strategy. Schmidt had little time for the old 1950s NATO doctrine, involving massive American nuclear retaliation and limited nuclear warfare in Europe. Not only would the latter be likely to escalate but such a war would turn Germany into the prime battlefield, leading to the country's devastation and the death of millions of its people. As a result Schmidt immersed himself in the contemporaneous debate and scholarship on military strategy, scouring the key American, English, and French literature which he considered much richer and of more 'conspicuous insight and impressive authority'[12] than anything yet to be found in Germany. He was impressed by the well-developed public discussion in the United States through the medium of serious periodicals and books. Schmidt felt particularly stimulated by the recent works of academics such as Kissinger and Robert Osgood, as well as defence experts including Klaus Knorr, Roger Hilsman, and Thomas Schelling.[13] Among Europeans, the British military historian Basil Liddell Hart struck a chord, as did the British Labour Party parliamentarian, Denis Healey—Britain's defence minister from 1964 to 1970.[14]

Schmidt was keen that the people of Germany, NATO's 'battlefield country', should be introduced to these current military-strategic controversies. Moreover, he wanted the Germans to participate actively in the West's public debate. By

1960, almost eight years after entering the Bundestag, Schmidt felt himself ideally placed to become a defence intellectual in his own right. He did so by embarking on a book project in the mould of those American and British defence intellectuals that he admired. His aim was not to write a detailed, technical manual but a work with real political impact. He wished to shake up his parliamentary friends, wider German political circles, the press, and the *Bundeswehr*, so that they would confront the issues of NATO's military strategy and West Germany's role within the Alliance. Some considered Schmidt to be engaged in a vanity project. Others such as the *Stuttgarter Zeitung* journalist Claus Heinrich Meyer suggested that Schmidt took up his pen as a means of 'venting' (*abreagieren*), because his party did not 'govern' (*regieren*). Frustrated by years in political opposition and driven by literary as much as political ambition, Schmidt—according to Meyer—was a man itching to do something ('*den es in den politischen Fingerspitzen gejuckt hat*'), who desperately wanted to be heard and to influence international politics in a concrete manner. As a reflection of this evident desire to design and make policy himself, Schmidt's wife and daughter called his book project 'Father's hand-knitted jumper' (*Vaters selbstgestrickter Pullover*).[15]

But this was no joke. Schmidt was already being taken seriously abroad by those whom he admired in the international strategic community. Denis Healey would later recall: 'In those days there was simply less interest in strategic and nuclear problems on the Continent. The outstanding German in the field was Helmut Schmidt, then a young senator from Hamburg, who wrote his first book on nuclear strategy...in 1961. He was my age, had fought in Russia while I was fighting in Italy, and had come to very similar conclusions.'[16] In similar vein, Kissinger described Schmidt in 1960 to General Charles Bonesteel, then Secretary of the US Army General Staff, as 'one of the most influential men in the German Social Democratic Party, and a specialist in military affairs. He is a very bright young man who I believe is destined to go far.'[17]

Schmidt set out his conception of the book in several letters during 1960. He told Kissinger he wanted to write a proper scholarly work on military strategy but one that would still attract a general audience. It should be not only informative but also interpretive—offering 'my own distinctive judgement'.[18] In a long, handwritten note to Willy Brandt, he elaborated on the book's essential thesis. Germany had a specific interest in the strategic conception of NATO, for several reasons. First, Bonn could not accept a strategy that would see Central Europe liberated only after a totally devastating final battle. The strategy was also problematic because, unless the Soviets were really planning a nuclear strike, it was doubtful that the West would even contemplate retaliating with nuclear weapons. And against non-nuclear Soviet aggression, NATO's current conventional forces were totally inadequate. Because Schmidt opposed nuclear first strikes, he advocated instead a strengthening of NATO's conventional forces. If the West managed to achieve a military balance of power in this way, future competition, so he hoped, would then in the long run shift to the ideological and economic planes.[19]

When Schmidt took his ideas on defence strategy to a potential publisher, the Seewald Verlag, they were greeted with delight. The director, Heinrich Seewald, replied that he had been seeking such a book for some time—actively trying to persuade Defence Minister Strauß to be its author—because strategy and foreign policy were too often muddled up and it was necessary to lay out each strand clearly and realistically, without prejudice, ideology, or emotion. Seewald was convinced that West Germany's 'strategic and foreign policy concept' should be 'reconceived anew and interpreted with real effect'. Moreover, the book had to be readable in order to reach the widest possible audience. Seewald wanted not a thin pamphlet but a substantial hardback book. To avoid the overstocked Christmas market of 1960, it should be published in the new year, when it would act as 'a wonderful cue' for the media at the start of a federal election year.[20]

Verteidigung oder Vergeltung duly appeared in January 1961, with an initial print run of 5,000 copies. It proved a publishing success and another 10,000 copies were printed in a special second edition using SPD funding, over the summer in the run-up to the federal elections. The book then came out in 1962 with Oliver and Boyd in Britain and Praeger in the United States under the title *Defense or Retaliation*. In the preface to these English-language editions Schmidt stated that his aim had been to 'give the German public a better picture of the strategic situation of their country'. That meant making available the conclusions of international specialists but then evaluating these from the German point of view. In other words Schmidt saw himself as an educator of his own people and also an interpreter between Germany and the world.[21]

In *Defense or Retaliation* Schmidt argued that 'the balance of power never stands still'. New forces affecting it were 'constantly making their appearance—the rise of China as a first-class military power, the economic growth of all the principal powers concerned, new developments in the field of military technology, and new strategic insights'. The West must therefore 'make sustained efforts in the political, military, and economic spheres aimed at the constant renewal of the balance at all levels if it is to be in a position to negotiate on all the subjects of dispute (e.g. German reunification, Berlin, disarmament and control)'. And because the struggle with Communism was here to stay, Schmidt believed that a 'constantly re-established balance of effective military strength' was necessary in Europe to prevent the struggle escalating into full-scale war: 'there would certainly be very little left of Germany after a war in Europe—particularly in view of NATO's present strategy' of massive nuclear retaliation. So the West needed to achieve a counterbalance of forces against the enemy, in order to sustain peace.[22]

Schmidt favoured credible deterrence ahead of the capacity for retaliation. The problem as he saw it was that the American threat of massive retaliation by strategic nuclear forces was losing its deterrent capability, due to 'the approach of a stable nuclear balance between the world powers'. Schmidt felt that superpower strategic parity would have to be matched by a move towards parity between NATO and the Warsaw Pact at the level of conventional forces. Only in this way could West Germany avoid political pressure from Moscow stemming from the overwhelming Soviet conventional presence in Central Europe.[23] In the 1950s NATO had tried to compensate for its conventional inferiority through the deployment of short-range battlefield nuclear weapons, but the Soviets were now developing so-called 'tactical nuclear weapons' of longer range. Schmidt warned starkly: 'Those who think that Europe can be defended by the massed use of such weapons will not defend Europe, but destroy it.'[24] In his view, NATO's development of tactical systems must be solely for the purposes of deterrence, rather than as instruments of war-fighting and retaliation, as many in the Pentagon believed. For him, deterrence was intended to prevent the escalation into nuclear warfare: the distinction between tactical and strategic weapons was mere casuistry. As he observed wryly, 'the peoples of Europe would not care whether it was tactical nuclear weapons or strategic missiles that brought about their extermination'.[25]

Yet Schmidt's position was complex. He was realistic enough to recognize that the scope of a conventional battle might widen and ultimately involve the use of nuclear weapons. NATO, he acknowledged, 'must therefore also have the means, should the enemy carry out locally or regionally limited acts of aggression with tactical nuclear weapons, of defending its territory with the same weapons... What is more, NATO must be able to fight a general or total war in the defence of Europe in case the enemy's attack is made at that level, i.e. includes the use of strategic nuclear weapons.'[26] Schmidt could therefore envisage NATO going nuclear if this was done in response to a Warsaw Pact nuclear attack, but he personally opposed the first-use of nuclear weapons. Given the insoluble nuclear conundrum, his priority remained the strengthening of conventional defence.

Schmidt's book was the first major, systematic study of strategic problems in the nuclear age that had been written by a German author from the perspective of German interests. Above all, this oeuvre moved Schmidt onto new levels as a defence intellectual. Now not merely a party defence nerd or 'expert'[27] but as the author of a book widely read on both sides of the Atlantic, he had placed himself on the international map and given much broader exposure to his perceptions of Western grand strategy and of West Germany's security position.

Around the same time, in 1961–2, Schmidt also became a figure of real standing in national politics. In November 1961 he was offered the newly created position of Senator for Internal Affairs (formerly Senator of the Police) in Hamburg, which he held until October 1965. This made him a member of the *Landeskabinett* or Senate of the city-state of Hamburg.[28] As Schmidt admitted in a private letter, he had not found it easy to leave the limelight of Federal politics in Bonn and so was keen to stay abreast of defence policy matters behind the scenes. But there were pluses as well as minuses. Whereas in Bonn he had been confined to the talking shop of opposition politics, in Hamburg as Senator he was actually able to do something—and this he found greatly rewarding. He was particularly determined to shake up Hamburg's bureaucratic structures and to reform the antiquated handling of public security, air-raid protection, and disaster management.[29]

And in a way he never expected, disaster was about to strike. On the night of 16 February 1962 Senator Schmidt returned from a *Länder*-Interior Ministers' conference in Berlin. He was being driven by his chauffeur to his bungalow in Langenhorn in the northern outskirts of Hamburg along one of the transit corridors through East Germany. The journey was slow and unsettling. As Schmidt stared out at the haunted Cold War landscape, he was increasingly alarmed by a horrendous storm blowing across the country, reaching speeds of 150 kilometres an hour. Trees were uprooted and branches kept falling onto the roads. Weather reports suggested that the full force of the hurricane would hit the North Sea coast a hundred kilometres or more from Hamburg. Little did Schmidt know of the horrific scenes that were actually unfolding in his city's heart when he finally got to bed at one in the morning.

He did not sleep for long. His phone rang at 6:20 a.m. and he was informed that the southern part of Hamburg (Wilhelmsburg, Finkenwerder, and Waltershof) was effectively drowning under 40,000 cubic metres of water. The storm surge along the coast had unleashed a tidal wave which then ploughed inland, its enormous force bursting dyke after dyke up the river Elbe. The wall of water, now nearly six metres above normal and with a propulsive force of thirty tonnes, had hit the city, crushed most wooden dwellings in its path, and swept away their inhabitants. The wave had struck shortly after midnight, when the city and its people were fast asleep.

Roused from his bed, Schmidt jumped into his official car and sped across town, blue light flashing. Twenty minutes later he reached Hamburg's police headquarters. Schmidt sensed a mood of raw terror. Policemen and civil servants were running around in panic without direction. The city's Mayor, Dr Paul Nevermann, was a thousand kilometres away enjoying a spa break in the ritzy Austrian resort of Bad Hofgastein. So Schmidt took charge alone, acting in a decisive, bold, and fearless manner—'*forsch, frech und furchtlos*' to quote *Der Spiegel*. He mobilized civilians and the military and brought them under his control. 'They have not been assigned to me', he admitted. 'I have taken them over.' He directed a motley crowd, including 5,000 policemen and thousands of civilian volunteers ranging from the Red Cross to sports divers. He also brought in 8,000 soldiers from the German *Bundeswehr* and another 4,000 allied troops—British, American, Dutch, Danish, and Belgian. Within moments, according to *Der Spiegel*, the 'Bundeswehr Reservehauptmann' mutated into 'Katastrophen-Generalstabschef Schmidt'.[30]

By enlisting the German and NATO armed forces to organize help in a catastrophic situation, Schmidt provoked controversy—at least in the short run.[31] He had overstepped existing laws—not least the federal constitution which technically forbade the *Bundeswehr*'s deployment in a civilian and internal issue, and especially by giving the soldiers 'police rights', including the use of force to remove people from their homes against their will.[32] He also spent money from the city-state's coffers without asking its parliament, and he resorted to such unorthodox measures as having dead bodies stored and cooled on an ice rink.[33] Schmidt justified all these actions by proclaiming that the Hamburg floods were an 'emergency outside the law' (*übergesetzlicher Notstand*).[34]

That morning he feared that anywhere between 5,000 and 25,000 people might die—by drowning or by freezing to death in the icy waters and the cold winter air. But thanks to the networks he had already established in Bonn among the defence community, he could exploit these channels now in a moment of utmost crisis. He personally called up all the military commanders that he knew and asked for immediate help. These included the American Supreme Allied Commander in Europe, General Lauris Norstad, German military figures such as Admiral

Bernhard Rogge and Major-General Christian Mueller, as well as the Federal Defence Minister Franz Josef Strauß. Phoned up so suddenly, they initially thought he was crazy, but, because he was so insistent and had their trust, they acted, and so did others. Schmidt's top priority was helicopters: he managed to get ninety from the Americans. With all electricity gone and telephone communication dead, the choppers allowed over-flight and over-sight as well as the wherewithal to lift people out of the swirling waters. He also got dozens of storm boats and rubber dinghies, 90,000 wool blankets (50,000 of them from the US forces), 40,000 air and foam matresses, 100,000 sandbags, plus tens of thousands of hot water bottles filled with drinking water. During the course of that epic day, 17 February, 315 people died. But almost 20,000 were rescued, many of them from imminent and mortal danger.[35]

Because Schmidt saved both the city and so many lives, his autocratic manner and erratic moods were forgiven. *Sonntagsblatt* depicted him as variously 'assertive, commanding, rough or friendly, sometimes in his shirtsleeves, sometimes arrogant, but never bureaucratic'.[36] And so he gained an enduring reputation as an effective 'crisis-manager' and political 'deliverer'—to quote words from the time that have resonated ever since.[37] In the great flood of February 1962, only three months after taking over as Senator in Hamburg, Schmidt showed himself to possess technical competence and political skills of the highest order. *Der Spiegel* dubbed him 'Lord of the Flood' (*Herr der Flut*).[38] The defence intellectual had become a popular figure, Hamburg's best-loved Senator.[39] The floods also swept him to national fame and elevated him into a man whose ideas should be taken seriously on all the critical issues of the day. Hence, it was no surprise that from now on his writings on military affairs would find an ever-widening audience.[40]

During the 1960s, *Verteidigung oder Vergeltung* went through several editions. By 1968 he and his publishers felt that, in view of the upcoming federal elections and also the stirrings of détente, the projected sixth edition needed a much broader approach and a radical rewrite.[41] Their intention was furthermore to convey to the public Schmidt's transformation in stature—from a politician focused primarily on defence matters to an 'all-rounder'.[42] In content, the new book entailed moving from a technical military-strategic perspective to the broader realm of East–West security relations and the FRG's role therein.[43] Hence the change of title—*Strategie des Gleichgewichts: Deutsche Friedenspolitik und die Weltmächte* (1969).

The new title became a bestseller. The first Seewald edition of 5,000 copies, released during the spring of 1969 in parallel with a licensed Bertelsmann Lesering edition of another 5,000, was followed by a second paperback special edition with a print run of a further 5,000 in September 1969—just ahead of the *Bundestag* elections.[44] By the time of the annual October book fair in Frankfurt, Seewald noted that on his list of political books Schmidt's aroused the greatest interest— with enquiries for translation coming from the English, Americans, French, Spanish, Italians, Dutch, and from all of Scandinavia. An amended third edition came out in mid November; a fourth only one month later.[45] A fully revised fifth edition of 5,000 copies plus a further Bertelsmann version (5,000 copies) as well as a licensed Ullstein pocket book edition of 20,000 followed suit.[46] Overall, some

50,000 German copies of the book had been sold within a year. And although no American version materialized, by 1971 the British publisher William Kimber brought out an English translation of the fifth edition entitled *The Balance of Power: Germany's Peace Policy and the Super Powers*. This version included a specially written English preface by Schmidt and a flattering foreword by Denis Healey, fresh from six years as Britain's minister of defence.[47]

The original book in 1961 had also been timed for a federal election, but then the SPD had not been successful. In 1969, however, the party won a landslide victory, ending two decades of CDU hegemony. Willy Brandt became chancellor and Helmut Schmidt was made defence minister. The strategist of balance now had a chance to put his ideas into practice.

THE DEFENCE MINISTER

One year after becoming defence minister, Schmidt announced in the English preface of *The Balance of Power*: 'This is not the book of a scholar but that of a practical politician.' He said he had drawn on the findings of political scientists and on his own political experience to analyse the 'actual development of political processes and the inherent opportunities for the future'. These words could be considered almost a policy manifesto for Schmidt the defence minister.[48]

In this new preface, he suggested that 1969 represented an historic moment because Brandt was the first Social Democratic chancellor in forty years. It also had momentous implications for the future because Brandt cherished the vision of a completely new relationship with the Federal Republic's communist neighbours. No post-war chancellor had 'espoused the cause of détente more vigorously than Brandt'. And indeed, since the building of the Berlin Wall in 1961 Brandt and Bahr had developed a policy of engagement with the Eastern bloc, which they sought to implement after taking office in 1969. This policy envisaged eventual unification via the gradual coming together of the two Germanies—what they called 'change through rapprochement' (*Wandel durch Annäherung*). In the short term, however, *Ostpolitik* involved recognizing the fact of division, both in Germany and in Europe; this would consolidate the international détente necessary for German rapprochement. Landmarks in the implementation of this policy included the 'Eastern Treaties' normalizing Bonn's relations with Poland (1970) and the Soviet Union and East Germany (1972), as well as the treaty to confirm four-power rights and responsibilities in Berlin (1971). These agreements were intended to bridge the East–West divide by easing tensions, promoting communication, and expediting trade, cultural exchange, and human contact among the people of divided Germany. For Brandt, a former mayor of West Berlin who had been distraught to see the Wall going up, the essence of *Ostpolitik* was human relations and personal connectivity—this was *Kontaktpolitik* adapted from high politics to the grass roots.

What was Schmidt's contribution during these dramatic years? As defence minister he was bound to concentrate on issues of security, but his formation during the 1960s as a defence intellectual also inclined him in this direction. He welcomed *Ostpolitik* as an opportunity for the FRG to take its own initiatives in foreign policy but also recognized the very real limits on West German agency, given its lack of sovereignty, the fact of German national division, and the continued Soviet threat. He was insistent, therefore, that the premises underlying German foreign and security policy should remain the same, namely NATO membership and American military protection. Brandt, for his part, never denied this but Bahr hoped and planned for a new pan-European security system, based ideally on full-scale disarmament leading to the dissolution of the two military alliances. Schmidt, the realist, never entertained these more utopian ideas. And so here was a fundamental philosophical divide that would define his relationship with Bahr right through the 1970s.[49] As he said in *The Balance of Power*, 'détente in Europe is impossible without the balance provided by NATO. To maintain the balance of power is a prerequisite of an effective defence as well as of an improvement in the relations between East and West...In this context security through deterrence is one side of the coin; and the other is security through détente.'[50] These concepts of security, deterrence, and balance were central to Schmidt's strategic thought, for Germany and for global politics.

Paralleling German *Ostpolitik*, there was a movement towards superpower détente as America and Russia evolved a new relationship, in particular by easing tension over nuclear weapons. In May 1972 they signed SALT I, the interim agreement on strategic arms limitations, confirming a shift from American nuclear superiority to strategic parity with the Soviet Union. This agreement on intercontinental missiles raised questions about the balance of power in Europe and thus about West German security. Strategic parity had long been been predicted by Schmidt. In his 1961 book he warned that the US strategic deterrent would inevitably lose its effectiveness 'with the approach of a stable nuclear balance between the world powers'.[51] He therefore pressed all through the 1960s for 'a mutual balanced reduction of military forces in Eastern and Western Europe' to minimize the danger of war on the Old Continent. And now, as he said in *The Balance of Power*, under the Brandt government 'for the first time, this goal is an essential element of German foreign policy'.[52]

But reaching this goal would be a slow process: the so-called mutual and balanced force reduction (MBFR) negotiations did not even get going until 1973. In the meantime, Schmidt concentrated on enhancing West German security by strengthening the country's own conventional deterrent. This was his major project as defence minister and it found expression in two so-called White Books, published in 1970 and 1971—of which the first was more important, setting a course that the FRG would follow through the ensuing decade.

This 1970 *Weißbuch* was the result of Brandt's announcement in his October 1969 inaugural address that the new government would undertake a 'critical stocktaking' (*kritische Bestandsaufnahme*) of the *Bundeswehr*. Such a self-exploration of the West German armed forces was unprecedented in both form and intensity. At the core of the White Book lay Schmidt's fundamental understanding of security policy, which was based on two pillars. First, the continued importance of Alliance solidarity in principle, together with West Germany's moral and financial commitment to embody this in an effective defence posture. Second, the need for arms control and arms reduction—in other words, halting the spiral of growth and seeking equilibrium at a lower level. Together these two pillars would sustain the kind of stable peace that Schmidt called *Frieden in Freiheit* (peace in freedom).[53]

The White Book was the product of more than a hundred hours of discussion, spread over several lengthy sessions of brainstorming and intensive editing, that involved Bonn's top politicians, the military leadership, and senior bureaucrats. Schmidt was fully engaged in the specifics of this process, far more than might have been expected of a defence minister. In fact, when presenting the White Book to the Bundestag, he stated that he personally identified himself with the overall concept of the volume and with its 120 concrete recommendations, adding, in a striking phrase: 'It carries not only my signature, but also my handwriting.'[54]

To construct Schmidt's first pillar—an effective West German defence posture within NATO—he needed to strengthen the *Bundeswehr*, which he and Brandt both regarded in 1969 as being in a lamentable state. In *The Balance of Power* he had identified the chronic shortage of trained leaders and the low morale of conscripts as key problems.[55] The White Book therefore highlighted the need for better pay and a fairer system of conscription. By reducing service time from eighteen months to fifteen, Schmidt not only addressed the morale problem but also increased the number of draftees—thereby enlarging West Germany's pool of trained manpower and reservists.

The second pillar—arms control and arms reduction—was more problematic. Within a few months of taking office, the Brandt government made a concrete negotiating proposal for mutual, simultaneous, and balanced reduction of all military forces in Europe. In May 1970 they presented it at the NATO Council meeting in Rome.[56] This reflected Schmidt's long-standing idea of 'a Central European zone of mutually limited level of armament' (*Mitteleuropäische Zone gegenseitig begrenzter Rüstung*). In Rome he now pressed for comprehensive reductions—both nuclear and conventional—that encompassed national and Alliance forces.[57] No immediate progress was made but the West German government had successfully laid the MBFR issue on the table. For this Schmidt was largely responsible. He proudly told the Bundestag in June that this policy of actively pursuing 'mutual, balanced, and equivalent arms limitations' constituted a major innovation in FRG defence policy, in contrast to the CDU line under Adenauer, Strauß, and others.[58]

East–West dialogue about SALT and MBFR constituted significant advances in détente. But this did not stop the Soviets from continuing to expand both their conventional and theatre nuclear forces and Schmidt was even more concerned now about the implications of all this for West Germany. He still abhorred the much-touted concept of 'limited nuclear war' but accepted the necessity for NATO to deploy theatre nuclear weapons as a deterrent against the Warsaw Pact's own deployment. The White Book also addressed the question of when, if at all, these weapons might be used. In line with Schmidt's earlier writings, it stated: 'As a means of defence tactical nuclear weapons must not be used except as a last resort and even then only with restraint and on a selective basis because of their escalating and destructive effect'. The White Book therefore expressed a clear preference for maintaining conventional forces of sufficient scale that NATO could undertake a non-nuclear counter-attack. However, given the Soviet Union's geo-strategic pre-dominance in Europe, conventional defence would be at best a delaying tactic. The hope was that this would 'leave time for negotiations concerning a termination of the conflict and for consultations among the allies about the first use of nuclear weapons, if negotiations were to fail'. It is noteworthy that the White Book of 1970 did not reject outright the principle of first use. This was, in fact, an essential part of NATO doctrine, from which Bonn's official defence policy could not afford to deviate.[59]

Here lay an underlying quandary. Schmidt's strategic concept focused on the necessity of balance at *all* force levels—from the conventional through the various steps on the nuclear ladder—ideally achieved through arms reduction. But the problem was that whenever the balance was upset by one side's escalation, the other side might feel it had to expand its own capabilities, fuelling an arms race. Potentially this could entail NATO's acquisition of modernized theatre nuclear weapons in order to deter the Soviet Union. Yet such weapons could be used to embark on limited nuclear warfare—an outcome that Schmidt regarded as totally unacceptable. In the early 1970s there seemed no need for a Western nuclear arms build-up to maintain the balance: SALT was making progress and Schmidt had high hopes for MBFR. But in the latter part of the decade, with the ebbing of détente and the stalling of arms-reduction talks, Schmidt would have to grapple in earnest, as chancellor, with the spectre of limited nuclear war.

OSTPOLITIK AS DEFENCE POLICY

Ostpolitik was almost synonymous with Brandt. So when Schmidt was catapulted into the chancellor's office, both media and public were intrigued to know how he would handle relations with the Soviet bloc. In his inaugural address he undertook to continue Brandt's policies. His aim, he said, was 'to go beyond resolutions with view to achieving practical results, in order to fill European détente policy with more substance'.[60]

But there were real differences of style and approach between these two Social Democrat chancellors. First, at the level of personality; 'The tempo of the new beginning', wrote one German journalist, 'expresses the temperament of the new man...to the point, concrete and realistic.'[61] The radio station Deutsche Welle spoke of 'more realism in politics, less idealism. More pragmatism in getting through the political tasks, less ideology...He is not a man for philosophizing. He is a man of action. He knuckles down.'[62] *The Observer* (London), entitling its pro-file 'A Man Who Can't Stop Working', depicted the new chancellor 'rushing up the steps of the Palais Schaumburg, and hastening from office to office of the chancel-lory...Helmut Schmidt is officer like. He believes in correct procedure, hard decisions and obedience.'[63] The officer analogy was apt: Schmidt took command in Bonn in May 1974 rather like the 'Lord of the Flood' who had seized control on that epic day in Hamburg in February 1962.

Some in the media linked Schmidt's character traits to the region he came from: stereotypically, claimed Deutsche Welle, Hanseatics were 'snappy and curt, well-groomed and clear-cut, self-confident and a little bit vain'. Schmidt's Hamburg roots mattered in a larger sense, too. Brandt, as a former Mayor of Berlin, felt *Ostpolitik* as a gut issue: the partition of Germany and of his city was a source of real pain. Schmidt, by contrast, was emotionally more remote from the country's great divide, seeing it as a problem of politics rather than an affair of the heart. Despite moments of real charm to offset his directness, Schmidt was primarily 'a technician of power', observed *Neue Züricher Zeitung*, whereas Brandt could move the masses and 'develop political goals that appealed to moral qualities'. In short, Brandt had a 'charisma' that Schmidt rarely seemed to project.[64]

Schmidt's realistic approach to foreign policy shaped his handling of relations with the East. Developing this theme in an article entitled 'Realism in *Ostpolitik*', the *Frankfurter Allgemeine Zeitung* suggested that there were now 'no vague visions of a pan-European security order, no false hopes about convergence or "change through rapprochement"'. Schmidt's formula, said the paper, was essentially 'we have to pursue interests in *Ostpolitik*, nothing else' because that was what the Soviets were doing and had always done.[65] There was no question, stated Deutsche Welle, that 'he was an architect of Ostpolitik'—a point made by other papers, who noted his vocal support for this policy as far back as 1966. Nevertheless, his approach was more hard-nosed because it was coloured by his outlook as a defence intellectual—so different from Brandt's. Schmidt always saw *Ostpolitik* as a problem of security policy.[66]

And Schmidt knew his adversary. His thinking was influenced by first-hand experience of the Soviet bloc—not least because of a remarkable trip across Eastern Europe in 1966, on which he kept extensive notes scribbled on pieces of paper.[67] He made clear that he was not on a special political mission, for himself or anyone else; this was a journey undertaken out of what he called 'pure touristic and political curiosity'. He wanted it to be a voyage of discovery, to get to know the opinions of 'the little man in the street' as well as those of high-ranking politicians, and above all to see the communist system in daily life and develop a sense of the different national cultures that lay beneath it. He was very conscious that whereas West German politicians would visit America once a year and West European states even more often, they rarely ventured beyond the Iron Curtain.[68]

On 13 July 1966 Schmidt piled his wife, Loki, his daughter Susanne, and a friend (the photographer Sven Simon)[69] into the family's Opel Rekord and set out across Eastern Europe. First stop was Prague; then Warsaw. But the most striking part of the trip was the approach to Moscow (see Figure 2.4). He had made this journey a quarter of a century earlier, under very different circumstances, as a junior officer in the First Panzer Division, which ended up in November 1941 on the outskirts of the Soviet capital. Although Schmidt made very little of this when talking to the media in the summer of 1966, the war experience was surely still

Figure 2.4 The Schmidt family in Red Square, June 1966.
Source: Sven Simon.

vivid in his mind. This time the journey from Warsaw to Moscow took only three days but he now had the leisure to reflect on what he was seeing. Schmidt wrote: 'Those three days' in the car, along the only major highway from the Polish border, 'gave us a real feeling for the vast space of the Soviet Union'. And in Moscow he was very struck by a huge map that depicted the whole country, from Brest to Vladivostok. By comparison the countries of Central Europe, from which they had started, seemed to slide off the edge of the map. Schmidt was painfully struck by the geographical smallness of Germany, despite the country's stature as a world-ranking economy. This image of Russia's almost incomprehensible vastness, first experienced as a soldier in 1941, conveyed to him anew the magnitude of Soviet power which, he insisted, 'must not be underestimated'.[70]

But the trip across Western Russia also brought home to him the USSR's grave socio-economic problems. Trying to find the right kind of petrol for a standard Western car proved highly challenging and the Intertourist hotels in which they were obliged to stay were 'miserable'. Even the most basic needs were hardly met: half a century later Schmidt still remembered twice having to mend 'loos that didn't work'. Villages appeared to have hardly changed in twenty-five years—housing conditions seemed positively 'intolerable' (*unzumutbar*)—and fruit was available only in big cities and then at extortionate prices. A pound of pears, for instance, cost about 5 DM (1 ruble and 25 copeks); a pound of tomatoes 2 DM. Clothing in GUM, the state's premier department store in Red Square, was a nightmare for Loki. She was appalled that a man's suit of shoddy quality, which nobody in the West would buy, cost 250 DM and a pair of high-heeled lady's shoes 50–120 DM, considering that a senior teacher's salary (her point of reference) in the USSR was no more than 800 DM per month. Dealing with such poverty and backwardness, Schmidt knew, would demand all the country's attention and resources. The inefficient and unproductive Soviet economic system, in contrast to West Germany's advanced state of development, was therefore a weakness that could be exploited in diplomacy. This dual sense of the Soviet Union's geopolitical power *and* economic vulnerability would define Schmidt's policy towards Moscow throughout his years in government.[71]

Based on the 1966 trip, Schmidt drew some specific conclusions for West German diplomacy. In his public comments he lent support to Brandt's proposals for opening treaty negotiations with the countries of the Soviet bloc, emphasizing that this should happen immediately. Given the situation he had seen with his own eyes, he also considered it an opportune moment to explore trade relations across the East–West divide (*Osthandel*).[72] In speaking out in this way, the SPD's 'defence expert' (*Wehrexperte*) propelled himself to the forefront of the architects of *Ostpolitik* within his party—a point often forgotten now in the conventional emphasis on Brandt and Bahr. But for Schmidt these policies could only be successful if grounded in a clearly formulated concept of security. Addressing the Bundestag on 23 September 1966, he argued that, in order to be in a position to promote eventual German unification, it was important to pursue détente while maintaining the balance of power. Ideally he wanted this balance to be achieved at a lower level of forces, through arms control. He called this 'the veritable strategic problem of the current epoch'. This linkage of creative *Osteuropapolitik* with arms control based on an equilibrium of military forces distinguished Schmidt from Brandt and Bahr.[73]

Schmidt's preoccupation with Moscow did not mean that he allowed himself to be intimidated. In an article entitled 'Fear is like a Fetter' for the newspaper *Sonntagsblatt*, he admitted that any German politician would feel insecure when faced with the immense power that Russia could project. Yet he was adamant that fear should not dictate Bonn's engagement with Moscow; on the contrary, he emphasized the importance of rationality and calculation. This required 'putting oneself in the other's shoes to study him, his interests and his needs, his aspirations and anxieties, his capabilities and potential – both imagined and actual'. Schmidt believed that the current Kremlin leadership did 'not want war' or 'the risk of the possibility of war'. In other words, Brezhnev was fundamentally different from Khrushchev, whose gambler mentality had led him into 'risky adventures' over Berlin and Cuba. Schmidt, moreover, agreed with Adenauer's aphorism—'the Soviet Union needs peace'—and therefore felt that, in principle, West Germany should be less worried.[74]

However, in the *Sonntagsblatt* article Schmidt also entered several caveats to this apparently sympathetic view of the Soviets. He recognized that the superpowers were world-wide competitors. Tensions between them anywhere on the planet could explode in Europe. Berlin was the crucial pressure point, not least because the East German regime could afford to play posture politics: it did not have the Kremlin's wider responsibilities for global stability and peace. Schmidt, despite his stress on Soviet rationality, also warned that even rational politicians can act irrationally, especially if provoked, and that what starts out as the most rational policy can lead to fateful mistakes. Above all, in line with his strategic thinking, he was sure that Brezhnev's cautious status quo policy in Europe was not merely an expression of the Soviet leader's character but was basically the result of the military equilibrium that the West had painfully achieved with the East. The lesson, said Schmidt in 1966, was clear: 'to keep this balance is a dictate of reason for the West'.[75]

As chancellor, Schmidt was conscious that this balancing act must now also be performed on a global stage. Richard Nixon's dramatic visits to Beijing and Moscow in 1972 had highlighted China's emergence as a force in world affairs and revealed the new strategic geometry stemming from the Sino-Soviet split. In his 1969 book Schmidt had already predicted a new global era of 'tripolarity', revolving around the United States, the Soviet Union, and the People's Republic. A visit to China had been on his wish list since the late 1960s—intended as an analogue to his voyage of discovery to Moscow in 1966—and he had actively encouraged Brandt to open diplomatic relations with the PRC; this was achieved in late 1972.[76] In October 1975 Schmidt finally paid his own visit to Beijing, meeting the ailing Mao Zedong, who warned of a looming world war as Moscow's influence rose while America's was on the decline following its defeat in Indochina. The Chinese leader asserted that détente served only Moscow's interests; Schmidt, by contrast, insisted that the FRG's armed forces were well equipped and that NATO felt confident of repelling a Soviet attack. Détente was therefore not to be taken as a sign of Western European weakness. He also had long conversations with Deng Xiaoping, especially about global strategy and the international economy, and was gratified by open Chinese support for the principle of German reunification at a time when both superpowers were wedded to the status quo. Although the chancellor's visit yielded few direct results, he left Beijing with the strong conviction that China had to be reckoned with not just politically and diplomatically—as Kissinger did—but also as a major future force in the global economy.[77]

China was a major player in Schmidt's conception of an interdependent world. It is often forgotten that, despite Nixon and Kissinger's obsession with triangular politics, their visit to China in 1972 did not result in any immediate transformation of the Sino-American relationship. Because full diplomatic relations were not established until 1979, trade contacts remained minimal. Consequently China's opening to the Western world concentrated primarily on Europe. In the years after Schmidt's visit, the Chinese intensified their fact-finding missions and shopping trips, especially to the FRG, exposing a larger number of party officials to the realities of an advanced economy and providing impetus for their drive to reform and modernize. With the Federal Republic becoming the PRC's main trading partner in Western Europe by 1978, thanks to its sophisticated technology and robust economy, Bonn was being taken seriously by the world's 'new, third Super Power'.[78]

Schmidt's engagement with China exemplified his growing sense of himself as a global statesman, interacting with each of the three big players. Of course he did not view the two great communist powers as equals: despite his interest in Beijing, Schmidt's principal diplomatic priority was always Moscow because of the unresolved German question. Nevertheless his policies towards the PRC and the USSR reflected his distinctive approach to the communist world, built around a combination of power politics and geo-economics. Unlike Brandt, Schmidt did not believe in grand visions for *Ostpolitik*: his métier was pragmatic progress rather than sweeping programmes. And compared with Bahr, he was much less optimistic about any rapid dissolution of the Iron Curtain. The two practical issues on Schmidt's agenda when he came to power in 1974 were deepening the rapprochement between the two Germanies and bringing to a successful conclusion the Helsinki discussions for a pan-European security agreement. Both of these would prove much more problematic than he had hoped.

It soon became evident that the recent normalization of relations had not resolved the underlying disagreements of Bonn and East Berlin over long-term outlooks and aims. The FRG wished ultimately to transcend the division of Germany, whereas the GDR wanted to cement that division and confirm its independence as a separate state.[79] To this end, the Honecker regime, supported by Moscow, increased the pressure on the highly sensitive issue of Berlin. To Schmidt's great annoyance, the Kremlin was not only unprepared to make any concessions but actively tried to weaken the links between the FRG and West Berlin and to undermine the rights of the three Western allies in the city—hammered out with great effort in the Quadripartite treaty of 1971. By 1976, Schmidt was forced to recognize that no substantive movement was possible for the moment at the bilateral level on the German question.[80] Bonn's relations with Moscow were also in difficulties over economic issues. The influx of investment in Russia by West German companies that Brezhnev had hoped for after his summit with Brandt in 1973 had not materialized. In short, *Osthandel* was stalling. Although the Kremlin invited Schmidt to Moscow in October 1974, the talks got bogged down on Berlin and only little progress was made on other important economic issues such as FRG credits, pipelines, and the construction of power stations in the USSR.[81]

On the multilateral plane, too, progress in East–West relations proved painfully slow. Negotiations for a pan-European agreement on security had been going on since 1973 in the form of the Conference on Security and Cooperation in Europe (CSCE). The signing of the Final Act in Helsinki on 1 August 1975 was seen by many as the pinnacle of détente in Europe and a highlight of *Ostpolitik*. This agreement embodied several basic aims of Bonn's *Deutschlandpolitik*—especially the principle of the non-use of force and that of human rights, the possibility of future peaceful change of borders, and the promotion of trade, cultural exchange, and practical humanitarian improvements to bridge the East–West divide. Helsinki was the first time during the Cold War that the countries of Europe had come together to create a framework for dialogue, and some Western politicians and pundits saw the CSCE as a forum for future détente. But, once the images of Helsinki had disappeared from the newspapers and TV screens, the momentum died. The follow-up conference was not scheduled until 1977 and in the short term the Helsinki accords made little tangible difference to daily life behind the Iron Curtain.

In fact, by the mid 1970s the general mood of détente had begun to fade. After the heady enthusiasm of the Moscow summit of 1972 and the SALT I agreement, the superpowers did not advance much further in strategic arms control. They became mired in the details of warheads and weaponry, and political will ebbed on the American side in 1973–4 with Watergate and the Nixon–Ford transition. Ford's brief meetings with Brezhnev in 1974–5 had little impact and SALT II did not appear on the table until 1979. Equally exasperating were the negotiations on MBFR which, after the inception in 1973, rapidly degenerated into a ponderous process of proposal and counter-proposal. This slow-motion diplomatic tennis game continued for the rest of the decade, without any conclusion.[82]

Frustrated on all fronts, Schmidt and his colleagues became profoundly suspicious of Soviet policy. The central problem was that détente was understood in fundamentally different ways in America, Germany, and the Soviet Union. For the United States, détente entailed accepting the reality of Soviet power while enmeshing the Kremlin in a network of relations with the West that would restrain any further expansion. Washington's central tactic was the concept of 'linkage'—a policy of carrots and sticks played out on a global chessboard that would enable it to manage every aspect of Soviet conduct. For Moscow, however, détente signified American recognition of the Soviet Union as an equal superpower. The achievement of nuclear parity, embodied in SALT I, removed the danger of Armageddon and made it safe for the Soviet Union, in rejection of linkage, to pursue its geopolitical and ideological objectives across the world. This would become clear later in the 1970s with Moscow's adventurism in Angola, the Horn of Africa, and Indochina. In other words, the Soviets' interpretation of 'peaceful coexistence' with America and Europe allowed them, as good Marxist–Leninists, a free hand to aid the revolutionary class struggle and accelerate the demise of capitalism across the globe.[83]

So, whereas Washington saw détente as an all-encompassing framework to control the Soviets, Moscow viewed it as a more limited, bilateral pact. This approach was also evident in its interaction with European states, especially West Germany. Just as the Soviets had codified the superpower nuclear balance in SALT I, so they sought to stabilize the territorial balance in Europe through the German treaties and the Helsinki accords. What mattered to Moscow about Helsinki were not human rights and freedom of movement, so important to Bonn, but international recognition of the post-war status quo through the principle that state boundaries were inviolable. Enshrining this in the Final Act was regarded by the Soviets as nothing less than a diplomatic triumph.

After Helsinki, Moscow declared that 'political détente' had been achieved 'in practice' in Europe and now pressed for what it called 'military détente'. This meant further arms limitation at the European level, to complement the superpower agreements. The Soviets particularly challenged the independence of the British and French nuclear deterrents (outside the SALT process), American strategies of limited nuclear warfare, and the modernization of US theatre nuclear forces in Europe.[84] They also put pressure on West Germany to loosen its ties with NATO, in return for some vague concessions on the German question. Bonn was quick to understand the implications of Moscow's new, hair-splitting rhetoric about 'political' versus 'military' détente.[85] While engagement with the Soviets was desirable, any Western negotiation position had to be anchored in NATO's solidarity and willingness to defend itself. At all costs the Soviets had to be prevented from breaking up NATO through bilateral tactics, and unilateral reductions in Western military strength were totally unacceptable.[86]

From Schmidt's perspective, Soviet demands for military détente laid West Germany open to political blackmail. Preoccupied as always with the balance of power, he kept promoting the strengthening of NATO's conventional forces, to ensure a credible deterrent at the sub-nuclear level. But he also had to fend off unwelcome pressures from his superpower ally. The Americans, led by Defense Secretary James Schlesinger, placed more emphasis on deterrence at the nuclear level. For some years they had wanted to strengthen NATO's own theatre nuclear forces (TNFs) posture as a counterbalance to the Soviet TNF arsenal that included ballistic missiles of medium range (2,000+ kilometres) and intermediate range (4,000+ kilometres) that targeted Europe—the SS-4 MRBMs and SS-5 IRBMs. The so-called 'Schlesinger Doctrine', announced in March 1974, even argued that, deterrence apart, NATO's nuclear force structure had to be credible in operational military terms. This raised Schmidt's bête noire of limited nuclear war in the German heartland. So his position on security was intellectually complex and politically delicate. He wanted to maintain dialogue with the Soviets and seek a military balance at a lower level. But, faced with Moscow's threats and its conventional superiority, he felt compelled to lobby for substantial rearmament by the Western Alliance. This set him at odds with Brandt, Bahr, and the left wing of his own party. Yet, in contrast to the nuclear strategy advocated by the Americans, he wanted NATO rearmament to concentrate on conventional forces.

Trying to keep the Americans, the Soviets, and the SPD left happy, the Schmidt government packaged all this as 'realistic détente policy' (*realistische Entspannungspolitik*).[87] The implications were spelled out by Foreign Minister Hans-Dietrich Genscher in a series of statements during 1976. At NATO's spring conference in Oslo in May he told colleagues that the Alliance had to revitalize itself, not just militarily but also politically.[88] At the NATO Council in November, Genscher went even further, highlighting the dichotomy between Soviet propaganda for arms reduction and a growing Soviet arms build-up.[89] He also pointed the finger at Soviet intervention in Angola, which belied the Kremlin's peace rhetoric.[90] In short, there could be no doubt that political and ideological expansionism remained integral to the Soviet conception of détente. Whatever Brezhnev said about détente 'overcoming the Cold War', in Bonn's eyes the Soviet Union simply 'pursued old aims with other means'.[91]

Helmut Schmidt had been an apostle for détente and one of the early architects of *Ostpolitik*. By late 1976, however, when facing re-election, the chancellor's security priorities had become deterrence and defence first, détente second. The principle of balance now dominated. *Ostpolitik* had become an aspect of defence policy.[92]

THE 1976 ELECTION AND ITS AFTERMATH

Schmidt had not been elected chancellor in May 1974: he gained that position because of a party vote after Brandt was forced to resign. The election of 3 October 1976—a contest against Helmut Kohl and the CDU/CSU—was therefore enormously important for Schmidt, both personally and politically. This was his chance to gain public endorsement as chancellor in his own right—a formidable task for at least two reasons. First, Brandt remained party leader, with a cult following on the left who hated nuclear weapons and lauded his détente policies. For many SPD members Schmidt lacked his predecessor's charisma and appeal. He remained the outsider from Hamburg—respected but not loved. Second, the SPD as a whole had been losing support among young voters, disillusioned with capitalism and established politics and passionate about direct democracy and green ideas. It looked unlikely that the SPD could coax this group of voters back into the party, as Brandt had managed in the aftermath of 1968. Schmidt deliberately campaigned on a personal platform, with slogans inviting the electorate to vote for the SPD in order to 'keep the better man' as chancellor (see Figure 2.5). Separating himself from the party in this way also allowed Schmidt to discourage centrist voters from backing the FDP and the CDU.[93]

Initially Schmidt remained aloof from electioneering, staying in Bonn and presenting himself as the statesman at the helm of the nation. He only threw himself

Figure 2.5 On the way to vote, Hamburg, 3 October 1976.
Source: Stern.

into campaigning over the last couple of weeks when it became clear that Kohl had considerable appeal with ordinary voters, coming over as an uncomplicated and approachable man whereas Schmidt seemed more remote.[94] In response, Schmidt zeroed in on Strauß as 'the real danger man' and Kohl as 'the man who would like to be Chancellor under Strauß'. Or, as he put it more pithily, Strauß was 'the cook' and Kohl 'the waiter'. SPD pamphlets played up Schmidt's virtues, asserting that the 'Chancellor works 16 hours a day…He is competent, fast-moving, decisive.' They added slyly: 'Helmut Schmidt is not the type of man who goes in for wine and beer festivals' (Schmidt was often photographed with a bottle of Coca-Cola). The lead SPD slogan at first (*Modell Deutschland*) featured the government's economic success in the face of the global economic crisis, but the party shifted in the last two weeks and asked the electorate to vote for peace (*den Frieden wählen*). This switch reflected concern at the Kohl factor but also resulted from pressure from Brandt and Bahr to feature their foreign policy achievements as a vote-winner. Brandt spoke publicly about the need to embark on a 'second phase of *Deutschlandpolitik*'; Schmidt promised a visit from Brezhnev as part of a 'new impulse to improve contacts with the East'.[95]

On one level the results of the federal elections might be seen as a setback for Schmidt and the SPD. The CDU/CSU emerged as the strongest party in the Bundestag, with 254 seats and 48.6 per cent of the vote. But the government coalition hung on with 264 seats and 50.5 per cent of the vote (the SPD's share being 224 seats and 42.6 per cent of the vote).[96] Internally the SPD judged that this narrow victory was due to the late emphasis on *Ostpolitik*. Nevertheless, Schmidt took the opportunity, as part of a Cabinet reshuffle, to move Bahr from the post of minister of economic cooperation to a non-Cabinet position as an executive party secretary. Although an apparent demotion, this left Bahr free from Cabinet discipline and able to exploit his closeness to Brandt as party leader. More in touch with the party base than the chancellor, he could now also play on his appeal as the man associated in public memory with the heyday of *Ostpolitik*. When asked by US ambassdor Walter Stoessel whether he would remain interested in foreign affairs, Bahr answered with a knowing smile: 'There is an old saying that the cat cannot forget mice—I might feel the same way about foreign affairs'. From this position Bahr would prove a thorn in Schmidt's side for the rest of his chancellorship.[97]

An early sign of these new personal dynamics was the private letter that Bahr sent to Schmidt on 19 October, laying out how he saw the next four-year electoral cycle. Bahr emphasized the need to make MBFR the dominant political theme. He predicted that troop reductions could have a major impact in the 1980 election, comparable to that of the Basic Treaty in 1972. Speaking of arms control generally, Bahr contended that the 'topic will have the same effect as the first phase of *Ostpolitik*. It will stir people's imagination, integrate the party, create solidarity within the coalition and split the opposition'—leaving Kohl in 'a difficult position'. Looking to highlight his own skill and significance, Bahr added: 'Tactically and technically a similar method could be chosen as the one that led to the Quadripartite Agreement, when prior, or rather in parallel, to the official negotiations we had some contacts with the Americans and Russians.' Having reminded Schmidt about his pivotal role as the backchannel and broker between the superpowers for the crucial agreement on Berlin, he added loftily: 'At some point I can tell you about it.' Here was a marker for the future: Bahr's consistent emphasis on disarmament and détente to move Europe beyond bipolarity, in tension with Schmidt's insistence on an East–West military balance as the basis for détente.[98]

For the chancellor, as we have seen, West Germany's whole approach to détente assumed a close bond with the United States, but this was also coming under strain in the aftermath of the election. If Egon Bahr was Schmidt's domestic bête noire, Jimmy Carter was the foreign counterpart. Both men challenged what the chancellor considered his balanced approach to foreign policy—Bahr through a utopian emphasis on disarmament and Carter by an overtly confrontational posture towards the Soviet Union. Schmidt's relations with the 'peanut farmer' never recovered from his explicit support of Ford during the American election campaign, and the consequences of this extraordinary gaffe were particularly fraught over security issues. Carter's Soviet policy was much more moralistic than Ford's, driven by a passionate human rights agenda and deep ambivalence about nuclear weapons. Speaking to the United Nations on 17 March 1977, eight weeks into his presidency, Carter called for 'deep reduction in the strategic arms of both sides. Such a major step towards not only arms limitation but arms reduction would be welcomed by mankind as a giant step towards peace.'[99]

Carter's key foreign-policy aides—Cyrus Vance, the secretary of state, and Zbigniew Brzezinski, his national security adviser—favoured moving rapidly to a SALT II treaty based essentially on the outline agreed between Brezhnev and Ford in Vladivostok in 1974, limiting the number of missile launchers on each side at their current levels of 2,400. That would then be the basis for a more radical agreement in SALT III. But the president wanted to present the Soviets straight away with a 'comprehensive proposal' embodying the 'deep cuts' that he favoured and setting limits at 1,800 to 2,000 launchers. This would entail genuine arms reduction instead of simply limiting future growth. Carter seems to have believed that a firm démarche at the start of his presidency offered the best chance of securing Soviet agreement and also the support of the Senate well ahead of the next election. Vance was therefore dispatched to Moscow at the end of March 1977.[100]

The American démarche was rejected out of hand. The Kremlin had already been irritated by Carter's moralizing about human rights, including statements about leading Soviet dissidents such as Andrei Sakharov. 'Stop your interference in our internal affairs', the Soviet ambassador in Washington Anatoly Dobrynin told Vance sharply. Vance's SALT proposals were seen by the Politburo as equally disturbing. Since they had been aired in advance to the American press, the Kremlin assumed the Vance mission was essentially a propaganda exercise and Dobrynin took the unusual step of telling the secretary of state before he left Washington that his mission would be a failure. The content itself was also unsettling for Moscow, because the Kremlin had regarded Vladivostok as virtually a done deal. 'If the United States wants to reopen questions that have already been solved', Brezhnev told Vance, 'then the Soviet Union will again raise such problems as the American Forward-Based Systems in Europe and the transfer of American strategic weapons to its allies'. These were references to US Air Force medium-range jets and the new cruise missiles. Brezhnev did not even allow Vance to present the detailed proposals in person. This may have been partly because of the Soviet leader's deterioration in health—something very evident to the American visitors—but it also reflected genuine anger at what seemed a total deviation in both style and substance from the pragmatic diplomacy of the Ford–Kissinger era, and raised basic questions about American trustworthiness.[101]

Carter's conduct was widely criticized at the time in the American press, abetted by leaks from disgruntled members of the administration. Rather than following the Carter line that 'hanging tough' with the Soviets would eventually elicit concessions, there was a general media consensus that the White House had 'seriously miscalculated' and 'overplayed its hand'. Reporters blamed Carter for not sending Vance on 'an exploratory mission', rather than making what seemed like 'a take it or leave it demand' for deep cuts. Vance, who had never met Brezhnev before, was placed in the position of 'making the strongest SALT demands any secretary of state ever put to a Soviet leader, proposing drastic changes in a negotiation that Vance's predecessor, Kissinger, had assured the Kremlin was "90 per cent complete"'.[102]

Vance left the Soviet Union deeply shaken by his rebuff in Moscow. En route home he stopped over in Bonn, where Schmidt closely questioned him. The chancellor expressed concern over press reports about differences of opinion between him and

Carter and did his best to avoid open criticism. But he nevertheless made it clear that, although sympathizing in principle with the president's idealistic objectives, he wondered if the Moscow setback was the result of merely a tactical error or represented a more fundamental failure of strategy. Vance insisted that the road was still open and this was only 'a tactical event'. Schmidt then indicated anxieties that if SALT II failed there would be military backlash in Moscow which would frustrate progress on MBFR in Europe. He also had reservations about Carter's direct approach on human rights. Again, he said, he sympathized in principle because détente did not mean that the West would refrain from challenging the Soviets ideologically and morally, but, on a practical level, he could not afford to indulge in human rights rhetoric because of West Germany's 'special situation' at the heart of Cold War Europe. Aware that the chances of serious Soviet–American dialogue were now receding, Vance said that a visit by Brezhnev to Bonn—pencilled in for the second half of 1977—would be 'useful and constructive from the Alliance perspective'. At the end of April, the Kremlin officially stated that Brezhnev would not hold a summit with Carter until SALT II was ready for signature. To Schmidt's chagrin, this would block any progress on arms control in Europe—his main concern.[103]

Schmidt wrote scathingly in his memoirs that 'Carter had no knowledge of Russian history, tradition and mentality' and made 'very serious mistakes' in his handling of Moscow in 1977. Despite his circumspection when speaking with Vance, he made these feelings abundantly clear at the time. For its part, the White House was equally angry with the chancellor: to quote National Security Adviser Zbigniew Brzezinski, his 'inability to keep his tongue under control soured American–German relations to an unprecedented degree'.[104]

After Carter's rebuff in Moscow, his allies looked forward to NATO's spring summit in London (10–11 May 1977) for clear American leadership on the Alliance's future defence and deterrence posture in Europe.[105] The president proposed that NATO defence ministers begin to develop a long-term defence pro-gramme (LTDP) and undertake an East–West study on the future trends in the Eastern bloc and their impact on the Atlantic Alliance.[106] Schmidt welcomed both these new initiatives in a speech at the summit that would prefigure ideas spelled out more fully in his IISS lecture in London in October (discussed in chapter 3). He told his NATO allies that strategic parity between the superpowers, codified in SALT I, had effectively turned strategic nuclear missiles into weapons of 'last resort'. It was thus necessary to work towards an acceptable balance of conventional forces between the Warsaw Pact and NATO, which Schmidt hoped to achieve via arms reductions in the forum of MBFR.[107] On the other hand, the chancellor also insisted that NATO must keep open the option of increasing its level of armaments if the Soviets did not cooperate in these arms-control negoti-ations. In this vein Schmidt lent his support to Carter's efforts to get the Allies to commit to greater defence spending. Here, in his London speech of May 1977, Schmidt sketched for the first time what came to be known as his 'two tracks' approach.[108]

A week later, NATO's Defence Planning Committee (DPC) issued ministerial guidance on the LTDP. In this context West German Defence Minister Georg Leber stressed that NATO's triad (conventional, tactical nuclear, strategic nuclear) had to remain credible at all levels in order to maintain a military balance. By putting it this way, Leber drew his colleagues' attention to the importance of the second element of the triad—US tactical nuclear weapons operating within the European theatre. At the end of its meeting the DPC affirmed that 'tactical nuclear weapons must be able to support conventional forces against a bigger [Soviet] attack and make evident to the enemy the risk of a nuclear escalation. The strategic nuclear weapons represent a "final sanction" for the total strategy.' Afterwards, NATO set up ten committees to address aspects of the long-term defence plan, of which the tenth, upgraded in October to the 'High Level Group' (HLG), was tasked with assessing 'the role of TNF in NATO strategy, the implications of recent Soviet TNF deployments, the need for NATO TNF modernization and the technical, military, and political implications of alternative NATO TNF postures'.[109]

By TNF the military planners at NATO HQ now signified not just tactical nuclear forces (of battlefield range, up to 500 kilometres) but also intermediate-range nuclear missiles, so that the acronym had been expanded to cover theatre nuclear forces of anything up to sub-strategic range. This element of the triad was attracting more attention because of the alarming Soviet build-up since 1976 of SS-20s—a new type of missile, with enhanced range, mobility, and accuracy. The special potency of SS-20s stemmed from their MIRV technology (multiple, independently targeted re-entry vehicles), meaning that each missile carried three warheads, each of which could be aimed at a different West European city. The SS-20s were omitted from the superpower strategic arms talks (SALT II) because, with a reach of up to 5,000 kilometres, they were classified as of intermediate range—weapons that could not reach the United States. But nor were they on the table in the MBFR talks in Vienna, being nuclear rather than conventional weapons. So the SS-20s slipped through the gaps in arms control. NATO was now putting its finger on what planners privately called the 'grey area' of nuclear arms control, between MBFR and SALT.[110]

The 'grey-area' problem would become the prime focus of Schmidt's approach to defence and diplomacy over the next couple of years—what he considered the key challenge to the security of West Germany and Western Euope. In addressing it he brought to bear his own distinctive philosophy of military balance, in which *Ostpolitik* was to be conducted as a function of defence policy. Bonn, he consistently argued, could safely reach out to the East only on the basis of its partnership with America. But this approach seemed threatened from two directions: by Bahr and the increasingly vocal SPD left who yearned for a 'second phase' of *Ost-* and *Deutschlandpolitik* in spite of the deteriorating international security situation; and also by Carter who had managed in his first few months in office effectively to derail further progress on realistic arms control in Europe. During the summer of 1977, as Schmidt turned to the grey area problem, the challenges posed by Bahr and Carter would come together in a major diplomatic crisis.

3

Defusing the Neutron Bomb

On 7 June 1977 the *Guardian* newspaper in London ran a story headlined 'US asks Congress for funds to make "people killer" neutron bombs'. The *Frankfurter Allgemeine Zeitung* printed a similar story entitled 'America Produces Neutron Bombs'. Both were recycling a piece from the *Washington Post* the day before. Its author, American journalist Walter Pincus, claimed to have discovered that the Carter administration was secretly planning the production of 'its first nuclear battlefield weapon specifically designed to kill people' through the release of 'great quantities of neutrons', rather than 'to destroy military installations through heat and blast'.[1]

Pincus' story started a furore in Washington. Carter knew little or nothing about what was officially designated the enhanced radiation warhead (ERW), which Ford had ordered one year earlier. Even top officials in his administration were taken by surprise at the news that the budget for the fiscal year 1978, which they had just reviewed, included allocations for ERW production. By the end of June the neutron bomb had become a major issue on Capitol Hill.[2]

Despite such pieces in the *Guardian* and *FAZ*, the story initially got little attention in the European media. But then, on 17 July, Egon Bahr published a short essay in the SPD's weekly paper *Vorwärts* entitled 'Is Mankind about to go Mad?'. In it he evoked lurid images of Hiroshima and the massive destruction by A- and H-bombs, and then lambasted what he called the 'N-bomb' as 'a symbol of the perversion of thought'. This, he declared, was a weapon that could 'cleanly' kill humans while leaving everything material unscathed—abhorrent to a socialist because it spared property but sacrificed people. In Bahr's eyes the 'scale of all values' had been 'turned on its head' so that, he said, 'feeling and conscience were rebelling' against the bomb. Hence his vocal public stance, which triggered a passionate debate in the West German media.[3]

The following day, *Der Spiegel* ran a nine-page spread on the neutron bomb and the history of nuclear weapons, entitled 'Bolt of Lightning over the Elbe'. Together with emotive pictures, the article featured a satellite photograph of Hamburg, Schmidt's home town, with graphics to compare the destructive power of neutron warheads and ordinary atomic weapons. The latter would destroy all structures within a radius of 2.2 kilometres, whereas the area of destruction from a neutron bomb would be confined to a mere 200 metres. For people, however, the death toll from blast and radiation would be little different: the following week *Der Spiegel* published a cartoon of two skeletons debating whether it was A- or N-bombs that were 'more humane' (see Figure 3.1).[4]

„ *FINDEN SIE DIE ATOM ODER DIE NEUTRONEN BOMBE HUMANER ?* ,,

Figure 3.1 'Do you find the A- or the N-bomb more humane?'
Source: Horst Haitzinger.

Over the next few weeks Bahr received dozens of postcards and letters sent by West Germans from all walks of life: housewives and architects, lawyers and priests, party members and undecided voters. These correspondents spoke their minds, hailing him as a 'strong' and 'brave' man who stood up to the Americans. They urged Bahr to hold firm and expressed overwhelming gratitude for his public stance against the 'devilish', 'monstrous', American weapon—'the result of capitalism'. Linking the N-bomb to the Schmidt government's nuclear power station programme (a response to the oil crisis of 1973), they branded the chancellor as being in bed with 'great capital', rather than listening to the sentiments of ordinary people and workers. Declaring themselves powerless, the letter writers appealed to Bahr as their spokesman and champion.[5]

Here was a challenge to Schmidt on several levels—as a man of peace, a true Social Democrat, and a defender of German interests. The neutron bomb was mainly intended by American strategists as a deterrent, to shore up the balance of power. But Bahr's intervention and the ensuing media storm conjured up images of what would happen if these weapons were actually used to resist a Warsaw Pact attack across the inner-German border. The neutron bomb brought traditional security issues back into popular debate at a time when the world economy had moved out of the acute crisis that had so preoccupied Schmidt in his first few years. But in his view the furore about the neutron bomb distracted the Alliance from what he had identified as the real challenge to the security of Germany and Western Europe, namely the grey-area problem caused by the Soviet SS-20s. In 1977–8 the chancellor would have to juggle his allegiance to the Atlantic Alliance, the highly volatile domestic situation, and his concern to sustain constructive dialogue with Moscow. It was a struggle that would test to the full Schmidt's talents as a statesman and a politician.

THE NEUTRON BOMB EXPLODES: WASHINGTON AND BONN IN TURMOIL

For both Washington and Bonn the neutron bomb exploded as a political issue in June and July 1977. It had, however, been under discussion among NATO strategists for several years and this background needs to be understood because of the coverage in Germany of the ERW as a novel and aggressive American intervention in nuclear politics. The warhead had been in research and development for nearly two decades and since 1974 the Pentagon and NATO's Nuclear Planning Group (NPG) had been treating the neutron weapon as one ingredient in the top-secret debate about modernizing theatre nuclear forces (TNFs).[6] The US Congress was informed about it in 1975, and the following year the NPG included ERWs in a formal package for modernizing shorter-range TNFs. Also under consideration by the NPG at this time was the Soviet production and deployment of SS-20s. Here was the crux of what Schmidt considered the sub-strategic imbalance in Europe. This came on top of the existing concerns about the consequences for Europe of superpower nuclear parity as codified in SALT I and the Soviets' increasing margin in conventional forces despite MBFR talks. However, Schmidt could not persuade Washington to take seriously this 'grey-area' sub-strategic imbalance until late 1977.[7]

For Schmidt the neutron bomb was a diversion from these fundamental issues, yet he had to take it seriously because of the massive political fallout from the explosive press reaction in July 1977. The Pentagon considered the neutron bomb as a possible war-fighting weapon (not primarily a device to enhance NATO's deterrence posture), but this was an unacceptable idea for the millions of Germans who saw Bahr as their spokesman. The most likely place for a Warsaw Pact attack was at the 'Fulda Gap'—an area between the East German border and Frankfurt am Main that contained two corridors of lowlands suitable for rapid tank advance. In the Pentagon's view the Alliance's ability to inflict significant military damage on the aggressor would be much improved with neutron warheads. Intended for short-range Lance missiles and 8-inch artillery shells, the function of ERWs was to destroy the Soviet tanks. Unlike ordinary nuclear bombs that produced massive blasts, neutron warheads would, due to their reduced heat and blast effect, only cause destruction within a very small radius, leaving buildings and infrastructure further afield more or less intact. This would allow NATO forces to be stationed much closer to areas of potential conflict and to respond much faster. Less collateral damage would also mean minimal casualties and fatalities among civilians and troops beyond the relatively restricted war zone. The ERW's increased precision thus made them in the eyes of the defence experts 'cleaner' and in fact 'less lethal' than the existing nuclear weapons already stockpiled.[8]

This Pentagon scenario was not, of course, how the issue was seen in West Germany. American strategists had always toyed with the idea of 'limited nuclear warfare' that would avoid the use of strategic nuclear weapons and the consequent destruction in the United States itself. Schmidt had jousted with Kissinger and others about this in the 1950s and 1960s (see chapter 2) because a nuclear war that seemed 'limited' to the Americans would be total and catastrophic for Germans. This was essentially the same point as the skeletons in *Der Spiegel* were making about the relative merits of the A-bomb and the N-bomb. But for Americans— three thousand miles or more from the Fulda Gap—the distinction between the two weapons was both meaningful and potentially life-saving.

Strategic 'logic' was, however, irrelevant to the popular debate that had erupted over the neutron bomb following Pincus' article on 6 June 1977. Carter was suddenly obliged to take a position on an issue about which he knew little. In doing so, however, he was caught in a bind. Although noted for his ambitions to achieve a nuclear-weapons-free world, he did not want to be seen as soft on defence questions—certainly not after the 'deep-cuts' debacle in Moscow. So he could not reject the ERWs outright, especially when the Pentagon and State Department supported the warhead's funding for military-strategic reasons. On 24 June Carter let it be known that he felt an emphatic 'abhorrence of nuclear weapons, period' but indicated that he was looking for the approval of ERW funding because he wished to 'keep his options open'.[9]

So, too, did Congress. The White House and Capitol Hill each wanted the other to make the commitment to production, thereby avoiding the political opprobrium for spending taxpayers' dollars on new weapons of mass destruction. In the event, the House passed the relevant funding in mid June, with the Senate Appropriations Subcommittee soon following suit. The latter, however, only approved monies for ERW production after a lengthy and highly contentious secret debate on 1 July. Among the supporters of the programme the powerful Democrat Senator John C. Stennis, chairman of the Armed Services Committee, claimed that 'the idea of having this weapon . . . with limited application is the best news I have heard in years'. To illustrate his point he likened the difference between the effects of ERWs and already-existing nuclear weapons to pistol and shotgun blasts—the one focused, the other scattergun in effect. But those opposed to the neutron warhead feared that the introduction of a more precise weapon would lower the nuclear threshold: 'there is more temptation to use it', declared one opponent. 'Once we introduce nuclear weaponry into conventional warfare, we're on our way.'[10] In the end, the Senate voted for ERW provision by the narrowest of margins: 43–2. But it included language by Stennis to 'freeze those funds until President Carter decides if he wants to go ahead with production and Congress is sent an arms control impact statement'.[11]

On 12 July, in a press statement, Carter was more forthcoming about the neutron weapon: 'It does not affect our SALT or strategic weapons negotiations at all.

It is strictly designed as a tactical weapon. I think that this would give us some flexibility.' But, he added, 'before I make a final decision on the neutron bomb's deployment, I would do a complete impact statement analysis on it, [and] submit this information to the Congress. But I have not yet decided whether to approve the neutron bomb. I do think it ought to be one of our options, however.'[12] By reserving his position until he had received the arms control impact statement, Carter showed that he had given the matter due consideration, and also bought himself time—perhaps another month—before having to take a decision that could seriously tarnish his anti-nuclear credentials.[13]

On the day of the Senate vote, 13 July, Schmidt arrived in Washington for a three-day state visit. His main aim was to overcome his general differences with Carter about how to deal with Brezhnev and Soviet *Westpolitik*. To little avail. The final German Foreign Ministry assessment of the talks acknowledged that no congruence of interests had been achieved. The pre-existing cracks in the Carter–Schmidt relationship had merely been papered over by the efforts of the American president to turn the visit into a publicity success by an extravagant 'charm-offensive' for the benefit of the media. To Schmidt's disappointment, neutron weapons and their implications for East–West relations had not been discussed. Nor had the chancellor got anywhere with his ambition to act as catalytic agent to re-animate superpower relations. Instead Carter claimed that progress was being made over SALT and he resisted German pressure to tone down his global human rights agenda—a policy that in Schmidt's eyes gratuitously rubbed up the Kremlin. Fearful of a Soviet peace offensive against the new 'capitalist weapon' that killed people but spared property, the chancellor got nothing from the White House that could placate domestic opposition and provide reassurance about America's security commitment to Germany and Europe. All in all Schmidt had little to show for his visit to Washington.[14]

He returned home just in time for the fallout from Bahr's article. So far Schmidt and the government had kept quiet about the neutron bomb. But after 17 July this was no longer possible. Bahr was the first major political figure to question openly the potential American deployment of neutron warheads on West German soil. And he had done so with panache and real domestic resonance. Divisions now began to emerge along ideological lines both within and also between the two governing parties. And this threatened to become yet another political problem for Schmidt, who since the 1976 elections had been operating on a mere ten-seat majority in the *Bundestag*. The chancellor tried to downplay the issue. He insisted that more information was needed and that the West German debate had to be conducted with less emotion and more analysis. He also said that he would reserve judgement until Carter made a clear decision on the weapon's development. SPD Defence Minister Georg Leber took a similarly cautious line.[15]

Internal party politics, however, were much more fractious. The SPD left wing came out strongly against, with the party's defence specialist, Alfons Pawelczyk, fiercely attacking the N-bomb for increasing the danger of nuclear war. Bahr also returned to the charge with a longer essay on 24 July, again published in *Vorwärts*, that responded to points raised by his critics and insisted the debate was not simply about defence strategy but about the upholding of universal ethical principles.[16] In these two essays, Bahr had also brought into public consciousness the idea of the 'nation'—or to be more precise the 'all-German nation' embracing the FRG and the GDR—by highlighting that ERWs meant warfare on German soil. The thought of millions of German dead in a future so-called 'limited' nuclear war that did not touch the territory of the superpowers deeply stirred people's imagination. Individuals wrote to Bahr about their personal wartime tragedies, their fears of 'losing all again', and of Germany once more being 'destroyed', as in World War Two.[17] The language was nationalistic in tone, urging Bahr for the sake of the 'people' (*Volk*) to conduct '*German* policies' (*deutsche Politik*).[18] ERWs endangered the 'Fatherland' and the lives of Germans on both sides of the border (*diesseits und jenseits der 'Staatsgrenze West*').[19]

Bahr's rhetoric of moralism and nationalism was genuinely felt but he was also playing to the gallery. Having managed to manoeuvre himself into the limelight with his *Vorwärts* articles and numerous media interviews, and realizing that his position as SPD executive party secretary could be turned into a pulpit, Bahr began to promote his own political agenda.[20] Whatever the intentions behind his original essay, Bahr knew that he was now in a position to promote his pet ideas on how the German question and *Deutschlandpolitik* ought to be handled. Considering that *Ostpolitik* was largely stagnant, over the coming months Bahr would keep reiterating that the 'German nation' depended more than ever on East–West détente rather than what he considered a confrontational Western nuclear policy.[21]

Adding complexity to the debate, Bahr's views also received support from some senior retired *Bundeswehr* generals, including Wolf Count Baudissin and Johannes Steinhoff. They rejected the American ERWs, pointing to their unsettling effect on the Soviets and speculating on the negative consequences this might have for progress in SALT, MBFR, and East–West relations generally.[22]

On the other side of the political divide, Manfred Wörner, the defence spokesman of the CDU/CSU, defended neutron weapons, asserting that they would benefit NATO's strategy and accord with 'German interests'. He, too, was playing the nationalist card but to different effect.[23] The opposition parties were firmly committed to the Atlantic Alliance and regarded the SPD left as almost traitorous; practically in bed with the Soviets. They noted that Bahr's language about the N-bomb bore marked similarities to the Kremlin's 'peace' rhetoric and were not impressed by Bahr's attempts to distance himself from the West German Communist Party (KPD).[24] Unsurprisingly, both the moderate wing of the SPD as well as the FDP coalition partner also expressed little enthusiasm for what they considered Bahr's impassioned grand-standing and his ideologically charged promotion of 'disarmament at all costs' (in Figure 3.2 a poster by the German Peace Union depicts the nuclear horrors highlighted by Bahr).[25] In fact, FDP Foreign Minister Hans-Dietrich Genscher had gone straight to the press after Bahr's second article to warn forcefully about an 'anti-American accent' to the ERW dispute and about how this could sow 'distrust between Europe and its most important ally'.[26]

In short, the neutron bomb articles had created fallout at all levels of West German politics. And Bahr's opportunistic use of the issue posed a fundamental

Figure 3.2 'NO to the neutron bomb', 1977.
Source: DFU, Bundesarchiv.

challenge to Schmidt's political authority. To make matters worse, the crucial decisions had to be taken by an American ally whose moves were difficult to predict. On 15 August, throwing another spanner in the works, Carter announced a further postponement of his decision about whether to produce ERWs. He stated that he first wanted to 'consult' with his European allies.[27] He appeared to want to pass the buck on ERW procurement to the Europeans, hoping to get them to declare (either individually or collectively) that they needed and desired ERWs on their territory. As Brzezinski recalled in his memoirs, the strategy was to 'press the Europeans to show greater interest in having the bomb and therefore some willingness to absorb some of the political flak'. If not, the administration would 'use European disinterest as a basis for a negative decision'.[28]

Carter's task was not easy. He felt genuine personal abhorrence for the neutron warhead. This idea of obtaining a European commitment to deploy as a precondition for deciding to produce ERWs can be traced back to advice offered earlier that month by the US permanent representation at NATO.[29] Similarly, on 13 August, the US ambassador in Bonn, Walter Stoessel, had written to Washington stating firmly that prior to any announcement of 'neutron warhead production or deployment' consultations with the FRG were, 'in the embassy view, absolutely essential'.[30] More generally, Carter's hesitation must be understood against the background of the public emotion generated by the weapon, in America and especially in West Germany. Since his July statements to the Senate the president had evidently grown increasingly uncomfortable with the idea of simply ordering the production of neutron warheads unilaterally. On the one hand, as Brzezinksi recalled, 'he did not wish the world to think of him as an ogre'.[31] On the other, Carter's August postponement announcement also revealed him as a political tactician. Having run his election campaign on the theme of nuclear arms reduction and non-proliferation, he could not introduce an expensive nuclear arms procurement programme without undermining his political credibility. It made sense to encourage the European partners to demand ERWs and thus take a larger share of the blame for an unpopular and emotionally charged decision.[32]

Yet the White House could see that its transatlantic allies were deeply ambivalent about the neutron bomb. Brzezinski tried to sum up the situation for the president: 'To the extent that the neutron bomb is perceived as modernizing NATO nuclear forces—and serving as a link between conventional and nuclear forces, making deterrence more credible—it is acceptable. To the extent that it is seen as lowering the nuclear threshold—that is, increasing the probability that nuclear weapons might actually be used—it is not.' Vance, he added, believed that, 'if pressed, the Europeans would accept the neutron bomb development, but for political reasons would be happy to see it cancelled'.[33]

No firm timetable was set for the consultative process. Still, in anticipation of a presidential decision by mid October, the White House lobbied permanent representatives to the Alliance's Nuclear Planning Group to hold consultations about the ERW on 13 September. There was also a need for a public show of Alliance steadfastness and cohesion in the face of increasing Soviet efforts to disseminate their anti-ERW peace propaganda.[34] But European governments were keen to resist what they perceived as unreasonable American pressure for a 'snap' Allied decision. In their view, Carter's attempt to link from the outset an express European commitment on ERW deployment to his decision to go ahead on production represented a major departure from the customary nuclear decision-making pattern among NATO allies—namely that the production of nuclear warheads remained an American decision alone. Moreover, they felt that the intrinsic military merits of the ERW had yet to be fully explored. In other words, the neutron bomb was not simply a problem of practical politics; it also had to be considered in terms of NATO's overall strategy.[35]

The Germans felt particularly exposed, for theirs was the territory earmarked as the prime location for deployment. Because of their strategic importance, Washington had singled them out for special bilateral consultation prior to the September NPG meeting, threatening to make US participation in the multilateral talks dependent on having this bilateral meeting.[36] Pushed into a corner, Bonn lobbied for a collective NATO opinion on ERW in advance of the NPG. The two allies were engaged in what Brzezinski called 'a diplomatic minuet'.[37]

American pressure prompted a major debate within the Federal government about how to construct an overall policy, further complicated by the Bahr-induced media furore. This persuaded the public to see the ERW as a 'bomb' that spread enhancing radiation—a new and more fearful American atomic 'wonder weapon'—rather than as an upgraded and more precise nuclear warhead that suppressed blast and burn.[38] On 23 August the chancellor asked the Foreign and Defence Ministries for a joint assessment of the N-bomb's effect on foreign and defence policy.[39] This was delivered a week later, on 1 September, and made several key recommendations. The overall point was that a flat rejection of neutron warheads might block the wider process of NATO TNF modernization. This process, both ministries emphasized, was essential for the Alliance's credibility. Within that context, the document argued that neutron weapons should be seen 'as a positive contribution to the Alliance's deterrence and defence capability', even if they potentially carried the risk of a regional nuclear war. However, the Federal Republic should not be forced to carry the can alone. ERW deployment must be made dependent on a decision of the whole Alliance, premised on the 'solidarity principle' of collective security. Equally important, West Germany should not be singled out as the sole territory on which these weapons should be stationed.[40]

The joint assessment was, in some respects, a compromise document. In tone and politics it clearly reflected the views of the Foreign Ministry and Genscher himself (and of the FDP as well).[41] They placed the onus squarely on the N-bomb's deterrence value, which was also emphasized by Defence Minister Georg Leber (a member of the SPD). But an internal Foreign Ministry analysis noted that some in the Defence Ministry as well as the Chancellery preferred neutron warheads to be considered primarily as bargaining chips, particularly in MBFR negotiations. The diplomats recognized that this latter approach (to produce in order to scrap) represented a position around which the majority of the SPD might rally, even though the party's hard left were going to reject the warheads altogether.[42]

The 1 September memo from the Foreign and Defence Ministries represented a serious attempt within the Federal government to come up with a clear policy on the ERW. Even this, as we have seen, was something of a fudge. Bridging the deep rifts that had opened in the national political debate would be a far greater challenge for Schmidt, as he tried to respond to the demands of his unpredictable American ally.

SCHMIDT AND CARTER: THE DIPLOMACY OF AMBIVALENCE

Politics aside, Schmidt had a deeper problem: he was divided in his own mind on the neutron bomb. At the NATO summit in May 1977 the chancellor had spoken in favour of an Allied military strategy that ensured a credible defence and deterrence posture. And while focusing on the need to achieve a mutually acceptable balance of conventional forces, he had also supported the Alliance's TNF modernization strategy in tandem with his suggestion that NATO keep open the option of raising the level of armaments if the Soviets did not cooperate on disarmament. One might, therefore, have expected him to support the Foreign Ministry's line on the value in principle of the neutron weapon.

Ever since the ERW story broke, however, Schmidt had abstained from any comment, other than seeking to calm public passions and promote a rational debate about the issue. By early September the chancellor had begun to harbour serious doubts about a policy that focused on the ERW as a useful new deterrent for NATO—in other words, to question the position of Genscher and the Foreign Ministry. For one thing, Carter's insistence on securing a European, and specifically German, deployment commitment *prior* to an American production decision made it impossible for Schmidt to sell ERWs to the German public as an American fait accompli.[43] Furthermore, he had grown increasingly concerned about German angst and the anti-nuclear crusade within the SPD—all of which was damaging his government's standing.[44] With this in mind Schmidt wrote a personal letter to Carter on 7 September about the neutron bomb conundrum: 'The Federal Government will have to handle this subject with great skill and circumspection. I shall as soon as possible put it before the Federal Security Council and I would be grateful if in the meantime your administration could exercise restraint vis-à-vis the public in this matter.' Following up on the ministerial recommendations of 1 September, he stressed that the issue 'should not be presented as a bilateral German–American problem but that the Alliance should find an answer which will have the common support of all its members'. But the letter carefully evaded the question of any German commitment to allow ERWs on German soil.[45]

The American–German bilateral meeting before the NPG proved inconclusive. The American delegation, headed by Assistant Secretary of Defense for International Security Affairs David McGiffert, emphasized the need for 'substantial support' from the Europeans for ERWs and stated that a positive production decision was inconceivable without German agreement to deploy. He also made clear that an ERW–MBFR deal with the Soviets was not on the American cards—thereby dashing the hopes of the SPD left. The Germans, for their part, sought to evade American pressure by pointing to the still awaited national decision by the Federal Security Council (*Bundessicherheitsrat*, BSR) and the importance of safeguarding Alliance solidarity.[46] Similar arguments were rehearsed at the formal NPG meetings on 13 and 27 September in Brussels. While all European allies, except for the Dutch, agreed that ERWs might be militarily desirable in principle, like the Germans they mainly wanted more time to forge a domestic consensus on the warheads and specifically on deployment on their own soil. And so the diplomatic minuet continued.[47]

But that was not how the situation was reported to Carter. After the McGiffert mission, Vance and Defense Secretary Harold Brown told the president that all allies were 'preparing themselves for a positive decision' by him. They claimed that the Germans and the British had 'already begun subtly to lean in favor of weapons' and warned that a US decision against the ERW 'would be read as evidence of a reduced American commitment to preserving a strong theater nuclear posture'. Carter's advisers were so keen to hammer out a NATO consensus on deployment 'within weeks rather than months', while maintaining domestic momentum towards a presidential production announcement, that they represented European reactions as more decisively pro-ERW than they were in reality.[48]

Schmidt, meanwhile, was trying to strip the emotion out of the ERW issue and to establish a coherent, realistic SPD position on the weapons.[49] This meant coming to some kind of modus vivendi with Bahr. When the two men met in late September, the chancellor made clear that he did not want to force Bahr into line. Acknowledging this freedom and accepting the chancellor's warnings against overly anti-American rhetoric, Bahr decided to refrain from further public comments on ERWs until the party congress in November.[50] Schmidt had no doubt that his relations with the White House had been harmed by Bahr's activities. But these, he also believed, had been consequent on mistakes made by Washington in handling the ERW affair.[51]

Some of these perceived American mistakes actually resulted from unfortunate, but fundamental, misunderstandings in American–German relations. Carter had evidently postponed his ERW production announcement in the hope of first securing a green light on deployments in Europe from his NATO allies, particularly the Germans. This policy was, however, a non-starter. As time went on, and the decision got further postponed, the president's dilemma worsened: on the one hand, he could not afford to be seen as giving in to the Soviets who actively sought to prevent the new warhead's procurement and to drive a wedge between the Western allies. On the other, he had to avoid, both at home and abroad, being seen as a warmonger who imposed new nuclear weapons on the Europeans and heated up the arms race. Given Vance and Brown's vaguely promising reports from their missions in Europe and the fact that Schmidt had not categorically excluded German acceptance of ERWs, Carter chose to believe that the chancellor's silence and non-committal stance signified that he wanted the weapon, but, because of domestic political difficulties, laid the responsibility for a production decision at the door of the White House. For his part, Schmidt also tended to assume that Carter's buck-passing diplomacy was mostly dictated by domestic considerations. In fact, he was getting very annoyed by what he took to be Carter's game plan of selling ERWs to the American public on the supposed basis of West Germany's desire to station the weapons, which would of course immediately render the FRG vulnerable to Soviet pressure.[52]

Neither man appreciated that, domestic politics aside, the other was genuinely ambivalent about the whole idea of ERWs. Had they done so, both Carter and Schmidt might in some ways have been content if the whole idea had been dropped in September. But by then the highly public controversy meant that it had become a major test of the Alliance's credibility and the issue could not now be quietly shelved. So Carter hesitated to pull the plug on ERWs. From his side, Schmidt remained concerned to redress the military imbalance in Europe and ensure America's continued commitment to NATO's defence and deterrence strategy. So he, too, was reluctant to issue a categorical 'no' to the ERW. The October target date for a NATO decision quietly disappeared, but the Allies kept on talking.[53]

In an effort to resolve this serious impasse in American–German relations, Carter sent Brzezinski to Bonn. At their meeting on 27 September, he and Schmidt tried to find ways of loosening the diplomatic knot. The chancellor suggested that the eventual introduction of ERWs in Germany was not entirely inconceivable. In fact, he said, in 'two to three years' Germans might well be ready to opt for deployment. But in the near future, Schmidt explained, it would be impossible to persuade a majority of the ruling coalition in the *Bundestag* to endorse this. In which case, Brzezinski replied, one might either simply abandon the neutron warhead project or introduce ERWs into MBFR negotiations. The latter was, of course, a view strongly held within the SPD but it had been rejected by McGiffert two weeks before. This time, however, Brzezinski said that he himself had proposed this idea to the National Security Council. Schmidt jumped at Brzezinski's offer, which he probably considered the best he could sell to both his party and the public— namely, keeping the production decision open and using ERWs as a bargaining chip to halt the Soviet conventional armaments build-up. Brzezinski promised to report Schmidt's views to the president.[54]

At the Federal Security Council meeting on 6 October, Schmidt's personal ambivalence regarding ERWs came fully to light. As previously, he did not speak out against the warhead per se. He merely remained adamant that he wanted nothing to do with what ought to be a purely national decision by the president of the United States on whether to produce the ERW and that, regarding deployment, Bonn should push for a collective NATO verdict. Singling out West Germany, he said, held numerous risks for European security, such as free-riding by the other allies, loosening Alliance cohesion, and provoking the Soviets into a new arms spiral. Schmidt also shared Bahr's fear that the introduction of improved nuclear artillery would mean greater likelihood of regional military conflict on German soil and the lowering of the nuclear threshold. Nevertheless, he proposed that the West collectively use 'its ability to technologically innovate' (i.e. ERWs) as a lever in the MBFR talks, whilst warning that an early NATO-wide rejection of ERWs might forfeit their leverage vis-à-vis the USSR. More intra-German consultations were needed. So the chancellor instructed Leber to avoid any statements at NATO's forthcoming Nuclear Planning Group in Italy that might prejudge Germany's future position on 'the bomb'.[55]

In the event, at Bari on 11 October, NATO postponed all decisions related to the ERW.[56] The Allies agreed that this warhead could offer a positive contribution to NATO's defence capabilities but felt that the public misrepresentation of the weapon had caused so much PR damage that the issue now needed handling with the utmost care. The Europeans expressed the need for a longer-term 'education process' of their publics and for further consultations at the highest political level, both nationally and within NATO. In response, Brown insisted that the West must not make itself dependent on Moscow's actions and misconstructions, and he repeated Washington's demand that without European consent to ERW deployment on their territory, the US would not sanction the weapon's production. He also expressed the hope that a decision by the Alliance as a whole could be taken by the end of the year. This was clearly pie in the sky: transatlantic talks on the neutron bomb had reached a complete stalemate.[57]

SCHMIDT LOOKS FOR A WAY OUT: THE ERW THREE-STEP

From late October Schmidt began to take the initiative. Over the next few months he would feel his way towards a compromise policy for the Alliance that took account of both German security needs and SPD party politics. But first the chancellor had to face six harrowing weeks of round-the-clock crisis management because of two interconnected acts of international terrorism.

On 5 September came the kidnapping by the Baader-Meinhof gang of Hanns Martin Schleyer, president of the Confederation of German Employers' Associations, and then on 13 October the hijacking of the Lufthansa airliner *Landshut* which was flown to Mogadishu, Somalia by four Palestinians in support of the Schleyer kidnapping. During these six weeks, which became known as the 'German autumn', Schmidt set up a crisis-management centre (*Krisenstab*) in the Chancellery itself, as his leadership came under its most severe public and media scrutiny of his whole time in office. He had to weigh up the value of one human life against the government's firm stance against terrorist blackmail. In the event Schmidt held firm, insisting that the Federal government would not do deals with terrorists. On his instructions the *Landshut* was stormed by German special forces on 18 October: all passengers remained unharmed; three hijackers were killed. On the same day the leading Baader-Meinhof terrorists who were incarcerated in Stammheim jail, including Andreas Baader, were discovered dead in their cells. Next day Schleyer himself was finally found, shot dead.[58]

These were extremely distressing and demanding weeks for the chancellor and naturally dragged his attention away from the neutron bomb issue. Yet he managed to keep cool in his decision-making, controlling his notorious impatience and hot temper. And, in political terms, he emerged well from both affairs—enhancing his reputation as a crisis-manager and an authoritative leader. The cover of *Der Spiegel* on 24 October featured him in statesmanlike pose above the caption 'After Mogadishu: the Admired German'.[59]

Four days later, on 28 October, Schmidt gave a major lecture at the International Institute for Strategic Studies (IISS) in London.[60] The speech had been planned for months and the chancellor had originally intended to feature the problems of the global economy—energy policy, East–West trade, and the stability of the industrial democracies—all familiar themes in Schmidt's definition of economic security. Early drafts of the lecture prepared by the Foreign Ministry's planning department in August 1977 did not include a section on military security in Europe. It was only in mid September, with the ERW now a serious transatlantic problem, that input on defence policy was requested from Leber and the Defence Ministry.[61] And it was the statements that Schmidt made on military issues which attracted global attention. The London speech would, in fact, propel him into the position of the foremost nuclear-strategic thinker among Western leaders of the 1970s. It would stand as a major reference point for years to come and therefore merits close reading and careful analysis.

In his remarks, the chancellor highlighted the emerging imbalance of military power in Europe. SALT, he said, 'codifies the nuclear strategic balance between the Soviet Union and the United States. To put it another way: SALT neutralizes their strategic nuclear capabilities. In Europe this magnifies the significance of the disparities between East and West in nuclear tactical and conventional weapons.' The latter, he hoped, would be dealt with by the MBFR talks in Vienna but 'nuclear tactical' weapons—by which Schmidt meant nuclear forces within the European theatre in which the Soviets enjoyed superiority—remained problematic. Underlining the centrality of NATO's double strategy of deterrence and détente, Schmidt stated that 'if we do not succeed in removing the disparities of military power in Europe parallel to the SALT negotiations...we must maintain the balance of the full range of deterrence strategy'. With these ideas, Schmidt had gone further than in his speech at NATO's May 1977 summit. He demanded not only renewed efforts to establish conventional parity but also to maintain balance at *all* levels—what he called the 'full range of deterrence'.[62]

From this position Schmidt asked his listeners 'to consider whether the "neutron weapon" is of value to the Alliance as an additional element of the deterrence strategy, as a means of preventing war'. But, he added, 'we should not limit ourselves to that examination. We should also examine what relevance and weight this weapon has in our effort to achieve arms control.' So he acknowledged that there was a military case for the neutron bomb on grounds of deterrence but also indicated sympathy for the argument that ERWs should be used as a bargaining chip in arms control discussions. Schmidt's policy of balance had always been intended to secure peace. Such a balance could either be achieved through arms build-up or arms reduction, and Schmidt's heart was always with the second of these options. This was clearly stated in those passages in the IISS speech about creating a conventional balance with the Warsaw Pact states. One option 'would be for the Western Alliance to undertake a massive build-up of forces and weapons systems; the other for both NATO and the Warsaw Pact to reduce their force strength and achieve an overall balance at a lower level. I prefer the latter.' In these remarks one can discern the germ of what would later become the chancellor's 'dual track' approach to achieving European security. These two strands, though still embryonic when he spoke in London, would become central to his future thinking.[63]

Ten days later, on 9 November, the two approaches—arms build-up or arms reduction—entered Bonn's policymaking process at the second Federal Security Council (BSR) meeting dedicated to the N-bomb issue. Genscher openly lobbied for the introduction of ERWs, although he did agree that they might have potential use as bargaining chips in MBFR talks with the Soviets. Importantly, he did not speak solely as head of the Foreign Ministry but also as the chairman of the coalition partner, the Liberals. Indeed, one month earlier, the FDP's Federal Expert Committee (*Bundesfachausschuß*) on 'peace and security politics' had voted for a resolution that the Liberal Democrats were, under certain conditions, willing to accept ERW deployment for deterrence purposes.[64] At the BSR, Genscher therefore highlighted the neutron weapon's importance for Germany on the grounds that it would enhance Europe's defence posture against the Soviet tank build-up. If the Europeans said 'no' to the neutron bomb, it would be the start of a slippery slope: Genscher conjured up the spectre of a nuclear-free Europe and American detachment from the continent.[65]

Schmidt also feared the possibility of American detachment but for very different reasons. Introducing neutron weapons might make the White House feel able to conduct a limited nuclear war in Europe that would not escalate to the strategic level and impinge on the United States. So the neutron bomb could have the effect of decoupling the New World from the Old and also feeding a new nuclear arms spiral at TNF level that would raise tensions in Europe. Having said all that, Schmidt nevertheless endorsed Genscher's view that West Germany could not afford to be seen as rejecting the ERW unilaterally (though equally, as he continued to underline, the FRG should not offer its unilateral approval). A German rejection would not only undermine Alliance unity but also raise doubts about Bonn's underlying Western loyalties. It would also grant Carter an alibi at home to abort ERWs and an opportunity to cast the FRG as scapegoat for his change of mind. All of this would directly play into the Kremlin's hands and make West Germany more vulnerable to Soviet blackmail. Unwilling to accept or reject outright the neutron bomb, the chancellor was ever more inclined to see the 'warhead option' used as a tool in East–West diplomacy. As he had explained privately to Callaghan in a meeting on 18 October, he wanted the United States to offer the 'discarding' of ERWs in return for 'appropriate Soviet concessions'. Few in the West believed the Soviets would actually make such concessions, but, in Schmidt's view, such intransigence would then make potential Western deployments more justifiable to their reluctant publics.[66]

While haggling with his Cabinet, Schmidt also had to obtain the support of his own party at the SPD's Hamburg Congress on 15–19 November, many of whom wished to reject the ERW in any form. Beforehand, the SPD had under-gone intense soul-searching, with its leadership determined to overcome the recent intra-party divide. In the spirit of fostering rational debate, *Vorwärts* had printed from late October a number of articles and commentaries laying out arguments for and against the ERW.[67] Once at Hamburg, all key party figures—including Schmidt, Leber, and, significantly, Bahr—pushed hard in their speeches for a compromise formula. Fudging the exact ways in which ERW pro-duction, arms control negotiations, and weapons deployment were to be tied together, the motion finally approved by the SPD stated: 'The Federal govern-ment is asked to establish, within the framework of her security and disarma-ment policy, the political and strategic prerequisites for ERW storage not to become a necessity on the territory of the FRG'.[68] Through this delicately worded sentence, the party's key aim had thus emerged: above all to prevent circumstances arising in which Germany felt compelled to accept ERWs. Yet, at the same time, the party leadership had at least managed to secure passage of a resolution that did not reject ERW deployments outright. In effect, the govern-ment had been granted freedom in its decision-making and thus the ability to further consult and negotiate with the Americans and other allies over acquiring neutron warheads.[69]

The crux, in Schmidt's eyes, however, remained that the ERW option could only be seriously pursued if in the first place the US president actually decided on pro-duction and did so independently of any prior European commitment to deploy. He told the BSR he was going to make this point to Carter yet again, adding that there would later be plenty of time for making deployment decisions within the Alliance.[70] Simultaneously, the Americans, in the light of Schmidt's IISS speech, were starting to take more seriously the arms control dimension of ERWs. On 16 November, the top-level Special Coordinating Committee (SCC) agreed that the president should indicate that the United States favoured the production of enhanced radiation warheads and should make another serious attempt to get the Allies, especially the FRG, to agree deployment in Europe as a precondition to announcing American production. Meanwhile, with a view to 'making the issue more palatable politically' for the Europeans, the Americans would initiate wider Allied consultations on the broad security issues including grey-area systems, and in this connection consider an arms-control trade-off package with the Soviets. Here the White House was picking up Schmidt's ideas.[71]

On 8 December, Defense Secretary Brown summarized for Carter the German position as a three-stage process with 'new German decisions before each of the later stages': (1) Carter's unilateral decision and announcement on ERW produc-tion; (2) a NATO ERW arms-control offer to the Soviets not to deploy, preferably within the MBFR framework; and (3) if these arms control negotiations failed, a collective Allied decision to deploy ERWs, without singling out West Germany as sole storage country. Brzezinski chose to interpret this as a sign that 'the Germans have moved toward our thinking', but, he added, they 'still want to *separate* the production and deployment decisions. They would support *our* decision on pro-duction and *then* face the question of deployment, but only after the failure of an arms-control linkage strategy. Hence we alone would have to take the political heat of a production decision.' This last point remained unacceptable to the Americans.[72]

For its part, Washington was now thinking hard about the arms-control dimension but along lines somewhat different from Bonn. The IISS lecture, with Schmidt's criticism of America for not addressing grey-area issues, forced the Carter administration to take seriously the SS-20s and this affected its attitude to what might be traded in return for non-deployment of ERWs. One option, advocated by the FRG, was for the Americans to forfeit ERW deployments in return for the Soviets withdrawing an additional number of tanks above those contained in the West's current MBFR proposal. This was suggested by Secretary of State Vance and America's MBFR ambassador Stanley Resor. But the other option, now emerging, was to link an ERW non-deployment deal to the Soviets' refraining from deploying SS-20s—as lobbied for by Brown and Brzezinski. The latter, Pentagon, position was accepted by the SCC on 16 November. Not only did the SS-20 proposal seem simpler than the MBFR route, while alleviating European opposition to ERWs, but the Soviets would also be forced to choose between retaining their highly prized missiles and blocking the hated American neutron warheads. Because Schmidt had already gone public in London with the idea of linking ERWs to MBFR, it was clear that great care was needed in advancing the SCC position and that, when talking to Schmidt, both arms-control options might have to be considered.[73]

Carter went along with the committee's recommendation. On 23 November, he addressed all these issues in a personal letter to the German chancellor. As part of his charm offensive, the US president began by emphasizing the centrality of Schmidt's London speech and expressed his willingness to follow up on a German government initiative calling for a meeting between Britain, France, America, and West Germany at high official level to explore 'grey-area' weapons and their relationship to the SALT negotiations. Then, after firmly reiterating his earlier conviction that European powers should 'explicitly' express support for ERW deployment *prior* to any US procurement decision, he stated that he also thought America should consider Schmidt's idea of linking deployment of these weapons to conventional arms control via MBFR. However, introducing the SCC's alternative option, Carter now proposed that the West approach the Soviets about an ERW–SS-20 *quid pro quo*.[74]

In his reply on 9 December Schmidt stuck to his guns, insisting that the ERW option be kept open, but stressing that of course the decision to produce lay with America alone. He agreed in principle on the idea of bargaining but refrained from committing himself to either strategy.[75] Privately, as is clear from British sources, he was not keen on an ERW–SS-20 deal, even though he had been so outspoken about the Soviet sub-strategic arms build-up and the resulting 'Eurostrategic' nuclear imbalance. In his opinion, the greatest and most pressing danger to Germany lay with a Soviet tank attack, and ERWs were the designated anti-armour weapon. The chancellor undoubtedly preferred an ERW–tanks arms-control package, while the SS-20s were to be dealt with in a different forum of negotiation.[76]

While juggling Cabinet, party, and his American ally, Schmidt also had to take account of the Kremlin. For the sake of the German question, Schmidt obviously wanted to avoid any further damage to the worsening state of West German–Soviet relations. No advances in *Deutschlandpolitik* had been made in the first half of 1977 and then the Kremlin kept deferring Brezhnev's state visit to the FRG originally planned for October or November. As justification for its action, Moscow blamed West German domestic issues—the lack of security given the constant threat of terrorism on German soil, as well as the consequent hostility towards West German Communist party officials. But it also cited the neutron bomb as another factor in the deteriorating relations between Moscow and Bonn.[77] Behind these duplicitous statements, the Kremlin was trying to apply political blackmail—making a Brezhnev–Schmidt summit conditional on West Germany's good behaviour. For Schmidt, of course, maintaining dialogue with the Soviets was an essential part of his long-term peace policy.

The Soviets also went on the offensive against Western 'warmongering'. On the public level they mounted a pro-peace, anti-nuclear propaganda campaign using the Western mass media, letters to Western parliamentarians, and Communist party channels.[78] They also targeted West European leaders, who were already under intense domestic pressure over the ERW. Between late November and late January Brezhnev sent numerous personal letters to Schmidt and Genscher, to other West European heads of government, and to Carter. Clearly seeking to frustrate NATO's TNF decision-making processes, the Soviet leader stated that deterrence against the USSR was not necessary and that ERWs, as new 'weapons of mass destruction', were harmful to détente and arms-control negotiations. Brezhnev threatened in response to instigate countermeasures.[79] In his 22 November note to Schmidt, he condemned American attempts to push ERWs onto the Europeans and went out of his way to praise the restraint of West Germany as the key country for any deployment. In singling out the FRG in this way, Brezhnev made a thinly veiled threat to the chancellor that a summit could only take place in the near future if he made a commitment to non-deployment.[80]

Bonn refused to be intimidated. As Genscher put it on 29 December in an end-of-year address, 'allies in their will for peace through the preservation of their own security must not allow their decisions to be subject to exogenous campaigns and threats'.[81] On the FRG's suggestion, the NATO governments coordinated the content and timing of their future responses. There was general agreement not to reply to Brezhnev's messages until a decision on ERW production had actually been taken.[82]

By the end of the year, Washington was also becoming more pro-active in the light of the Soviet propaganda offensive. It sought to steer public opinion towards what it now thought *really* mattered—Soviet nuclear rearmament, and in particular their SS-20 deployments. The Kremlin had so far been lucky that the latter development became buried in the negative Western publicity on the American N-bomb and played its cards well in exploiting the anti-American comments of Bahr and others. There was now a general recognition in the White House that the neutron bomb affair had become a test of the president's perseverance and of his ability to lead NATO in the face of formidable Soviet pressure.[83]

FROM DIPLOMATIC BREAKTHROUGH TO
PRESIDENTIAL COP-OUT

The year 1978 began with the Schmidt–Carter impasse on ERWs unresolved. Having both hoped in September 1977 that the whole issue might quietly go away, they now found themselves locked into going ahead in some way with ERWs. But, crucially, neither had so far conceded on the big question: who would make the first commitment? The Germans stuck to Schmidt's phased three-step approach, whereas the Americans continued to favour an integrated strategy under which Carter's production decision had to be preceded by an Allied expression of willingness to accept ERW deployments, before the President would enter into arms-control negotiations with the USSR.[84] To escape the deadlock, both Bonn and Washington looked to bring other Allies into the discussion—above all Britain because of its 'special relationship' with America and its distinctive status as the only other nuclear power that was within the NATO command structure.[85]

West Germany's precise ERW position was established at the BSR meeting on 20 January 1978. This was significant because it made explicit the chancellor's three-step logic, clearly revealing the underlying rationale behind it, and also now offered a partial green light on future neutron weapons deployment on West German soil. The three stages were spelled out as follows. First, on the premise that non-nuclear states such as West Germany had never previously been part of NATO decision-making on nuclear weapons production, the ERW procurement decision should remain with the US president alone. Second, NATO should within two years achieve conclusive results in arms-control negotiations. But, third, if satisfactory Soviet concessions in these talks were not forthcoming, Bonn would then allow ERW deployment on West German territory. The German commitment to deploy, however, would depend on a joint Allied agreement and on a pledge from at least one other European state also to accept the weapons. The thinking behind the last point was that West Germany as an ERW host did not want to be elevated alone to a special position among the NATO nuclear powers—America, Britain, and France—and thus become distinct from the other non-nuclear allies. Bonn remained acutely aware of the sensitivities of the Soviets, West European neighbours, and the domestic opposition towards any change in the FRG's non-nuclear status; little more than thirty years since the demise of the Third Reich.[86]

If the president accepted the German plan, Schmidt would have succeeded in asserting his prime aim of breaking Carter's deployment–production linkage. But the BSR insisted that these decisions should be relayed to the White House in utmost confidence: Carter must not refer to them in public debate or even to the Senate.[87] Far from seeking a visible role in shaping Western nuclear politics, Bonn was anxious not to give the impression that ERWs were a bilateral German–American affair, in order to keep the Alliance harmonious. The BSR conclusions were relayed to the White House not via diplomatic channels but on the occasion of US Deputy National Security Advisor David Aaron's visit to Bonn on 30 January. Even London, closely consulted by Bonn as a trusted NATO ally, was kept entirely in the dark.[88]

Three weeks later, on 20 February, the Americans presented their own 'three-part scenario' on ERW decision-making to the Germans, British, and French in the form of a discussion document. The new American proposal stated that the president would announce N-bomb production on his own, with a view to the weapon's deployment in Europe in about two years. At the same time, he would make an arms-control offer to the USSR to forego deployment of the ERW in Europe in return for Soviet agreement not to deploy its SS-20. The Alliance in a separate but concurrent statement would support this approach, and indicate its willingness to eventually station the neutron warheads in Europe as a force-modernization step made necessary by Soviet improvements, if the Kremlin failed to respond to the arms-control offer. This American scenario was thus not entirely identical with the FRG's three-stage plan in January, but nevertheless a significant American alignment with German thought had clearly occurred.[89]

Washington's ideas were then presented formally to the NATO Council on 24 February. The Germans were keen for this to be done simply as a fresh American initiative (without any reference to the BSR paper), so that the discussions remained as uncontroversial as possible. Bonn envisaged officially introducing Allies to the German position in the form of a 'response' to the American initiative at the next NATO Council meeting in March.[90]

Schmidt's desire for the Germans to be publicly seen as taking a low-key, reactive approach to American ideas and decisions stemmed not only from the difficult international context, but from the persistently tense political situation over the N-bomb question at home. Opposition towards neutron weapons remained strong within the SPD and among the leftist grassroots. Worse still, the seemingly patched-up ideological rift on security between Bahr and Schmidt had dramatically reopened on 4 February when Bahr published a lengthy article on neutron weapons and détente policy in the *Flensburger Tageblatt*. Having promised Schmidt in the autumn not to stir up further debate, he denounced the neutron warhead anew with his characteristic blend of ethical reflection and strategic analysis. For Bahr, an ERW–tanks–MBFR linkage as part of a disarmament strategy was desirable; hence he found this facet of the government's thinking to be acceptable. But in his judgement, disarmament and arms control were absolutes and must not be combined with nuclear arms build-up in order to establish a military balance, as Schmidt suggested. In other words, Bahr preferred the idea that the United States use the threat of ERW production (rather than of their future deployment) as a bargaining tool with the USSR. Bahr's intervention reopened the ideological rift in the SPD and reignited public controversy.[91]

These domestic difficulties were another reason for Schmidt to downplay the FRG's role at the top table. And yet, it was in no little part due to the chancellor's leadership and vision that the original American–German stalemate appeared to have been broken. By March 1978 German diplomatic tactics looked to be paying off as NATO moved towards consensus on a three-step procedure. As regards the arms-control package, the German government was now ready to accept America's preferred SS-20–ERW deal, if only because this seemed the quickest route to an all-Allied decision.[92] This deal was included in a British–American draft proposal for the NATO Council meetings scheduled for 20 and 22 March. The following day, it was hoped, Carter could then make his announcements on production, arms-control, and deployment intentions. In response, NATO Secretary General Joseph Luns would express the Alliance's support, or at least acquiescence. Those who were against deployments would keep silent.[93] Ultimately however, all depended on the president making his announcements. The ball was now firmly in Carter's court.

At 7:30 on the morning of 17 March, a few days before the planned NATO Council meetings, Carter left Washington for his remote retreat on St Simons Island, off the coast of Georgia. Desperate to escape the relentless pressures at the White House, he was looking forward to a quiet Easter fishing holiday with his family. Next day he received a chatty message from Brzezinski: 'Hate to spoil your fishing with thoughts like these but you should know that we are about to take the final steps to implement with the Allies the three-part policy on Enhanced Radiation Warheads (ERW) which you set in motion with your November letter to Schmidt.' Brzezinski enclosed a detailed memorandum from Vance and Brown on the procedures proposed for the NATO meetings, concluding: 'Harold, Cy and I are in unanimous agreement that the time has come to put this issue behind us and we have a good chance of doing it in the next few days'. The national security adviser considered this a routine communication. To his surprise, the documents came back to him with brief, blunt, presidential annotations: 'Re production, etc. Do not act until after consultation with me', and 'Do not issue any statement'.[94]

The NATO meeting on 20 March was duly deferred and that evening, on his return to Washington, the president met with Vance, Brown, and Brzezinski for ninety minutes. The latter found Carter 'very displeased' that, as he saw it, the bureaucrats had been 'moving forward', putting him under intense pressure to take a decision. As the President put it in his diary, 'they had generated a lot of momentum, including an immediate agreement for me to produce these neutron weapons. My cautionary words to them since last summer have pretty well been ignored, and I was aggravated'. It was clear to his advisers that the president 'would have preferred to back out of this issue', but they told him bluntly that 'he could not do so'. Vance felt that Carter 'appeared not to appreciate the enormous damage to his prestige and U.S. leadership that would result from backing away from the alliance consensus that had been worked out in his name'. Brzezinski said that for Carter 'not to go through with what we had proposed earlier to chancellor Schmidt would contribute to a sickness and then weakening of the alliance'. The main beneficiary would be the Soviet Union, which would be handed a huge propaganda victory. But none of this impressed Carter. Brzezinski reflected in his diary: 'I don't think that I have ever seen the President quite as troubled and pained by any decision item. At one point he said: "I wish I had never heard of this weapon".'[95]

How to explain Carter's sudden paralysis? In retrospect it is clear that the entire Allied consultative process up to this point had never rested on a firm presidential commitment. Poor communication between the president and his aides and his own reticence in saying what he wanted had created a gap between Carter's thought and the goals of his Cabinet. In fact, as we know, the president had from the outset agonized over ERWs on moral grounds. And he also had real doubts about the three stages because he would have to commit to an expensive production process that could easily be undercut by either later Soviet arms reductions or a West European refusal to deploy. Hence his obsession with securing a cast-iron European commitment to deploy before he decided to start manufacturing the weapons.[96] Ironically, Carter's dilemma had been exacerbated by the Germans' quiet January ERW stationing offer. Not only did this decouple production from the ERW deployment decision, but it included the condition of German non-singularity.[97] ERWs were only of military use if stationed close to the potential war theatre in and around West Germany's eastern border. In the winter of 1977–8, only the Netherlands and Belgium looked like realistic co-deployers and by early March both of them had backed out. By now Britain had offered to act as the other ERW host—even though it was not of course a continental, non-nuclear state and was therefore not strictly comparable as a risk-sharer. Still Bonn accepted this as a compromise. Even so all of this was insufficient to quell the surge of doubt and loathing that now seems to have overwhelmed the US president.[98]

The 20 March meeting at the White House did not yet abandon the ERW. Under intense pressure from his advisers, Carter shifted ground once again and agreed to defer an announcement in the hope of soliciting 'more explicit statements of support' from the Europeans, especially Schmidt. The NATO Council was still expected to meet in the week beginning 3 April. But at their morning briefing on 26 March, according to Brzezinski, Carter 'said, in effect, that he did not wish to go through with it; that he had a queasy feeling about the whole thing; that his administration would be stamped forever as the administration which introduced bombs that kill people but leave buildings intact; and that he would like to find a graceful way out'. Brzezinski replied that leadership meant 'making the decisions which the Europeans are not prepared to make' but Carter was 'unconvinced'. The next morning he told his advisers that he was dropping the whole idea.[99]

The president then dispatched Deputy Secretary of State Warren Christopher to Bonn, Hamburg, and London to inform Genscher, Schmidt, and Callaghan. The challenge was now to find a face-saving public formula to cover his retreat. On 31 March Christopher sat in Schmidt's living room explaining that Carter was 'leaning strongly' against the decision to produce ERWs. He did not wish to lay the blame on anybody, Christopher added; on the contrary, the administration acknowledged it had received tremendous aid from the FRG. He explained that Carter justified his change of heart for a series of reasons: disagreement persisted in the Alliance (with the Netherlands, Belgium, Denmark, and Norway still opposed to the ERW); public opinion in NATO countries was divided; the ERW was no 'panacea'; the Pentagon considered the weapon marginal for defence purposes; the ERW–SS-20 link was not convincing; and Soviet arms-control concessions were uncertain.[100]

Schmidt listened to Christopher's rag-bag of arguments in total disbelief. During the previous summer Carter had, after all, insisted that the neutron weapon would improve deterrence. And the decision-making trajectory as well as public statements by American defence officials over the past months certainly contradicted Christopher's claim that the Pentagon was sceptical towards the ERW. The reasoning surrounding Allied disagreement also struck Schmidt as dubious: the Germans and Americans (together with the British) had effectively achieved a 100 per cent consensus over 'substance' and an almost 100 per cent congruence over the 'wording' on all ERW-related matters prior to the planned late-March NATO meetings. But the chancellor kept his cool. He ended the conversation by urging Carter at least to await Genscher's impending visit to Washington before making any announcement.[101]

The White House had managed to keep things under wraps for a while. Only on 28 March did reports appear in the press that Carter had called off the NATO meetings. Even so, nobody was sure whether a temporary delay or full-scale reversal was in the offing.[102] But then on 4 April the *New York Times* stated categorically that Carter had definitely decided to ban the N-bomb and that he had done so 'against the advice of most of his top foreign policy advisors'. Worse still, Michael Getler, the *Washington Post*'s correspondent in the FRG, declared that the neutron warhead was 'becoming the most politically bungled major weapons project in NATO history. As seen from Bonn, it has sown more confusion and bewilderment among members of the Western alliance than anyone in this capital can remember.'[103]

So, by the time Genscher arrived in Washington on 4 April, the game was up. All he could do now was to mount a damage-limitation exercise to persuade the administration to acknowledge publicly that it had not been the FRG that had impeded a pro-ERW presidential decision. And also, trying to avoid the impression that NATO had capitulated to Soviet propaganda, Genscher urged the president to use the language of postponement or deferral rather than flatly announcing the ERW's cancellation.[104]

On the same day in Bonn, the chancellor finally vented his frustrations with US ambassador Stoessel. He had gone out of his way, he exclaimed, to work in tandem with the White House toward an ERW decision ahead of the March NATO Councils, even though he had never shared the military's high estimation of neutron warheads. And underlining his personal efforts, he claimed that 'in the FRG's 29-year history' he was probably the chancellor who cultivated the closest ties with the United States. More still, he said he had knowingly risked his 'personal amity' with two of the central figures of his party—Brandt and Wehner—by keeping in step with the Americans over the neutron bomb; now they were no longer on speaking terms with him. Many things would have been easier, he fumed, had he known the president's true position at an earlier stage. Taking a deep breath, he made appropriate noises about keeping intact personal relations between Bonn and Washington and reminded Stoessel that the FRG preferred the Americans to announce an official 'deferral' rather than an outright cancellation.[105]

In this at least the Germans gained a small victory. On 7 April Carter told the world that he had decided to defer ERW production. Brzezinski called it 'the worst presidential decision of the first fourteen months'.[106]

* * * * *

The damage for Schmidt was considerable. He may in a way have been saved by Carter's N-bomb deferral announcement from ending up in open confrontation with Bahr and other nuclear sceptics within the SPD.[107] But because of the president's cop-out, Bahr now appeared vindicated in meddling in the government's foreign and security policy-making by airing his own visions in the media. In doing so he had publicly gained stature in the FRG as *the* political figure showing real concern for the future of the German nation and for the people's true security. Bahr's supporters and many ordinary citizens consequently saw the chancellor as a misguided and weakened leader.

There was also more general political fallout. The leadership of the governing coalition that had lobbied for the N-bomb to strengthen deterrence and bargain with the Soviets had found the rug pulled from under its feet. In the FDP, antagonism was now rife against the 'arms-control wing' of the SPD and this too undermined Schmidt's authority. Moreover, the Christian Democrats pilloried the chancellor mercilessly: for failing to control the SPD left, for offering Carter merely conditional acceptance of eventual ERW deployments in Germany which had proven insufficient to persuade the president, and for shying away from making public his government's position. All this, the CDU claimed, had contributed to the worsening climate of German–American relations and shown up the governing coalition as an unsteady Alliance partner. On the diplomatic front, Brezhnev seemed to have been proved right in his brazen 'peace diplomacy', thereby apparently having prevented a major NATO decision to procure a new American nuclear weapon. CSU party leader Franz Josef Strauß pontificated to *Die Welt* that in the post-war era 'this is the first time that an American president has openly and visibly lain down in front of a Russian tsar'.[108]

Carter's deferral was also a major personal embarrassment for Schmidt. Despite his initial ambivalence about the ERW, he and Genscher had spent nine months crafting an intricate compromise formula in the hope of satisfying the president, the Alliance, the German government, and their own parties. And he had done all this despite feeling that, in essence, the neutron bomb was an irritating diversion from the fundamental challenge to European security posed by the Soviet SS-20s. Having invested so much time, energy, and political capital in the issue, only to be humiliated by the president's last-minute *volte face*, his overwhelming reaction was one of incandescent rage. Schmidt had absolutely no doubt that the blame for this whole sorry mess lay with Carter personally, and this was also the general view within the coalition. Once again, they felt, the peanut farmer from Georgia had demonstrated his unreliability as a man and his unpredictability as a policymaker. As Klaus Kinkel—Genscher's political adviser—put it, the Carter administration was nothing better than a 'leaderless hen-coop'.[109]

Genscher himself likened the farcical end of the neutron bomb affair to 'a second-class burial'.[110] The president's sudden dumping of the whole idea left West Germany looking like America's poodle. This was all the more galling since it was Schmidt who, during the winter of 1977–8, had taken the lead in shaping a solution to the ERW conundrum. What started as a debate over strategy had become an issue of personal prestige and national status. The chancellor regarded the president's sudden killing-off of the neutron bomb as nothing less than a personal betrayal. The affair turned his long-standing doubts about Carter into an abiding resentment that threatened to poison Bonn's whole relationship with Washington. It also exposed the FRG's minimal leverage in Cold War security politics just at a time when, through the G7 process of global economic governance, the country was being taken seriously as a diplomatic equal of the United States.

When all was said and done, however, Schmidt knew that the United States remained West Germany's most important ally. As he told the *Bundestag*'s Foreign Affairs and Defence Committee in the aftermath of Carter's deferral: 'Without the US there is no security for Western Europe. We must thus always try to look to maintaining a vital consensus with America at all levels.'[111] Carter, too, was eager to pick up the pieces and to reinstate American leadership. The contorted ERW debate at least had the effect of finally pushing the 'grey-area' issue to the top of NATO's agenda. Over the next two years Schmidt and Carter would thus be drawn into a new battle over nuclear politics in the European theatre, now focused on the Soviet SS-20s. This time, however, the outcome would be very different.[112]

4

Constructing the Dual Track

The year 1979 would mark the high point of Schmidt's diplomacy. After the fiasco of the neutron bomb, he faced an even tougher problem: the general imbalance of theatre nuclear forces in Europe. In crafting a solution, he brought West Germany to the top table of Western nuclear powers—America, Britain, and France—in an unprecedented 1 + 3 summit in Guadeloupe. And NATO's dual-track policy, which he was instrumental in creating, would eventually play a crucial part in the dénouement of the Cold War.

After the ERW debacle, Carter knew that he urgently needed to reassure the Europeans, particularly Schmidt. On 10 April 1978 Brzezinski noted: 'We will have to develop some initiatives in the arms and security area to fortify the president's image'.[1] NATO's prime concern was the ongoing Soviet build-up of intermediate-range ballistic missiles (IRBMs), notably SS-20s, which threatened Western Europe and was not being discussed in either SALT or MBFR negotiations. This was the underlying grey-area problem that Schmidt highlighted publicly in his IISS speech of October 1977. To enhance stability and peace he wanted to re-establish the equilibrium of military forces in Europe. As he had argued in his writings since the 1960s, this balance could be created either via nuclear arms limitations by both superpowers (the outcome he preferred), or through building up a Western counterweight to the Soviet grey-area arsenal, if arms control talks failed. With the removal from NATO's diplomacy of ERW as a bargaining chip, the Allies were looking to the modernization of America's longer-range theatre nuclear forces—cruise and Pershing II (PII) missiles. These grey-area weapons framed the second round of the Carter–Schmidt debate about European security, conducted in 1978–9, which is the subject of this chapter.

Schmidt's conceptual approach to this issue was the same as over ERW and he faced similar political problems at home, especially the opposition of Bahr and the SPD left to new American nuclear deployments. But he approached this round on the basis of tactical and conceptual lessons learnt from the neutron bomb affair. On the tactical level, Schmidt considered it essential to improve communication between the Allies, which he felt could only be achieved by direct, face-to-face dialogue. To this end he pioneered a new 'Big Four' Western European security summit at Guadeloupe—informal in character, yet candid in content—similar to his original ideas for the G5 in economic affairs. On the conceptual side, he had to resolve the dilemma of which should come first: an American commitment to produce or a European commitment to deploy. Over ERW Schmidt had proposed a sequential three-step process, which had ended up leaving Carter feeling too dependent on the contingency of future Allied decisions. So now Schmidt developed a dual-track approach, which committed both America and its NATO allies from the outset to produce *and* deploy cruise and Pershing missiles, while linking the scale of the eventual deployment to the outcome of proposed negotiations over the reduction of Soviet intermediate-range nuclear forces. Based on this model, in December 1979 the NATO allies committed themselves in a single act—what Bonn called *uno actu*—to produce, deploy, and negotiate, with an automatic, built-in pledge that the level of deployment in the future would be proportionate to the success of arms control negotiations. Instead of a three-stage process that lacked any certainty of America and its allies keeping in step, the dual track was one tightly wrapped package.

So, over cruise and Pershing, unlike the ERW, NATO managed to hammer out a firm, consensual decision. Schmidt played a leading role in crafting such an outcome, all the more remarkable because he had to do so from the back seat. West Germany was not a fully sovereign state or a nuclear power (unlike the other three at Guadeloupe—America, Britain, and France), so in a strict sense he was the junior partner. And he was very careful not to take an overt leadership role, lest this awaken among Germany's neighbours the ghosts of the country's militaristic past.

In contrast with the saga of the neutron bomb, the dual-track decision proved a success story for Schmidt: he helped design it conceptually and implement it diplomatically. The skills he had shown in global economic governance (the G7) and had developed as a defence-intellectual politician finally came together when he forged this coherent NATO dual-track policy. In the process he elevated himself to the position of a world leader in defence and security politics, engaging in what he unashamedly called *Weltpolitik* (world politics). But he achieved this at the cost of renewed strains within his party—strains that were gradually eroding his political base and would eventually destroy his chancellorship.

LAYING DOWN TRACK ONE: TNF MODERNIZATION

The grey-area problem and NATO's TNF posture had been addressed in private since the autumn of 1977 by the Alliance's High Level Group (HLG). This was a small and exclusive circle of top Defence and Foreign Ministry officials with direct access to national leaderships but no obligation to present fully approved government positions. As such, the HLG soon developed a dynamic of its own. At its February 1978 meeting in Los Alamos, to explore 'Alternative TNF Postures', the experts quickly decided to prioritize the modernization of longer-range theatre nuclear forces (LRTNFs) over improvements in battlefield weaponry, both conventional and nuclear.[2] This downplayed ERWs just at the time when, at the political level, NATO leaders were trying to sew up their package on the neutron bomb. The HLG's emphasis on LRTNFs held a particular attraction for the West Germans. They wanted so-called 'deep strike' capabilities—systems that could reach into the Soviet Union (though short of Moscow)[3] and would also serve as a direct counter to the new Soviet SS-20s and Backfire bombers. If visible, their presence would reassure German public opinion and display the reality of this deterrent to the Warsaw Pact.[4]

At this stage, Washington was not willing to commit itself to the LRTNF option. But after the president ditched the ERW in April 1978, allowing the Soviets to claim a major diplomatic victory, he accepted Brzezinski's advice on the need to show clear Alliance leadership and reinforce NATO's defence posture in another way. At the NPG's meeting in Frederikshavn on 18–19 April, NATO defence ministers agreed unanimously on the enhancement of American TNF systems in Western Europe with a range over 1,000 kilometres.[5] Nevertheless, German Foreign Ministry officials lamented the Americans' unwillingness to identify specific weapon systems for modernization.[6] At NATO's Washington Summit of 30–31 May Carter remained vague. He simply called for the general replacement and modernization of nuclear weapons and declared American willingness to discuss the SS-20 problem whilst emphasizing the strengthening of NATO's conventional forces in line with the Alliance's long-term defence plans.[7]

The British shared Bonn's dislike of America's evasiveness on TNFs but also had issues with Schmidt's perspective. To their mind the chancellor was overly attracted to an exact mirroring of Euro-strategic nuclear capabilities on each side—something they believed to be 'practically impossible, politically divisive and militarily unnecessary'. But they felt there was 'nevertheless a good case for maintaining and strengthening the present in-theatre capability within NATO's total nuclear armoury'.[8] We can see here two different European motivations behind the emergent consensus in the High Level and Nuclear Planning Groups on the need for longer-range theatre nuclear forces: the Germans' primary concern with the political and military threat posed by the Soviet SS-20s, as opposed to the British belief that there was a general structural weakness in the Alliance's deterrence posture that needed offsetting via LRTNF enhancements. The Germans were concentrating on their vulnerable geo-strategic position within NATO as a non-nuclear power at the front line, whereas the British, as an offshore nuclear power, tended to consider the Alliance at large.[9]

The grey-area problem and NATO's internal debate about TNF modernization could not, however, be disentangled from strategic arms limitation negotiations (SALT II). These in turn were part and parcel of the overall superpower relationship which, to Schmidt's chagrin, was in limbo after Carter's surprise attempt to rewrite the basis of SALT II with his deep cuts proposal in spring 1977, provoking the Soviets to postpone any future superpower summit. Moscow had then gained a clear propaganda victory over the neutron bomb. Despite his concern about the European balance, Schmidt did not expect crisis hot spots (*krisenhafte Zuspitzungen*) or a serious degeneration of East–West relations to arise from the growing conventional and nuclear arms disparities in Europe or from the modernization of weaponry. Instead, he feared that dangerous tensions would arise from the spread of armaments to Third World countries via commercial or state-controlled arms exports and through great-power involvement, direct or indirect, in regional conflicts. He was particularly concerned about the extension of the Cold War to post-colonial Africa in the mid 1970s, with the Soviets or their proxies exploiting the power vacuums in Angola, Ethiopia, Eritrea, and Somalia and the Americans then being drawn in. With both superpowers increasingly entangled in the global Cold War and geo-ideological adventurism, Schmidt feared that heightened mutual distrust over motives and actions would damage their mutual engagement, leaving arms-control negotiations in a continuing freeze. In short, European security could not be insulated from the climate of global affairs, or what Schmidt referred to as the *weltpolitische Lage*.[10]

Schmidt's global view of security politics went together with his global conception of economic affairs. It was this conceptualization of Germany's place within an interdependent world that led the chancellor to start speaking from the spring of 1978 about engaging in *Weltpolitik*. This was, of course, a historically loaded term because of its association with the belligerent foreign-policy rhetoric of Wilhelmine Germany, but Schmidt felt justified in using it not only because the Cold War had become increasingly global but also because West Germany itself had now achieved the rank of 'world power' (*Weltmacht*). It was the Bonn G7 summit in July 1978 that made this status clear—a point picked up by commentators, as we saw in chapter 1. The *Wall Street Journal*, for instance, categorically stated that under Schmidt West Germany had 'developed into a world power', both 'economically and also increasingly politically'.[11]

With this legitimation, Schmidt resorted more frequently to the language of *Weltmacht* and *Weltpolitik*. Speaking off the record to leading editors that October, he said that over the last few years West Germany had risen to become not just 'world-economically but also world-politically a rather weighty state'.[12] This was not an unmitigated benefit, he admitted. Sometimes it was positively 'scary'—because in Europe, and also globally by the Soviet Union and China, the FRG was seen as the next power 'behind the United States'. This provoked 'envy' and 'ill-will' as well as raising the demands placed on West Germany's government, society, and economy—all of which, he felt, was the consequence of the FRG's increased room for manoeuvre thanks to its 'self-liberation through *Ostpolitik*' and its 'relatively successful economic management' compared with other states. *Weltpolitik* discourse also remained problematic for historical reasons: Schmidt was always painfully aware that the scope of West German foreign policy was limited by the nation's haunted past. He told the editors bluntly that the *Bundeswehr* was now 'qualitatively one of the best armies in the world' and 'quantitatively one of the biggest in the West, including the USA'. But, he added, this must never be mentioned in public because it would conjure up memories of 'Auschwitz and Hitler'. So, in Schmidt's view, for the FRG to engage in *Weltpolitik* in the 1970s was fraught with difficulties; yet he had no doubt that such an engagement was both essential and inevitable now that the country had come of age.[13]

At the heart of Schmidt's *Weltpolitik* was the search for political stability and the preservation of peace in order to make progress on the German question. And peace and stability, as he always said, hinged on the establishment of a balance in the politico-military arena. Indeed, this equilibrium of military forces (*Gleichgewicht*) between East and West—what he called the 'Archimedean point' in all efforts at arms control—was a precondition for further détente (*Entspannung*). In an era of global Cold War this should not be a détente limited merely to Europe and the two Germanies but one that was global in scope. In sum, Schmidt considered it a 'world-political necessity that an approximate equilibrium existed'.[14]

How could such an equilibrium be achieved? Given the gravity of Cold War antagonisms, Schmidt believed that the world-leading powers (the superpowers and those of 'global weight') ought to engage with each other in a calculable and predictable way, showing willingness to compromise with their opponents. Because the Soviets were not willing to talk to the Americans, this placed the onus, in his view, on a power of global weight such as the FRG, which in any case had its own interest in dialogue with Moscow for the sake of the German question. A meeting seemed all the more urgent because he had not been able to hold a summit with Brezhnev since October 1974 on account of Soviet foot-dragging.[15] After the ERW fiasco, however, the Soviet leader was much happier to come to West Germany, and the visit[16] was duly arranged for 4–7 May 1978 in Bonn and Hamburg.

This was the fourth meeting between the two of them. Brezhnev arrived an ailing man, with numerous heart and lung problems, but he was buoyed up by the strengthening position of the USSR in world affairs. The main item of business was to sign a 'framework agreement'[17] on economic and industrial cooperation, which covered a variety of areas, from energy and trade to finance and credits. These were long-standing desiderata for Moscow but Brezhnev's keenness was accentuated by Soviet anxiety about the increasing pace and intensity of China's economic opening to the West, especially the recent flurry of visits to West Germany. In April Bonn had hosted China's Minister of Foreign Trade, Li Qiang, and, three weeks after Brezhnev, Vice-Premier Gu Mu would arrive on a top-level fact-finding mission. Captivated by the FRG's level of modernization and hoping to emulate the German post-war 'economic miracle' through rapid technology transfer, the Chinese were soon deep in talks for a steel rolling mill, four chemical plants, and machinery for exploiting coalfields and iron ore—deals worth billions of DMs. Brezhnev feared that Chinese competition would diminish Soviet opportunities: he therefore saw real urgency in embedding Soviet–German commercial relations in a governmental agreement.[18]

Schmidt, for his part, ever since the 1966 Moscow trip, had believed in the economic benefits and political opportunities that lay in trade and technological ties with the USSR. And the specific conception of a wide-ranging and long-term deal dated from his days as finance minister in 1973, building on the policy of *Osthandel* that had been integral to the Brandt government's *Ostpolitik*. With so little having come from his 1974 summit with the Soviet leader, Schmidt was especially glad now in 1978 to conclude the 'framework agreement'. The chancellor placed particular emphasis on the length of this cooperation treaty, which spanned a full twenty-five years, a longevity 'without parallel in the world' and that endowed the agreement with an 'incredibly high economic and political significance'. His aim, he told Brezhnev, was 'to overcome the past and to turn our relations into a factor of international stability'. Speaking to the Bundestag, he made the same point publicly: 'the economic agreement extends far beyond the range of economic affairs. It provides an orientation for the development of political relations in general, for long-term peaceful development which presupposes that the people in both countries acquire a permanent interest in one another's economic welfare'.[19]

Contemporary commentators saw the summit's achievements in political and security affairs as less substantial. There was little progress over the problems of Berlin and this also prevented the signing of three other German–Soviet agreements. Brezhnev also studiously evaded discussion of the unilateral Soviet build-up of SS-20s. Claiming that the Soviet Union did not seek military superiority, he implied that a certain military equilibrium in Central Europe already existed, rather than being to date just an aspiration—as Schmidt saw the situation. But despite these obvious roadblocks, there was some underlying clarification of key issues. Brezhnev stated that the USSR was willing to discuss reductions of all weapons categories, including 'grey-area' armaments, as long as neither side's security would be affected. And the German–Soviet joint communiqué included for the first time language about 'parity' in military forces and 'equality' as the criterion for security. Schmidt and Brezhnev agreed that

> further steps in the field of disarmament and arms limitation must be accelerated in order to ensure that the process of détente is not impaired but rather supplemented by developments in the military sector. The two sides regard it as important that nobody should aspire to military superiority. They proceed on the assumption that approximate equality and parity are adequate guarantees of defence.[20]

Schmidt seized on this language as a promising sign. On this basis, he hoped, Brezhnev would realize that if he now continued SS-20 deployments, he would be violating the principles of their public communiqué.[21] His hopefulness was increased by the personal ethos of the summit, fostered especially by a visit to Schmidt's home in Hamburg on the final day. As Schmidt explained before the summit, 'given my knowledge of the person of Leonid Brezhnev, I have confidence in the potential for understanding that lies in personal discussion'[22]. The two leaders chatted over a lunch of ham and asparagus, well lubricated by vodka, about Russian literature and Hamburg's history. Brezhnev was particularly impressed by the forty-volume collected works of Marx and Engels that adorned Schmidt's bookshelves. In this way the visit ended on what Schmidt called 'a harmonious note'. The chancellor told the press that the Soviet leader was a safe pair of hands and a man from whom West Germans had no reason to fear a military attack. He regarded Brezhnev as a pragmatist, not a warmonger, and noted that the two men had established a certain rapport as human beings when sharing their experiences of fighting in the Second World War, as they had in 1974 (see Figure 4.1).[23]

This new German–Soviet *Tuchfühlung* did not, however, change the facts of nuclear life in Europe. Brezhnev's willingness in principle to negotiate over arms reductions in Europe did not stop Moscow continuing to deploy SS-20s. Although the Bonn meeting showed that for the Soviets West Germany's political value had clearly risen, Schmidt knew that, in regard to his desired goal—the elimination of Euro-strategic disparities—he depended entirely on negotiations that would have

Figure 4.1 Schmidt and Brezhnev, Moscow, 30 October 1974.
Source: DPA.

to be conducted by Carter with Brezhnev, which were stymied by the American–Soviet deadlock over SALT II. And this impasse prevented any superpower discussion on other nuclear issues, including the grey-area problem that so preoccupied Schmidt. The latter would only be addressed in the follow-up round of negotiations, known as SALT III.[24]

Schmidt was concerned that the Americans were jeopardizing a key German interest for SALT III by a concession they were prepared to make in SALT II. This was the protocol offered in May 1977, after the failure of the Vance mission to Moscow, which would prohibit for three years the deployment of cruise missiles, both ground-launched (GLCMs) and submarine-launched (SLCMs) with a range of over 600 kilometres. Cruise was a new system that the Carter administration treated principally as a tradeable bargaining chip in negotiations over Soviet ICBMs but which Schmidt regarded as a direct counter to the Soviet SS-20s. He therefore considered the American draft protocol a major threat to West German security.[25]

To sum up his concerns in the wake of Brezhnev's visit and before the upcoming NATO summit in Washington at the end of May, the chancellor first spoke to Carter on the phone and then wrote him a long letter. In the phone call, Schmidt noted the cordial atmosphere of his talks with Brezhnev and highlighted the Soviet leader's stated willingness to negotiate over grey-area weapons.[26] In his letter the chancellor reiterated the FRG's concern that

> with the growing Soviet medium-range capacity, even given the possibility of a quantitative equalization through the overhang in terms of warheads of nuclear strategic systems, the continued existence of the deterrence capacity could be in jeopardy. To counteract this it will be necessary to secure either an adequate offset of the Soviet medium-range potential in and for Europe or find a solution with the corresponding effects in terms of arms control. The Federal Government gives preference to the latter.[27]

Schmidt accepted that the draft protocol was on the table for SALT II but he did not want its temporary moratorium on longer-range cruise missiles to become a permanent ban: 'To the Federal Government it is of crucial importance that, after the expiry of the three-year validity of the protocol, the cruise missiles should be retained as a defensive counterweight and possibly as a "contrepartie" as regards arms control'. This letter was another early intimation of Schmidt's dual-track approach—of reinforcing deterrence while also promoting dialogue.[28]

The message to Carter also reveals how unsatisfactory Schmidt found the HLG's narrow focus on LRTNF modernization without reference to arms control. The chancellor's concern was now belatedly being recognized in Washington.[29] In anticipation of a future phase of serious inter-Allied political consultations that would link LRTNF procurement *and* arms control, the German Foreign and Defence Ministries began seriously to coordinate their views on the general grey-area conundrum and to work towards the preparation of a German government position.[30] The French and British, for their part, now thought it an opportune moment to announce that their own national nuclear systems should definitely not be included in future SALT rounds.[31]

In Washington, too, the tempo of debate intensified. In response to a request from Carter, the Special Coordination Committee advised on 19 August that the intricate politico-military problems of European security dictated an 'integrated strategy'. This concept represented a crucial development in the American position. The committee suggested that the United States lend its support to the HLG's recommendation for an increase in LRTNF capabilities but also stated that *if* the Alliance decided ultimately to make such deployments these 'would have to be accompanied by a strong arms control effort'. Pure deployment or pure arms control—each of these approaches alone was to be ruled out. Here we can see Washington feeling its own way towards a dual-track solution.[32]

In view of European concerns about the grey area, the committee advised that development of new cruise missiles should go ahead, together with an upgrade of the Pershing IA system (to be known as Pershing II). This weaponry was seen as a 'political necessity'—to offset continued Soviet TNF deployments, rebuild NATO's credibility, and help reassure the Germans.[33] As far as the president was concerned, the arms-control track acted merely as a 'cover' to secure Bonn's support of new nuclear weapons deployments. By adopting this premise, however, Washington totally misunderstood Schmidt's balance of power policy (*Gleichgewichtspolitik*).

As was clear from his conversations with Brezhnev and his correspondence with Carter, the chancellor did not look to arms-limitation diplomacy as a mere 'cover'. He wanted to keep NATO's nuclear deterrence viable but, on grounds of principle and not just politics, he preferred options that would facilitate reductions in Soviet IRBMs. For Schmidt, arms control was essential—at the very least as a complement to deployment.[34]

In the autumn of 1978 Washington informed London that it now recognized the need for a hardware solution to the TNF problem. The Americans were aiming for a NATO decision by the summer of 1979.[35] At this stage, it is worth noting, the German coalition government's precise public position on TNF modernization and the grey area was not yet clear.[36] Despite Schmidt's own emphasis on Soviet arms reductions, within the HLG German defence experts from both the Foreign and Defence Ministries sought to dispel the impression that the LRTNF issue was approached in Bonn above all from an arms-control perspective. At the Brussels HLG meeting on 16–17 October, Germany's Major-General Wolfgang Altenburg lobbied for LRTNFs as the means to redress the deficiency in NATO's deterrence spectrum, *not* as a counterweight matching SS-20 and Backfire. In other words, NATO's strategic case came first; the public policy case about countering the SS-20 threat came second. LRTNFs should not be dispensable arms control bargaining chips, for this would give the wrong signal to the Soviet Union about NATO's resolve to shore up its deterrence and defence capabilities.[37]

So far no exact LRTNF systems had been earmarked by the High Level Group. The Germans favoured submarine-launched cruise missiles, based offshore, because the prospect of ground-launched cruise missiles on German soil raised the spectre of renewed major popular controversy akin to that over neutron bombs only a year earlier. Yet, what mattered most to Bonn were not weapon types but the FRG's non-singularity status—not being the sole continental country to deploy—and the principle that West Germany would never operate LRTNFs under a dual-key system. 'There could be no German finger on the trigger', the HLG was firmly told—so as not to upset the Soviet Union, and also Germany's smaller Western neighbours, for obvious historical reasons.[38] The Brussels HLG meeting ended with a consensus to develop LRTNF weapons systems. This was to do be done on the basis of widespread 'participation' (to share the cost and risk) and on the clear assumption that the Allies were not seeking to build up a position of 'essential equivalence' in TNFs with the Soviet IRBMs. The envisaged extra NATO capability was only 300 to 500 systems, of which a minimum number (as yet unspecified) must be deployed irrespective of the outcome of any arms-limitation talks.[39] With this emphasis on sufficiency, the HLG was moving away from Schmidt's earlier idea of an exactly mirrored parity at all levels of the deterrent triad (*Schichtenparität*).[40]

As 1978 drew to its close the High Level Group proposed that specific LRTNF systems should be identified at the April 1979 nuclear planning group meeting in Florida.[41] Even if that happened, nobody expected a clear programme of action in the spring. In fact, Washington appeared to many as over-optimistic in aiming for a final political Alliance decision on TNF modernization by the end of 1979. Nevertheless, the White House seemed finally to be embracing a policy of LRTNF enhancements, based on military and political need. But so far, none of its European allies had volunteered to deploy.[42]

And there was still no clear, harmonized line within West Germany's coalition government. Foreign Minister Hans-Dietrich Genscher and his party, the FDP (together with the CDU/CSU opposition), believed that military-strategic necessity dictated reinforcement of the American TNF arsenal in Europe, in order to keep NATO's flexible response doctrine credible. Any arms-control negotiations with the Soviets ought to be undertaken from a position of strength, *after* a modernization decision had been implemented. Arms-control efforts without new TNFs would allow for an ever-increasing imbalance in the Soviets' favour. By contrast, SPD Defence Minister Hans Apel, as well as some of his senior bureaucrats, tended to look at TNFs primarily as a way of resolving the 'grey-area problem' via arms limitations. Although they recognized the importance of loyalty to NATO and the Alliance's need to update its weapons arsenals, they were fixated on the Soviet SS-20s and mainly wanted LRTNFs as a bargaining chip to re-establish a Euro-strategic balance via arms limitations if not reductions.[43]

Schmidt hovered between these two positions, at times supporting and on other occasions inhibiting the processes of NATO's LRTNF decision-making. On the whole, however, the chancellor still hoped to get more weight placed on arms-control diplomacy. Arguments within the coalition apart, there were of course the much more deep-seated ideological quarrels within the SPD between the Schmidt and Bahr camps, which had erupted during the ERW controversy and continued to simmer. This left the chancellor perennially worried, whatever policy was finally agreed, how party and public would react. What exactly should be the link between LRTNF modernization and arms control? Here was the dilemma now facing Schmidt.[44]

SCHMIDT AT THE TOP TABLE: GUADELOUPE, OR 1+3

In trying to address this quandary, the chancellor wanted to prevent a repeat of the neutron bomb disaster. His thinking developed on two levels—international and domestic. First, he wanted to improve policy coordination between West Germany and NATO's three nuclear powers—America, Britain, and France. In particular, he sought better communication with his fellow leaders, especially Carter, with whom relations remained fraught. To ease the tensions he used Callaghan and Giscard, with both of whom he had cordial and cooperative relations. Following the tried and tested formula of the Library Group, on which the G5 had been based, he wanted the meeting to take place informally and away from bureaucrats and the press. In October he proposed the idea of a summit to Brzezinski, and, as a result of his initiative, NATO's 'Big Four' eventually agreed to meet on the French Caribbean island of Guadeloupe on 5–6 January 1979. Their venue would be the exclusive beach hotel *Hamak*.[45]

At home, meanwhile, Schmidt entered into private correspondence with Egon Bahr, hoping to avert another round of political sniping while he was trying to thrash out a nuclear policy for NATO. In a letter on 15 December 1978 the chancellor laid out some of his central strategic considerations and asked Bahr not to tie the SPD to a course totally critical of new armaments. He was quite frank about wanting 'to avoid an anti-TNF modernization campaign similar to the one of summer 1977' against the neutron bomb—which, he noted, had 'started from within the SPD' and 'without pre-consultation' among the party's leaders. Not only could such a campaign lead the FRG into an unpredictable clash with America but it would also expose the SPD to claims that the party was dancing to the Kremlin's tune.[46] Bahr, however, was unimpressed. Deep down, he remained wedded to his visions of an all-European security structure. He therefore replied that mutual and balanced force-reduction talks had to have absolute priority in West German diplomacy because, he believed, these talks would be entering a critical stage in 1979. A decision to deploy cruise missiles, he told Schmidt, would only alienate the Russians, hamper progress on MBFR, and damage détente.[47]

The Schmidt–Bahr exchange of letters in December 1978 revealed the familiar differences in the two men's security outlooks. Ultimately, these could not be bridged. Whereas Schmidt, along the lines of the 'flexible response' doctrine, saw the European nuclear balance endangered by the new Soviet IRBM deployments, Bahr continued to argue that the European balance was guaranteed by the strategic equilibrium between the two superpowers. German security depended simply on the American strategic guarantee. He did, however, make two concessions to Schmidt. First, he said that, if American LRTNF deployments could not be stopped, Washington ought to be pressed to consider submarine-launched cruise missiles, for these would at least not be stationed on German soil.[48] Second, Bahr did not go public with his misgivings, in contrast with the *Vorwärts* articles of summer 1977.

With the home front quiet, Schmidt was able to concentrate on his upcoming summit in the Caribbean. In fact, he disliked the term 'summit diplomacy' (*Gipfeldiplomatie*) because, in his view, formal summits came with the paraphernalia of a PR machine and official statements, layers of government bureaucracy, and an entourage of advisors—not to mention intense public pressure to produce concrete results. What mattered to Schmidt, by contrast, was the personal exchange of ideas and the fostering of candid discussion. He was always driven by the desire to fathom his partner's motives and thoughts. 'Only in this way', he argued, was 'the foundation laid for a reliable cooperation and partnership, for predictability, for political accountability, personal trust.'[49]

In preparing for Guadeloupe, Schmidt was also conscious that West Germany was moving into uncharted waters. For the first time, his country would be sitting at the top table with NATO's three nuclear powers, even though the country had renounced nuclear weapons and lacked full sovereignty. Even more striking, the FRG would be bargaining as an equal with the three Western victor powers from World War Two. Given the sensitivities of this 1 + 3 situation, Schmidt was therefore keen to avoid the limelight as much as possible. Not wanting to be publicly identified as the instigator of the summit, he shifted responsibility for its organization on to the White House. And he lured Giscard into participating in a meeting that would deal primarily with NATO's defence planning, even though the French had pulled out of the Alliance military command structure in 1966. Paris had

Figure 4.2 Guadeloupe: '1 + 3' in beach hut, 5 January 1979.
Source: Jimmy Carter Library.

originally resisted a quadripartite summit on nuclear issues, to avoid bringing into the equation their *force de frappe*, but the chancellor successfully baited his hook by persuading Giscard that France should be the host nation.[50]

And so, on 5 January 1979, the four leaders found themselves sitting in an open, thatch-roofed beach hut, under palm trees in the light Caribbean breeze (see Figure 4.2). Ahead of them of were two days of uninterrupted discussion about global security.[51] Although Giscard, as host, acted as formal chairman of the sessions, the mood was relaxed; the leaders were attired in short-sleeved shirts, and there were no position papers or fixed agenda. Translators were not required because English served as the common language. In free moments the leaders gossiped and sunbathed, jogged and snorkelled, played tennis and went sailing.[52] Despite the holiday atmosphere of what one journalist called this 'swimming pool summit', the discussions were intense and differences of opinion were expressed with the candour that Schmidt desired.[53]

The chancellor was in no way abashed by his inclusion in the West's nuclear inner circle. In the first substantive discussion of European security, he offered a lengthy overview of the strategic situation. Giscard called it 'an impressive exposé', showing Schmidt's 'competence and powers of synthesis'. The chancellor occasionally turned the pages of his briefing papers, collated in an elegant black moleskin folder, but 'he hardly ever looked at them', Giscard noted, 'for he knows his subject so intimately'.[54] In his presentation, Schmidt was at pains to reject any 'special position' (*Sonderposition*) for the FRG: this was clearly a major point of his intervention, to highlight the sensitivities of the German situation. Yet, in a more personal sense, Schmidt *was* asserting a special position for himself amongst his partners at Guadeloupe. This became especially apparent in a long afternoon session, with advisers, devoted to LRTNFs and SALT when the chancellor spoke for a full forty-five minutes. The central issue was the question of West Germany being singled out in any commitment to deploy, on which he and Carter had already locked horns over the neutron bomb. Schmidt said he had been 'appalled' recently to read the scenario for a NATO exercise, which postulated 'fighting taking place in Germany alone'. Nevertheless, the chancellor said he would accept GLCMs on German soil 'provided at least one other European NATO ally did also'. He pledged that he would stick to this promise, despite the mounting anti-nuclear pressures within West Germany, not least from within his own party.[55]

The chancellor spoke with a mixture of intellectual superiority and emotional intensity that had the effect of winding up some of his interlocutors. Giscard recalled that Schmidt took 'visible pleasure in going into all the details' of SALT II, and 'expressing critical judgements' on the way these negotiations were being handled, 'which visibly irritated Jimmy Carter'. The president considered Schmidt 'very contentious' and did not conceal his annoyance. If Germany was not prepared to accept outright the necessary deployment of GLCMs and Pershing IIs, he said pointedly, it was difficult to see why others should do so on Bonn's behalf. Schmidt reiterated this was an *all-Allied* problem, revolving around a crucial gap in NATO defences. Carter replied testily: 'but *you* won't agree to fill it'. For his part, Brzezinski was 'very disappointed' by Schmidt, who, he said, delivered a 'rather elementary lecture on nuclear strategy' and 'kept saying that he has a political problem and that he is not in any position to make any commitments'.[56]

The two days at Guadeloupe resulted in a degree of consensus. Carter successfully prioritized LRTNF modernization. And his European nuclear allies, Giscard and Callaghan, shared his view at this stage that NATO should first improve its defence and deterrence posture before beginning to tackle arms control with the Kremlin.[57] Nevertheless, the president did concede, under pressure from Schmidt, that the grey area was a problem and needed to be tied into the arms-control agenda of SALT III. This was also acceptable to Giscard and Callaghan as long as their own national nuclear deterrents were excluded from SALT III and the SS-20s were included.[58] Carter promised that he would raise the grey-area issue with Brezhnev at their next summit, currently scheduled for February, and assured his allies that he would tell the Soviet leader of 'his concern about the increasing deployment of SS-20 and would say he would like negotiations about this'. He said he 'would not be specific about whether these discussions should take place in SALT III or a separate negotiation'.[59] The two tracks were therefore now becoming more clearly defined in Carter's mind, but, worryingly for Schmidt, the negotiation track was left vague and pushed into the future. This would be his main concern over the next few months.

Guadeloupe ended with a relaxed press conference in the lush hotel grounds. Clad now in business suits, the four leaders stressed the harmony among them for the benefit of several hundred media representatives.[60] The conclusions of

Guadeloupe were presented to the world as a simple pro-American and pro-SALT II consensus. Little was made of the conundrum of 'grey-area' weapons and of the work needed to make progress with the specific questions of how to proceed on LRTNF modernization and deployment and how to get the Soviets to decommission their SS-20s. The two tracks surfaced in the media only in late January 1979 when the *New York Times* reported that 'the question whether the West needs to field a new class of long-range missiles in Europe has emerged as a major issue in European–American relations because it is viewed as having enormous implications for the future of alliance unity as well as for prospects of further progress in Soviet–American arms control'.[61]

The press also picked up on the FRG's prominence in these discussions. As the *New York Times* noted, there was 'widespread comment in European newspapers that the real significance of the Guadeloupe meetings was West Germany's consecration as a mature Western power whose prerogatives now extend beyond a significant economic role to matters of global strategy'. Asked directly about this, Schmidt commented: 'The fact that we are involved in consultations that involve matters other than economic problems is no novelty. But, of course, through Guadeloupe it's entered the public consciousness.' While acknowledging the FRG's growing role as 'a world decision maker', Schmidt was at pains to avoid the impression of vaunting ambition. 'We don't want to stand out in any way', the chancellor said. 'Our economic strength is often overrated, and we'll never be a political giant.' He reminded reporters that his country carried many burdens, including its Nazi past, its difficult relationship with East Germany, and the problematic position of Berlin—so vulnerable to attack from Eastern Europe. And he restated the familiar mantra that West Germany 'does not want to become a nuclear power or leave the impression that it does'. Despite Schmidt's attempted diffidence, the media clearly identified his country as one of 'the Big Four of the Western world'.[62]

Such talk, however, was not popular among the other NATO allies. Italy, in particular, took exception to Guadeloupe as a four-power directorate.[63] Although the informal, quadripartite discussions had, in Brzezinski's words, 'contributed a great deal to the shaping of a strategic consensus'—in contrast with the constant miscommunication over ERWs—Guadeloupe would not be repeated. Other means had to be developed to reach a NATO decision that would satisfy all fifteen members and prove 'politically enforceable' across the whole Alliance.[64]

The Big Four had, therefore, no illusions of the work that lay ahead of them and their bureaucrats. In Bonn, the West German government now began to brace itself to accept at least a few LRTNFs. Desperate not to lose sight of the arms-control track and SALT III, they pressed for a parallel forum to NATO's HLG, within which arms-reduction options could be seriously explored.[65] When David Aaron, Brzezinski's deputy, secretly visited Bonn in early February, the Germans proposed the creation of a Special Working Group (SG).[66] After further discussion between Washington, Bonn, and London,[67] NATO duly launched the SG in early April. Its establishment showed that the Alliance was following through on the arms-control track that Schmidt had so forcefully pursued at Guadeloupe.[68]

Nevertheless, this second track was not unanimously welcomed within the Alliance. Significantly the British and American delegates even began the SG discussions by questioning its basic premise—asking whether the TNF modernization decision should indeed be accompanied by an arms-control initiative, lest the latter delay the former. In any case, the Americans considered the arms control approach merely a means to garner political support for deployments: they were convinced that negotiations would elicit only Soviet attempts to stall Western modernization rather than genuine Kremlin moves towards arms control.[69] The Americans, supported by the British, considered it imperative that 'TNF arms control' must be 'a *supplement* to, *not a substitute* for, TNF modernization'. Otherwise there was always a danger 'that some Allies, in an effort to cope with internal political debate over modernization, would seek to make actual deployments hostage to the outcome of arms control negotiations'.[70]

The Anglo-American 'deployments-first' stance in the SG was backed in part by West German representatives, who believed that only this would get the Soviets to the negotiating table. Their rationale was 'arm to disarm', although they acknowledged the morally offensive nature of this phrase.[71] It was the Belgians, Danes, Dutch, and Norwegians in the SG who were single-mindedly committed to 'arms control above all else'. Doubtful that their governments would participate in future deployments, they looked to arms control either as an end in itself or as a means to postpone the TNF decision.[72] Despite these differences of nuance, however, broadly speaking all the SG participants from continental Europe were in agreement that the question was not *whether* to accompany the modernization decision with an arms-control proposal, but *how* to do so. It was this position (and not the Anglo-American one) that would animate the group's future work.[73]

While track two was being debated, the HLG presented its latest report on modernization to the NPG meeting in Homestead, Florida on 24–25 April 1979. There NATO defence ministers agreed that in order to show strength and unity and to avoid a repetition of the N-bomb debacle, NATO should make its decision by the end of the year. They asked the HLG to prepare a final, fully costed LRTNF paper, which, while taking into account the SG's work, should be based on the accepted parameters of 200–600 ground-launched systems in a mix of Pershing II and cruise missiles. NATO ministers were moving towards a firm political decision based on the two tracks.[74]

At Homestead, Hans Apel, the German defence minister, made a fundamental point about how to connect the two tracks, seeking to avoid a repeat of the ERW mess. He said it would be fatal for NATO if the Allies did not unanimously reach an *uno actu* decision on a TNF modernization programme and on arms control—in other words, one combining these two elements into a single package. Apel said this having closely consulted Schmidt a few days earlier. His carefully chosen language was the first clear sign of a harmonized and fine-tuned German government stance in response to the Carter administration's 'integrated approach'.[75] Crucially, it also indicated that Bonn was actively trying to shape Allied opinion around Schmidt's particular rationale.[76] This would entail that NATO's collective decision for an evolutionary modernization of LRTNFs—involving from the outset a commitment both to produce and deploy—would be combined with a *simultaneous* offer to the Soviets to negotiate limits on both new American and Soviet TNF systems. The inbuilt automaticity within and between the two tracks was intended to prevent the sole selection or prioritization of either. This *uno actu* concept represented a clear difference from the sequential approaches adopted in the ERW debate and touted at Guadeloupe.[77]

The intricate, tightly packaged solution that was now on the diplomatic table had clear benefits for Schmidt on the domestic front. As he had told the SPD *Bundestagsfraktion* on 6 February, he was following a middle path between Germany's right and left. On the one hand, he wanted to avoid too close an association with those on the right, such as the CDU's Manfred Wörner, who favoured new weapons systems and then hoped to achieve arms-reduction negotiation successes from a position of strength. On the other hand, he would keep his distance from those on the left who betted variously on pacifism, unilateral arms cuts, or negotiations that might prove endless and fruitless. In navigating between these extremes the chancellor saw what he called real 'opportunities of politics'. The two tracks, inextricably bound together in the *uno actu* formula, offered a compromise with the potential to satisfy both sides.[78]

In the event Schmidt won support for his position from the BSR and the SPD's party congress in May.[79] This did not, however, stop Bahr from agitating behind the scenes because he objected to any kind of automatic deployments. In a letter of 2 June he warned Schmidt against TNF modernization and urged him to lobby NATO at least for the same sequencing logic as proposed for ERWs a year before: arms-control talks with the Soviets first, inter-Allied discussions and decisions regarding deployments later, if these talks failed.[80] The chancellor, drawing very different lessons from the N-bomb affair, stood firm. On 4 July 1979 he delivered a statement to the *Bundestag* in support of the upcoming NATO dual-track decision. This included a clear commitment to modernization: 'The Allies must undertake all measures necessary to preserve their security'. But, Schmidt added, using sentences he had deftly crafted with the Bonn bureaucracy: 'The extent to which we can adjust the scale of concrete measures aimed at meeting the continuous armament effort of the Warsaw Pact will depend on the degree of success in achieving effective and balanced limitations of LRTNF systems on both sides through arms-control negotiations'.[81] This carefully worded formula reflected the chancellor's personal desire for a military balance at a lower level of armaments but it also represented an olive branch to Bahr and the SPD left. Yet, by emphasizing that the ultimate size of Western deployments would depend on future American–Soviet negotiations, Schmidt cleverly reminded Bahr that the outcome was not in Bonn's hands.

Bahr was torn between his loyalty to party and chancellor on one side, and his own convictions on the other. As he later explained in his memoirs, he did not want to undermine Schmidt's government, especially with an election due the following year. And there was also nothing to be gained by alienating the Americans, who were of course essential for any arms-control negotiations. After June 1979 he desisted from criticism of Schmidt's defence policy in public and in private. The persistent sniping during the ERW affair would not recur.[82]

And so, during the first half of 1979, the chancellor developed a distinctive dual-track policy, which won the approval of his key allies and the endorsement of his own party. All the while, however, he continued to downplay in public Germany's new global role. 'Germany is not a world power; it does not wish to become a world power' he told *Time* magazine in June. 'I am rather cautious that nobody in Bonn overplays Germany's hand.'[83] Much of this was disingenuous, however. Schmidt had stamped his mark on NATO's nuclear diplomacy. He knew it, and so did the world.

PACKAGING THE DUAL TRACK

The dual track had now taken clear form but a lot of work still had to be done on the details of the package and how it would be sold diplomatically to the whole of NATO. Many of the non-nuclear Allies had growing reservations about LRTNF deployments as the issue entered public debate, and this made them dither over track one.[84] The Dutch, Danish, and Italian governments feared alienating leftist voters and the Turks did not want to jeopardize an economic aid package from the Soviet Union. So West German ministers spoke out strongly in favour of the dual track. At NATO's Eurogroup ministerial meeting in May, Apel stressed the importance of the upcoming decision, both for strengthening NATO's defence and deterrence and, even more, demonstrating the Alliance's ability to take a collective decision. If this failed, he said, NATO would lose face with the USSR and the public.[85] Genscher, too, went on the offensive. Two weeks later, at NATO's spring summit of foreign ministers in The Hague,[86] he underlined the significance of simultaneity in the proposed package: the Allies would commit to future LRTNF deployments at the same time as proposing arms-control negotiations to the Soviets. At The Hague a general NATO consensus seemed to emerge that TNF modernization must go ahead, at least at some minimum level, independently from the results of the arms-control talks. In other words, although 'downward adjustments' of the number of new LRTNFs to be deployed were possible, the option of non-deployment should be ruled out.[87] But this was not yet a definitive conclusion.

The general drift of NATO thinking tended towards ruling out a possible 'zero-option' dénouement for the whole dual-track process: in other words, the total removal of Soviet IRBMs and no deployment of new American LRTNFs. This certainly was a divisive issue in Bonn, with intense debate about the merits of minimum deployment and no deployment at all. Schmidt tried to fudge the matter, as was evident in the ebb and flow of a letter he sent to Carter on 19 May:

> It will of course be necessary to take into account the effects of modernization measures on ongoing arms control negotiations. This does not mean, however, that the necessary LRTNF modernization measures should be placed in jeopardy by mere hope for balanced results in the field of arms control. On the contrary, the modernization measures must be carried out as decided, as far as scope, methods, time, and phases are concerned, unless changes are justified or rendered necessary by progress made in arms control.[88]

In his response on 1 June, the president put his own spin on the issue, spelling out that 'some *essential* deployments [would] be needed in any case'.[89] The administration was clearly determined to pin down its allies into accepting a minimum number of missiles—not least to avoid a costly arms-for-scrap outcome. On grounds of personal preference as well as political expediency, Schmidt refused to be tied down by Carter on this point, continuing to propose looser formulations. Not only would such vagueness keep open the 'zero option' but it would also seem less provocative to the Soviets and ease the political problems of other Western European leaders. Whatever Schmidt's personal hopes for a zero solution, he shared the general view in Bonn that Moscow was hardly likely to make arms-control concessions on a scale that would obviate the Alliance's military-strategic need for TNF modernization. But his preference, and that of his government, was not to spell this out because of domestic sensitivities and, equally important, the need to bring all NATO member states on board.[90]

Even with close allies things were difficult. The new Conservative British Prime Minister Margaret Thatcher, elected in May, was no supporter of the German chancellor's dual-track proposal. Her government was interested in TNF modernization alone, and hence proposed that Britain and the FRG speed up the decision-making processes of the HLG at ministerial level. To Schmidt, however, NATO's decision had to be Alliance-wide *and* embody an integrated two-track approach.[91] The problem for him, as usual, was that he felt the need to stay in the background. As *Time* magazine put it, 'Always sensitive to historic European misgivings about the Germans, Helmut Schmidt is careful to play down Bonn's emerging political strength'.[92] Fortunately for Schmidt, the Carter administration was finally beginning to take a clear lead, at least on the LRTNF modernization track.[93] Carter had put his signature on what could be considered an American 'action plan'—a document drafted by Brown and Vance after the Homestead NATO Nuclear Planning Group meeting that outlined an American road map towards a dual-track decision.[94]

With the December deadline getting ever nearer, the Germans and Americans now worked in tandem to push their allies towards a firm commitment to carry the NATO decision.[95] The FRG focused particularly on its continental, non-nuclear neighbours, some of whom would have to share the burden of nuclear basing. Bonn felt encouraged that the Allies were slowly coming round to its dual-track *uno actu* approach but several fundamental questions remained unresolved. Was it possible to complete on time the parallel SG and HLG processes and bring them together in a single integrated decision document? Could the other European leaders secure parliamentary consent ahead of December? And would the number of European countries committing to deploy be sufficient to make the decision credible?[96]

The chancellor was particularly anxious about burden-sharing and the singling out of West Germany for deployments. Given the political uncertainties in Belgium and the Netherlands, he continued to entertain hopes that Norway and Denmark might act as hosts. Although they had always refused to accept NATO nuclear hardware on their soil, he floated the idea that they take submarine-launched cruise missiles. But Carter explicitly rejected SLCM deployments altogether, arguing that other Allies might consider this an easy way to evade their responsibility to station land-based missiles, which were essential to make the modernization visible to the Kremlin. So Schmidt had to abandon this idea.[97] By July the Carter administration had drawn a draft deployment programme for ground-launched missiles, covering five key countries[98]:

West Germany	108 PII & 28 GLCM launchers (112 missiles)
Netherlands	12 GLCM (48)
Belgium	12 GLCM (48)
United Kingdom	36 GLCM (144)
Italy	28 GLCM (112)

The British were on the whole positive, while the Dutch and Belgian governments—although prepared in principle to deploy—remained doubtful about securing domestic political consent. Italy responded enthusiastically, but, with elections looming, nobody could prejudge the next government's standpoint.[99] Nevertheless, Rome welcomed its inclusion in LRTNF policymaking, especially after its resentment at being excluded from Guadeloupe, and, come September, Italy's new coalition government was promising to vote for the dual track and to accept deployments on Italian soil.[100] Schmidt had thus finally secured a non-nuclear European deployment partner, in addition to Britain, which he had always deemed essential.[101]

With track one clearly defined, the Germans now emphasized the need for an equally detailed arms-control proposal under track two.[102] Since cruise missiles, integral to LRTNF modernization, were already under discussion as strategic weaponry, the second track could not be disentangled from the SALT process. Schmidt was pleased that on 18 June Carter and Brezhnev had finally signed the SALT II treaty at their long-delayed summit, held in Vienna. But he remained unhappy at the asymmetry of the agreement because the Soviet SS-20s were not included while the treaty contained the detested protocol prohibiting for three years (until 31 December 1981) the deployment of long-range ground- and submarine-launched cruise missiles. This weakened the strength of track one. Worse still, Schmidt discovered that Carter, in his discussions about SALT III at Vienna, had not even mentioned the SS-20s—despite his pledge at Guadeloupe to do so.[103] Once again, it seemed, the American president could not be relied upon. And then, when meeting Soviet Foreign Minister Andrei Gromyko a week later, Schmidt realized that Moscow was utterly unwilling to address SS-20s—despite Brezhnev's cooing noises at their Bonn summit in 1978.[104] In fact, the Soviets saw future arms-control initiatives and negotiations primarily as a tactical device to 'forestall NATO nuclear modernization'.[105]

For Schmidt this was a sobering moment. His key ally was not supporting him and the adversary he had tried so hard to cultivate proved obdurate. Irrespective of

Bonn's *Ostpolitik* interests, the chancellor knew that for the moment all his efforts had to be geared to NATO. It was imperative for the Alliance to project political and military strength and to be seen to be acting in unison.[106]

For the rest of the summer, American and German officials haggled over the specifics of the Western arms-control proposal and how to link it with the TNF modernization strand.[107] This culminated on 28 September, when the HLG and the SG had their first joint meeting, thereby formally bringing together the two tracks which had hitherto been constructed separately. The representatives of the Allies accepted the American deployment plan, modified at the request of Bonn, to reduce West Germany's overall total of GLCMs from 112 to 96. The representatives also welcomed the SG report that set out a series of principles along which arms-control negotiations should proceed.[108]

The first principle, that *arms limitation must be a complement to, not a substitute for, TNF modernization*, had been the subject of intensive last-minute fine-tuning between Washington and Bonn. This followed serious pressure by the German Defence Ministry and the SPD left, who had wanted the Western 'zero option' stated explicitly in the SG report's proposal on arms control—in other words, no LRTNF deployments in return for a Soviet offer of sufficiently substantial, if not total, arms reductions. The German Foreign Ministry had sought to suppress such radicalism, pointing to the relatively open formulations used by Schmidt in his July *Bundestag* declaration, which neither explicitly mentioned nor excluded the 'zero option'.[109]

Sorting out this issue took a month of hard bureaucratic argument. In the end, Schmidt himself got involved, authorizing a request to include a sentence referring to the possibility of what would effectively be a 'zero–zero' option: 'theoretically, total elimination of Soviet LRTNFs would make it unnecessary for NATO to deploy such weapons in Europe'.[110] Washington and Bonn then kicked around various drafts for the rest of September.[111] The Carter administration stuck to its guns, determined to avoid any wording that could be interpreted as denying the need for some degree of Western LRTNF modernization.[112] The final version of the contentious paragraph contained in the SG report on 28 September read as follows:

> One could postulate an arms control outcome so successful that the Soviet modern long-range theatre nuclear threat was eliminated. Thereby permitting NATO to consider suspending its own LRTNF modernization plans. As a practical matter, however, such an outcome is highly unlikely, and posing it as a realistic possibility could lead to an immediate and lasting impasse, while Soviet deployments grew.[113]

This language was clearly a fudge. For the moment, it suited both the Americans and Germans, but the idea of a zero option would prove a bone of contention in the future.

The HLG–SG joint meeting proposed that the texts of their two reports should now be combined into an integrated decision document for discussion by the NATO Council and NPG during October and November. This would then be presented for approval and decision by NATO ministers in December.[114]

Just as NATO looked to be on the home straight, in early October the Soviets launched a long-anticipated propaganda campaign against LRTNF modernization— as they had done against the neutron bomb two years before. Instead of letters to key Western leaders, however, its centrepiece this time was two carefully calibrated speeches by Brezhnev himself.[115]

First, in an address to the Committee on Disarmament of the Socialist International in Moscow on 1 October, the Soviet leader condemned those NATO countries that were developing the LRTNF deployment plan and accused them of 'playing a dangerous game with fire'.[116] He targeted in particular those Western social democratic delegates whose parties were in government in NATO countries and pointed to the special responsibility of the West German SPD. This immediately set alarm bells ringing in Bonn because it raised the spectre of German singularity and Soviet blackmail.[117]

Given Brezhnev's personal involvement and fierce tone, his 1 October speech stood in sharp contrast to the conciliatory statements made in Bonn in 1978. Five days later, in case the FRG had not got the message, Brezhnev delivered a similar speech right on its doorstep in East Berlin. Criticizing NATO's planned LRNTF deployments as an attempt 'to destroy the existing balance of power in Europe', the Soviet leader threatened the introduction of new Soviet arms if NATO implemented its plans and even nuclear counterstrikes against West Germany. On arms limitation, Brezhnev's counter proposal offered little detail and skirted the SS-20 issue. So with NATO on the road to a unanimous decision that would give the Alliance a much-needed political boost, there was little desire in Allied capitals to let a rather uncertain prospect of any diplomatic agreement with the Kremlin imperil a hard-won success in Alliance decision-making. Brezhnev's proposal was thus quickly rejected.[118]

At the same time, track two came under threat from the American side, where Senate ratification of the SALT II treaty was now in question. This concerned Schmidt because the TNF systems were on the agenda for SALT III, which could only be addressed once SALT II had been completed. In August accusations by Idaho Democrat Senator Frank Church that the CIA had recently discovered the existence of a Soviet brigade of 2,600 men in Cuba were picked up by the media. Carter had used this incident as an opportunity to show the American public his steadfastness by telling the Kremlin that the brigade's presence was unacceptable. But it soon come to light that the brigade merely trained Cuban forces and had been on the island since 1962, in fact with President John F. Kennedy's secret consent. All Carter could therefore achieve was a Soviet promise that the brigade would never be turned into a combat unit. This rather farcical episode not only distracted Senators for almost a month but also turned many against the SALT II treaty, fuelling arguments that the presence of the brigade proved Soviet deceitfulness and showed the difficulty of verifying Soviet compliance with agreements.[119] Moscow, in turn, felt that the Carter administration had played politics with the 'Cuban brigade', aggravating its doubts about American reliability and commitment to SALT II. In all likelihood the timing of Brezhnev's propaganda offensive was a reaction to events on Capitol Hill, while his speeches in turn intensified anti-Soviet feeling in Washington. By late 1979 superpower relations seemed trapped in a process of cyclical decline.[120]

Bonn watched from the sidelines with growing concern. Defence Minister Apel told reporters after a meeting with Brzezinski at the White House on 2 October that NATO would be in 'real crisis' if the Senate failed to ratify SALT II.[121] In a letter to Carter on 8 October, Schmidt voiced his own anxiety over 'the turn the political debate on SALT II ratification [was] taking'. He saw the treaty as 'a crucial element of Western security'. Non-ratification would jeopardize Allied joint 'endeavors of enhancing NATO's defence posture' and cause a 'serious adverse effect within the Alliance, as well as regarding its credibility looked upon from the outside'.[122]

Despite his anxieties over the viability of track two, the chancellor had no doubt that NATO must proceed with its decision. He made this clear to Gromyko when the Soviet foreign minister visited Bonn in late November. Gromyko asserted that there already existed an equilibrium in intermediate-range nuclear forces (INFs) and that the proposed NATO deployment would upset this. Schmidt gave as good as he got, showing Gromyko tables to prove his claim that the Soviets were the ones upsetting the balance with their SS-20 missiles and Backfire bombers. The chancellor acknowledged that the USSR had legitimate security interests but said that the FRG demanded Soviet respect for German security interests. He also emphasized that West Germany had taken the lead in developing an arms-control strand to balance essential nuclear modernization. In private Gromyko assured Schmidt that the Kremlin remained interested in détente and arms control but then proceeded to blast NATO in a press conference.[123]

The chancellor also emphasized for the benefit of German opinion his commitment to the dual track in various speeches and interviews during November, stressing that the whole coalition was behind it. Reporting in secret on his meeting with Gromyko to the SPD's parliamentary party, he noted that mistakes had been made by both superpowers. But, looking into the future, he asserted that by 1985 the Soviets would enjoy marked superiority in both theatre-nuclear and conventional forces unless the West acted now to shore up the balance. This line of argument, he told his party colleagues testily, was based on twenty years of thinking and writing, alluding explicitly to his 1969 book on the balance of power, *Strategie des Gleichgewichts*. Some 'comrades' (*Genossen*) had labelled him a mere 'doer' (*Macher*), but Schmidt reminded them that he had also worked with his mind (*geistig gearbeitet*) and that their cherished policy of *Ostpolitik* had only been feasible because of the power balance that then existed between East and West. Against this background, Schmidt said that the Alliance decision had to be taken now: delay would not only upset the balance further but also erode NATO's cohesion. But he also told his party he was sure that it remained a fundamental security interest of the FRG to continue the policy of cooperation with the Soviet bloc. Here was one of his clearest statements of the philosophy behind the dual track.[124]

Despite continued rumblings from the left, the SPD party conference on 3–7 December endorsed the dual-track policy. The mood in other NATO countries was, however, less propitious. Growing anti-nuclear popular protest and heated parliamentary debates—fuelled by Soviet propaganda—had pushed several European governments to the brink, even forcing political leaders to make last-minute trips to Washington. The Danes proposed a six-month moratorium on the dual-track decision, while the Norwegians wanted a review of NATO's decision after two years. The Dutch, for their part, were keen to postpone their national deployment decision and toyed with a NATO proposal of halving the modernization programme as well as again raising SALT II ratification as a precondition.[125]

In the end, however, on 12 December 1979 at a Special Meeting of NATO defence and foreign ministers in Brussels, all the Allies acquiesced in the dual track, as had been hoped.[126] But this was only possible because the ministerial communiqué had been carefully worded:

> The Ministers have decided to pursue these two parallel and complementary approaches in order to avert an arms race in Europe by the Soviet TNF build-up, yet preserve the viability of NATO's strategy of deterrence and defence and thus maintain the security of its member States.
>   a. A modernization decision, including a commitment to deployments, is necessary to meet NATO's deterrence and defence needs, to provide a credible response to unilateral Soviet TNF deployments, and to provide the foundation for the pursuit of serious negotiations on TNF.
>   b. Success of arms control in constraining the Soviet build-up can enhance Alliance security, modify the scale of NATO's TNF requirements, and promote stability and détente in Europe in consonance with NATO's basic policy of deterrence, defence and détente...[127]

This wording reflected a number of American concessions, firstly on deployments and host nation status and, secondly, on arms-control negotiation procedures. On the deployment question, no country was specifically mentioned in the final NATO statement. And among the five who had been previously identified as hosts, the Netherlands reserved the right to withhold its decision until 1981 while the Belgians said they would review their situation in mid 1980. As for the arms-control track, thanks to their diplomatic overtures in Washington, the Norwegians achieved two aims: the establishment of a high-level special consultative body to support the US arms-control negotiation effort,[128] and the addition of an extra sentence at the very end of the ministerial communiqué, which read, 'NATO's TNF requirements will be examined in the light of concrete results reached through negotiations'. Against the Americans' original wishes, but to the satisfaction of Schmidt and his government, who had quietly liaised with Norway, this phrasing implied that the 'zero option' remained a possibility, even if in practice such an outcome of the negotiations still seemed unlikely. The added sentence certainly acted as a palliative for large sections of the German SPD around the Bahr wing, considering that it had been only on this basis that the December party conference had grudgingly voted for the dual-track decision.[129]

Helmut Schmidt could feel considerable satisfaction about his conduct of defence and security policy during 1979. The construction of the dual track had been a huge advance on the shambles of the neutron bomb: a 'decision' rather than a 'deferral'; an Alliance consensus instead of an American cop-out. In its construction, the chancellor had played a leading role—facilitating international communication at the highest level, especially at Guadeloupe, and also neutralizing his party through canny politics and persuasive argument. Key to progress in both the foreign and domestic arenas was the mechanism of simultaneity and automaticity between the two tracks, embodied in Schmidt's *uno actu* concept—a significant improvement on the sequential approach that had failed to secure consensus over the ERW.

Reflecting on his achievements in early December 1979, Schmidt told the SPD that without German pressure the second track would not have come into existence. It had been leveraged by West Germany's growing international clout over the past decade. Previously, he said, Bonn had been obliged to 'run every two weeks to the West to ask for support', but now, thanks to the growth of its relative independence in foreign policy, the Federal Republic had emerged as an equal partner on the transatlantic stage. This had been apparent to the world in January when he had been one of what he called the 'Guadeloupe 4'—sitting with the former Western victor powers of 1945 at the nuclear top table.

But none of this was intended to prejudice what he frankly described as 'a policy of cooperation with the Soviet Union'. This policy he fully intended to continue, despite the deterioration of East–West relations during 1979, evident in his recent set-to with Gromyko.[130]

Yet relations would soon get a whole lot worse. Once NATO announced its decision, the Soviets declared it to be 'unacceptable', the party newspaper *Pravda* stating flatly that the Alliance had completely 'destroyed the basis for talks on medium-range weapons' in Europe.[131] With SALT II unlikely to be ratified, East–West dialogue on arms control now seemed to have been suspended. On New Year's Eve 1979 the *Frankfurter Allgemeine Zeitung* wrote off the 1970s as a decade of 'fear and uncertainty' and foresaw the possible end of the long post-war peace. In a deliberate echo of British Foreign Secretary Sir Edward Grey's famous words on the eve of war in August 1914, the *FAZ* journalist Johannes Gross added that, although 'there is little evidence that the lights are about to go out', nevertheless 'they are flickering'.[132]

Gross was writing in the wake of a bombshell on Christmas Day—the Soviet invasion of Afghanistan. This triggered a superpower crisis that would test as never before Schmidt's capacities as a global statesman.

5

The Double Interpreter

Helmut and Loki Schmidt spent Christmas 1979 at their home in Hamburg, together with their daughter Susanne, and Helmut's brother Wolfgang and father Gustav. The Christmas tree stood not in their living room but hundreds of miles away in Bonn, covered with Loki's hand-made decorations, in the entrance hall of the Chancellery. As always, the normal quiet rituals of Christmas Eve followed the jollities of the chancellor's birthday party the day before. Schmidt then went to the NDR studios in Hamburg to pre-record the chancellor's New Year's speech, before heading off on vacation on 28 December. Following family tradition, the destination for a couple of weeks' rest was the balmier and sunnier shores of the Mediterranean, this time Majorca, where Schmidt could read, play chess, and reflect on current affairs.[1]

Jimmy Carter also left the capital for the festive season, in his case to Camp David, the presidential retreat in Maryland. It was a rather solitary Christmas, spent only with his wife and daughter, without their extended family who were usually present. For the president, like the chancellor, Christmas came as a welcome break from the turmoil of politics—not least because both men had to face the rigours of an election year—for Schmidt in October, for Carter in November.

But Carter's vacation, unlike Schmidt's, proved short-lived. On 27 December the President had to rush back to Washington because of the news that, over Christmas, the Soviets had mounted a massive airlift of troops into Afghanistan, which was wracked by mounting unrest. Soviet Special Forces quickly eliminated the existing Afghan leader Hafizullah Amin and installed their own client, Babrak Kamal, to head a friendly regime intended to stabilize this key country on the USSR's southern border. But what the Kremlin hoped would be a quick fix turned into a quagmire: the new government could not impose its grip, the Afghan army fell apart, and the whole country collapsed into anarchy. The Soviets were sucked into a protracted civil war.

The fallout from Afghanistan would cloud the rest of Schmidt's chancellorship. Superpower relations degenerated into a 'New Cold War' and Schmidt's hopes of arms-control negotiations—the second track of NATO's December 1979 decision—vanished. After that fateful Christmas, the German chancellor began to play what he would soon describe as the role of 'double interpreter' between two nuclear superpowers that were not merely estranged but, he feared, on the brink of war. This work as diplomatic interlocutor would be another feature of what made him a global chancellor.

AFGHANISTAN: TO PUNISH OR TO TALK?

With the Soviet intervention in Afghanistan, Schmidt immediately knew that his hopes of meaningful arms talks were going up in smoke. He summoned a camera team to Majorca and interrupted his holiday so that he could alter a passage in his New Year's speech that dealt with détente and Moscow's role therein. Although he did not want to seem out of step with the chorus of Western denunciation of the USSR, he avoided the word 'invasion'—saying instead that Soviet 'actions' in Afghanistan were wrong and that there had to be diplomatic consequences.[2]

Carter's reaction was much more extreme and this would set the tone for Western diplomacy. The president left Brezhnev in no doubt that he regarded the Soviet intervention in Afghanistan as 'a clear threat to the peace' and potentially 'a fundamental and long-lasting turning point in our relations'.[3] On 4 January 1980 Carter took a similar line in a televised address to the American people, calling the invasion 'a serious threat to peace' and insisting that it was not possible to 'continue to do business as usual with the Soviet Union'. He went on to announce that he had recalled the US ambassador from Moscow and had imposed economic sanctions, especially on grain exports and technology transfers. And despite proclaiming the negotiation of the SALT II treaty as 'a major achievement' of his administration, he said that he was asking the Senate to defer further consideration of whether to ratify the agreement in order to 'assess Soviet actions and intentions'. The President's determination to punish the Kremlin for invading Afghanistan was rooted in his reading of the past. 'History teaches, perhaps, very few lessons', he said. 'But surely one such lesson learned by the world at great cost is that aggression, unopposed, becomes a contagious disease.'[4]

Here Carter, like many of his Cold War predecessors, was invoking the so-called lessons of appeasement from the 1930s, namely that it was essential to stand up to aggressive dictators. During a 'Meet the Press' TV interview on 20 January he asserted that 'this in my opinion is the most serious threat to world peace since the Second World War'. To justify his claim he added: 'It's an unprecedented act on the part of the Soviet Union. It's the first time they have attacked, themselves, a nation that was not already under their domination, that is, a part of the Warsaw Pact neighborhood.'[5] By this time the President was also calling on the US Olympic Committee not to participate in the upcoming Moscow Olympics—a hugely important prestige project for the Kremlin. Elaborating on his geopolitical reasoning, Carter declared that the invasion 'endangers neighboring independent countries and access to a major part of the world's oil supplies. It therefore threatens our own national security, as well as the security of the region and the entire world.'[6]

The reference to oil was significant. During 1979 the United States had lost control of its long-standing client regime in oil-rich Iran—in January Islamic revolutionaries had toppled the Shah; then in November they seized fifty-two American hostages from the US embassy in Tehran. Getting the hostages out alive became Carter's main political obsession: the White House Christmas tree had been left unlit as a symbol of national solidarity. The Soviet invasion of Afghanistan was therefore inextricably linked for the Carter administration with the stability of the whole of South West Asia, running from the Persian Gulf to the Horn of Africa where Soviet proxies were already installed. This became known in Washington as 'the arc of crisis', a concept that fused regional tensions into the whole East–West relationship. With the United States on the defensive in so many areas, Carter—facing re-election against very negative opinion poll ratings—was determined to prove his toughness on national security. He told television viewers 'I am still committed to peace, but peace through strength'.[7]

Schmidt agreed with the White House that Iran and Afghanistan were bound up in what he called a 'double crisis'. But he did not want in his words a 'Third World conflict to be turned into an East–West conflict': this could transform Central Europe into a crisis zone, as had happened in 1962 during the Cuban missile crisis. Seriously perturbed by Carter's hawkish rhetoric and actions, the chancellor declared: 'We will not permit ten years of détente and defence policy to be destroyed'. Talking to Walter Stoessel, the US ambassador to Bonn, on 10 January, Schmidt made clear that he would follow 'two basic principles'—solidarity with the United States and keeping open lines of communication with Moscow. Stoessel warned that an early Schmidt visit to Moscow would be regarded as 'business as usual', but the chancellor said that a summit was not imminent and, in any event, he would go to Washington first. Writing to Carter a week later, Schmidt developed this approach. He stressed the need to maintain 'direct US–Soviet dialogue on a high level' and also urged Carter that further sanctions against Iran, especially military measures, 'would destabilize the entire region' to Soviet benefit. In February, lunching with Vance in Bonn, he complained with some vigour about Carter's intent to 'punish' the Soviets. What, he asked, did the Americans 'wish to achieve'? He lamented the lack of prior US consultation and poor communication, while expressing his fears of a dangerous escalation of tensions between East and West. Speaking to the press, Schmidt indicated that he saw the invasion of Afghanistan as mainly a matter of installing a friendly regime on a sensitive border, rather than as the first step towards controlling the Persian Gulf and its oil. He felt that the Kremlin's motivation was complex and 'ambivalent'—a mix of imperialist power politics and an exaggerated need for security. He therefore repeated his mantra that the West needed a style of crisis management 'that took the reaction of the other side into account'. The chancellor believed that talking was valuable, indeed essential, in its own right at times of crisis, whether or not it yielded any substantive results.[8]

Although anxious to maintain dialogue with the Kremlin, Schmidt was ready to make concessions to the White House, especially over the Olympic boycott, which quickly became a loyalty test for its allies in American eyes. Personally, Schmidt was unhappy that Carter was using what he deemed a PR issue as a substitute for meaningful diplomacy and he was concerned that if West Germans boycotted the Moscow games this would undermine ten years of normalization efforts with both East Berlin and the Kremlin. Nevertheless, he promised Carter as early as 24 January that ultimately Bonn would 'come down on the right side' on the Olympics, whatever the political difficulties. As an article in *Der Spiegel* put it, Bonn had to show 'solidarity with its protector power' (*Schutzmacht*): times of crisis showed how little room for manoeuvre (*Spielraum*) it enjoyed and revealed the full extent of the country's political and military dependence on the United States. The article quoted an acerbic comment from a high-ranking Bonn official about 'Finlandization' (usually a disparaging Western reference to Helsinki's subservience to Moscow): 'Now we have the Finlandization of the Federal Republic' by the United States.[9]

Schmidt was under pressure domestically in an election year. Although opinion polls indicated that his popularity matched that of Adenauer at the height of the latter's appeal, they also showed that more than half of West Germans feared that the superpowers were about to envelop the globe in another war. The SPD left was particularly vociferous that a peace policy was imperative. Criticizing Schmidt for showing excessive solidarity with Carter, Brandt, still party leader, warned that 'we shouldn't be more American than the Americans'. Peter Conradi, a left-winger from Stuttgart, declared that 'we mustn't go with the Americans into death'. And leading leftist authors, including Günter Grass, told the chancellor that America had lost all its moral authority following Vietnam and that Germany should not be dragged into a policy leading to 'the destruction of all life on this planet'. Herbert Wehner, leader of the party in the Bundestag, even went so far as to declare that he objected to cruise and Pershing II deployments on German soil—a standpoint totally at odds with the official line of both the government and NATO. Clearly, European disarmament remained fundamental for the German left.[10]

For Schmidt, this balancing act between East and West was, as always, a fraught business. On 5 March he met Carter at the White House in a public front of Alliance unity. In a joint press statement the two leaders reiterated their condemnation of the Soviet invasion and 'agreed that participation in the Olympic Games would be inappropriate as long as Soviet occupation in Afghanistan continues'. Schmidt, however, did not explicitly commit to an Olympic boycott—all the while insisting that West Germany's more distanced course made Bonn no less a staunch ally of the United States. On the contrary, so Schmidt stated, his talks with Carter confirmed that even if there were differences in some fields, these were 'nuances' which 'disappear behind the large measure of agreement, behind our common convictions'. According to *Newsweek*, Schmidt, in his 'new activist role in world affairs', was seen by the US administration in 'a very strong leadership position'—a man who 'can bring a number of countries with him on anything he decides to do'. As a result the German chancellor managed to secure Carter's commitment to 'maintain the framework of East–West relations that has been built over two decades' and a declaration of his 'continuing support for the arms control negotiations'. But this display of solidarity did not prevent Schmidt from using the visit to air his anxieties about US policy. In a major speech in New York, in what *Time* magazine described as 'something of a Deutsch-uncle lecture on how the US ought to conduct international relations', Schmidt said: 'Partnership means teamwork. Consultation is no one-way street.' He reminded Americans that West Germans, 'living in the shadow of Russian might and vulnerable to pressures on West Berlin', were wary of American actions that might provoke the Soviets in Europe. Then he spoke candidly about the White House's lack of consistency and predictability, asserting that Carter had first ignored the danger to Afghanistan and then over-reacted. Europeans, he declared, were therefore 'nervous about walking out on a limb that might be sawed off behind them'.[11]

Meanwhile, the chancellor tried to keep open contacts with the Kremlin, looking towards a possible meeting with Brezhnev. In a letter on 4 March the Soviet leader sounded discouraging—adopting what Schmidt called 'a critical tone' about the current state of international relations and saying that a summit with Schmidt should occur only as 'the crowning moment' of careful preparations. For his part, given current international tensions, the chancellor was not willing to go to Moscow without some sign of Soviet movement on arms control. Through the secret *Ostpolitik* backchannel, Egon Bahr and SPD foreign policy adviser Eugen Selbmann managed to make progress. On 24 March Selbmann suggested that it would be a positive step if Moscow could declare its readiness to halt further SS-20 deployments and to negotiate on the TNF issue. A Soviet commitment to making such a declaration at a summit, he said, would encourage Schmidt to fix a date. The Soviets did not respond directly, but on 31 March the Soviet ambassador to Bonn delivered a formal invitation for Schmidt to visit Moscow in the middle of June. The motivation for this change of heart is unclear but the reasons were probably Schmidt's success in standing alongside Carter and the Kremlin's growing isolation. And by 10 April the Soviets in the backchannel, talking rather candidly about 'a distinction between politics and propaganda', said that Brezhnev 'in principle is willing to halt further production and deployment of SS-20s' and even, 'as a final consequence, to destroy existing stockpiles'.[12]

Although rumours of the summit began to leak into the press,[13] the chancellor delayed an official announcement for two weeks, until mid April. For him, backchannel whispers were not enough to justify a trip to Moscow in the current global crisis. He had to find a public rationale for the summit, to demonstrate that he was in step with America and not simply engaged in appeasement or self-aggrandizement. Specifically, he needed to show both the Americans and the Russians that there was some basis for East–West dialogue on TNFs without, however, selling out on NATO's dual-track decision. Schmidt had now dropped the phrase 'policy of détente' (*Entspannungspolitik*) but spoke instead of a 'military equilibrium' on which alone, he felt, a policy of 'cooperation with the East' could be constructed.[14] In the middle of April he made four major speeches, each delivered to an SPD election rally but all intended to address the international situation. In Essen on 12 April he set out that situation in the starkest possible terms—depicting a world that was teetering on the brink of war. He was speaking just days after the United States had broken off diplomatic relations with Iran over the unresolved hostage crisis (7 April), warning its allies privately that it would now resort to military action. But Schmidt's image of how war might come was rooted in a very different historical analogy from that of Carter, with the latter's talk about the lessons of appeasement from the 1930s. Schmidt had in mind not the origins of World War Two but of World War One.

The chancellor began his Essen speech with what he called 'the concerns of world policy and peace policy' (*welt- und friedenspolitische Sorgen*). He likened the current crisis to that of July 1914. None of the powers wanted war then, he argued, but, because they got 'trapped in the logic of military calculations', the result was 'the First World War with its hecatombs of death'. Of course, he admitted, the analogy was not exact. In 1980 there were only two world powers, not five, and neither of them was dominated by the military, but he believed that 'military thinking' nevertheless played 'too big a role, especially in the Soviet Union'. Both superpowers, he acknowledged, 'consciously want to avoid war', but he feared that they did not have 'a sufficient war-avoidance strategy' and might therefore unintentionally slither into war, as he felt had happened in 1914. For Schmidt, the root problem was a lack of open communication between Washington and Moscow about their aims and interests. He identified four global flashpoints—the Middle East, the hostage crisis in Teheran, the 'ongoing occupation of Afghanistan', and the danger of a massive superpower arms race, especially with regard to TNFs. Without sensitive handling, these could easily fuse together and ignite a third world war.[15] And this was not mere rhetoric: in a private letter to Brandt he also spoke of his fears that a variety of small crises 'could escalate quickly into a direct military confrontation between the great powers'.[16]

The text of Schmidt's speech was sent to German embassies around the world, but it was at home that his analogy with 1914 really hit the headlines. The cover of *Der Spiegel* on 21 April showed a photo of helmeted soldiers above a question (in old Prussian script) 'Like August 1914?' (*Wie im August 1914?*). The subhead read, 'Fear of the Great War'—a deliberate allusion to the British term for 1914–18. Whether or not they read what was inside *Der Spiegel*, millions of Germans saw this cover in news kiosks and bookshops across the country for a whole week. Not surprisingly, Schmidt, the interpreter of history, stirred up a firestorm. SPD leader Willy Brandt reminded the chancellor of Fritz Fischer's trenchant indictment of the *Kaiserreich* in his book *Griff nach der Weltmacht?* Was Schmidt trying to diminish Germany's burden of war guilt? And, Brandt insinuated, was he trying to elevate semi-sovereign West Germany to the rank of a world power? From the right, political rival Franz Josef Strauß sneered that 'the Peace Chatterer has turned out to be a Panic Chancellor'—accusing him of crass electioneering and seeking to show up what he considered the hollowness of the SPD's long-standing peace policy. Much of the German press debated whether Schmidt was simply whipping up emotions for political ends. The chancellor could hardly afford to ignore the domestic setting (not least in an election year), but what he said was entirely in keeping with his lifelong philosophy of statecraft, in which notions of balance, stability, and communication had always been axiomatic.[17]

Furthermore, at Essen and in the other April speeches Schmidt coupled his bleak analysis of the global situation with some clear prescriptions for crisis management and even resolution, at least in Europe. He prefaced his comments by emphasizing that he was not a 'neutral observer'—the core of West German security lay in its alliance with the United States—but he also stressed the need at times of crisis to put oneself in the shoes of all parties, in order to keep the peace.

He spoke specifically of the deadlock over theatre nuclear forces, which allowed the Soviets to continue their INF deployment (running at one new SS-20 every week). Since general arms-control negotiations had lapsed because of the failure of SALT and Soviet rejection of the dual-track decision, Schmidt now pushed a more modest basis for superpower discussions. To quote his Essen speech again: 'A first possible step to resolve this conflict would be that both sides simultaneously desist for a specific number of years from any new, additional or modernized INF deployments and use this interim period for negotiations and mutual limitations—in order to establish a balance at a lower level.' Five days later, in Düsseldorf, he indicated that his timeframe was a period of three years, in other words up to 1983.[18]

To allies who questioned his reasoning, such as Belgian Foreign Minister Henri Simonet, Schmidt said this apparent mutual pause offered a face-saving way for the Soviets to come back to the negotiating table. If the Americans explicitly stated that they would not deploy before 1983, then American and Soviet behaviour would look essentially the same. It was, he said, 'merely a question of presentation', or what Simonet called 'cosmetics'.[19] Schmidt felt that the cosmetics were to Western benefit: the Americans could not deploy before 1983 anyway, because the cruise and Pershing missiles were currently only in the process of production. The Soviets, by contrast, would have to stop a deployment process that had been going on since 1976. In other words, the Soviets would have to halt their build-up at 1980 levels, whereas NATO would not change its intended policy in any way and would therefore hold firm to the dual-track decision. Bonn made this point clear in letters to its NATO allies, and to the wider German public at the SPD Congress in Cologne. Despite earlier friction, the party leadership at the Congress now came out publicly in support of Schmidt's position.[20] For the moment, this propitiated his left wing.[21] Having affirmed his Alliance credentials and secured political support, the chancellor felt ready to announce the Moscow visit. This was done on 15 April.[22]

To keep the Americans happy, Schmidt took the issue of the Olympic boycott to the Bundestag a week later. On 23 April it voted in favour by an overwhelming majority of 98 per cent.[23] This enabled Schmidt to ask West Germany's National Olympic Committee to follow suit when it met on 15 May. After a four-hour meeting, televised nationwide, the committee succumbed, though the margin was narrow: 59 for and 40 against. Immediately afterwards, Carter called Schmidt to praise the chancellor's leadership, calling the German vote a 'major step toward tying our countries even closer together'.[24]

But Schmidt was conscious that West Germany's Olympic boycott—not emulated by either France or Britain—risked alienating the Soviets. He was also aware that the balance of power in the White House had shifted in favour of anti-Soviet hawks, led by Brzezinski, because Secretary of State Cyrus Vance had resigned in opposition to Carter's (failed) attempt to rescue the hostages in Iran on 24 April. The mood in the Bonn–Moscow backchannel became more cautious. The Soviets wanted a face-saving formula for negotiations, based on mutuality. They felt trapped by their own previous insistence that the dual-track decision must be revoked before they would be willing to engage in any arms-control talks. Schmidt therefore sought to give them some wriggle room by reviving his April proposals. On 9 June, once again in Essen, he told the annual SPD party conference: 'It would serve the cause of peace if during the next three years both sides were to desist from any further deployments and begin negotiations on mutual limitations soon.'[25]

In April Schmidt's call had attracted little attention in America because the media was obsessed by the US Olympic Committee's vote to boycott the Moscow games and the failed mission to rescue the Tehran hostages. But his 9 June speech did hit the headlines in the United States. The *New York Times*, for instance, headed its report of his speech 'Schmidt urges missiles freeze'. The emotive word 'freeze' was the term bandied around in the American press because of fears that Schmidt's proposal might imply a complete halt to Western production. This was never the chancellor's intention. He did not use the words 'freeze' or 'moratorium' in any of these speeches in April and June because, in his view, it was only the Soviets who would be doing the freezing—at the level of current deployments.[26]

Concerned about the swirl of media comment, Carter decided to send Schmidt a cautionary message. Drafted by Brzezinski but agreed with the new Secretary of State Ed Muskie, this letter on 12 June referred to 'conflicting press reports' of the Essen speech that had caused 'confusion in Europe' and which, if continued, could 'only undermine allied solidarity on this central security issue, and have hard consequences for the future of the alliance'. Carter acknowledged that stories suggesting that Schmidt had proposed a 'freeze' were incorrect but he went out of his way to reiterate that the United States would 'not agree to any proposal for a freeze, moratorium, or renunciation of a new and additional missile deployments [sic], even for a fixed period of time'.[27]

Schmidt was nettled. 'Quite frankly', he told Carter on 16 June, 'I was astonished that you were worried about press reports concerning my remarks.' Clearly implying that Carter could easily have picked up the phone to discuss the matter in private, he included the text of his Essen remarks to 'help eliminate any misunderstandings which might have arisen'. He asked for a private meeting when they were together at the upcoming G7 summit in Venice later in the month. But the confrontation escalated. Carter's letter was immediately leaked to the press in Washington[28] and Schmidt exploded in his Cabinet meeting on 18 June—accounts of which in turn were leaked to the German press. According to *Der Spiegel*, Schmidt called the letter 'outrageous'—again the White House could have discussed the issue orally—and he got increasingly wound up during the meeting about how Carter was treating him, eventually exclaiming: 'We are not America's 51st state.' The general feeling in Bonn was that it was America's indiscretions, not Germany's, that were damaging the West. Schmidt was particularly concerned that these public signs of German–American discord would undermine him when he went to Moscow. His ability to deal firmly with the Kremlin depended on an assumption of underlying transatlantic unity.[29]

Schmidt's anger had still not abated when the two leaders met in a hotel room in Venice on the evening of 21 June, together with Muskie, Brzezinski, Genscher, and Berndt von Staden (former German ambassador in Washington). The atmospherics were not helped by the cramped conditions: the two sides sat face to face with their knees almost touching. In his diary, Carter called it an 'unbelievable meeting' with Schmidt 'ranting and raving' about the letter and about being treated as 'the 51st state'. Brzezinski called the encounter a 'humdinger': at one point Schmidt exclaimed 'Well, I don't mind a fight', to which Brzezinski retorted, 'if a fight is necessary I am quite prepared not to shrink from a fight'. This was remarkable behaviour for a German chancellor, facing off against an American president and his entourage as if they were equals. Schmidt, to be sure, had lost his cool, but, at a deeper level, this encounter was another sign of his growing self-image as a global statesman. The chancellor was particularly riled by the leaks and public insinuations that he was now breaking his word just to win an election. He went back over the history of the TNF decision, emphasizing that not only was he the author of the original dual-track position but also that, as over the neutron bomb, he had always stuck to his Alliance commitments, despite opposition within his own party.[30]

To some extent the verbal pyrotechnics helped clear the air. By the end of the meeting, at Schmidt's request, Carter agreed to make a brief press statement to demonstrate German–American unity. The President insisted 'we have no differences between us about how to deal with Afghanistan' and that 'we have absolutely no doubt that he and the Federal Republic of Germany are completely committed to carry out the agreement that was reached back in December concerning the deployment of theater nuclear force for Western Europe'. Although not offering an explicit endorsement of Schmidt's Moscow visit, as the chancellor had requested, Carter did mention that they had 'discussed the agenda' for the trip in 'outline form'. Despite the display of harmony, the press were not convinced. Schmidt hardly said a word, while Carter had to fend off questions about why he wrote the letter in the first place if he had 'no doubt' about Schmidt's commitment to the dual-track position. He was also asked whether the journalists should write that the two men now liked each other. 'Always have', said Carter briskly, before bringing proceedings to an end.[31]

All through June, in fact, Schmidt had hardly troubled to conceal his irritation with Carter. 'The chancellor, who had kept his famous lip buttoned for well over a year on the subject of Jimmy Carter', noted American journalist Elizabeth Pond shortly after Venice, 'pointed out that he had been used to thinking for himself and expressing his opinion for 30 years and that he did not propose to be instructed now by any newcomer with a lot less political experience.' Repeatedly Schmidt underlined to the media his authority as a veteran statesman. He reminded them of his numerous writings as a transatlantic defence intellectual as well as his lengthy dealings across more than a decade with the Russian leadership and with 'three consecutive American administrations – Nixon, Ford and Carter'. He was equally blunt about the purpose of his talks with Brezhnev: 'I do not intend to undertake to negotiate arms control when I go to Moscow', adding that he was 'neither an idiot nor an illusionist' but 'a realist'. He would be speaking there only as a German because he had 'no mandate to talk for the West' with the Soviets—'that's just a little bit too big for the rather small stature of my country'—but he insisted, 'I will certainly not say a single word which couldn't be subscribed to by my western friends.'[32]

Schmidt's priority was to get back into dialogue with the Soviets, whereas Carter was determined to avoid anything that smacked of appeasement. At root, neither had confidence in the other. On the surface, however, the cracks had been papered over in Venice. At the end of the summit Carter offered the clear endorsement of Schmidt's Moscow trip that the chancellor had sought. 'I think it's coming at a good time', he said, adding that he was sure Schmidt would make a 'forceful presentation' of the Western position. Indeed, he claimed it would be helpful for the Kremlin 'to hear in an unvarnished fashion directly from European leaders the same kind of message they've been hearing by various means from us', thereby showing that it was 'fruitless for them to try to drive a wedge between us and our European friends and allies'. Schmidt was finally in a position to go to Moscow.[33]

SCHMIDT IN MOSCOW

Schmidt and his party landed at Vnukovo airport on 30 June 1980. A vivid sense of their experiences is conveyed in the private notes by Berndt von Staden. During the flight, they were struck by the endless Russian plains—the sense of the country's vastness that had overwhelmed Schmidt during his journey to Moscow in 1966. On the ground there was a friendly and rather chaotic welcome from a large group of Soviet leaders, including Brezhnev, Alexei Kosygin, and Gromyko. Schmidt had last been to the Kremlin in 1974, von Staden in 1970: both immediately noticed the new apartment blocks that had been built—similar in style to those erected in the 1960s in the West. Another hint of Westernization detected by von Staden was the fabric used in the well-cut suits of the Soviet leadership.

En route to Red Square, Brezhnev also pointed out to Schmidt the Olympic village—the only mention during the visit of the upcoming Games which West Germany had decided to boycott. Once in the Kremlin, they got down to business in the 'intoxicating' (*berauschend*) environs of St Catherine's Hall amid an 'orgy of white, gold, and green'. The meeting seemed to be staged for maximum effect. Each delegation entered simultaneously through a double door of its side of the room and then spread out along the conference table, ten on either side. Across the table Schmidt saw what seemed to be the whole Soviet Politburo ranged in front of him—testimony to the importance that the Kremlin attached to this meeting. Brezhnev opened with a one-hour statement; Schmidt responded in kind. In these exchanges little emerged that was new—the chancellor was saving his detailed points for the substantive meetings—but he was at pains to stress his loyalty to NATO and the United States and also West Germany's continued contribution to the military equilibrium in Europe. At one point he explicitly represented himself as Carter's messenger, putting to Brezhnev 'two essential points' about SALT. At the subsequent dinner Schmidt spoke about the need for arms-control negotiations, but he did not mince his words about Soviet responsibility for the crisis in Afghanistan and demanded complete withdrawal of the Red Army. His dinner comments were widely reported in the Western press and even termed 'surprisingly forceful'.[34]

Although the war in Afghanistan coloured the whole meeting, echoes of an earlier conflict added emotional depth at a human level. Their public references at the dinner to the need for peace cited their personal experiences of the 'horrific' Russo-German war of 1941–5. This became more meaningful the following morning, 1 July, when they laid wreaths at the Memorial to the Soviet Unknown Soldier and then at a military cemetery where German and Japanese dead were buried.[35]

After that, they returned to the serious business of what the Germans were keen to stress was a 'working visit'. Schmidt and Brezhnev held two meetings, with Genscher, Kosygin, and Gromyko in attendance. At the first, Brezhnev made a significant concession, namely that the Soviets were willing to talk to about TNFs in Europe without waiting for ratification of SALT II or the dropping of NATO's dual-track decision. On the other hand, the Soviets also insisted that any such talks would have to include not just missiles but also American nuclear-armed aircraft— the so-called forward-based systems that Washington refused to discuss as strategic weaponry. In which case, Schmidt retorted, the Kremlin should include in the discussions not only the SS-20s but also the SS-4 and SS-5 missiles, plus the Backfire bombers. After a brief word in Brezhnev's ear, Gromyko responded: 'This widens the question.' Laughing, he added: 'As they say, appetite grows as you eat!'[36] By putting forward-based systems on the table, one might say, the Soviets had given with one hand and taken back with the other. But it is clear that overall some movement had occurred, even though the two sides agreed not to make it public at this stage for fear of negative media comment in the West. Prompted again by Gromyko, Brezhnev agreed with Schmidt's suggestion that he should first share what had been discussed with Carter.[37]

During his Moscow visit, the chancellor also had a chance to speak for the first time to the Soviet chief ideologue Mikhail Suslov, who sat next to him at the state dinner, and to meet with Soviet top brass, in particular Marshals Nikolai Ogarkov and Dmitri Ustinov (the Soviet defence minister). He had specifically asked to talk with the Russian military leadership—to get to know them personally and have a professional exchange 'from expert to expert'. Perhaps at the back of his mind was that anxiety, so vivid in his April comments on 1914, about the influence of the military mindset in current Soviet foreign policy-making. In line with his determination to pursue dialogue with Moscow at all levels, he proposed the development of contacts and new networks between the Soviet and West German defence establishments. He even issued a general invitation to Ustinov and officers of the Soviet Defence Ministry to visit West Germany. This the Soviet Marshal welcomed cautiously but not with a full affirmative. Schmidt's two hours of discussions with Ustinov and Ogarkov spanned the topics of his 1969 book on the balance of power (which Ustinov claimed to have read parts of in Russian translation) and dwelled particularly on arms-control negotiations, the contentious issue of SS-20s, the motivation of soldiers, and specific details of military materiel. In this way Schmidt was able to highlight his background as a defence intellectual and former defence minister—presenting himself as a political leader who could discuss strategy and weaponry on equal footing with the generals. And, by talking as a German, Schmidt was keen to make clear that Bonn was not simply 'America's continental dagger' pointing at the Soviet Union, as critics in Moscow had asserted.[38]

Behind the scenes, however, there was another side to the Moscow summit. Building on their 'framework agreement' of May 1978, the two governments signed a formal programme for trade cooperation over the next twenty-five years, whereby the Germans provided technology and equipment for the development of Soviet energy deposits, and in return the USSR would supply oil and gas to the Federal Republic. It was significant, however, that the trade deal was signed by the German ambassador to the USSR: Schmidt was determined not to be photographed doing so himself with Brezhnev. That would not go down well with the White House, given its embargo on West–East technology transfer.[39] The deal reflected Schmidt's long-standing belief in the FRG's need to diversify its sources of energy, accentuated by the second oil shock of 1979. It also embodied his abiding conviction that economic contacts were essential for normalizing relations with the East and thereby promoting peace; these contacts should continue even when political ties were disrupted. In general, he saw the Olympic boycott as a high-profile but low-cost way to show diplomatic solidarity with America, while effectively continuing 'business as usual' at the economic level. 'Compared to economics', he told the Soviet ambassador to Bonn in March, the Olympics were 'merely of passing significance'. Although no FRG athletes went to Moscow, ironically West German companies provided much of the equipment for the games—from a new airport at Sheremetyevo to the cutlery in the Olympic canteen.[40]

Media reception of the summit was cool—not least due to Schmidt's deliberately vague comments in the press conference about what had been achieved. He was quoted as saying that he was 'satisfied with the results of the visit' and that it had lived up to his expectations, but observers saw little accomplished over Afghanistan. Brezhnev had refused to declare that he intended to make a complete troop withdrawal, as Schmidt had wanted.[41] Hostile papers like the *Chicago Tribune* spoke of Schmidt going home 'with hardly anything to show for his efforts'. Even David K. Willis of the generally friendly *Christian Science Monitor* entitled his piece simply 'Schmidt and Brezhnev Talk At–and Past–Each Other'.[42] In truth, as agreed with Brezhnev, Schmidt was keen to get Carter's response to the Soviet proposal on INF talks before going with a full analysis of the summit. So, although Schmidt, as soon as he got back to Bonn late on 1 July, celebrated the re-opening of dialogue over a few beers with SPD cronies in the Kessenicher Hof,[43] otherwise reaction was deliberately muted (even his Cabinet was told very little the following morning). And for his foreign minister there was no time even for a beer: at 7 am on 2 July Genscher was already on the plane for Washington, to play out the German role of 'double interpreter'. His task was to brief the White House on the talks, establish an agreed public position and, more generally, manage the atmospherics (*das klimatische Umfeld*) between the two governments after the storm at Venice. A negative public reaction from the White House would not only undermine the gains Schmidt had made in Moscow but also prejudice any chance of reviving détente. What if the Kremlin's 'movement' on arms-control dialogue—for Bonn, the essential significance of the Moscow summit—was dismissed by the United States as a fake concession (*Scheinkonzession*)?[44]

In fact, Genscher received a warm welcome in the American capital. As soon as he arrived in Washington on the evening of 2 July, he saw both Secretary of State Edmund Muskie and Carter himself, setting out in detail the course of the conversations in Moscow. In response, the President said he felt Schmidt had conveyed Carter's messages effectively and had spoken to Brezhnev, particularly on the key issue of Afghanistan, 'with firmness and clarity'. The chancellor, he added, 'had represented not only the Federal Republic of Germany but the Allies, ably'. Carter even expressed what he called 'admiration and appreciation' towards Schmidt. To some extent this was another PR exercise to mollify the prickly German, but Carter and Muskie were genuinely relieved that Brzezinski's dark predictions of a West German sell-out had not come true. Genscher, in return, sought American endorsement for what the Germans considered their key gain from Moscow, namely the idea of a resumed dialogue over arms control. He and Muskie haggled over the appropriate wording for a joint public statement. Avoiding, at American behest, any reference to a Soviet 'proposal' (*Vorschlag*), they agreed to say that NATO would 'study this *reaction* in a constructive spirit' and that the ideas contained therein were 'worthy of that kind of consideration'. Soon the agreed German–American account of Moscow was spinning its way out into the American press, resulting in comment that was generally positive. 'Soviets Said To Modify Arms Stance', headlined the *Washington Post* on its front page. 'Muskie Sees Hint of a Softening on Missiles in Europe.'[45]

Schmidt's strategy of, in effect, using the Americans to announce the results of his Moscow meeting seemed to have paid off. Despite the friction with Carter in June, he had managed to maintain his delicate balancing act as mutual interpreter. But little substantive progress had been made about resuming superpower dialogue. For the Americans, no moves were even conceivable until the Olympics were over (3 August) and by then both West Germany and the United States were immersed in the last stages of national election campaigns, so foreign policy was on the back-burner.

On 5 October Schmidt and his FDP partners were returned to power. An additional benefit to the chancellor was the clear defeat of his CDU opponent Franz Josef Strauß, who had challenged Schmidt for many years over *Ospolitik* and defence policy. But it took Schmidt a month to finalize his new Cabinet and by then Carter had been ignominiously swept from power by his Republican challenger, Ronald Reagan. This time, unlike 1976, Schmidt had managed to keep his mouth shut about American electoral politics but he viewed the results with mixed feelings. On the one hand, Carter had been—or at least had become—a known quantity, while Reagan was renowned as a hardline Cold Warrior. But, on the other hand, the Carter–Schmidt relationship had been so fractious that opening a new chapter held a certain attraction.[46] Whatever Schmidt's private thoughts, it was clear in November 1980 that his work as mutual interpreter would have to begin anew.

And it did so amid another international crisis. The long face-off between the Polish communist government and striking workers, especially in the shipyards on the Baltic coast, resulted in the government's concession in August 1980 of independent trade unions. Forming an umbrella organization, Solidarity, which soon claimed to represent 80 per cent of Polish workers, mounted a series of general strikes during the autumn. Poland occupied a key strategic position between the USSR and Germany: the collapse of communist power there would destabilize the whole Soviet bloc. Bonn and other Western governments feared that Moscow would intervene militarily, as in Czechoslovakia in 1968. On the other hand, the Polish crisis blew up less than a year after the calamitous Red Army invasion of Afghanistan. Suslov warned the Politburo that a second use of Soviet troops would be 'disastrous' and that 'world public opinion would not permit us to do so'. In December 1980 the Warsaw Pact drew back from the use of force.[47]

For Schmidt, the Polish crisis clouded the last months of 1980. The chancellor felt obliged to cancel his summit with Erich Honecker, the East German leader, intended for August. Even after the Warsaw Pact pulled back, Schmidt wondered how long the Kremlin could talk tough and yet allow the Polish situation to deteriorate before losing its prestige as a world power. With Poland boiling up, Afghanistan unresolved, and no progress on arms control, Schmidt ended 1980 in a gloomy mood. In an off-the-record discussion with chief editors in Bonn on 18 December he reflected again on his April anxieties about the world being in a 1914-style situation. Now, he told them, he actually felt more concerned about 1981 than he had originally been about 1980.[48]

'THE ACTIVIST BETWEEN EAST AND WEST'

The new American President took the oath of office on 20 January 1981, the day the US hostages were finally freed in Tehran. Although one crisis therefore eased, Reagan made clear that he was even more hawkish than Carter towards the Soviet Union. In his first news conference on 29 January he said that 'so far détente's been a one-way street that the Soviet Union has used to pursue its own aims'. Its leaders had consistently stated 'that their goal must be the promotion of world revolution and a one-world Socialist or Communist state, whichever word you want to use' and had 'openly and publicly declared that the only morality they recognize is what will further their cause, meaning they reserve unto themselves the right to commit any crime, to lie, to cheat, in order to attain that'. Insisting that America had to regain its status and power, he backed up his rhetoric with a massive new arms build-up.[49]

In such circumstances, it seemed hard to discern any scope for dialogue with Moscow, and peace groups in Europe were deeply alarmed. Schmidt, however, believed he had seen a more nuanced Reagan when the two men met in Washington just after the election. This was supposed to be a brief courtesy call but the chancellor strung it out for a full hour, without interpreters. Back home Schmidt told journalists off the record that Reagan came over as a cautious man and 'not a

cowboy who shoots from the hip'. The president-elect said that Carter had negotiated 'too softly and too inconsistently': America needed to build up its arms in
order to negotiate from a position of strength. This conversation satisfied Schmidt
that, despite Reagan's hard-line rhetoric and his denunciation of SALT II as a hol-
low treaty, he wanted to conduct meaningful arms-control talks with the Soviet
Union, even if these took time. Reagan insisted: 'I am willing to sit down again and
again and again and again.' This was not a man in Schmidt's mould but the clarity
was refreshing after all the flip-flops in Washington over the last few years. Publicly
his advisers played up the meeting in almost euphoric terms suggesting that
American policy would now be more predictable than under Carter and also based
on closer consultation with NATO allies.[50]

Despite making these positive noises, Schmidt was well aware that it would
probably take a year for a new administration to prepare for substantive arms-
control talks.[51] (He did not want a repeat of Carter's half-baked 'deep cuts' proposal
in 1977, just three months into his presidency.) Even this prognosis proved optimistic: on 30 March Reagan was shot and nearly killed by a maverick gunman,
taking weeks to recuperate, and his administration was riven by feuds between
hawks and doves in the NSC, the Pentagon, and the State Department. Time was
no longer on Schmidt's side. At home leftists and pacifists were increasingly exercised
by Reagan's policy and by Schmidt's commitment to the dual track, which, for them,
meant new American nuclear missiles in West Germany within a couple of years
(see Figure 5.1). Protestors took to the streets and criticism became unrestrained

Figure 5.1 Protests against the 'armaments chancellor', Duisburg, 1 May 1981.
Source: Bundesbildstelle.

within the SPD, so much so that on 17 May, at the SPD *Landesparteitag* in Wolfratshausen (Bavaria), Schmidt reprimanded the leftists for failing to see that it was the Soviets who had initiated an arms build-up (*Vorrüstung*), to which the West had to respond (*Nachrüstung*). He even threatened publicly to resign if the party did not implement the dual-track decision. A reliable German government could not keep changing its policies almost ad lib. And in any case, Schmidt insisted, it too had a conscience—not just the pacifists, who in the chancellor's opinion were misguided with their ideas about unilateral disarmament. Their demands, driven by emotion, would lead to Western nuclear inferiority vis-à-vis an ever-strengthening Soviet Union and hence to a weakened American negotiating position. In a nutshell, Schmidt appeared still to believe what he had stated so bluntly in 1962: 'Anyone who is a pacifist has no political mind' (*Wer Pazifist ist, hat keinen politischen Verstand*). He felt it was imperative to grasp that the Americans were the Germans' friends; the Soviets were at best neighbours.[52]

The domestic political crisis hung over his visit to Washington later in May 1981 (see Figure 5.2). But in America Schmidt at least felt confirmed in his earlier perceptions of Reagan as a more predictable ally than Carter, and he secured the President's commitment to keep talking while rearming—as promised under the dual-track process. The chancellor, however, urged Reagan that, when doing the talking, he should not rely on the 'Dobrynin channel'—a reference to the Soviet ambassador in Washington—because 'Dobrynin can't...talk to Brezhnev,...he must report to Gromyko'. Schmidt thus lauded the president's initiative for doing

Figure 5.2 Schmidt and Reagan, White House, 22 May 1981.
Source: Bundesbildstelle.

the 'right thing by writing' directly and in personal terms to the Soviet leader. Schmidt was candid about Brezhnev's idiosyncracies, calling him 'cruel, abrupt, a great host, and emotional'. But, the chancellor continued, 'he is given to thinking about peace and war, and is fed up with war, having seen too much in his life'. Schmidt believed that Brezhnev could be relied upon to come to grips with the issue because in forming his coalition with the military (and Suslov in particular) the Soviet leader had not only extracted their support for his policy towards America but had also managed to shore up his power in the Kremlin. In short, Schmidt was arguing, Brezhnev was a leader who was inclined to talk peace and was also in a political position to do so.[53]

In a joint press statement on 22 May, Reagan and Schmidt affirmed their 'resolve to implement both elements of the NATO decision of December 1979 and to give equal weight to both elements'. Behind the scenes Schmidt had already made clear to Washington that any deployments in late 1983 could only take place if the necessary bases and infrastructure had been constructed in 1981–2, which would require legislation in the Bundestag. This would not be passed, he insisted, given the state of German opinion, if no progress had been made along the negotiations track. Succumbing to his pressure, Washington committed itself to start talks with the Soviets on Euromissiles by the end of the year, as had also been announced in a NATO communiqué on 5 May.[54]

Although worried that the White House was not ready to talk, Schmidt also dreaded that before long there would be no one in the Kremlin with whom to hold conversations. Brezhnev was now clearly on his last legs, pumped up by drugs and unable to walk unaided. Once he disappeared from the scene, Schmidt feared another policy vacuum—this time in Moscow—and thought that the next generation of Soviet leaders might be more inclined to take risks. Hence the importance he attached to getting Brezhnev to Bonn soon, reciprocating his own Moscow trip of July 1980. The visit was eventually fixed for late November 1981. For his part, the Soviet leader was keen to come, anxious to head off the deployment side of the dual-track decision. Seeking to exploit the anti-nuclear and anti-American public mood in West Germany—some 300,000 peace protestors had just overrun the Hofgarten in Bonn (the largest demonstration in German history to date)— Brezhnev gave a lengthy interview to *Der Spiegel*, published on 2 November. Citing the German–Soviet declaration of May 1978 that neither side aspired to military superiority, he castigated NATO for 'not being serious about negotiating'. The Reagan administration, he claimed, did not want agreements 'on the basis of parity and equal security' but as 'a diktat of military superiority'. Whereas the Americans had no interest in ending the arms race, the Soviets genuinely wanted to 'stabilize peace on the planet'.[55]

The pressures from Western Europe, especially the FRG, as well as from Soviet propaganda finally got to Washington, still locked in bureaucratic turf fights about policy and position. The State Department was alarmed at the potency of the Soviet 'peace offensive' and Reagan was persuaded to make a dramatic speech along the lines of Kennedy's 'Ich bin ein Berliner' address of 1963. He spoke live on 18 November 1981, just days before Brezhnev's visit to Bonn, in an address timed for maximum exposure to European TV audiences. The President's core message was simple: 'The United States is prepared to cancel its deployment of Pershing II and ground-launch cruise missiles if the Soviets will dismantle their SS-20, SS-4, and SS-5 missiles.' If the Soviets agreed, he continued, 'we could together substantially reduce the dread threat of nuclear war which hangs over the people of Europe. This, like the first footstep on the Moon, would be a giant step for mankind.' What Reagan proposed was, essentially, the zero option championed by Schmidt in 1979 and backed by the SPD. After much internal bickering in Washington, it had been picked by Pentagon hawks, notably Richard Perle, but only as a tactical ploy to propitiate Allied opinion. For Schmidt, however, a zero option would be the ideal outcome because it would remove all the Euromissiles that threatened Germany with nuclear obliteration rather than simply controlling their growth in a balanced way. He was delighted that the Reagan administration had finally been prodded into a public proposal for arms talks that was congruent with thinking in Bonn and that his own efforts had been critical in pushing them to this position. Publicly he endorsed what he called 'the American peace strategy', adding that it gave him 'a very firm basis on which to talk to the Soviet General Secretary'.[56]

Schmidt was in fact now describing himself as a 'double interpreter' between East and West—a term also picked up in the press. Talking off the record, he stressed that no West German leader could be a 'negotiator'—only the two super-powers could negotiate on nuclear weaponry—or stand equidistant between the two of them, because Bonn was an ally of Washington. But, he said, 'we Germans can play the interpreter's role'—to 'help each side understand the other', adding that 'we Germans are perhaps the best interpreter in both directions'—not least because the FRG was 'a non-nuclear middle power' that had 'a keen national interest in peace and security in Europe due to its geographic place and its history'. Schmidt also believed that he had special credentials for the job of interpreter. To quote one American journalist: 'As the Western leader who thinks he knows Mr. Brezhnev best–Mr. Schmidt never tires of noting that he has talked to the Soviet leader six times over the last eight years–the Chancellor feels uniquely qualified to do the job'. Even SPD critics grudgingly acknowledged the international stature he had achieved. 'Schmidt talks to the big shots', said Karl-Heinz Hansen, a vocal opponent of the dual-track decision. 'We are somebody in the world again. That helps our sense of self.' Veteran *New York Times* columnist Flora Lewis observed that it was 'the virtually complete break in Soviet–American relations after the invasion of Afghanistan, deepened by the Reagan administration rhetoric, that opened the way for Mr. Schmidt. He became the activist between East and West, first persuading Moscow to agree to talks on Euromissiles, then persuading Washington to come up with a dramatic bargaining offer.'[57]

Brezhnev's visit to Bonn on 23–24 November was his first trip to the West since the Soviet invasion of Afghanistan, nearly two years before. It was also significant that he chose the Federal Republic as his privileged interlocutor. In Bonn the Soviet leader dismissed Reagan's zero option as unfair to the USSR—failing to take account, for instance, of the British and French nuclear forces—and offered instead his own 'moratorium' proposals to appeal to Western peace opinion. Behind the scenes he and Foreign Minister Gromyko were anxious to get Schmidt's take on the Washington enigma. What were the aims and intentions of the president and what was the power balance between hawks and doves around the White House? This played to Schmidt's self-conception as the superpowers' mutual interpreter. To his Russian visitors, he insisted on Reagan's basic sincerity about arms limitation but he also reminded them that, if negotiations failed, the dual-track deployments would take place by the autumn of 1983. By now the superpowers had agreed to start INF talks in Geneva at the end of November. These would be conducted at the level of senior officials and arms-control experts and not, as Schmidt would have liked, by the two leaders. But he was still pleased that some kind of superpower dialogue would resume and, regarding Soviet–German relations, he spoke of a new 'security partnership' between the two governments.[58]

As with the Moscow summit of July 1980, there was also an economic dimension to the Bonn meeting in November 1981. Once again, the Germans handled this discreetly, to minimize offence to the United States. Just before Brezhnev's arrival, a West German consortium had signed a series of contracts for equipment, materials, and labour, worth an estimated $4.5 billion, as part of a Europe-wide $10-billion deal to construct a 3,500-mile pipeline that would in return bring natural gas for the next twenty-five years from Siberia to Central Europe. The Soviets wanted the contracts signed as the highlight of Brezhnev's visit but the West Germans insisted on doing so two days before. They also treated the contracts as commercial agreements, even though the government was backing the whole project. The Reagan administration intensely disliked what the media called 'the deal of the century', sending over an eleventh-hour mission to try to dissuade the Germans. But Schmidt denied American accusations of energy dependency on the Soviets, with the concomitant potential for Soviet blackmail. Even though the FRG would double its reliance on Soviet gas to 30 per cent, overall the country would only depend on the USSR for 5 per cent of its energy needs. The deal was part of Schmidt's economic strategy since the 1973 oil shock of diversifying the FRG's sources of imported energy. On the political front, as usual, he insisted on the value of trade for stabilizing East–West relations. As he told a British journalist, 'we want to have not only juridically a state of peace in the centre of Europe, but all the kind of trade and neighbourly traffic that goes with the idea of peace'.[59]

With the superpowers moving towards dialogue once again, Schmidt felt it feasible to resume momentum on relations with the GDR. Inner-German relations were, in his view, an integral part of his European 'peace policy'. The summit with Erich Honecker, deferred from August 1980 because of the Polish crisis, finally went ahead on 11–13 December 1981; the talks took place fifty kilometres north of Berlin at Werbellinsee. This was the first formal summit between the leaders of the two Germanies since 1971. Schmidt did not expect any substantive progress on key issues, let alone treaties or agreements. Indeed he believed that Germany would still be a divided country in the twenty-first century. Given this assumption, he was keen simply to keep open channels of communication, speaking of a 'readiness to talk without pre-conditions' and of the need to understand one another 'as Germans'.[60]

The final day of his visit to the GDR was, however, overshadowed by dramatic news from Poland, where the communist government, after months of prevarication, finally imposed martial law. This enabled it to round up Solidarity leaders and suspend civil liberties. Schmidt tried to play down the crisis, stressing that the Red Army had not invaded (unlike in Czechoslovakia in 1968) and stating that the FRG believed in 'strict non-intervention and non-interference'. He said publicly that 'this was a good occasion to stress the need for continuing contacts in times of East–West distrust'. Reagan, however, took a very different line—asserting that Moscow bore 'a heavy and direct responsibility for the repression'—and Washington hawks seized the opportunity to try to sabotage the centrepiece of European economic détente, the Siberian pipeline, by banning the export of oil and gas equipment directly or indirectly to the USSR. This hit European companies such as AEG-Kanis in West Germany who relied on components from General Electric, Caterpillar, and other US manufacturers. And so, ironically, American sanctions against the Kremlin had the almost unique effect of uniting all West European leaders against the White House, including Margaret Thatcher in Britain.[61]

With the Atlantic now seeming more of an abyss than a bridge, Schmidt could no longer maintain his credibility as Cold War intermediary. His visit to Washington in early January 1982 was close to a disaster. For a leader who liked to say that he had been to the United States forty or fifty times, it came as a rude shock to see anti-German pickets outside the White House. There were questions about his resolve and credentials as a 'man of the West', accusations of being 'lukewarm and selfish' on Poland, and even sneers that he was actually 'Brezhnev's buddy'. The Bonn delegation was asked why the Italian communist party had been more critical of the Polish regime than the government of the Federal Republic. The chancellor's own touch also seemed less sure, his restlessness displayed in constant smoking and excessive garrulousness. He 'talked and talked', wrote one journalist—about China, economics, Brezhnev, and even Frederick the Great—'as if he thought [that] if he only kept talking everything would be fine'.[62]

But now the talking was coming to an end: 1982 was a story of sustained decline, which can be dealt with briskly. Schmidt's health was deteriorating—he had in fact been fitted with a pacemaker in October because of problems with his heart—and, after eight years in power and repeated medical crises, he was close to exhaustion.[63] At home he faced renewed SPD efforts to derail the dual-track policy. The left wanted to veto the deployment of Pershing and cruise missiles whether there was progress in arms-control negotiations or not. This forced Schmidt to put his chancellorship on the line. At a SPD party convention in Munich in April 1982, for instance, he claimed that, if the left got its way in blocking deployments, this would be a clear victory for the Soviets that would 'shake the foundations of the Atlantic Alliance' and actually 'increase the likelihood of nuclear war'. He also tried to remind his party that the dual track had not proved a vote-loser in the 1980 election. Reiterating his arguments to the Euro-American workshop in Bonn in June, he underlined that NATO's aim was a 'negotiated equilibrium' and cautioned that 'reason, not emotion, has to govern strategy'.[64]

Schmidt's problems were exacerbated because anti-nuclear feeling increasingly manifested itself in anti-Americanism—even though the United States was the

FRG's protector power, as Schmidt kept reminding fellow Germans. When President Reagan addressed the Bundestag on 9 June, insisting that 'we must continue to improve our defenses if we're to preserve peace and freedom', he was heckled by several parliamentarians—most unusual treatment for a foreign head of state. Two days later in West Berlin, when the president asked why the Soviets walled in their people to stop them enjoying freedom, 100,000 people massed in protests bearing banners proclaiming 'Reagan is a Fascist' and even 'Kill Reagan'.[65]

Nor had the Soviet–American arms-control talks in Geneva made much progress. There was one apparent breakthrough in mid July: the so-called 'Walk in the Woods' by the American and Soviet negotiators, Paul Nitze and Yuli Kvitsinsky. This deal, sketched out on their own initiative, would have reduced the Soviet SS-20 deployment by two-thirds to 75 in return for the same level of cruise missile launchers, together with no deployment of Pershing IIs. The deal was, however, done without authorization from their governments, both of which rapidly disavowed the whole package. The Reagan administration stuck adamantly to NATO's full track-one deployment and Assistant Secretary of Defense Richard Perle even tried to use Schmidt as a pretext. He predicted that West German politicians would say, 'See! The Americans were willing to eliminate the Pershing II'—trying to pull the rug from under Schmidt as Carter had done over the neutron bomb. Perle argued that Pershing II deployment was essential to back up the chancellor: 'We can't leave him high and dry, and at the mercy of his opponents, by reneging on our own commitment to deploy it'. In fact, when Schmidt found out that the White House had ditched the deal, he was indignant, regarding Perle's arguments against it as spurious because the FRG would still have been deploying cruise missiles.[66]

Amid all these domestic and foreign problems, Schmidt's own government was falling apart over the economy. With 7.5 per cent of the workforce unemployed (1.8 million people, the highest figure since the 1950s), the SPD left and the unions demanded higher taxes on top earnings and cuts in the working week—all financed by increased government borrowing. Such rampant Keynesianism appalled the monetarist-minded FDP Liberal Democrats, Schmidt's junior coalition partners. Their leader, Genscher, despite his largely harmonious relations with the chancellor on foreign policy, was now convinced that the SPD was no longer a responsible party of government. This reinforced the FDP's alienation from the SPD pacifist left wing over security policy. Genscher started courting the opposition CDU to see if they could together form an alternative coalition government. The two parties finally combined in a successful constructive vote of no confidence on 1 October 1982—the only example in the history of the Federal Republic to date—which brought to an end Schmidt's chancellorship.[67]

Seeing the writing on the wall, Schmidt prepared his exit carefully. He pushed the FDP before they jumped, blaming the collapse of the coalition squarely on their 'dishonesty'. In keeping with his style, ever since the 'Lord of the Flood' moment in Hamburg twenty years before, he wanted to seem in control. And he put a huge effort into his speech on 17 September formally dumping the FDP. Even the *Frankfurter Allgemeine Zeitung*, in no way a pro-SPD paper, called it 'a great rhetorical masterpiece...fully controlled, every word sharply calculated for its propagandistic purpose but coldly presented – as cold as steel'.[68] During his last twenty-four hours he conducted his final cabinet meeting with what was said to be almost 'spooky' normality, and, as the veteran defence intellectual, made a point of saying farewell to the *Bundeswehr* in a parade near the Defence Ministry. Only there was he close to tears.[69]

Schmidt also devoted much time and thought in composing his last speech to the Bundestag as chancellor, on 1 October, which would be televised live. He sat late into the night with press spokesman Klaus Bölling, intent not on settling political scores but on charting the future direction for his party. In familiar vein, Schmidt stressed the need for international peace, good neighbourliness in the heart of Europe, and loyalty to both the Atlantic Alliance and the European Community. The text was composed in an office already stripped bare—surrounded by boxes full of his beloved books and photographs of himself with German and foreign VIPs. Bölling felt one could almost sense the emptiness of his soul. Schmidt's wife Loki, a biologist, was away in the Amazon jungle collecting specimens and he told her firmly not to return because she had looked forward to the trip for so long, saying he had to endure this alone and she could not help him anyway. His solitariness seemed even starker because his CDU successor, Helmut Kohl, was surrounded in the Bundestag by his whole family.[70]

When Schmidt had spoken his last words, there were a few valedictory remarks before Kohl was formally elected the sixth chancellor of the Federal Republic. Schmidt had been in power for eight and a half years, longer than any of his predecessors apart from Adenauer. Emotions only came to the surface when Wehner, as SPD leader in the Bundestag, hesitantly presented him with a bunch of red roses in plastic foil, muttering 'I'm rather embarrassed'.[71]

After the speech, Schmidt sat with Bölling for a couple of hours in his empty office, ruminating on what he had achieved. *Ostpolitik*, he said, should be seen as Brandt's 'great achievement'. But he was proud of getting West Germany through the world economic crisis. And he gave particular weight to the Moscow summit of 1980 when, face to face with Brezhnev in the Kremlin, he felt he had 'for a few hours' transcended the limits of West Germany's geopolitical condition, speaking for once 'like the representative of a great power'. By facilitating this renewal of superpower dialogue, Schmidt had proved his credentials as broker or interpreter between East and West. And so, reflected Bölling ironically, 'the lieutenant of the great German army who in 1941 stood on the edge of Moscow had managed a successful reconnaissance mission for the West'. Schmidt sat back and looked at Bölling: 'All in all, we haven't done too badly'.[72]

Later that evening (see Figure 5.3) he walked alone—except for a security guard carrying his roses—through the garden for the last time and out to the chancellor's car.

Figure 5.3 The Departure, 1 October 1982.
Source: AP, Fritz Reiss.

Conclusion

How, then, to evaluate Helmut Schmidt as a statesman? Did *Der Spiegel*, for instance, get it right in 1982 when Schmidt left office, in claiming that his foreign policy had not been shaped by 'concepts' or 'intellectual models' but was essentially reactive? He was a mere 'doer' (*der Macher*), a safe pair of hands in times of crisis, who lacked broader vision and primarily concerned himself with trying to solve immediate problems, so that 'little endured of historical significance'.[1] This clichéd image of his chancellorship persists to this day, as the obituaries in November 2015 revealed. Even essentially sympathetic biographers, such as Hartmut Soell, Hans-Joachim Noack, and Martin Rupps, have praised his diverse talents, political skill, and persuasive rhetoric while leaving open his place in history. Much of the writing has evaluated Schmidt in a tightly German/European setting, focusing on his political conduct and ethical precepts, without contextualizing him in the global arena or comparing him with other international statesmen of the 1970s.[2]

According to Henry Kissinger, 'any statesman is in part the prisoner of necessity. He is confronted with an environment he did not create, and is shaped by a personal history he can no longer change.' Given these constraints, Kissinger argued in 1979, 'the public life of every political figure is a continual struggle to rescue an element of choice from the pressure of circumstance'. The room for manoeuvre is limited; any success is precarious. 'Yet there is a margin between necessity and accident, in which the statesman by perseverance and intuition must choose and thereby shape the destiny of his people.' For Kissinger, 'the statesman's responsibility is to struggle against transitoriness', and just occasionally—if the environment is sufficiently 'malleable'—the statesman has 'the chance to shape events' and 'build a new world'. At such moments he has the opportunity for greatness.[3]

Reflecting on Schmidt from this perspective in 1999, Kissinger lavished faint praise on the chancellor as a leader with 'knowledge', 'character', 'competence', and 'even flair'. But, he argued, Schmidt lacked the attributes and opportunity for greatness. Time and place conspired against any real chance to shape history. 'It was not given to him to repeat the drama of Brandt or carry out the fulfillment of Kohl', especially in advancing a resolution of the German question. For Kissinger, Schmidt was always 'destined to be a transitional figure'.[4]

This book has taken a much more positive view of Schmidt's modus operandi and of his legacies. Admittedly he was catapulted into power in 1974 at a moment of crisis—both domestically over a spy scandal at the heart of government and internationally over the feared disintegration of the capitalist system. For Schmidt, prosperity was inseparable from political stability: he feared that continued economic crisis would undermine liberal democracy and threaten Western survival in the Cold War. So his first months in office were often a frantic attempt to steady the ship at home and abroad; he was indeed reacting to what was thrown at him. But, as I have shown, he was no mere crisis-manager: Schmidt acted with a clear conceptual framework derived from his direct engagement with politics and also from his thinking and writing over two decades. This gave him a sense of Germany's past and a vision of Germany's future, which served as a platform for attempting to shape history. And, as this book has also argued, the 1970s were not simply a transitional phase.[5] They were a period of genuine transformation in which Schmidt the statesman was able to play a significant part, seizing creatively the opportunities of the moment to help reshape the global order.

What, in summary, did he achieve? And what in his background had made this possible? A seminal moment was his experience as a twenty-two-year-old soldier in Hitler's First Panzer Division, fighting its way to Leningrad and Moscow in 1941. This left him with an enduring sense of Russia—both its enormous size and its glaring backwardness—and a real awareness of what war was actually like. After 1945 he could have gone in several directions. He had always dreamed of being an architect; he was also an accomplished musician. But, already a married man, Schmidt had to start earning a living as soon as possible and so he took a degree in economics before working in local government in his native Hamburg. Here he dealt first-hand with the huge problems of reconstruction after the Second World War. He joined the SPD in 1946 and moved into national politics from 1953 as a member of the *Bundestag*. Part of his brief was to speak for his party on transportation and economic affairs.

Although trained in economics, once Schmidt was in Bonn his passion became military security and he soon made his name as one of the SPD's leading defence experts. Unlike most Social Democrats he supported German rearmament within NATO and the country's alliance with America—even serving as a reserve officer in the *Bundeswehr*. Two major books in 1961 and 1969 proved his entrée into what he liked to call 'the American defence community', gaining him a respectful readership among scholars, strategists, and policymakers.[6] A regular visitor and speaker in America and Britain, Schmidt enhanced his visibility and appeal as a defence intellectual by impressive fluency in the English language. Underpinning all his speeches and writings was the pursuit of peace and stability, founded on key strategic ideas such as the military balance of power and the avoidance of even limited nuclear warfare. This reflected a clear understanding of divided Germany's vulnerability astride the front line of Cold War Europe. Schmidt therefore came to the Defence Ministry in 1969 with clear concepts and visions that he then implemented self-consciously in the *Bundeswehr* White Papers of 1970–1. This was one of the most important stocktakings of the German armed forces since their inception in 1955 and a benchmark for their reform in the context of détente and *Ostpolitik*.

Suddenly thrown into the position of finance minister in 1972–4, Schmidt was forced back to his intellectual roots as an economist. But the issues were now of global scope and existential urgency: the Bretton Woods financial system had collapsed, the first oil crisis exploded, and the world economy was sliding into the alarming disease of stagflation that defied all the verities of post-war Keynesianism. So Schmidt had to apply his expertise and conceptual thinking to a situation for which there were no textbook solutions or reliable institutions. In the Finance Ministry and then as chancellor he was able to employ his economic skills on an international plane and to lasting effect as he developed a truly global vision, expressed in new notions of 'interdependence' and innovative practices of 'policy coordination'.

In place of the Bretton Woods-era regulatory mechanisms, Schmidt helped create a milder form of international discipline in the form of 'surveillance' administered via personal diplomacy between key political leaders. His model was the Library Group of four key finance ministers in 1973–4, including Giscard. This took on new significance as a tool of world economic governance once these men had become political leaders, and their inner circle was gradually institutionalized as the G7 through the summits of 1975–8. The credit for this does not lie exclusively with Schmidt, but his rapid emergence as a 'world economist' (*Weltökonom*) was a critical part of the process. To be sure, the G7 was no panacea and these summits later degenerated into bureaucratic routine and media spectacle, but, between Rambouillet in 1975 and Bonn in 1978, the G7 did play a significant role in stabilizing the West economically. This, together with his initiative in co-founding the European Monetary System, should be recognized as part of the chancellor's enduring institutional legacy.[7]

Despite this preoccupation with the crisis of capitalism in the early years of his chancellorship, Schmidt—the strategist of balance—did not lose sight of traditional Cold War issues. He continued to emphasize the centrality for the FRG of the American alliance, but, building on Brandt's *Ostpolitik*, he was convinced that the country needed to keep extending relations with the Soviet bloc—a conviction first formed during his epic trip to Moscow in 1966. *Ostpolitik* was, however, harder to conduct than in the détente era of the early 1970s because Brandt had achieved most of the immediately feasible objectives in his Eastern Treaties and also because superpower relations deteriorated sharply in the second half of the decade. Yet Schmidt did notch up two significant achievements during his last five years as chancellor. He was crucial in shaping NATO's 'dual-track' decision, through the ideas in his IISS lecture in London in 1977 and through his diplomacy during and after the Guadeloupe summit of 1979. And, as the New Cold War deepened in 1980–2, he carved out for himself the special role of what he called a 'double interpreter' between Washington and Moscow. In consequence, Schmidt advanced West Germany's status to what American journalist John Vinocur characterized as an 'associate superpower'.[8]

That claim is perhaps too extravagant but one may reasonably say that, among the Western allies, Schmidt took the Federal Republic to a seat at the top table— in security as well as economics. Its new rank was strikingly evident in Guadeloupe, where the three Western victor powers (America, Britain, and France), all members of the nuclear club, engaged with the FRG as an equal. Schmidt may not have achieved so much on the German question compared with

Brandt and Kohl, but the international environment in which he had to operate was not conducive to significant progress. These national and Eurocentric criteria, in any case, constitute too narrow a yardstick for judging his performance. In an era of global crisis, Schmidt, through the G7 economic summits and the looser 1 + 3 forum in Western security, enabled the Federal Republic to come of age in international affairs. This was no mean achievement.

Moreover, the 'dual-track' decision deserves note as a significant episode in the story of the Cold War as a whole. Of course, it was in part a stop-gap measure to maintain the cohesion of the Alliance against a continued Soviet arms build-up in Europe. But this was not merely reactive politics. The dual-track concept reflected Schmidt's basic belief in the need for an equilibrium of military forces, not for its own sake alone but as an instrument of peacemaking. This equilibrium could be achieved either by a Western nuclear build-up to counter the Soviet advantage in theatre nuclear forces, or by negotiating a reduction of these weapons—ideally, for Schmidt, their complete elimination on each side. Negotiations got nowhere in the short term and so, under the automaticity built into the dual-track decision, NATO deployed cruise and Pershing II missiles in 1983, especially in the FRG, Britain, and Italy. The German deployment occurred only after huge domestic political battles within the SPD and on the streets, which helped to bring down Schmidt, and it was his successor, Christian Democrat Chancellor Helmut Kohl, who pushed it through. Kohl later gained the credit, together with Margaret Thatcher, for sustaining NATO's credibility during the New Cold War. Yet he was in large measure simply carrying through the policy that Schmidt had designed. Moreover, the other facet of the dual-track policy—negotiation—was also realized a few years later, when the firmness of the Western alliance in the early 1980s facilitated the 1987 INF treaty between the superpowers. As a result, a whole category of nuclear weapons was removed on both sides, for the first time since 1945; this had always been Schmidt's hope and aim. He therefore deserves more credit than he is usually granted for this major step in dispelling the nuclear nightmare in Europe and thus in defusing the Cold War.

Schmidt's diplomacy and real achievements—in both the areas of economics and finance as well as security and defence—grew out of a long history of thought and action. Henry Kissinger has noted, in an observation that certainly could be applied to Schmidt, that 'the convictions that leaders have formed before reaching high office are the intellectual capital they will consume as long as they continue in office'.[9] For both of these men, of course, the balance of power was one of their guiding concepts. Yet Schmidt's *Gleichgewichtsstrategie* focused primarily on a military equilibrium in Europe, whereas Kissinger was more concerned with the balancing acts of global geopolitics between Washington, Moscow, and Beijing. Even so, Schmidt's vision of the world did embrace the challenges of an emerging China in what he called 'tri-polarity' and 'the world triangle'. Above all, he was forced to think globally because of Germany's sensitive place in a matrix of power and vulnerability between the United States and the Soviet Union: any problem in the global Cold War could easily backfire in Berlin. Schmidt, no less than Kissinger, was therefore a thinker as well as a doer in the security politics of the 1970s.

Kissinger, of course, is now renowned as what biographer Jeremi Suri calls 'the foreign policy celebrity of the 1970s, the only figure who appeared to make sense of a rapidly changing world'. To be sure, Schmidt did not enjoy the cult status of Kissinger, who was acclaimed as 'Super K' (*Newsweek*) and even as 'the world's indispensable man' (*Time*).[10] Nor did Schmidt win the Nobel Peace Prize.[11] And yet it has been a central claim of this book that as a statesman-intellectual who conceptualized, articulated, and even tackled the big issues of his age, he was Kissinger's equal. What is more, unlike Kissinger, Schmidt understood the problematic of foreign policy in the 1970s to include not only power and diplomacy but also the global economy. Kissinger's most recent biographer, Niall Ferguson, concedes that his subject was 'deeply skeptical about the claims of economics'. According to Suri, 'Kissinger's knowledge of economics was notoriously limited' and he 'frequently neglected crucial global topics' such as finance and monetary affairs. Schmidt, by contrast, was a serious macro-economist turned politician who saw the global economic crisis as the most pressing international problem of the mid 1970s. He also made a significant contribution to addressing it through his conduct of *Weltwirtschaftpolitik* and the creation of the G7—an institution that barely figures in Kissinger's voluminous memoirs. In Schmidt's opinion, Kissinger approached the world economic crisis 'from the traditional viewpoint of power politics', whereas the German chancellor developed ideas of interdependence that were foreign to Kissinger's more traditional approach to state relations, constructed around a hierarchy of powers playing a complex chess game at a distance. Interdependence of the sort Schmidt envisaged entailed multilateral engagement in a cooperative approach to global challenges; a theme he further developed in a series of lectures on grand strategy that he gave at Yale soon after the end of his chancellorship, published with the subtitle *The Anachronism of National Strategies in an Interdependent World*. He was, it might reasonably be said, more attuned than Kissinger to what many scholars now see as the key challenge of the 1970s, 'the shock of the global'.[12]

Not only was Schmidt at home in global economics as well as security policy, but in further contrast to Kissinger he was also a political leader rather than merely an adviser. To be sure, Kissinger exerted huge influence in American foreign policy making as national security adviser and secretary of state from 1969 to 1977 but he never held elective office, let alone supreme power within his country. It is noteworthy that Kissinger regularly describes himself as a 'statesman', even though he lacked this crucial attribute of political power, and equally notable that his biographers have perpetuated this perception. Kissinger designed policy, he acted as high-level intermediary, he was a consummate backchannel manipulator, but he did not carry ultimate responsibility for the decisions of the state or have to account for his actions to a domestic electorate. Schmidt as chancellor, by contrast, bore responsibility and faced accountability. In these fundamental respects he was a statesman; on that definition Kissinger was not.

Yet being a party politician can be a source of weakness as well as strength. This was definitely the case for Schmidt. He was a Social Democrat by class background and personal conviction, yet his advocacy of strong defence and the Atlantic

Alliance placed him at odds from the outset with the dominantly pacifist tenor of the SPD. And his enthusiasm for European integration and *Westbindung* pulled him in a different direction from his party comrades' preoccupation with German unification. These tensions were not hugely significant while the SPD was in opposition and Schmidt was merely a member of the Bundestag. But once the party assumed power and he took over the helm of the nation, the ideological conflicts within the SPD soon hampered policymaking and increasingly eroded his authority as chancellor. In the long run it did not help that the party leadership remained with his predecessor, Willy Brandt—icon of East–West détente, acclaimed for his *Ostpolitik*. From mid 1977 Brandt's former aide, Egon Bahr, came out in open opposition to Schmidt's defence and security policy; by 1983 it was Brandt himself who led the SPD's turnaround against implementing Schmidt's dual-track policy.

This growing left/right split within the SPD mattered in a larger sense because Schmidt was the leader of a coalition government. Divergent economic priorities always made the SPD–FDP partnership an unholy alliance: the SPD was a party of workers and employees, favouring higher government spending on welfare and public works, whereas the FDP represented professionals and employers with more of a liberal, market orientation. From 1977 ideological differences over foreign policy aggravated tensions between the two parties. And in the end the persistent challenges to Schmidt from pacifists and anti-Americanists in the SPD wore down the coalition and eventually forced him from power in 1982. In short, Schmidt the world statesman could never fully rise above the problems of Schmidt the party politician. In these circumstances, what he managed to achieve on the international stage was striking.

Of course, Schmidt's political problems were often of his own making. As we have seen, he tended to speak intemperately and did not hesitate to lecture people, especially those he considered intellectually inferior. The 1950s tag 'Schmidt the Lip' stuck with him all his political life. Although charming with friends, Schmidt was certainly not the cosiest of politicians. 'He had no gift for small talk', said Kissinger, 'and no patience with it.'[13] Schmidt's prickly manner made him many enemies, notably Franz Josef Strauß in domestic politics; but the really problematic personal relationship was the one with Jimmy Carter. For Schmidt, the American alliance was axiomatic, yet from the start he felt little but contempt for the 'unknown farmer governor'. His public intervention on the side of Ford in the 1976 election was not merely tactless but a diplomatic faux pas of major proportions—exacerbated by the chancellor's refusal to make a personal apology to Carter. When on the defensive, with his intellectual vanity at stake, Schmidt could be unbearable. And in such situations his *Oberlehrer* tendency became particularly pronounced, using language that was caustic and even offensive. Schmidt's affront to Carter was never forgiven, and, even after the election, the chancellor did not trouble to conceal his disdain for the president, conveying the impression that he considered Carter unfit to be leader of the West.

This personal friction between Schmidt and Carter proved diplomatically poisonous, especially over the neutron bomb and Euro-strategic missiles. Yet one should also note that Schmidt proved sufficiently pragmatic to transcend his personal failings, maintain his focus on the issues that mattered, and do the hard graft that is essential for diplomatic success. Despite his allergy to Carter and his dislike of Brzezinski, he thrashed out deals with the Americans that sustained both German security and the cohesion of NATO. This is also part of his achievement and it deserves further comment. From Schmidt's perspective, Carter foisted the neutron bomb on the West Germans and then, after months of negotiations, dropped the whole idea, humiliating Schmidt personally and snubbing his country. The chancellor was particularly aggrieved because he had laboriously worked out a package that sought to sustain *Ostpolitik*, shore up NATO's credibility, and placate his party's left wing. The chancellor's basic transatlantic commitment, however, was not shaken by the clash of personalities. He adapted his ERW package to the broader, ongoing debate about theatre nuclear weapons, forging a compromise with Carter at Guadeloupe in January 1979 and establishing the foundations for NATO's dual-track decision the following December. Schmidt the Diplomatist had managed to control his temper and construct this compromise solution, repairing some of the damage caused by Schmidt the Lip.

His ineptitude in dealing with Carter was not, therefore, fatal. In fact, Schmidt's practice of international relations generally placed a very high value on good personal communication and this theme should also be underlined in any balance sheet on his chancellorship. As Schmidt reflected in a speech at Harvard in 1979, 'partnership in security involves trust and predictability. For that reason personal and direct contact between political leaders is indispensable.' This meant face-to-face meetings, because they were the only real way to gauge the other side; to get a feel for his counterpart's character, concerns, and reactions. Out of such meetings, regularly conducted, he claimed, came a clear estimation of the people you could rely on, and how far they would remain loyal despite all the other pressures.[14]

Schmidt believed that in special circumstances one could even speak of 'political friendships'. The supreme example was what he called his 'belle entente' with Valéry Giscard d'Estaing. Through their meetings, he reflected in 1985, the two became so close that they could intuit each other's reactions, making a telephone call necessary only as final confirmation. Aside from Giscard, Schmidt also developed genuine political friendships with Gerald Ford and Jim Callaghan, both of whom he liked, respected, and trusted. Indeed, the four men continued to meet annually at Ford's house in Vail, Colorado, long after they had left office—at least a dozen times by 1996. It also mattered immensely that these statesmen could communicate freely and easily in the shared language of English, dispensing with interpreters and thereby allowing franker and more intimate conversations. Even though Schmidt did not trust Carter, and vice versa, they also spoke the same language—making the relationship intense but candid. Especially after the ERW fiasco, Schmidt was convinced they must talk face to face: true statesmanship meant rising above personal animosities for the greater good—hence the importance of Guadeloupe. Communication in this free, informal, and direct manner at the highest level was fundamental to the 1 + 3 network that Schmidt helped to establish between West Germany, France, America, and Britain.[15]

The roots of 1 + 3 lay in the Library Group of 1973, out of which evolved the G6/7 summits. Schmidt disliked the term 'summit', because it suggested something rather pompous and out of the ordinary. He preferred and privileged informal meetings that were 'regular', 'personal', and 'confidential'—key words in his diplomatic lexicon. Schmidt was convinced that summitry in this form, again conducted in the common working language of English, fostered understanding of the interests and motives of other nations and forced the participants to define and present their own positions in plausible ways. Even more importantly, the leaders had to go further and discern shared interests, reach compromise positions, and advance common action. But Schmidt also valued the communication that went on at the margins of the G7 and other similar summits. There, during what Schmidt called 'fireside chats', it was possible to have useful conversations with other leaders that went beyond the official agenda to deal with the wider problems of *Weltpolitik* and *Weltstrategie*.[16]

These dialogues took place between allies and friends. But Schmidt was convinced that such personal communication was equally necessary on a bilateral basis, especially with adversaries—all the more so when the international climate was cool, if not outright hostile. He told two American journalists in 1981 that his 'basic philosophy in foreign policy' was to be 'calculable, put yourself in the shoes of the other guy, on the other side of the table, and try to evaluate the situation from his point of view'. In 'normal times', Schmidt went on, 'this sounds trivial, but not when there are tensions'. And the tensions were very real by the end of his chancellorship, as superpower relations degenerated in the Second Cold War. 'It's dangerous to be an enigma to the Russians', he stressed, and for 'the Russians to be an enigma to us is very, very dangerous'. With adversaries, personal communication might not create trust, as it did with allies, but it did at least bring predictability to the table.[17]

Knowing the 'Other' had, in fact, been Schmidt's aim ever since his first journey to Moscow in 1966. But by the end of his career this idea had been refined into his concept of the 'double interpreter', not merely observing the superpowers from the sidelines but acting as interlocutor between them. Schmidt did not like the word 'intermediary' (*Vermittler*). For one thing, he insisted, the FRG was not equidistant between the two superpowers, but, instead, operated as a full partner in the Western alliance. And he did not wish simply to act as messenger boy; he sought to 'help each side understand the other'—to 'translate, in both directions'. Even more than this: to influence their actions, especially over theatre nuclear weapons. He hoped 'to open up the Soviet Union in its very heart to negotiations', and to persuade the Americans to take seriously German interests. The chancellor's objective, going beyond mere mutual translation, was to draw the two superpowers away from maximalist, megaphone diplomacy and prepare them for compromise (*Kompromissbereitschaft*). This, he believed, could be effected only through face-to-face dialogue of a sort that had become normal between Nixon and Brezhnev in the early 1970s but then had stopped completely after the Vienna summit of 1979. Hence his own efforts at shuttle diplomacy in 1980–2, because, he insisted, 'political cooperation requires personal relationships'. And political cooperation, in turn, would enhance stability, thereby promoting the cause of peace, which for Schmidt was the ultimate objective of foreign policy.[18]

Yet the chancellor always understood that, for West Germany, foreign policy had to be conducted with circumspection. That was the country's unique predicament stemming from the burdens of its history: the *Kaiserreich*, the Hitler era, and what he called 'the Auschwitz past'. Schmidt was consequently at pains to avoid any impression of over-assertiveness, frequently letting others take the front seat—especially his close ally, Giscard, in the cases of the Rambouillet G6 and the 'Guadeloupe 4'. Nor did he ignore the legacies of 1945, which had left his country occupied, divided, and denied the trappings of power, including nuclear weapons. Schmidt the statesman always worked within these historical parameters, even at his zenith on the world stage. As one of his party buddies from Hamburg remarked: 'He is convinced most of the time that he's the only real leader in the western world. He is also probably right. The problem is he's German.'[19]

* * * * *

So, to come back to the clichés at the start: Schmidt the diplomatist was not, merely reactive. He held firm ideas about international relations, both with regard to method (conducting them through personal communications between political leaders) and also in terms of goals for West Germany in an increasingly interdependent world. He set out these ideas in speeches and writings that place him on a par with Henry Kissinger as a policy intellectual. Unlike the US national security adviser, however, he handled economics as well defence with equal facility. And he did so from the position of a political leader.

Yet Schmidt came to an ignominious end, deserted by his coalition partners and denounced by much of his own party. Walking out of the Chancellery in Bonn on the evening of 1 October 1982 with his bunch of roses, he cut a forlorn figure.

Should we then accept Kissinger's verdict in 1999 that Schmidt was destined to go down in history as 'a transitional figure', rather than the equal of great German chancellors like Otto von Bismarck and Adenauer, Brandt and Kohl? As this book has shown, Schmidt did live in an era of profound transition, economically as well as geopolitically. But he was not merely the object of these systemic changes and not just a short-term crisis-manager. Schmidt helped shape global affairs in the directions that he believed would best serve West German security and global stability. The G7 not only created a new forum for global management, it added diplomatic clout to West Germany's position as an economic *Weltmacht*. In security matters, the FRG could never be a world power because of its divided nature and semi-sovereign status. Yet, through Schmidt's pro-active involvement in nuclear politics and his role as double interpreter between the superpowers, he elevated West Germany to the top table in international politics. Schmidt thus conducted what he called *Weltpolitik*—giving this historically charged term new meaning in an era of global Cold War and economic interdependence.

In the process, he also contributed to the eventual resolution of the German question, though not to the same degree and with the same visibility as Brandt or Kohl. Schmidt transformed West Germany's 1 + 3 relationship with the Western victor powers into an equal partnership of the Big Four. And as double interpreter, maintaining both Adenauer's allegiance to *Westbindung* and Brandt's commitment to *Ostpolitik* in unpropitious international circumstances, he succeeded in raising the FRG's credibility with both superpowers. In the event it fell to Kohl to seize the historical moment for German unification, which he grasped with both hands. Unity was accomplished peacefully through the 2 + 4 formula, whereby the two Germanies negotiated their future in partnership with all the victor powers—from East as well as West. But one could reasonably claim that 2 + 4 was made possible because of what had been achieved via 1 + 3 and double interpretation. This, too, was part of Helmut Schmidt's rich legacy as the global chancellor.

Notes

ABBREVIATIONS

AAPD	*Akten zur Auswärtigen Politik der Bundesrepublik Deutschland*
AdsD	Archiv der sozialen Demokratie, Bonn
BA	Bundesarchiv, Koblenz
DEB	Depositum Egon Bahr
DzD	*Dokumente zur Deutschlandpolitik*
EA	Eigene Arbeiten
FAZ	*Frankfurter Allgemeine Zeitung*
FD-NOR	Det kgl. Forsvarsdepartementet, Oslo
GWU	George Washington University
HSA	Helmut Schmidt Archiv
HSPA	Helmut Schmidt Privatarchiv, Hamburg
JCL	Jimmy Carter Presidential Library, Atlanta
NARA	National Archives and Records Administration, College Park
NSA	National Security Archive, Washington, DC
PAAA	Politisches Archiv des Auswärtigen Amts, Berlin
TNA	The National Archives, Kew, London
US DDRS	US Declassified Documents Reference System
ZA	Zwischenarchiv

EPIGRAPHS

From John Vinocur, 'The Schmidt Factor', *New York Times*, 21 September 1980; from Henry Kissinger's speech at the state funeral of Helmut Schmidt in St Michaelis, Hamburg, 23 November 2015, <https://www.ndr.de/fernsehen/Henry-Kissinger-wuerdigt-Helmut-Schmidt,staatsaktschmidt100.html>.

INTRODUCTION

1. 'Dreizehn Jahre geliehene Macht (I)', *Der Spiegel*, no. 39/1982, 27 September 1982, 40; Archie Brown, *The Myth of the Strong Leader: Political Leadership in the Modern Age* (London, 2014), 101, 128–39, at 136.
2. Ronald J. Granieri, 'Building a Social Democratic Hall of Fame', H-German (October 2005), <http://www.h-net.org/reviews/showrev.php?id=11199>.
3. See also Kristina Spohr, 'Helmut Schmidt–a German leader with a global vision', *The Guardian*, 10 November 2015, <http://www.theguardian.com/commentisfree/2015/nov/10/helmut-schmidt-german-chancellor-europe>.
4. Helmut Schmidt, *Verteidigung oder Vergeltung: Ein deutscher Beitrag zum strategischen Problem der NATO* (Stuttgart, 1961) and *Strategie des Gleichgewichts: Deutsche Friedenspolitik und die Westmächte* (Stuttgart, 1969).
5. The term 'doer' (*Macher*) was often used about Schmidt in a slightly pejorative manner, to convey the sense that he was a crisis-manager. 'Kanzler Schmidt: Hoffen auf den Macher', *Der Spiegel*, no. 20/1974, 13 May 1974, 19–34.

6. Among major studies of Kissinger, see Niall Ferguson, *Kissinger: 1923–1968—The Idealist* (London, 2015); Jussi Hanhimäki, *The Flawed Architect: Henry Kissinger and American Foreign Policy* (New York, 2004); and Jeremi Suri, *Henry Kissinger and the American Century* (Cambridge, MA, 2007). For contemporary comment see also 'Krisenmanager, Mann der Krise', *Der Spiegel*, no. 24/1974, 10 June 1974, 73–80.

7. Robert D. Putnam, 'Diplomacy and Domestic Politics: The Logic of Two-Level Games', *International Organization* 42 (Summer 1988), 427–60.

8. Hartmut Soell, *Helmut Schmidt, 1918–1969: Vernunft und Leidenschaft, vol. 1* (Berlin, 2003); *Helmut Schmidt, 1969 bis Heute: Macht und Verantwortung, vol. 2* (Berlin, 2008); Gunter Hofmann, *Helmut Schmidt: Soldat, Kanzler, Ikone* (Munich, 2015); Hans-Joachim Noack, *Helmut Schmidt: Die Biographie* (Berlin, 2010); Martin Rupps, *Helmut Schmidt: Eine politische Biographie* (Stuttgart/Leipzig, 2002); Idem, *Troika wider Willen: Wie Brandt, Wehner und Schmidt die Republik regierten* (Berlin, 2004); Michael Schwelien, *Helmut Schmidt: Ein Leben für den Frieden* (Hamburg, 2003); Astrid Zipfel, *Der Macher und die Medien: Helmut Schmidts politische Öffentlichkeitsarbeit* (Tübingen/Stuttgart/Heidelberg, 2005). Cf. Klaus Wiegrefe, *Das Zerwürfnis: Helmut Schmidt, Jimmy Carter und die Krise der deutsch-amerikanischen Beziehungen* (Berlin, 2005); Dominik Pick, *Brücken nach Osten: Helmut Schmidt und Polen* (Bremen, 2011); Gunter Hofmann, *Willy Brandt und Helmut Schmidt: Geschichte einer schwierigen Freundschaft* (Munich, 2013).

9. Enrico Böhm, *Die Sicherheit des Westens: Entstehung und Funktion der G7-Gipfel, 1975–1981* (Munich, 2014); Johannes von Karczewski, *'Weltwirtschaft ist unser Schicksal': Helmut Schmidt und die Schaffung der Weltwirtschaftsgipfel* (Bonn, 2008); Emmanuel Mourlon-Druol and Federico Romero, eds, *International Summitry and Global Governance: The Rise of the G7 and the European Council, 1974–1991* (London, 2014); Elizabeth J. Benning, 'Economic Power and Political Leadership: The Federal Republic, the West and the Re-Shaping of the International Economic System, 1972–1976', unpublished PhD dissertation, London School of Economics and Political Science, 2011.

10. Niall Ferguson, Charles S. Maier, Erez Manela, and Daniel J. Sargent, eds, *The Shock of the Global: The 1970s in Perspective* (Cambridge, MA, 2010), 60, 61, 358; cf. Konrad H. Jarausch, ed., *Das Ende der Zuversicht? Die siebziger Jahre als Geschichte* (Göttingen, 2008).

11. See, for example, M. Weinachter, *Valéry Giscard d'Estaing et l'Allemagne: Le double rêve inachevé* (Paris, 2004); Hélène Miard-Delacroix, *Partenaires de choix? Le chancellier Helmut Schmidt et la France, 1974–82* (Frankfurt, 1993); Mathias Waechter, *Helmut Schmidt und Valéry Giscard d'Estaing: Auf der Suche nach Stabilität in der Krise der 70er Jahre* (Bremen, 2011). See also Emmanuel Mourlon-Druol, *A Europe Made of Money: The Emergence of the European Monetary System* (Ithaca, NY, 2012); Guido Thiemeyer, 'Helmut Schmidt und die Gründung des Europäischen Währungssystems 1973–1979', in Franz Knipping and Matthias Schönwald, eds, *Aufbruch zum Europa der zweiten Generation: Die europäische Einigung 1969–1984* (Trier, 2004); Kiran Klaus Patel and Kenneth Weisbrode, eds, *European Integration and the Atlantic Community in the 1980s* (Cambridge, 2013).

12. Bernhard Blumenau, *The United Nations and Terrorism: Germany, Multilateralism, and Antiterrorism Efforts in the 1970s* (London, 2014); Matthias Dahlke, *Demokratischer Staat und transnationaler Terrorismus: Drei Wege zur Unnachgiebigkeit in Westeuropa, 1972–1975* (Munich, 2011); Tim Geiger, 'Die "Landshut" in Mogadischu: Das außenpolitische Krisenmanagement des Bundesregierung angesichts der terroris-

tischen Herausforderung 1977', *Vierteljahrshefte für Zeitgeschichte* 57, no. 3 (2009), 413–56; Bernd Rother, *Willy Brandts Aussenpolitik* (Wiesbaden, 2014); Independent Commission on International Economic Development, *North/South: A Programme for Survival* (London, 1980).

13. Kenneth N. Waltz, *Man, the State and War: A Theoretical Analysis* (New York, 1959); John L. Spanier, *Games Nations Play: Analyzing International Politics* (New York, 1972).

14. Dieter Rebentisch, 'Gipfeldiplomatie und Weltökonomie: Weltwirtschaftliches Krisenmanagement während der Kanzlerschaft Helmut Schmidts, 1974–1982', *Archiv für Sozialgeschichte* 28 (1988), 307–32; Raymond Cohen, *Negotiating across Cultures: International Communication in an Interdependent World* (2nd revised edn, Washington, DC, 1999).

15. Helmut Schmidt, *Weggefährten: Erinnerungen und Reflexionen* (Berlin, 1996), 251–2, 306.

1. THE WORLD ECONOMIST

1. Flora Lewis, 'Rifts Reported in Bonn Coalition', *New York Times*, 11 May 1974, 1, 7; Craig R. Whitney, 'Storm over Brandt Clouds Presidential Election', *New York Times*, 14 May 1974, 10 and 'The Painful Road to Brandt's Resignation', *New York Times*, 23 May 1974, 16.

2. Neal Ascherson, 'A Man Who Can't Stop Working: Profile', *The Observer* (London), 19 May 1974, 15.

3. 'Authority in Bonn', *New York Times*, 19 May 1974, 22.

4. Helmut Schmidt Privatarchiv, Hamburg (henceforth HSPA), HS privat, Presse-Echo, 18.–24. Mai 1974, Thomas Meyer, 'Hier steht ein Mann, der die Kaffeepause abschafft', *Frankfurter Allgemeine Zeitung*, 18 May 1974, 3.

5. HSPA, HS privat, Presse-Echo, 13.–17. Mai 1974, Chefredaktion Politik, Do. 16.05.1974, 12:40—Kommentar zur Wahl von Bundeskanzler Helmut Schmidt von Oswald Hirschfeld.

6. HSPA, HS privat, Presse-Echo, 13.–17. Mai 1974, Hans Barbier, 'Der Superschatzkanzler— Schmidt betont die Wirtschaftspolitik', *Frankfurter Allgemeine Zeitung*, 15 May 1974.

7. Address of 17 May 1974 (*Regierungserklärung*), printed in Helmut Schmidt, *Kontinuität und Konzentration* (2nd edn, Bonn–Bad Godesberg, 1976), ch. 1, 9–30, at 9, 16. 'Schmidt Pledges Continuity of West German Foreign Policy', *New York Times*, 18 May 1974, 2.

8. An expurgated version was published as 'Der Politiker als Ökonom', in Schmidt, *Kontinuität und Konzentration*, 36–52, at 41. The original may be found in HSPA, HS privat, Pz, öknomisches Papier 1974 mit Unterlagen Bd 1.

9. Since the 1940s American leaders had seen the connection between the Great Depression and dictatorship in exactly the same terms. See John Lewis Gaddis, *The United States and the Origins of the Cold War, 1941–1947* (New York, 1972), 18–20. See also Bundesarchiv, Koblenz (henceforth BA), B136/17765, BuMin für Wirtschaft an das BKamt, Betr.: Antwort der Bundesregierung auf den NATO-Fragebogen 1974, Economic Section, 29 July 1974; and National Archives and Records Administration, College Park, Maryland (henceforth NARA), RG 59, Entry 5177, Office of the Secretary of State, Transcripts of Henry Kissinger's Staff Meetings, 1973–77, Box 2, Secretary's Staff Meeting, 8 January 1974.

10. HSPA, HS privat, Eigene Arbeiten (henceforth EA) 21.6.–14.9.1974, Nr. 4, NATO Rat—Rede vom 26.6.1974; Schmidt, 'Der Politiker als Ökonom', 42.

11. James Callaghan (Prime Minister of the UK, 1976–9), Valéry Giscard d'Estaing (President of France, 1974–81), and Takeo Fukuda (Prime Minister of Japan, 1976–8).

12. Johannes von Karczewski, '*Weltwirtschaft ist unser Schicksal': Helmut Schmidt und die Schaffung der Weltwirtschaftsgipfel* (Bonn, 2008), 78.

13. HSPA, HS privat, Pz, öknomisches Papier 1974 mit Unterlagen Bd. 1, points 3 and 4; Schmidt, 'Der Politiker als Ökonom', 46; HSPA, HS privat, EA 21.6.–14.9.1974, Nr. 7, Speech and handwritten notes, Parteirat Bonn, 29.6.1974—Diskussion zu Helmut Schmidts wirtschaftpolitischem Vortrag.

14. Willy Brandt, *People and Politics* (Boston, 1978), 438; *Foreign Relations of the United States, 1969–1976, Volume E-15, Documents on Western Europe, 1973–1976*, <https://www.history.state.gov/historicaldocuments/frus1969-76ve15p2/ch7>, (henceforth *FRUS 1969–76, vol. E-15*), doc. 279; Ascherson, 'A Man Who Can't Stop Working', 15. In 1982, at the end of his chancellorship, Schmidt would look back and consider it 'a mistake' that he had not taken on the party-chief role. See Willy Brandt and Helmut Schmidt, *Partner und Rivalen: Der Briefwechsel (1958–1992)* (edited and introduced by Meik Woyke) (Bonn, 2015), docs 650–3; and cf. docs 664–6.

15. Helmut Schmidt, *Menschen und Mächte* (Berlin, 1987), 166–7; George P. Shultz, *Turmoil and Triumph: My Years as Secretary of State* (New York, 1993), 146–7.

16. Hartmut Soell, 'Zwischen reaktivem und konzeptionellem Handeln', in Konrad H. Jarausch, ed., *Das Ende der Zuversicht? Die siebziger Jahre als Geschichte* (Göttingen, 2008), 288; Gerald R. Ford, *A Time to Heal* (London, 1979), 221. Cf. Helmut Schmidt, *Weggefährten: Erinnerungen und Reflexionen* (Berlin, 1983), 300–6; Schmidt, *Menschen und Mächte* (Berlin, 1987), 200–21.

17. Address of 17 May 1974, in Helmut Schmidt, *Kontinuität und Konzentration*, 15.

18. Enrico Böhm, *Die Sicherheit des Westens: Entstehung und Funktion der G7-Gipfel (1975–1981)* (Munich, 2014), 84; Robert Gildea, *France Since 1945* (Oxford, 2002), 258–9. On Franco-German cooperation in line with the Elysée Treaty, see Archiv der sozialen Demokratie, Bonn, Helmut Schmidt Archiv (henceforth AdsD, HSA),1/ HSA009010, Carlo Schmid (AA, Koordinator für dt-frz. Zusammenarbeit) to Helmut Schmidt, 12 July 1974; and C. Schmid to H. Schmidt, 14 January 1975.

19. Haig Simonian, *The Privileged Partnership: Franco-German Relations in the European Community, 1969–1984* (Oxford, 1985), 249; HSPA, HS privat, EA 20.5–21.6.1974, Nr. 14, Entwurf einer Eingangserklärung des Bundeskanzlers für die Bundespressekonferenz am 5.6.1974.

20. Daniel J. Sargent, *A Superpower Transformed: The Remaking of American Foreign Relations in the 1970s* (New York, 2015), 186–7; Böhm, *Die Sicherheit des Westens*, 90–1. See also NARA, RG 59, Entry 5177, Office of the Secretary of State, Transcripts of Henry Kissinger's Staff Meetings, 1973–77, Box 2, Acting Secretary's Staff Meeting, 10 June 1974.

21. Helmut Schmidt, 'The Struggle for the World Product: Politics between Power and Morals', *Foreign Affairs* 52, no. 3 (April 1974), 437–51, at 438.

22. 'Bonn: "Radnabe der Allianz"' and 'Wir sind ein erstklassiger Partner', *Der Spiegel*, no. 1–2/1975, 6 January 1975, 22–9, 30–4, at 29, 31. It is noteworthy that earlier, in 1969 in his book *Strategie des Gleichgewichts*, Schmidt had written that in international trade and the world economy West Germany was a *Weltmacht*. See Helmut Schmidt, *Strategie des Gleichgewichts: Deutsche Friedenspolitik und die Weltmächte* (Stuttgart, 1969), 236.

23. Printed in Schmidt, *Kontinuität und Konzentration*, 138–54, at 139.
24. Böhm, *Die Sicherheit des Westens*, 97, note 266. The speech of 24 March 1975 can be found in HSPA, HS privat, EA 19.3.–25.4.1975, Nr. 2a, Heft 'Bergedorfer Gesprächskreis zu Fragen der freien industriellen Gesellschaft, Protokoll–Nr. 50, 1975–Kooperation oder Konfrontation – Stürzt die Wirtschaft in eine weltpolitische Krise?, Referat: Helmut Schmidt'; plus an earlier draft version with Schmidt's handwritten amendments.
25. Horst Möller et al., eds, *Akten zur Auswärtigen Politik der Bundesrepublik Deutschland 1975, Band I: 1. Januar bis 30. Juni 1975* (Munich, 2006) [henceforth *AAPD 1975/I*], doc. 173, 812.
26. *AAPD 1975/I*, doc. 173, 809–11; *AAPD 1975/II*, doc. 222, 1034. BA, B136/16765, Sanne to AL IV, Betr: Gedankenskizze für Bundeskanzler über wirtschaftspolitische Probleme auf der NATO-Gipfelkonferenz, 28./29. Mai, 20 May 1975; and Statement by Schmidt at NATO Summit Meeting, 30 May 1975. Cf. Jeremi Suri, 'Henry Kissinger and the Geopolitics of Globalization', in Niall Ferguson et al., eds, *The Shock of the Global: The 1970s in Perspective* (Cambridge, MA, 2010), 173–88, here esp. 173.
27. Bonn meeting of 27 July 1975, quoted variously from the German and American record in *AAPD 1975/II*, doc. 222, 1035–6, and *Foreign Relations of the United States, 1969–1976, Volume XXXI, Foreign Economic Policy, 1973–1976*, <https://www.history.state.gov/historicaldocuments/frus1969–76v31>, (henceforth *FRUS 1969–76*, vol. 31), doc. 94. See also Böhm, *Die Sicherheit des Westens*, 105–8 and Elizabeth Benning, 'The Road to Rambouillet and the Creation of the Group of Five', in Emmanuel Mourlon-Druol and Federico Romero, eds, *International Summitry and Global Governance: The Rise of the G7 and the European Council, 1974–1991* (London, 2014), 49–50.
28. *AAPD 1975/II*, doc. 222, 1036–7, and *FRUS 1969–76*, vol. 31, doc. 94; Böhm, *Die Sicherheit des Westens*, 107–8.
29. 'Helmut Schmidt: Private Memorandum on International Concertation of Economic Action, 30 July 1975', in Hartmut Soell, ed., *Helmut Schmidt—Pioneer of International Economic and Financial Cooperation* (Heidelberg, 2014), 73–5.
30. 'The West's Summit', *New York Times*, 1 August 1975, 19.
31. 'Memorandum of Conversation, Bonn, 27 July 1975', and 'Memorandum of Conversation, Washington, 17 September 1975', *FRUS 1969–76*, vol. 31, docs 94 and 102.
32. 'Memorandum of Conversation, Washington 17 September 1975', *FRUS 1969–76*, vol. 31, doc. 102; NARA, RG 59, Office of the Counselor—Helmut Sonnenfeldt, Entry A1 5339A—Box no. 3, Economic Summit—Shultz (2 of 2), Hillenbrand at US emb. Bonn to State Department, Subject: Conversation with Chancellor Schmidt, 25 September 1975. Benning, 'Road to Rambouillet', 54; Kissinger, 'The Industrial Democracies and the Future', speech at Pittsburgh, 11 November 1975, 1–12, here 2, 5, Gerald R. Ford Library, White House Press Releases, box 17—digitized, <http://www.fordlibrarymuseum.gov/library/document/0248/whpr19751111-012.pdf>. See also Sargent, *A Superpower Transformed*, 190–2.
33. Clyde H. Farnsworth, 'Shaky Europe looks to the Summit for Aid', *New York Times*, 14 November 1975, 1.
34. James Callaghan, *Time and Chance* (London, 1987), 479–80; Henry Kissinger, *Years of Renewal* (London, 1999), 693–4.
35. 'Memorandum of Conversation, Rambouillet, 15 November 1975', *FRUS 1969–76*, vol. 31, doc. 122; Robert Mauthner, 'Rambouillet: Did the Summit Work?', *The Spectator*, 22 November 1975, 8; Klaus-Peter Schmid, 'Wir fanden einen neuen Geist', *Die Zeit*, 21 November 1975, 2; Ford, remarks to the press, 17 November 1975, The

American Presidency Project (henceforth APP) website, <http://www.presidency.ucsb. edu/ws/index.php?pid=5383&st=&st1>.

36. Cf. NARA, RG 59, Office of the Counselor – Helmut Sonnenfeldt, Entry A1 5339A, Box no. 3a, Economic Summit, Shultz (1 of 2), Economic Summit—Second Session, Sunday, 16 November 1975, 10:45 am; and, Economic Summit—Third Session, Sunday, 16 November 1975, 4:00 pm; and, Economic Summit—Fourth Session, Monday, 16 November 1975, 10:45 am.

37. Callaghan, *Time and Chance*, 479; Harold James, *International Monetary Cooperation since Bretton Woods* (Oxford, 1996), ch. 10, at 263. For the American position at the summit, see NARA, RG 59, Entry 5403, Records of Henry Kissinger 1973–77, Box 2, Thomas Enders to Kissinger, Economic Summit Preparations—Briefing Memorandum + attachments, 4 November 1975.

38. 'The Rambouillet Declaration, 17 November 1975', in Margaret Thatcher Foundation, <http://www.margaretthatcher.org/document/110957>.

39. Kissinger, 'The Industrial Democracies', 8; Robert D. Putnam and Nicholas Bayne, *Hanging Together: Cooperation and Conflict in the Seven-Power Summits* (2nd edn, London, 1987), 35, 42.

40. 'Memorandum of Conversation, Washington, 26 March 1976' and 'Message from Ford to Schmidt, Washington, undated', *FRUS 1969–76*, vol. 31, docs 133 and 137, note 2 (reference to Schmidt's reply to Ford on 22 April 1976); von Karczewski, *'Weltwirtschaft ist unser Schicksal'*, 212, 216.

41. 'Memorandum of Conversation, Washington, 19 May 1976' and 'Editorial note', *FRUS 1969–76*, vol. 31, docs 138 and 139; von Karczewski, *'Weltwirtschaft ist unser Schicksal'*, 215–17; 'Schmidt: Die Rezession ist überwunden', *Frankfurter Allgemeine Zeitung*, 19 June 1976, 11. *AAPD 1976/I*, docs 134 and 138, 610–12, 627.

42. Cf. NARA, RG 59, Office of the Counselor—Helmut Sonnenfeldt, Entry A1 5339A, Box no. 3a, Economic Summit—Puerto Rico (July 1976), Political Setting of the Puerto Rico summit, Department of State, June 1976.

43. Putnam and Bayne, *Hanging Together*, 42–4; Joint Declaration Following the International Summit Conference in Puerto Rico, 28 June 1976, APP website, <http://www.presidency. ucsb.edu/ws/index.php?pid=6157&st=&st1=>; von Karczewski, *'Weltwirtschaft ist unser Schicksal'*, 260.

44. 'Den Deutschen aus der Seele gesprochen', *Der Spiegel*, no. 31/1976, 26 July 1976, 19–23.

45. 'Ford Cabinet meeting, 29 June 1976', *FRUS 1969–76*, vol. 31, doc. 150.

46. See NARA, Office of the Counselor—Helmut Sonnenfeldt, Entry A1 5339A, Box no. 3a, Economic Summit—Puerto Rico (July 1976), Robert Hormats to the White House—Preparatory Meeting for the Puerto Rico Summit, 16 June 1976.

47. AdsD, HSA, 1/HSA006688, Betr.: Wirtschaftsgipfel III, 14 January 1977. Putnam and Bayne, *Hanging Together*, 44–5, 48–9; von Karczewski, *'Weltwirtschaft ist unser Schicksal'*, 262–3; Böhm, *Die Sicherheit des Westens*, 148–53. On the link between the G7 and NATO summits, see BA, B136/16769, Briefing by STS van Well and Dr Terfloth—NATO-Ministerratssitzung, 11 May 1977, 2. For the American position in December 1976—shortly after Jimmy Carter's election to the presidency—in support of a summit meeting in principle but at a later date (namely 'late spring or early summer', by when US economic stimulus policies ought to have been formulated), see Jimmy Carter Presidential Library, Atlanta, Georgia, Office of Staff Secretary, Handwriting File—1976 Campaign Transition File, Foreign Policy 12/76–1/77, Memorandum from W. Michael Blumenthal (Office of the Secretary of the Treasury) to President-elect, 23 December 1976.

48. BA, B136/16769, Downing Street Summit Conference: Declaration + Appendix, May 1977; cf. London Economic Summit Meeting—Joint Declaration Issued at the Conclusion of the Meeting, London, 8 May 1977, APP website, <http://www.presi-dency.ucsb.edu/ws/index.php?pid=7480&st=&st1=>, *AAPD 1977/I*, doc. 114, 587–99; Putnam and Bayne, *Hanging Together*, ch. 4, esp. 69 and 72; Callaghan, *Time and Chance*, 485–6.

49. Fukuda quoted from 'Minutes of the London Economic Summit Meeting, 7 May 1977', in *Foreign Relations of the United States, 1977–1980, Volume III, Foreign Economic Policy*, <https://www.history.state.gov/historicaldocuments/frus1977-80v03>. (hence-forth *FRUS 1977–80*, vol. 3), doc. 27.

50. Memoranda from Henry Owen (US ambassador at large for economic summit affairs) to Carter, 4 February and 8 April 1978, *FRUS 1977–80*, vol. 3, docs 101, 125; von Karczewski, *'Weltwirtschaft ist unser Schicksal'*, 373–6; John Vinocur, 'West Germany Seen Facing a Slowdown in Economic Growth', *New York Times*, 25 April 1978, 49; 'Letter from Carter to Schmidt, 11 April 1978', in Margaret Thatcher Foundation, <http://www.margaretthatcher.org/document/111478>.

51. Terence Smith, 'Reporter's Notebook: Neither All Work Nor All Play at the Economic Conference', and Flora Lewis, 'President of "the Club"', *New York Times*, 17 July 1978, A3 and A1.

52. von Karczewski, *'Weltwirtschaft ist unser Schicksal'*, 374–5; Putnam and Bayne, *Hanging Together*, 79–82, quoting Schmidt on 81.

53. Bonn Economic Summit Declaration Issued at the Conclusion of the Conference, 17 July 1978, APP website, <http://www.presidency.ucsb.edu/ws/index.php?pid=31093& st=&st1=>. Flora Lewis, '7 Industrial Nations Pledge to Spur Jobs, Curb Inflation; U.S. Ready to Cut Oil Imports', *New York Times*, 18 July 1978, A1;. 'Die Weltwirtschaft ist unser Schicksal', *Die Zeit*, 25 February 1983, <http://www.pdf.zeit.de/1983/09/Die-Weltwirtschaft-ist-unser-Schicksal.pdf>.

54. 'Das Wichtigste: Den Absturz vermeiden', *Die Zeit*, 21 July 1978, <http://www.pdf. zeit.de/1978/30/das-wichtigste-den-absturz-vermeiden.pdf>. Callaghan, *Time and Chance*, 495, 497; Nicholas Bayne, 'The Foundations of Summitry', in Mourlon-Druol and Romero, eds, *International Summitry and Global Governance*, 26–7.

55. Theo Sommer, 'Nach dem Gipfel: Eine neue politische Wirklichkeit?', *Die Zeit*, 21 July 1978, 1; Peter Jenkins, 'Schmidt leads the summit party', *The Guardian*, 17 July 1978, 11; 'Summit Message: The U.S. Can No Longer Call the Shots', *New York Times*, 23 July 1978, 15; Paul Lewis, 'Economic Summit Signals Bonn's New Diplomatic Clout', *New York Times*, 23 July 1978, E4; von Karczewski, *'Weltwirtschaft ist unser Schicksal'*, 418–20; Simonian, *Privileged Partnership*, 277–83. For the German Foreign Ministry's positive verdict on Bonn, see *AAPD 1978/II*, doc. 225, 1133–5.

56. 'Memorandum of the Chairman of the CEA (Schultze) to President Carter, Washington, 11 July 1978', *FRUS 1977–80*, vol. 3, doc. 143; 'Schmidt notes for Copenhagen European Council, 7 April 1978, <http://www.margaretthatcher.org/document/111534>; AdsD, HSA, 1/HSA006725, Vermerk—verschlossen, by Schulmann, AL4, 6 November 1978. See also Matthias Schulz, 'The Reluctant European: Helmut Schmidt, the European Community, and Transatlantic Relations', in idem and Thomas A. Schwartz, *The Strained Alliance: U.S.–European Relations from Nixon to Carter* (Cambridge, 2010), 301–5.

57. Quotations from 'Kanzler Schmidt: "Dynamisch wie Napoleon"', *Der Spiegel*, no. 32/1978, 7 August 1978, 19–20. On the relationship between Carter and Byrd, see Jimmy Carter, *Keeping Faith: Memoirs of a President* (New York, 1982), 72–3.

58. Böhm, *Die Sicherheit des Westens*, 145–6; Schmidt, *Menschen und Mächte*, 204; HSPA, EA 24.9.–31.10.1976, Nr. 24, 'I am not a newcomer', *Newsweek*, 18 October 1976, 15.

59. 'Bonn: Nach Carters Wahl ratlos', *Der Spiegel*, no. 46/1976, 8 November 1976, pp. 25–6.

60. See Ford, *A Time to Heal*, 221, where he states 'Both of us [HS and GF] understood the necessity of controlling inflation. Politically, we couldn't tolerate high unemployment, yet we recognized that if we accelerated our economies precipitously to reduce the jobless rate, we would just rekindle the fires of inflation...The course both countries were following now wasn't glamorous, but it was the only path to real recovery.' On Schmidt's views on economic policy in 1976/7, see AdsD, HSA, 1/HSA009302, Erwägungen für 1977 (Marbella Papier), 5 January 1977. This 'economic' paper was originally one of Schmidt's annual letters as chancellor to Herbert Wehner, written during his Christmas holidays as he identified the challenges that awaited him in the new year. This particular letter, nicknamed the 'Marbella Papier' because it was composed in the Spanish resort town of said name, was later polished over Easter 1977 and then sent out to the party leadership and confidants on 22 April 1977, who discussed its conclusions.

61. 'Front gegen den "religiösen Schwärmer"', *Der Spiegel*, no. 15/1978, 10 April 1978, 23–5 (Genscher and Schmidt).

62. Peter Jenkins, 'Schmidt leads the summit party', *The Guardian*, 17 July 1978, 11.

63. For the reference to Schmidt as *Weltökonom*, see for example 'Bonn: Nach Carters Wahl ratlos', *Der Spiegel*, no. 46/1976, 8 November 1976, 25, and 'Der Saisonarbeiter', *Der Spiegel*, no. 47/1976, 15 November 1976, 44.

2. THE STRATEGIST OF BALANCE

1. Helmut Schmidt Privatarchiv, Hamburg (henceforth HSPA), HS privat, Eigene Arbeiten (henceforth EA) 20.5.–21.6.1974, Nr. 21, Rede vor den Lehrgangsteilnehmern der Führungsakademie der Bundeswehr, 11.6.1974.

2. Politisches Archiv des Auswärtigen Amts, Berlin (henceforth PAAA), Zwischenarchiv (henceforth ZA) 113456, 'Die Sicherheitspolitik der Bundesrepublik Deutschland 1974' (undated).

3. See HSPA, HS privat, EA 21.6.–14.9.1974, Nr. 32, Bundespresseamt an BK, fsnr 5113, 12.8.1974—Welt Interview mit Bundeskanzler Schmidt.

4. Helmut Schmidt, *Verteidigung oder Vergeltung: Ein deutscher Beitrag zum strategischen Problem der NATO* (Stuttgart, 1961); Idem, *Strategie des Gleichgewichts: Deutsche Friedenspolitik und die Westmächte* (Stuttgart, 1969). Cf. HSPA, HS privat, EA 20.5.–21.6.1974, Nr. 21, Rede vor den Lehrgangsteilnehmern der Führungsakademie der Bundeswehr, 11.6.1974.

5. Alice Siegert, 'Schmidt Stresses Atlantic Alliance', *Chicago Tribune*, 18 May 1974, 4; Joe Alex Morris Jr, 'Schmidt Shifts Focus from Détente to NATO', *Los Angeles Times*, 18 May 1978, 2.

6. It is noteworthy that Kissinger remembers meeting Schmidt for the first time in Germany in 1957, whereas Schmidt thought it was in Harvard six months later in 1958. See Matthias Naß, '"Ich finde Helmut ziemlich sentimental" – Henry Kissinger über seinen alten Freund Helmut Schmidt, den er noch immer siezt', *Die Zeit*, 19 February 2009, <http://www.zeit.de/2009/09/Zigarette-09>.

7. Henry Kissinger's speech at St.-Michaelis-Kirche on 23 November 2015, in *Zeit online*, <http://www.zeit.de/hamburg/stadtleben/2015-11/helmut-schmidt-staatsakt-rede-henry-kissinger>.

8. Cf. Jussi Hanhimäki, *The Flawed Architect: Henry Kissinger and American Foreign Policy* (New York, 2004); Jeremi Suri, 'Henry Kissinger and the Geopolitics of Globalization', in Niall Ferguson et al., eds, *The Shock of the Global: The 1970s in Perspective* (Cambridge, MA, 2010), 173–88.

9. Helmut Schmidt, 'Politischer Rückblick auf eine unpolitische Jugend', in Helmut Schmidt and Hannelore Schmidt, eds, *Kindheit und Jugend unter Hitler* (Munich, 1994), 209–82.

10. HSPA, HS privat, Presse-Echo, 13.–17. Mai 1974, Chefredaktion Politik, Do. 16.05.1974, 12:40—Kommentar zur Wahl von BK Helmut Schmidt von Oswald Hirschfeld. See also David Binder, 'Helmut Schmidt An All-Round Politician', 8 May 1974, 16. The reference to Schmidt-Schnauze as a 'Markenartikel-Bezeichnung' or an '"ehrenvoll" empfundener Beiname' can be found in HSPA, Presse-Echo 1962 iv, Claus Heinrich Meyer, 'Von Bonn nach Hamburg und zurück? Hellmut [sic] Schmidt wird Innensenator der Hansestadt', *Stuttgarter Zeitung*, 13 December 1961.

11. Fritz Erler (1913–1967) was the SPD's foremost defence expert in the 1950s. He was then the party's defence spokesman, deputy chair of the Bundestag's defence committee in 1953–7, and later leader of the SPD parliamentary party in 1964–7. Schmidt looked up to the more senior and rhetorically gifted Erler as their abundant correspondence reveals. See HSPA, HS privat, Fritz Erler 14.7.1913–22.2.1967—Unterlagen/Korrespondenz 1950–1992.

12. Helmut Schmidt, *Defense or Retaliation: A German View* (New York, 1962), 6.

13. Henry Kissinger, *Nuclear Weapons and Foreign Policy* (New York, 1957) and *The Necessity for Choice: Prospects of American Foreign Policy* (New York, 1960); Robert E. Osgood, *Limited War: The Challenge to American Strategy* (Chicago, 1957) and *NATO: The Entangling Alliance* (Chicago, 1962); Klaus Knorr, *On the Use of Military Power in the Nuclear Age* (Princeton, 1966); Thomas C. Schelling, *The Strategy of Conflict* (Cambridge, MA, 1960); Matt Schudel, 'Roger Hilsman, foreign policy adviser to JFK, dies at 94', *Washington Post*, 8 March 2014.

14. Schmidt, *Defense or Retaliation*, 5–6; B. H. Liddell Hart, *Deterrent or Defence* (London/New York, 1960).

15. HSPA, Presse-Echo 1962 iv, Claus Heinrich Meyer, 'Von Bonn nach Hamburg und zurück? Hellmut [sic] Schmidt wird Innensenator der Hansestadt', *Stuttgarter Zeitung*, 13 December 1961.

16. Denis Healey, *The Time of My Life* (New York, 1990), 247.

17. HSPA, Korrespondenz privat politisch, 1959–1961, A–Z Band 2, Abt. 1960, Nr. 6, Kissinger an Major General C. H. Bonesteel, Secretary of the General Staff, Dept of the Army, Washington, 26.8.1960.

18. HSPA, Korrespondenz privat politisch, 1959–1961, A–Z Band 2, Abt. 1960, Nr. 6, Schmidt an Prof. Dr. Henry Kissinger, Harvard Univ., Center of International Affairs, 8.7.1960. See also HSPA, HS privat, Schriftwechsel—Verteidigung oder Vergeltung, engl. Ausgabe 1961–Allgemeiner Schriftwechsel, Schmidt an Heinrich Seewald 1.7.1960: Here he suggested that 'Meine Hoffnung ist, nicht nur bei den der Sozialdemokratie anhängenden Leser mehr Verständnis für militärische Realitäten zu wecken als auch insbesondere bei den übrigen Lesern Verstädnis zu erwecken für den militärischen Realismus sozialdemokratischer Vorstellungen. Zweifellos wird aber vieles in dem Buch stehen, das auch für meine sozialdemokratischen Freunde im Bundestag überraschend sein mag.'

19. HSPA, HS privat, Schriftwechsel—Verteidigung oder Vergeltung, engl. Ausgabe 1961—Allgemeiner Schriftwechsel, Schmidt to Brandt, Spätherbst 1960 (handwritten).

20. HSPA, HS privat, Schriftwechsel—Verteidigung oder Vergeltung, engl. Ausgabe 1961—Allgemeiner Schriftwechsel, Heinrich Seewald to Schmidt, 4.7.1960.

21. Schmidt, *Defense or Retaliation*, ix. See also n. 40 in this chapter.

22. Schmidt, *Defense or Retaliation*, 206–7.

23. Schmidt, *Defense or Retaliation*, 210.

24. Schmidt, *Defense or Retaliation*, 100–1.

25. Schmidt, *Defense or Retaliation*, 103.

26. Schmidt, *Defense or Retaliation*, 184–5.

27. See HSPA, Presse-Echo 1962 iv, Meyer, 'Von Bonn nach Hamburg und zurück?', *Stuttgarter Zeitung*, 13 December 1961. Meyer commented scathingly: 'In Bonn war er "Experte". Als Verkehrsexperte hat er angefangen, als Militärexperte [im Herbst 1961] aufgehört...'. See also 'Atomwaffen–Wo, was, wie, wann', *Der Spiegel*, no. 14/1961, 29 March 1961, 18–20.

28. On the creation of the new position of Hamburg Senator for Internal Affairs and the issues of public security and disaster management at *Länder*-level, see HSPA, Korrespondenz privat politisch, 1962–1965, A–Z, Bd. 3, 1962, Nr. 5, Friedrich Schäfer (SPD Fraktion) to Schmidt, 15.3.1962 (earlier letter Schmidt to Schäfer, 7.12.1961).

29. HSPA, Korrespondenz, privat politisch 1962–1965, A–Z, Bd. 3, 1962, Nr. 3, Schmidt to Oberst I G Dr Fritz Beermann, Washington, 18.5.1962. Cf. HSPA, Presse-Echo 1962 iv, 'Helmut Schmidt bleibt im Vorstand', *Frankfurter Allgemeine Zeitung*, 4 January 1962; and, 'Helmut Schmidt, Innensenator – In Hamburg: "Alles in einer Hand" – auch Notstandsaufgaben', *Die Andere Zeitung*, 11 January 1962.

30. HSPA, Presse-Echo 1962 iv, Sozialdemokratischer Brief 3/62 Informationen, 7; 'Katastrophen, Rettungs-Einsatz – Herr der Flut', *Der Spiegel*, no. 10/1962, 7 March 1962, 17–30, esp. 26–30.

31. HSPA, Presse-Echo 1962 iv, 'Katastrophen/Sturmflut–Stadt unter', *Der Spiegel*, no. 9/1962, 28 February 1962, 26; 'Katastrophen, Rettungs-Einsatz—Herr der Flut', *Der Spiegel*, no. 10/1962, 7 March 1962, 28. See also HSPA, Material: Flutkatastrophe Febr. 1962, Kopien—EA, Korrespondenz, Presse-Echo, Letter by Konteradmiral Rogge to Der Spiegel, 2 March 1962, re: Titelgeschichte Stadt Unter, 28.2.1962, Nr. 9/1962. Here Rogge praised Schmidt's responsible behaviour in a situation of crisis, and his short and clear orders. He added, 'Es kann gar nicht die Rede sein, daß der Senator "den Anwesenden, vom Admiral bis zum Amtsleiter, über den Mund fuhr"....Ich zitiere aus dem amtlichen Protokoll der Lagebesprechung am 23.2.1962 um 12.00 Uhr:...Er [Rogge] hebt besonders hervor, daß die Art in der Senator Schmidt die bisherigen Lagebesprechungen geführt hat, auch für Vertreter der Bundeswehr beispielhaft gewesen sei.'

32. See Federal Basic Law (Grundgesetz) articles 143, as well as 11 and 13; HSPA, Korrespondenz, privat politisch 1962–1965, A-Z, Bd. 3, 1965, Nr. 9, Schmidt to Jahn MdB, 24.5.1965; Jahn to Schmidt, 14.5.1965.

33. HSPA, Presse-Echo 1962 iv, 'Für Notfälle gewappnet sein—Hamburgs Innensenator sprach über "Notstand und Notverordnung"', *Hamburger Echo*, 28 April 1962.

34. HSPA, Material: Flutkatastrophe Febr. 1962, Kopien—EA, Korrespondenz, Presse-Echo, BK Helmut Schmidt zu seinen Erlebnissen bei der Sturmflut in Hamburg vor 20 Jahren, NDR II, 12:40, 16.2.1982.

35. HSPA, Material: Flutkatastrophe Febr. 1962, Kopien—EA, Korrespondenz, Presse-Echo, Bandabschrift Hamburger Journal (Sturmflut) NDR, 15.2.1982; Günter Stiller,

'Ein Mann der Tat im Heer der Kopflosen', *Hamburger Abendblatt*, 8/9 February 1992.

36. HSPA, Material: Flutkatastrophe Febr. 1962, Kopien—EA, Korrespondenz, Presse-Echo, 'Das Porträt - Der Senator', *Sonntagsblatt*, 6 May 1962.

37. HSPA, HS privat, Presse-Echo, 13.–17.5.1974, 'Bundeskanzler Helmut Schmidt (SPD)', *Hamburger Abendblatt*, 15 May 1974; 'Kanzler Schmidt: Hoffen auf den Macher', *Der Spiegel*, no. 20/1974, 13 May 1974, 19–34.

38. *Der Spiegel* wrote: 'Helmut Schmidt. Kette rauchend, war Herr der Flut'. The article was titled accordingly: 'Katastrophen, Rettungs-Einsatz – Herr der Flut', *Der Spiegel*, no. 10/1962, 7 March 1962, 30.

39. HSPA, Material: Flutkatastrophe Febr. 1962, Kopien—EA, Korrespondenz, Presse-Echo, 'Das Porträt – Der Senator', *Sonntagsblatt*, 6 May 1962; HSPA, Presse-Echo 1962 iv, Sozialdemokratischer Brief 3/62 Informationen, 7.

40. See for example, Oliver B. Hemmerle, 'Explaining NATO to the West Germans: Helmut Schmidt as a Military Affairs Writer in the 1960s', in Christian Nünlist and Anna Locher, eds, *Transatlantic Relations at Stake: Aspects of NATO, 1956–1972* (Zürich, 2006), 219.

41. By 1969 *Verteidigung oder Vergeltung* had appeard in five editions—with twenty thousand copies sold altogether. The English language edition by Oliver & Boyd had sold 4,000 copies, 2,000 of which via the American imprint by Praeger. See HSPA HS privat, Schriftwechsel—Strategie des Gleichgewichts, R. Sommer to Schmidt, 2.12.1969; and, Seewald to Schmid, persönlich/handwritten from *Plättig Hotel*, 3.12.1969.

42. HSPA, HS privat, Schriftwechsel—Strategie des Gleichgewichts, Seewald to Schmidt, 8.5.1969.

43. HSPA, HS privat, Buchmanuskript, Strategie des Gleichgewichts 1969, Paul J. Friedrich (Schmidt's personal assistant) to Schmidt, Notiz for HS—Betr: das neue Buch 'Strategie des Gleichgewichts', 19.12.1968.

44. HSPA HS privat, Schriftwechsel—Strategie des Gleichgewichts, Paul J. Friedrich to Alfred Nau (SPD Parteivorstand) re: Paperback Sonderausgabe, 28.8.1968.

45. HSPA, HS privat, Schriftwechsel—Strategie des Gleichgewichts, Seewald Verlag (R. Sommer) to Schmidt, 16.10.1969; Sommer to Friedrich, 13.11.1969.

46. HSPA, HS privat, Schriftwechsel—Strategie des Gleichgewichts, Seewald to Helmut Schmidt, 11.2.1970; Seewald to Schmidt, 9.3.1970; and, Lieferschein 21663, 15.5.1970.

47. HSPA, HS privat, Schriftwechsel—Strategie des Gleichgewichts, Seewald to Schmidt (on Denis Healey foreword), 26.10. 1970; Löwke to Schmidt, 16.11.1970 re: HS's preface to the English edn.

48. Helmut Schmidt, *The Balance of Power: Germany's Peace Policy and the Super Powers* (Foreword by Denis Healey) (London, 1971), 23.

49. Andreas Vogtmeier, *Egon Bahr und die deutsche Frage zur Entwicklung der sozialdemokratischen Ost- und Deutschlandpolitik vom Kriegsende bis zur Vereinigung* (Bonn, 1996); Gottfried Niedhart, Revisionistische Elemente und die Initiierung friedlichen Wandels in der neuen Ostpolitik 1967–1974, *Geschichte und Gesellschaft* 28, no. 2 (2002), 233–66. See also Oliver Bange, 'An Intricate Web–Ostpolitik, the European Security System and German Unification', in Oliver Bange and Gottfried Niedhart, *Helsinki 1975 and the Transformation of Europe* (Oxford/New York, 2008), 43–64.

50. Schmidt, *The Balance of Power*, 14, 19.

51. Schmidt, *Defense or Retaliation*, 210.

52. Schmidt, *The Balance of Power*, 14.
53. HSPA, Presse-Echo Verteidigungsweißbuch 1970, Minister, Helmut Schmidt (Bundesminister der Verteidigung) zum Inhalt des Verteidigungsweißbuchs, DFS, 22:25, 5.5.1970.
54. HSPA, HS privat, EA 1970, März–2.6.1970, Nr. 50, Rede vor dem Bundestag, 2.6.1970 [Weißbuch Vorwort 20.5.1970 + Endfassung in: *Bulletin der Bundesregierung*, Nr. 77, 4.6.1970, 758]; and Nr. 52, *Weißbuch 1970: Zur Sicherheit der Bundesrepublik Deutschland und zur Lage der Bundeswehr*.
55. Schmidt, *The Balance of Power*, 245–8. See also '*Weißbuch*–Nicht nur Schießen', *Der Spiegel*, no. 21/1970, 18 May 1970, 33–4.
56. HSPA, HS privat, EA 1970, März–2.6.1970, Nr. 38, HS Bundesminister der Verteidigung zum Inhalt des Verteidigungsweißbuchs, DFS, Tagesschau, 22:25, 5.5.1970. See also HSPA, Presse-Echo 1970, Juni, 'Rüstugskontrolle – Bundesverteidigngsminister Helmut Schmidt setzte sich erneut für einen Abbau der militärischen Kräfte in Europa ein', *Bergedorfer Zeitung*, 3 June 1970.
57. HSPA, Presse-Echo zur NATO Ratstagung am 26./27.5.1970 in Rom, Das aktuelle PPP-Interview mit Helmut Schmidt, Truppenreduzierung—Konsequente politische Linie, Bundesregierung gibt Initialzündung für römische Erklärung, 27.5.1970. See also his 1959 speech 'Militärisch "verdünnte" Zonen in Mitteleuropa', in Helmut Schmidt, *Beiträge* (Stuttgart, 1967), 485–503.
58. HSPA, HS privat, EA 1970, März–2.6.1970, Nr. 50, Rede vor dem Bundestag, 2.6.1970; and Nr. 52, *Weißbuch 1970: Zur Sicherheit der Bundesrepublik Deutschland und zur Lage der Bundeswehr*.
59. Bundesministerium der Verteidigung, ed., *Weißbuch 1970: Zur Sicherheit der Bundesrepublik Deutschland und zur Lage der Bundeswehr* (Bonn, 1970), 28 (quotes), 29, 40, 41. For earlier drafts of the White Book, see also HSPA, HS privat, Pz, Dokumentation Weißbuch 1970.
60. 'Regierungserklärung von Helmut Schmidt', 17. Mai 1974, in Deutscher Bundestag, *Stenographische Berichte no. 7/100*, 6593C–6605D.
61. HSPA, HS privat, Presse-Echo 13.–17. Mai 1974, Jens Feddersen, 'Das Tempo Schmidt – Mehr Realismus – weniger Idealismus', *Neue Ruhr Zeitung*, 14 May 1974.
62. HSPA, HS privat, Presse-Echo 13.–17. Mai 1974, Helmut Schmidt—der neue deutsche Bundeskanzler/Porträt, Deutsche Welle, 14.5.74.
63. Neal Ascherson, 'A Man Who Can't Stop Working: Profile', *The Observer*, 19 May 1974, 15.
64. HSPA, HS privat, Presse-Echo, 13.–17. Mai 1974, C.K. in Bonn, 'Helmut Schmidt – ein Realist und Pragmatiker', *Neue Züricher Zeitung*, 15 May 1974.
65. HSPA, HS privat, Presse-Echo, 18.–24. Mai 1974, Fritz Ullrich Flack, 'Realismus in der Ostpolitik', *Frankfurter Allgemeine Zeitung*, 24 May 1974.
66. HSPA, HS privat, Presse-Echo 13.–17. Mai 1974, Helmut Schmidt—der neue deutsche Bundeskanzler/Porträt, Deutsche Welle, 14.5.74; Bernhard Wördedorff, 'Atlantiker, Europäer oder was? Auch dieser Bundeskanzler orientiert Außenpolitik am Staatsinteresse', *Vorwärts*, 16.5.1974; Süddeutscher Rundfunk, Chefredaktion Politik, Do. 16.05.1974, 22:15–22:30—Militärpolitischer Kommentar zur Wahl von Oswald Hirschfeld. The address to the SPD Parteitag in Dortmund on 3 June 1966 was entitled 'Deutschlandpolitik im Wandel der weltpolitischen Bedingungen' and is printed in Schmidt, *Beiträge*, 545–78, esp. 569–78. See also HSPA, HS privat, Presse-Echo, Mai/Juni/Juli 1966, II, 'SPD Parteitag: Schmidt fordert aktive Entspannungspolitik', *Die Welt*, 3 June 1966; 'Schmidt fordert aktive Entspannungspolitik', *Stuttgarter*

Zeitung, 4 June 1966; Norman Crossland, 'SPD takes new line in quest for reunification', *The Guardian*, 4 June 1966.

67. These notes can be found in: HSPA, HS privat, EA 2.6.–31.8.1966, XV. On the *Ostreise*, see also Hans Georg Lehmann, *Öffnung nach Osten: Die Ostreisen Helmut Schmidts und die Entstehung der Ost- und Entspannungspolitik* (Bonn, 1984), esp. ch. 1.

68. Quotes from HSPA, HS privat, EA 2.6.–31.8.1966, XV, Nr. 24, 'Hier und heute – Enttäuscht aus drei Ostblockländern zurück: SPD Politiker Helmut Schmidt', *Quick*, August 1966 (no exact date), 5–9. See also, HSPA, HS privat, EA 2.6.–31.8.1966, XV, Nr. 22, Gedanken in Moskau, 3.8.1966; Nr. 23, Gastfreundschaft im Osten, 9.8.1966; HSPA, HS privat, Presse-Echo, Juli/August/September 1966, III, 'Kurz berichtet: Helmut Schmidt besucht Osteuropa', *Die Welt* 8. July 1966; 'Informationsreise durch Osteuropa, Helmut Schmidt macht erste Station in Prag', *Frankfurter Allgemeine Zeitung*, 18 July 1966; Werner Baumgartner, 'Helmut Schmidt als Tourist in Warschau – "1000 Jahre polnischer Staat" – Massenaufmärsche und Militärparade', *Rhein-Zeitung* (Koblenz), 23/24 July 1966; 'Warschau am Kontakt kaum interessiert – Nur wenige Gesprächspartner für Helmut Schmidt – Keine Illusionen', *Frankfurter Allgmeine Zeitung*, 25 July 1966; 'Helmut Schmidt heute in Moskau', *Hamburger Abendblatt*, 25 July 1966.

69. See Dominik Pick, *Brücken nach Osten: Helmut Schmidt und Polen* [Studien der Helmut Schmidt und Loki Schmidt Stiftung, Bd. 7] (Bremen, 2011),18. N.b. Photographer Sven Simon, son of Axel Springer, joined the Schmidts on their trip; not—as Pick claims—Wolfgang Schulz of the SPD Bundestagsfraktion.

70. HSPA, HS privat, EA 2.6.–31.8.1966, XV, Nr. 22, Gedanken in Moskau, 3.8.1966; Nr. 24, 'Hier und heute – Enttäuscht aus drei Ostblockländern zurück: SPD Politiker Helmut Schmidt', *Quick*, August 1966 (no exact date), 5–9.

71. HSPA, HS privat, EA 2.6.–31.8.1966, XV, Nr. 22, Gedanken in Moskau, 3.8.1966; Nr. 23, Gastfreundschaft im Osten, 9.8.1966; Nr. 24, 'Hier und heute – Enttäuscht aus drei Ostblockländern zurück: SPD Politiker Helmut Schmidt', *Quick*, August 1966 (no exact date), 5–9 and three drafts, 12 August 1966 (Schmidt wanted 'Als Tourist im Osten' as the main title). Author interview with Helmut Schmidt, Hamburg, 15 October 2015.

72. HSPA, HS privat, Presse-Echo Juli/Aug/Sept 1966, III, 'Helmut Schmidt erteilt Ratschläge für Ostpolitik', *Frankfurter Neue Presse*, 16 August 1966; 'Schmidt: Moskau und Prag für stärkeren Handel mit Bonn', *Münchener Merkur*, 16 August 1966. In these public comments Schmidt specifically advocated opening treaty negotiations with the East on the renunciation of force (*Gewaltverzichtsabkommen*) and lobbied for economic and trade relations.

73. 'Rüstungsbegrenzung als Bestandteil außenpolitische Strategie', in Schmidt, *Beiträge*, 597–603.

74. HSPA, HS privat, EA 2.6.–31.8.1966, Nr. 28, Helmut Schmidt, 'Wie gefährlich sind die Russen? – Angst ist eine Fessel', *Sonntagsblatt*, 21 August 1966.

75. HSPA, HS privat, EA 2.6.–31.8.1966, Nr. 28, 'Wie gefährlich sind die Russen? – Angst ist eine Fessel', *Sonntagsblatt*, 21 August 1966.

76. Helmut Schmidt, *Was ich noch sagen wollte* (Munich, 2015), 139–40. *AAPD 1972/III*, doc. 328.

77. Schmidt, *Strategie*, 48–53; Horst Möller et al., eds, *Akten zur Auswärtigen Politik der Bundesrepublik Deutschland 1975, Band II: 1. Juli bis 31. Dezember 1975* (Munich, 2006) [henceforth *AAPD 1975/II*], docs 322, 323 and 326; Helmut Schmidt,

Menschen und Mächte (Berlin, 1987), 356–68; Martin Albers, 'The Policies of Britain, France and West Germany towards the People's Republic of China, 1969–1982', unpublished PhD dissertation, Cambridge University, 2014, 148–52.

78. Albers, 'The Policies of Britain, France and West Germany towards the People's Republic', 251–3, 277–8. *AAPD 1978/I*, doc. 177, 879–81. Schmidt, *The Balance of Power*, 48–53, at 52.

79. *AAPD 1976/I*, doc. 260, 1193. Bundesministerium des Innern and Bundesarchiv, eds, *Dokumente zur Deutschlandpolitik, VI. Reihe, Band 4: 1.1.1975–31.12.1976* (henceforth *DzD 1975–6*), (Munich, 2007), doc. 186, 660; See also *DzD 1975–6*, doc. 219. For the amendment in the GDR's constitution in 1974, eliminating references to the '(all)-German nation', see Bundesministerium der innerdeutschen Beziehungen (ed.), *Zur Lage der Nation* 1975 (Coburg, 1975), 144–5.

80. Archiv der sozialen Demokratie, Bonn, Helmut Schmidt Archiv (henceforth AdsD, HSA), 1/HSA006611 Ausländische Regierungen: R (1975–82), Ref 212 LR I Peters to BK, Betr: Sow Berlin-Pol; Hier Würdigung zum 5. Jahrestag der Unterzeichnung des Vier-Mächte-Abkommens, 7 September 1976; *AAPD 1976/I*, doc. 66, 320–3; doc. 84, 398–9; doc. 149, 669–75; *AAPD 1976/II*, doc. 308, 1405; doc. 321, 1466.

81. 'Bonn Continues Approach to East: Schmidt Expected to Visit Moscow', *New York Times*, 1 June 1974, 5; *AAPD 1974/II*, docs 309, 311–16; Michael Parks, 'Brezhnev Issues Tough Bonn Stand', *The Sun*, 29 October 1974, A4; Christopher S. Wren, 'Schmidt's Talks in Moscow Slow', *New York Times*, 30 October 1974, 5. Cf. HSPA, HS privat, Pz, Helsinki Gespräche, 29.7.–1.8.1975, Nr. 6, Vermerk (von AL II)— Gespräch von Schmidt mit Breschnew in Helsinki am 31.7.1975, 1 August 1975.

82. Cf. National Archives and Records Administration, College Park, Maryland (henceforth NARA), RG 59, Entry 5304, Records of H. Kissinger, 1973–77, Box 2, Winston Lord to Kissinger—Beyond Détente, 10 December 1975; and Lord to Kissinger—Alternative SALT Proposals, 23 Octber 1975.

83. See generally Raymond L. Garthoff, *Détente and Confrontation: American–Soviet Relations from Nixon to Reagan* (Washington DC, 1985), 36–53; Odd Arne Westad, *The Global War* (Cambridge, 2005), 194–7, 241.

84. *AAPD 1976/I*, doc. 152, 686–7, esp. note 7.

85. *AAPD 1976/II*, doc. 350, 1581. See also *AAPD 1975/II*, doc. 315, 1815.

86. 'Ostpolitik: Nichts mehr zu verschenken', *Der Spiegel*, no. 51/1975, 15 December 1975, 21–3.

87. Cf. 'Genscher: Entspannung allein schafft noch keine Sicherheit', *General-Anzeiger*, 23 August 1974; 'Rede des BM Genscher in der 183. Sitzung des Dt. Bundestages am 25.7.1975', in Deutscher Bundestag, ed., *Verhandlungen des Deutschen Bundestages— Stenographische Berichte, 7. Wahlperiode, Bd. 94* (Bonn, 1975), 12797–874, esp. 12798C. See also Dieter Bingen, 'Realistische Entspannungspolitik: Der mühsame Dialog mit dem Osten—die Bundesrepublik und ihre östlichen Nachbarn (1974–1982)', in Hans-Dieter Lucas, ed., *Genscher, Deutschland und Europa* (Baden-Baden, 2002), 155–84; Agnes Bresselau von Bressendorf, *Frieden durch Kommunikation: Das System Genscher und die Entspannungspolitik im Zweiten Kalten Krieg 1979–1982/83* (Berlin, 2015), 83–98.

88. *AAPD 1976/I*, doc. 152, 686–9.

89. *AAPD 1976/II*, doc. 321, 1464.

90. *AAPD 1976/II*, doc. 356, 1599; doc. 321, 1464, note 10; and 1466, note 16.

91. Garthoff, *Détente and Confrontation*, 36; *AAPD 1976/II*, doc. 321, note 16, 1466.

92. *AAPD 1976/I*, docs 45 and 152, 207 and 686–7, note 7. See also Schmidt, *Menschen und Mächte*, 64, 204.

93. See R. E. M. Irving and W. E. Paterson, 'The West German General Election of 1976', *Parliamentary Affairs* 30, no. 2 (1977), 209–25; Geoffrey Pridham, 'Ecologists in Politics: The West German Case', *Parliamentary Affairs* 31, no. 4 (1978), 436–44. 'Keine guten Noten für die Werbemanager: Werner Kaltefleiter über den Bundestagswahlkampf (VII)', *Der Spiegel*, no. 42/1976, 11 October 1976, 26. Cf. Wolfgang Jäger and Werner Link, *Republik im Wandel 1974–1982: Die Ära Schmidt, vol. 5/II* [Geschichte der Bundesrepublik Deutschland] (Stuttgart, 1994), 90–5, 149–55, 162–3.

94. 'Wahlkampf: Maßnehmen und bolzen', *Der Spiegel*, no. 37/1976, 6 September 1976, 21; 'Statt des Duells ein Ball paradox', *Der Spiegel*, no. 40/1976, 27 September 1976, 26–7.

95. Irving and Paterson, 'The West German general election of 1976', 216–17; 'SPD erwartet neue Impulse zur Verbesserung der Ostkontakte: Schmidt verspricht sich Anstöße vom Besuch Breschnews in Bonn', *Frankfurter Allgemeine Zeitung*, 27 September 1976, 1–2.

96. On the CDU and the 1976 election, see Frank Bösch, 'Die Krise als Chance: Die Neuformierung der Christdemokraten in den siebziger Jahren', in Konrad H. Jarausch, ed., *Das Ende der Zuversicht? Die siebziger Jahre als Geschichte* (Göttingen, 2008), 288–301. See also Helmut Kohl, *Erinnerungen, 1930–1982* (Munich, 2004), 378–418. Cf. National Archives and Records Administration, College Park (henceforth NARA), RG 59, Office of the Counselor—Helmut Sonnenfeldt, Entry A1 5339B—Box no. 1, FRG, Mr Hartmann to The Secretary: The FRG after the election, 26 October 1976.

97. Egon Bahr, *Zu meiner Zeit* (Munich, 1996), 509–10; Georgetown University Library Special Collections, Washington, Walter John Stoessel, Jr, Papers, Box 1, Memorandum of Conversation with Egon Bahr, 21 December 1976 (Bahr quote).

98. AdsD, Depositum Egon Bahr, Box 427, Letter Bahr to Schmidt, 19 October 1976; cf. Bahr, *Zu meiner Zeit*, 501.

99. Carter at the United Nations—Address to the General Assembly, 17 March 1977, The American Presidency Project (henceforth APP) website, <http://www.presidency.ucsb.edu/ws/index.php?pid=7183&st=&st1=>; Christian Philip Peterson, 'The Carter Administration and the Promotion of Human Rights in the Soviet Union, 1977–1981', *Diplomatic History* 38, no. 3 (2014), 628–56.

100. Zbigniew Brzezinski, *Power and Principle: Memoirs of the National Security Adviser, 1977–1981* (London, 1983), 156–65; Jimmy Carter, *Keeping Faith: Memoirs of a President* (New York, 1982), 215–19.

101. Anatoly Dobrynin, *In Confidence: Moscow's Ambassador to America's Six Cold War Presidents, 1962–1986* (New York, 1995), 390, 392; cf. 'Gromyko Blasts U.S. for "Cheap" Arms-Talk Tactics', *Los Angeles Times*, 31 March 1977, A2.

102. Murrey Marder, 'Some Aides Feel U.S. Miscalculated', *Washington Post*, 2 April 1977, A1, A14; cf. Brzezinski, *Power and Principle*, 162.

103. *AAPD 1977/1*, doc. 82, esp. 413–19; Raymond L. Garthoff, *Détente and Confrontation*, 575.

104. Schmidt, *Menschen und Mächte*, 222–4; Brzezinski, *Power and Principle*, 291; cf. Michael Getler, 'Much Rides on Outcome of Carter–Schmidt Encounter', *Washington Post*, 6 May 1977, A13.

105. *AAPD 1977/II*, doc. 108, 544.

106. *AAPD 1977/I*, doc. 121, 625; cf. *AAPD 1977/I*, doc. 141, 727–36. The National Archives, Kew, London (henceforth TNA), FCO 46/1486 Speeches at NATO Council Meeting, London (May 1977), Telegram (telno 135) by Owen regarding Carter's speech at 'NATO Ministerial meeting: Morning of 10 May', 10 May 1977; and The White House: Remarks of President Jimmy Carter at NATO Ministerial Meeting, Lancaster House, of Carter's speech, Tuesday, May 10 1977, 10 May 1977.
107. *AAPD 1977/I*, doc. 121, 626; cf. *AAPD 1977/I*, doc. 141, 727–36; TNA, FCO 46/1486, Telegram (telno 136) by Owen regarding Schmidt's speech at 'NATO Ministerial meeting, 10 May', 11 May 1977.
108. *AAPD 1977/I*, doc. 121, 624–7; TNA, FCO 46/1486, Owen's telegram regarding Schmidt's speech, 11 May 1977. See also *AAPD 1977/I*, doc. 108, 544–51.
109. Quote from Christoph Bluth, *Britain, Germany, and Western Nuclear Strategy* (Oxford, 1995), 230.
110. *AAPD 1977/I*, doc. 123, 632; *AAPD 1977/I*, doc. 141, 727–36; TNA, DEFE 13/1141 NATO Defence Planning—Long Term Defence Programme (May 1977–April 1978), Letter from Quinlan to the Private Secretary/Secretary of State on 'NATO Ministerial Guidance 1977', 2 June 1977. The reference to the 'grey area' was first used, it appears, in 1976. See, for example, Gerald R. Ford—Remarks and a Question-and-Answer Session in Portland With Members of the World Affairs Council of Oregon, 22 May 1976, APP website, <http://www.presidency.ucsb.edu/ws/index.php?pid=6028&st=&st1=>; Ford, Presidential Campaign Debate, 6 October 1976, APP website, <http://www.presidency.ucsb.edu/ws/index.php?pid=6414&st=&st1=>. See also Richard Burt, 'The Gray Area', *New York Times*, 25 June, 1976, 22. The 'grey area' then entered public discourse more visibly, after Schmidt's interventions on the issue in 1977 (see chs 3 and 4). Cf. Paul Doty and Robert Metzger, 'Arms Control Enters the Gray Area', *International Security* 3, no. 3 (Winter 1978–1979), 17–52; Treverton, Gregory F., 'Nuclear Weapons and the "Gray Area"', *Foreign Affairs* 57, no. 5 (Summer 1979), 1075–89.

3. DEFUSING THE NEUTRON BOMB

1. Walter Pincus, 'Neutron Killer Warhead Buried in ERDA Budget', *Washington Post*, 6 June 1977, A1; Walter Pincus, 'US asks Congress for Funds to Make "People Killer" Neutron Bombs', *The Guardian*, 7 June 1977, 4; 'Amerikaner stellen Neutronen-Bomben her', *Frankfurter Allgemeine Zeitung*, 7 June 1977, 1.
2. Walter Pincus, 'Senate Pressed for Killer Warhead', *Washington Post*, 21 June 1977, A2; Walter Pincus, 'Carter Urges Production Funds for Neutron A-Weapon', *Washington Post*, 13 July 1977, A1.
3. Egon Bahr, 'Ist die Menschheit dabei, verrückt zu werden', *Vorwärts*, 21 July 1977, 4; Michael Getler, 'Bonn Party Chief Says U.S. Bomb A "Perversion"', *Washington Post*, 17 July 1977, A1.
4. 'Lichtblitz über der Elbe', *Der Spiegel*, no. 30/1977, 18 July 1977, 19–27; 'Wir wissen nun, was auf uns zukommt', *Der Spiegel*, no. 31/1977, 25 July 1977, 22; Michael Getler, 'Bonn Steps Up Debate Over Neutron Bomb', *Washington Post*, 24 July 1977, A6.
5. Archiv der sozialen Demokratie, Bonn, Depositum Egon Bahr (henceforth AdsD, DEB) Boxes 13 and 22 Zuschriften N-Bombe (1977–78). See also Boxes 17 and 20, Neutronenbombe I and II (1977–79). On the concept of an 'attentive public', see Thomas Risse-Kappen, *Die Krise der Sicherheitspolitik: Neuorientierungen und*

Entscheidungsprozesse im politischen System der Bundesrepublik Deutschland 1977–1984 (Munich, 1988), 87. AdsD, DEB, Box 13, Letters by Deckert, 21 July 1977; NRW Minister Deneke, 18 August 1977; Drenger, 6 August 1977; Foitzik, 26 July 1977; SPD Ortsverein Weilhein, 19 July 1977; Bohne, 18 July 1977. AdsD, DEB, Box 22, Letters by Harbig, 21 July 1977; Rausch, 18 July 1977; Sandreczki, 22 July 1977.

6. Horst Möller et al., eds, *Akten zur Auswärtigen Politik der Bundesrepublik Deutschland 1977, Band II: 1. Juli bis 31. Dezember 1977* (Munich, 2008) (henceforth *AAPD 1977/II*), doc. 232, 1149, note 12. See also National Archives, Kew, London (henceforth TNA), DEFE 68/353 Improving the effectiveness of NATO's theatre nuclear forces 1.1.–31.12.1976 and FCO 46/1825 Theatre Nuclear Force (TNF) modernisation: long term defence planning 1.1.–31.12.1978 [Part A].

7. Jimmy Carter Presidential Library, Atlanta, Georgia, Carter Presidential Papers Staff Offices, NSA–Brzezinski Material, Subject File (henceforth JCL, CPPSO, NSA–BM, SF), Box 16, ERW and Radiological Warfare (RW), 6–8/77, Vance to President, Subject: European Attitudes toward the Neutron Bomb, 25 July 1977. See also Politisches Archiv des Auswärtigen Amts, Berlin (henceforth PAAA), B150 1977, Dr Hofstetter to Bundesminister, 19 July 1977.

8. Ibid.; *AAPD 1977/II*, doc. 198, 996, note 15. See also JCL, CPPSO, NSA–BM, SF, Box 16, ERW and RW, 6–8/77, Carter to Stennis, 12 July 1977.

9. Walter Pincus, 'Pentagon Wanted Secrecy on Neutron Bomb Production', *Washington Post*, 25 June 1977, A1; see also Olav Njølstad, *Peacekeeper and Troublemaker: The Containment Policy of Jimmy Carter, 1977–1978* (Oslo, 1995), 101–2.

10. Quotes from Martin Tolchin, 'Neutron Bomb Fund Debated by Senate in a Secret Session', *New York Times*, 2 July 1977, 1, 5.

11. Ibid.; Walter Pincus, 'New Bomb Advances in Senate', *Washington Post*, 2 July 1977, A1.

12. 'It is…Not a New Weapon', *Washington Post*, 13 July 1977, A14. See also *AAPD 1977/II*, doc. 198, 997.

13. Congressional Record (13 July 1977), S11757. See also Bernard Weinraub, 'Senate Votes For Neutron Bombs, Heeding Carter Plea', *New York Times*, 14 July 1977, 5.

14. *AAPD 1977/II*, doc. 186, 950–60; doc. 197, 992–4; doc. 198, 995–7; cf. 'Schmidt-Reise: Kleines Mirakel', *Der Spiegel*, no. 30/1977, 18 July 1977, 28–30.

15. JCL, CPPSO, NSA–BM, SF, Box 16, ERW–RW, 6–8/77, Vance's memorandum for the president, 'European Attitudes toward the "Neutron Bomb"'. See also 'Bonn schaltet sich in die Diskussion über Neutronen-Bombe ein', *Frankfurter Allgemeine Zeitung*, 19 July 1977, 1.

16. Egon Bahr, 'Es geht um die Skala unserer Werte', *Vorwärts*, 28 July 1977, 9.

17. AdsD, DEB, Box 22, Letter by Haase-Wunderlich, 28 July 1977.

18. AdsD, DEB, Box 13, Letter by Diedrichs, 18 July 1977.

19. AdsD, DEB, Box 13, Letter by Goebel, 27 July 1977.

20. AdsD, DEB, Box 20, file 1 Kommentare Neutronenbombe I (1977–79). See also Sherri L. Wasserman, *The Neutron Bomb Controversy* (New York, 1983), 68.

21. See Deutscher Bundestag, 79. Sitzung (9.3.1978), 6125–32, esp. 6127.

22. See, for example, Michael Getler, 'Bonn Steps up Debate over Neutron Bomb', *Washington Post*, 24 July 1977, A6. AdsD, DEB, Box 20, Mappe 2, 'Neuer Antrieb für das Wettrüsten? Vorwärts-Interview mit General a. D. Wolf Graf Baudissin', *Vorwärts*, 15 September 1977, 8. Die Angst der SPD vor der Bombe', *Süddeutsche Zeitung*, 11 October 1977. See also former General Steinhoff's press statements in *AAPD 1977/II*, doc. 257, 1251, note 7.

23. Michael Getler, 'Bonn Steps up Debate over Neutron Bomb,' *Washington Post*, 24 July 1977, A6.

24. AdsD, DEB, Box 20, Mappe 2, 'Egon Bahr bekräftigt sein "Nein" zur Neutronenbombe', *Die Welt*, 17 August 1977. On linguistic similarities between Bahr and West German Communists (and the latter's positive references to Bahr's activities), see copies of articles from the German Communist Party's (DKP) newspaper *Unsere Zeit* during August and September 1977. On suspicions regarding Bahr's language, see also Deutscher Bundestag, 67. Sitzung (24.1.1978), 5162.

25. See Hans-Dietrich Genscher, *Erinnerungen* (Berlin, 1995), 404. Cf. Egon Bahr, *Zu meiner Zeit* (Munich: 2006), 484–6.

26. 'Neutron critic', *The Guardian*, 26 July 1977, 6.

27. Walter Pincus, 'Carter Delays Decision on Neutron Weapons', *Washington Post*, 16 August 1977, A6.

28. Zbigniew Brzezinski, *Power and Principle: Memoirs of the National Security Adviser, 1977–1981* (London, 1983), 302. See also JCL, CPPSO, NSA–BM, SF, Box 16, ERW–RW, 6–8/77, Hunter and Utgoff to Brzezinski, Subject: Consultations on the neutron bomb, undated.

29. JCL, CPPSO, NSA–BM, SF, Box 16, ERW–RW, 6–8/77, DTG 0412212 Aug 77, Perez to Sec state, Subject: Handling the neutron bomb issue in NATO, 4 August 1977.

30. JCL, CPPSO, NSA–BM, SF, Box 16, ERW–RW, 6–8/77, 130056Z Aug 77, Stoessel to State Department, Subject: German attitudes on neutron warhead, 13 August 1977.

31. Quoted in Brzezinski, *Power and Principle*, 302.

32. Njølstad, *Peacemaker*, 107–11.

33. JCL, CPPSO, NSA–BM, SF, Box 16, ERW–RW, 6–8/77, Brzezinski to President (cover letter with Vance memo), undated (July 1977?).

34. JCL, CPPSO, NSA–BM, SF, Box 17, ERW–RW, 9/77–1/78, Thomson and Utgoff to Brzezinski, Subject: Neutron Bomb Consultations, 8 September 1977; Kevin Klose, 'Neutron Plans Belie US Pleas – Kremlin', *The Guardian*, 1 August 1977, 7; 'Gromyko Calls for a UN Ban on the Neutron Bomb', *The Guardian*, 28 September 1977, 6; cf. Politisches Archiv des Auswärtigen Amts, Berlin (henceforth PAAA), B150 1977, Meyer-Landrut to Staatssekretär, Betr.: Auswirkungen der Neutronenwaffe auf das Ost–West Verhältnis + Annex, 29 September 1977.

35. TNA, DEFE 11/810 Enhanced Radiation Weapons: The Neutron Bomb 1.1.1977–31.12.1978, P. M. Stanford, Attachment: Enhanced Radiation Warheads—Draft DOP Paper: Note by Ministry of Defence Officials, 4 October 1977; Owen to MOD, Telno. 2596, 23 September 1977.

36. PAAA, B150 1977, DG20 to Bundesminister, Betr.: Neutronenwaffe, 30 August 1977.

37. PAAA, B150 1977, Abteilung 2 to Bundesminister, Betr.: Neutronenwaffe, Annex: draft letter to the chancellor, 1 September 1977. For Schmidt's, Genscher's, and Leber's early views and cautiousness, see AdsD, DEB Box 20, Mappe 1, Stichworte zur Sicherheitspolitik Nr. 8/77 (August 1977); Brzezinski, *Power and Principle*, 302.

38. PAAA, B150 1977, Dr Dannenbring to Bundesminister, Betr.: Neutronenwaffen, 29 August 1977; TNA DEFE 11/810, PM's visit to Bonn 9.–10.9.1977. N.b. in UK government documents reference was also made to the reduced blast (RB) warhead/weapon. But considering how the warhead gained publicity, it was the 'enhanced radiation' aspect that became emphasized and notorious.

39. PAAA, B150 1977, Wischnewski to Genscher, 23 August 1977.

40. PAAA, B150 1977, Abteilung 2 to Minister, incl. attachment 'Nationale Bewertung der verteidigungs-, außen- und rüstungskonrollpolitschen Implikationen der Neutronenwaffe', 1 September 1977. See also AdsD, DEB Box 412B, Mappe 1, Chef BKA, Schüler, to Bahr. Betr.: BSR am 6.10.1977, 5 October 1977.

41. See Wasserman, *Neutron Bomb*, 71.

42. PAAA, B150 1977, DG20 to Bundesminister, Betr.: Neutronenwaffe, 6 September 1977.

43. PAAA, B150 1977, DG20 to Minister, Betr: Neutronenwaffe, 14 September 1977.

44. See, for example, AdsD, DEB, Box 20, Mappe 2, 'Bundesweite Aktionen gegen Neutronenbombe', *Unsere Zeit*, 3 September 1977.

45. JCL, CPPSO, NSA–BM, President's Correspondence with Foreign Leaders File, Fiji–FRG, Box 6, Letter Schmidt to Carter, 7 September 1977; cf. JCL, CPPSO, NSA–BM, SF, Box 17, ERW–RW, 9/77–1/78, Memorandum: David Aaron to President, Subject: report on Enhanced Radiation (ER) Warhead Consultations, undated.

46. PAAA, B150 1977, Dannenbring to Washington, Betr: Neutronenwaffe, Hier: Deutsch-amerikanische Gespräche im BMVg am 12. September 1977, 14 September 1977; and, Pfeffer to Bundesminister, Betr: Neutronenwaffe, 14 September 1977.

47. PAAA, B150 1977, Pauls to Bonn AA, Telno. 1144, Betr.: Nukleare Planungsgruppe (NPG), 28 September 1977. TNA, DEFE 11/810, Killick to MODUK, Telno. 312, 13 Sept. 1977; and, Killick to MODUK, Telno. 332, 27 September 1977.

48. JCL, CPPSO, NSA–BM, SF, Box 17, ERW–RW, 9/77–1/78, Memoranda by Vance and Brown for President, 16 September 1977 and 23 September 1977. TNA, DEFE 11/810, Killick to MODUK, Telno. 332, 27 September 1977.

49. AdsD, DEB, Box 20, Mappe 2, 'Die Angst der SPD vor der Bombe,' *Süddeutsche Zeitung*, 11 October 1978.

50. AdsD, DEB, Box 22 Zuschriften zur N-Bombe (H–Z), Letter Bahr to Schmude, 28 Sept 1977.

51. AdsD, DEB, Box 413, Mappe 2 Verschiedenes 15.3.1978–7.5.1979, Letter Schmidt to Bahr, 13 September 1978. On tactical mistakes made in Washington, cf. *AAPD 1977/II*, doc. 198, 995–6, note 9.

52. Cyrus Vance, *Hard Choices: Critical Years in America's Foreign Policy* (New York, 1983), 67–9; *AAPD 1977/II*, doc. 257, 1252–3; Klaus Wiegrefe, *Das Zerwürfnis: Helmut Schmidt, Jimmy Carter und die Krise der deutsch-amerikanischen Beziehungen* (Berlin, 2005), 187.

53. AdsD, DEB, Box 20, Mappe 1, Bundesministerium der Verteidigung, Informations- und Pressestab—Material für die Presse: Die Neutronenbombe, 14 October 1977, 8.

54. *AAPD 1977/II*, doc. 257, 1250–3; PAAA, B150 1977, Bonn AA to Washington, Telno. 4309, 28 September 1977.

55. *AAPD 1977/II*, doc. 275, 1331, 1329.

56. *AAPD 1977/II*, doc. 286, 1385–7, esp. 1387.

57. *AAPD 1977/II*, doc. 286, 1387. TNA, PREM 16/1576 DEFENCE: Deployment of Enhanced Radiation Weapons (ERW) in Europe, part 1, 15.9.1977–22.2.1978, Letter R. L. L. Facer to B. G. Cartledge—Enhanced Radiation Warheads, 13 October 1977.

58. Tim Geiger, 'Die "Landshut" in Mogadischu: Das außenpolitische Krisenmanagement des Bundesregierung angesichts der terroristischen Herausforderung 1977', *Vierteljahrshefte für Zeitgeschichte* 57, no. 3 (2009), 413–56.

59. 'Nach Mogadischu: Der bewunderte Deutsche', *Der Spiegel*, no. 44/1977, 24 October 1977. See also Schmidt's own reflections in Helmut Schmidt, *Was ich noch sagen wollte* (Munich, 2015), 27–8.

60. Helmut Schmidt, 'The 1977 Alastair Buchan Memorial Lecture', *Survival* 20, no. 1 (Jan.–Feb. 1978), 2–5.

61. AdsD, HSA, Bundeskanzler, Auslandsreisen (1976–7), Bd. 154, Box 1/HSAA006791, Correspondence relating to IISS Lecture (letters and drafts of speech) dated 14 December 1976; 11 January 1977; 1 and 18 March 1977; 10 and 19 August 1977; 12 September 1977. See also Helmut Schmidt Privatarchiv, Hamburg (henceforth HSPA), HS privat, Eigene Arbeiten (henceforth EA) 20.10.–15.11.1977, Nr. 8, Bulletin der Bundesregierung, no.112, 1013 [Volltext IISS Rede] and internal communication over the making of the speech with Rolf Breitenbein, Walther Stützle, Dr Konrad Seitz, and Dr Udo F. Löwke.

62. Schmidt, 'The 1977 Alastair Buchan Memorial Lecture', 4.

63. Schmidt, 'The 1977 Alastair Buchan Memorial Lecture', 4.

64. PAAA, ZA 109383, Bundesfachausschuß für Friedens- und Sicherheitspolitik, 14./16.10.1977—Vorschlag für die Beschlußfassung der FDP Fraktion zum Thema Neutronenwaffe.

65. *AAPD 1977/II*, doc. 318, 1529.

66. *AAPD 1977/II*, doc. 318, 1529–30; Wasserman, *Neutron Bomb*, 91.

67. See the issue *Vorwärts*, 27 October 1977, 10–11. See also *Vorwärts—Beilage*, 27 October 1977, 1–8; *Vorwärts*, 19 November 1977, 15–18. AdsD, DEB, Box 20, Mappe 2, Christian Potyka, 'Die Angst der SPD vor der Bombe', *Süddeutsche Zeitung*, 11 October 1977.

68. *AAPD 1977/II*, Doc. 345, 1659, note 27.

69. *AAPD 1977/II*, Doc. 345, 1659, notes 26 and 27. Rückriegel to BM, Betr: Neutronenwaffe, hier: Empfehlung des SPD Parteitags in Hamburg (15.–19.11.1977), 25 November 1977, PAAA, ZA 109383. Cf. TNA, FCO 46/1811—United States Neutron Bomb: Enhanced Radiation Warheads (ERWs) 1.1.–31.12.1978 [Part A], Wright to FCO, Telno. 46, 19 January 1978.

70. *AAPD 1977/II*, doc. 318, 1530; cf. PAAA, B150 1978, Van Well to Abteilung 2, Betr.: Gespräch BK mit Carter, 3.1.1978, 2 January 1978.

71. JCL, CPPSO, NSA–BM, SF, Box 17, ERW–RW, 9/77–1/78, Special Coordination Committee Meeting, 16 November 1977; Brzezinski, *Power and Principle*, 302.

72. JCL, CPPSO, NSA–BM, SF, Box 17 ERW–RW, 9/77–1/78, Brzezinski to President, 'FRG Position on Enhanced Radiation', undated—as covering note to memo from Brown to President, 8 December 1977, 8.

73. PAAA, B150 1977, Abt. 2—Staatssekretär, 28 November 1977, Sprechzettel, Betr.: Sitzung des BSR am 29. November 1977; JCL, CPPSO, NSA–BM, SF, Box 17, ERW–RW, 9/77–1/78, Special Coordination Committee Meeting, 16 November 1977; Brzezinski, *Power and Principle*, 302–3; cf. Wasserman, *Neutron Bomb*, 94–7.

74. *AAPD 1977/II*, doc. 366, 1762, note 3. Cf. Brzezinski, *Power and Principle*, 303.

75. *AAPD 1977/II*, doc. 318, 1530, note 23.

76. TNA, DEFE 11/810—Enhanced Radiation Weapons: The Neutron Bomb 1.1.1977–31.12.1978, Wright to MoD, Telno. 1071, 23 November 1977.

77. *AAPD 1977/II*, doc. 331, 1542–5, doc. 354, 1707. Cf. *AAPD 1977/I*, doc. 36; PAAA, ZA 113115, Stand der deutsch-sowjetischen Beziehungen (August 1978).

78. PAAA B150, Wieck to Bonn AA, Telno. 148, 12 January 1978. Cf. 'If U.S. Builds Neutron Bomb, So Will We, Brezhnev Says', *Chicago Tribune*, 24 December 1977, 1; 'Whither SALT', *Chicago Tribune*, 1 January 1978, Section 2, 4; 'Warnke Scoffs at Russ threat on Neutron Bomb', *Chicago Tribune*, 7 January 1978, 5.

79. *AAPD 1977/II*, doc. 354, 1706–7, notes 6–10. PAAA, B150 1978, Pfeffer to Bundesminister, Betr.: Neutronenwaffe, 11 January 1978.

80. *AAPD 1977/II*, doc. 354, 1705, note 3.

81. *AAPD 1977/II*, doc. 362, 1746, note 8; see also doc. 338, 1620. PAAA, B150 1978, Pfeffer to Bundesminister, Betr.: Neutronenwaffe, 11 January 1978; Van Well to Abteilung 2, Betr.: Gespräch zwischen BK und Carter am 3.1.1978, 2 January 1978.

82. *AAPD 1978/I*, doc. 6, 48–54. PAAA, B150 1978, Staden to Bonn AA, Telno. 327, 25 January 1978; Boss, NATO to Bonn AA, Telno. 164, 8 February 1978. TNA, FCO 46/1812—United States Neutron Bomb: Enhanced Radiation Warheads (ERWs) 1.1.–31.12.1978 [Part B], Brief notes by Kieran Prendergast of Owen's reactions to telegrams (no 35 and 74) by Holmer, 3 January 1978.

83. *AAPD 1977/II*, doc. 374; doc. 366, 1762, note 5.

84. JCL, CPPSO, NSA–BM, SF, ERW–RW, 9/77–1/78, Brown's Memorandum to President, 8 December 1977.

85. De Gaulle pulled France out of the military command structure in 1966. On breaking the German–American deadlock, see PAAA, B150 1978, Van Well to Abteilung 2, Betr.: Gespräch zwischen BK und Carter am 3.1.1978, 2 January 1978.

86. *AAPD 1978/I*, doc. 23, 139, esp. note 3; doc. 29, 176, esp. note 5. PAAA, B150 1978, BSR Beschluss, 30 January 1978. See also *AAPD 1978/I*, doc. 104, 502.

87. PAAA, B150 1978, Staden to Bonn AA, Telno. 327, 25 January 1978. AdsD, DEB, Box 356, Graf Rantzau, Betr.: Amerikanischer Vorschlag zur Behandlung der Neutronenwaffe im Bündnis, 23 February 1978.

88. PAAA B150, Van Well to Ruhfus, 30 January 1978 plus Annex on BSR decision. *AAPD 1978/I*, doc. 23, 138–43 and esp. 139, note 3; doc. 43, 237–8. Cf. TNA DEFE 11/810, Bullard to Wilberforce, Telno. 74, 30 January 1978; TNA, FCO 46/1812, Owen to Wright, Telno. 43, 3 February 1978.

89. PAAA, B150 1978, D2 an Bundesminister, Betr.: Neutronenwaffe, 10 March 1978; *AAPD 1978/I*, doc. 55.

90. TNA, DEFE 24/1656—Nuclear Policy: Enhanced Radiation Warheads (Neutron Bomb); Concerns of NATO Members 1.1.1978–31.12.1979 [Part F], Draft paper on ERWs by Tebbit, 10 February 1978; Mendelsohn to Jung, 27 February 1978 plus annex on the 'US ERW arms control proposal'. PAAA, B150 1978, Abteilung 2 to Bundesminister, 21 February 1978; Blech an Botschaft Washington, Plurez 23 February 1978; Abteilung 2 to Bundesminister, Betr.: Neutronenwaffe—Operative Überlegungen im Hinblick auf BSR Sitzung am 14.3.1978, 14 March 1978.

91. AdsD, DEB, Box 13, Mappe 1, 'Neutronenwaffe und Entspannung'—Bahr's typeset, published in *Flensburger Tageblatt*, 4 February 1978; see also TNA, PREM 16/1577, Wright to FCO, Telno. 168, 3 March 1978.

92. PAAA, B150 1978, Abteilung 2 to Bundesminister, 21 February 1978; Staden to Bonn AA, Telno. 836, 3 March 1978; To Minister, 7 March 1978; Ruth to Staatssekretär, 15 March 1978; AAPD, doc. 77, 381. Cf. TNA, PREM 16/1577, Wright to FCO, Telno. 179, 10 March 1978.

93. PAAA B150, Staden an Bonn AA, Telno. 760, 27 February 1978; Dannenbring, Betr.: Neutronenwaffe, 3 March 1978; Memorandum by Lewalter, 15 March 1978.

94. JCL, CPPSO, NSA–BM, SF, Box 17, ERW–RW, 2–4/78, Memorandum Brzezinski to President, 18 March 1978. See also President Carter's Vacations while in Office, <http://www.jimmycarterlibrary.gov/documents/jec/trips.phtml>.

95. Jimmy Carter, *Keeping Faith: Memoirs of a President* (New York, 1982), 226–7; Vance, *Hard Choices*, 94; Brzezinski, *Power and Principle*, 304–5.

96. Brzezinski, *Power and Principle*, 303–4; Vance, *Hard Choices*, 93–5.
97. *AAPD 1978/I*, doc. 76, 376–80.
98. PAAA B150, Betr.: Neutronenwaffe; hier: Haltung der Verbündeten, 2 April 1978; cf. TNA, FCO 46/1816—United States Neutron Bomb: Enhanced Radiation Warheads (ERWs), 1.1.–31.12.1978 [Part F], Clay to Private Secretary, 3 April 1978; PAAA, B150 1978, Abt. 2 to Bundesminister, Betr.: Deutsch–Niederländische Konsultationen, 8 March 1978; Blech to London embassy (Drahterlaß) + attachments, 5 April 1978. Carter, *Keeping Faith*, 226.
99. Brzezinski, *Power and Principle*, 304–5.
100. PAAA, B150 1978, Dg22 an Staatssekretär, Betr.: Neutronenwaffe, 28 March 1978; Betr.:Neutronenwaffe, hier: Sprechzettel für die BSR-Sitzung, 3 April 1978. *AAPD 1978/I*, doc. 93.
101. Ibid. See also Jonathan Steele, 'Arms Talks Swing Carter against Neutron Bomb,' *The Guardian*, 5 April 1978, 1.
102. Walter Pincus, 'U.S. Pulls Back From NATO Neutron Weapons Discussions', *Washington Post*, 28 March 1978, A3; 'Neutron Bomb Discussion', *Washington Post*, 31 March 1978, A26. See also TNA, PREM 16/1577, Jay to FCO, Telno. 1289, 28 March 1978.
103. Richard Burt, 'Aides Report Carter Bans Neutron Bomb: Some Seek Reversal', *New York Times*, 4 April 1978, 1, 4; Bernard Gwertzman, 'Neutron Policy and Diplomacy: Administration Facing Difficult Explanations', *New York Times*, 5 April 1978, 1, 6, 9; Michael Getler, 'Carter Given Alternatives to Barring Neutron Arms', *Washington Post*, 6 April 1978, A1.
104. *AAPD 1978/I*, doc. 96, 480–3. See also Hans-Dietrich Genscher, *Erinnerungen* (Berlin, 1995), 405–9.
105. *AAPD 1978/I*, doc. 94, 476–8. See also PAAA, ZA 112971, Leitfaden für Hintergrundsgespräch am 7. April (rüstungskontrollpolitischer Teil), 7 April 1978; Sprechzettel für die Unterrichtung des Auswärtigen und Verteidigungsausschusses am 10. April 1978, undated.
106. Brzezinski, *Power and Principle*, 305; Vance, *Hard Choices*, 94–6. Richard Burt, 'Carter Said to Favor Delay in Production of the Neutron Bomb', *New York Times*, 7 April 1978, 1, 6, 11; Harry Kelly and Jack Fuller, 'Neutron Weapon Put Off,' *Chicago Tribune*, 8 April 1978, 1, 4. On the whole deferral episode and backchannel politicking, cf. *AAPD 1978/I*, docs 92–8, 103, 104, 106, 108, 109. TNA, PREM 16/1577, Carter to Callaghan, 6 April 1978; Robinson to FCO, Telno. 1456, 7 April 1978.
107. It is noteworthy that the FDP was the first party to publicly announce, on 21 February 1978, its firm willingness to support a positive US production decision (on the basis of the January BSR caveats). At equidistance from the entirely positive CDU/CSU party declaration of the same day and the more hesitant SPD position, it is furthermore significant that the FDP for the first time in its history signed up to a deployment of nuclear weapons under certain preconditions. For the declarations, see see AdsD, DEB, Ordner 20, Mappe 1, fdk Tagesdienst (FDP) and Deutschland-Union-Dienst (CDU/CSU).
108. TNA, PREM 16/1577, Bullard to FCO, Telno. 257, 8 April 1978. Cf. PAAA, B150 1978, Betr.: Neutronenwaffe; hier: Mögliche Konsequenzen der Entscheidung des amerikanischen Präsidenten, 2 April 1978. '"Jämmerliche Haltung" – Interview mit Strauß', *Die Welt*, 8 April 1978.
109. Kinkel quoted in TNA, PREM 16/1577, Bullard to FCO, Telno. 259, 11 April 1978. See also Walter Ellis, 'Germans Are Fed Up With US Demands', *The Guardian*, 16 April 1978, 6.

110. Genscher, *Erinnerungen*, 408.
111. HSPA, HS privat, EA 21.2.–14.4.1978, Nr. 20, Sprechzettel für die Unterrichtung des Auswärtigen und Verteidingungsausschusses am 10.4.1978.
112. PAAA, B150 1978, Dannenbring, Drahterlaβ to embassies in London, Paris, Moscow, and Brussels, 10 April 1978.

4. CONSTRUCTING THE DUAL TRACK

1. Zbigniew Brzezinski, *Power and Principle: Memoirs of the National Security Adviser, 1977–1981* (London, 1983), 206.
2. The National Archives, Kew, London (henceforth TNA), FCO 46/1825 Theatre Nuclear Force (TNF) Modernisation: Long Term Defence Planning (January–May 1978); Woodworth's Discussion Paper, 7 February 1978, 3; Loose Minute by Tebbit incl. paper: 'Theatre Nuclear Weapons Modernisation: Task force 10 – Record of NPG High Level Group Meeting held at Los Alamos 16/17 February 1978', 1 March 1978, 5–8, 10. Cf. the slightly less detailed Norwegian HLG record, Det kgl. Forsvarsdepartementet, Oslo (hereafter FD-NOR), FD 200.18 MNW 1978, Letter from John A. Lunde to Det Kgl. Forsvaresdepartemente incl. 'NPG-High Level Group on TNF modernization – hovedpunktene fra møtet i Los Alamos 16–17 februar 1978 (28/2/78)', 2 March 1978. Cf. H. H. Gaffney's recollections, 'The History of the Euromissiles', 1 Sept. 2003, <http://www.worldsecuritynetwork.com/NATO/Gaffney-H.-H/The-History-of-the-Euromissiles>; and Henry H. Gaffney, 'Euromissiles as the Ultimate Evolution of Theater Nuclear Forces', *Journal of Cold War Studies* 16, no. 1 (2014), 180–99.
3. TNA, FCO 46/1825, Loose Minute by Tebbit incl. paper: 'Theatre Nuclear Weapons Modernisation: Task force 10 – Record of NPG High Level Group Meeting held at Los Alamos 16/17 February 1978', 1 March 1978, 1–5.
4. Ibid., 8–9.
5. N.b. France was not a member of the NPG, due to its historical self-exclusion from NATO's military structures under Charles de Gaulle. TNA, FCO 46/1825, Loose Minute—HLG report—by Tebbit, 28 March 1978; Loose Minute—Task Force 10—by Tebbit, 31 March 1978, including copies of comments sent to Tebbit by Anding (29 March 1978) and by Kristina Heidenstroem (Norwegian Delegation to NATO) (29 March 1978). See also, Jimmy Carter Presidential Library, Atlanta, Georgia (henceforth JCL), Agency File, NATO 12/77–5/78, Carter Presidential Papers—Staff Offices, NSA—Brzezinski Material Information, Memorandum from Zbigniew Brzezinski for the President; Subject: NATO NPG Meeting + Memorandum for the President by Harold Brown; Subject: NATO NPG (9 April 1978), 17 April 1978; Memorandum, National Security Council—from Jim Thomson for Zbigniew Brzezinski; Subject: NATO NPG Meeting, 13 April 1978. Politisches Archiv des Auswärtigen Amts, Berlin (henceforth PAAA), B 150 1978, Dannenbring to Bundesminister, Betr.: Vorschau auf die 23. NPG-Ministerkonferenz am 18./19. April 1978 in Fredrikshavn/Dänemark, 13 April 1978.
6. TNA, FCO 46/1825, Letter from E. W. L. Hedley (UK delegation to NATO) to Tebbit incl. cover note + report 'Nuclear Planning Group, Long-Term Defence Programme, Improvements to NATO's Theatre Nuclear Force Posture' (25 April 1978), 26 April 1978, 2 and NPG draft report paragraph 19. Horst Möller et al., eds, *Akten zur Auswärtigen Politik der Bundesrepublik Deutschland 1978, Band I: 1. Januar bis 30. Juni 1978* (Munich, 2009) [henceforth *AAPD 1978/I*], doc. 124 + doc. 159, 601 + 783.

7. *AAPD 1978/I*, doc. 170, 847.

8. TNA, FCO 46/1826 Theatre Nuclear Force (TNF) Modernisation: Long Term Defence Planning (May–September 1978), Letter from Fred Mulley (UK Defence Minister) to Prime Minister, 15 May 1978. In the same file see also, Letter from Fred Mulley to the Prime Minister on 'NATO Theatre Nuclear Forces (TNF)', 9 June 1978; and Letter from David Owen (UK Foreign Minister) to the Prime Minister, 30 May 1978. Cf. *AAPD 1978/I*, doc. 151, 735; *AAPD 1978/I*, doc. 159, 783.

9. See n. 8; and TNA, FCO 46/1826, Memorandum by W. J. A. Wilberforce (Head of the Defence Department, FCO) for Private Secretary 'NATO's Theatre Nuclear Forces', 18 May 1978.

10. Helmut Schmidt Privatarchiv, Hamburg (henceforth HSPA), HS privat, Eigene Arbeiten (henceforth EA) 18.5.–20.6.1978, Nr. 6, Wolf J. Bell, 'Gleichgewicht der Kräfte ist Voraussetzung für die Entspannung', *General-Anzeiger*, 24 May 1978.

11. Quoted in Johannes von Karczewski, *'Weltwirtschaft ist unser Schicksal': Helmut Schmidt und die Schaffung der Weltwirtschaftsgipfel* (Bonn, 2008), 419–20.

12. HSPA, HS privat, EA 11.10.–15.11.1978, Nr. 11, Bundeskanzler Schmidt—off the record—im Bundeskanzleramt mit deutschen Chefredakteuren, 31 October 1978.

13. Ibid.

14. HSPA, HS privat, EA 18.5.–20.6.1978, Nr. 6, Wolf J. Bell, 'Gleichgewicht der Kräfte ist Voraussetzung für die Entspannung', *General-Anzeiger*, 24 May 1978. Cf. HSPA, HS privat, EA 29.6.–28.9.1981, Nr. 7, 'Ich glaube nicht, daß irgend jemand morgen Krieg anfängt ...', *Hannoversche Allgemeine Zeitung*, 7 July 1981.

15. On the evolution of German–Soviet relations and the postponement of visits, see PAAA, Ref. 213—ZA 133094, Der Breschnew-Besuch 1977 in Bonn im Gesamtzusammenhang der deutsch-sowjetischen Beziehungen, undated (signed off VLR I Dr Kühn, 25 August 1977).

16. On the Schmidt–Brezhnev talks generally, see Hartmut Soell, *Helmut Schmidt: Macht und Verantwortung* (Berlin, 2008), 721–7.

17. On the nature of the 'framework agreement' (as a government agreement, *Regierungsabkommen*) as well as the question of signatories and of avoiding the need for *Bundestag*-approval, see PAAA, Ref. 213—ZA 133096, Hermes an Frank (undated, signed off on 2 May 1978); and, Vermerk, 4 May 1978.

18. Bundesarchiv (henceforth BA), Koblenz, B136/1677, Betr: Deutsch–sowjetische Beziehungen, 15 December 1978, 3; *AAPD 1978/I*, doc. 177, 879–85. Martin Albers, 'The Policies of Britain, France and West Germany towards the People's Republic of China, 1969–1982', unpublished PhD dissertation, Cambridge University, 2014, 251–64; cf. Ezra F. Vogel, *Deng Xiaoping and the Transformation of China* (Cambridge, MA, 2011), 221–7.

19. HSPA, HS privat, EA 17.4.–17.5.1978, Nr. 8, 'Unser Mann in Bonn: Breschnew Besuch – ein Beitrag zum Frieden', *Bergedorfer Zeitung*, 27 April 1978. *AAPD 1978/I*, doc. 142, 690–1. Angela Stent, *From Embargo to Ostpolitik: The Political Economy of West German–Soviet Relations, 1955–1980* (Cambridge, 1981), 205. See also BA, B136/17748, Bundeskanzler Schmidt on Brezhnev's visit—interview with 'Panorama', 21:00, 9 May 1978. PAAA, Ref. 213—ZA 133095, Betr.: Gespräch des Herrn Bundesministers mit dem amerik. Botschafter 27.4.1978—hier: Breschnew-Besuch in Bonn, 27 April 1978; and, Ref. 213—ZA 133096, Bewertung des Breschnew-Besuchs von STS van Well, 8 May 1978.

20. 'Breschnews Gespräche mit Schmidt "nützlich, sachlich" und ohne konkretes Ergebnis', *Frankfurter Allgemeine Zeitung*, 6 May 1978, 1. *AAPD 1978/I*, doc. 136, 657–9, and

doc. 137, 663–5.On the formulations used in the communiqué, see AAPD *1978/I*, doc. 698, note 19; PAAA, B150 1978, Abt. 2 to Bundesminister, Betr.: Deutsch–sowjetische Deklaration—hier: Begriff der annähernden Gleichheit, 3 May 1978. Helmut Schmidt, *Menschen und Mächte* (Berlin, 1987), 94.

21. Cf. HSPA, HS privat, EA 18.5.–20.6.1978, Nr. 11, Bundeskanzler Rede im Nordatlantik Rat, Washington, 30.5.1978.

22. HSPA, HS privat, EA 17.4.–17.5.1978, Nr. 8, 'Unser Mann in Bonn: Breschnew Besuch – ein Beitrag zum Frieden', *Bergedorfer Zeitung*, 27 April 1978.

23. Schmidt, *Menschen und Mächte*, 96–8; HSPA, HS privat, EA 17.4.–17.5.1978, Nr.15, Bundeskanzler Interview: Schmidt zum Staatsbesuch Leonid Breschnews, 'Panorama', 9 May 1978; and EA 18.5.–20.6. 1978, Nr. 9, 'Schmidt: After You'—Interview with *Newsweek*, 29 May 1978. 20–2. See also *AAPD 1978/I*, doc. 136, 654–9; Jürgen Leinemann, 'Wie schafft man Vertrauen?', *Der Spiegel*, no. 19/1978, 18 May 1978, 25–6.

24. HSPA, HS privat, EA 17.4.–17.5.1978, Nr. 15, quotes from 'Panorama', 9 May 1978. See also Michael Getler, 'Schmidt Says Brezhnev Willing to Expand Arms Talks with West', *Washington Post*, 10 May 1978, A24. *AAPD 1978/I*, doc. 136, 657–9, and doc. 137, 663–5. PAAA, B150 1978, Abt. 2 to Bundesminister, plus Anhang—Rüstungskontrollpolitische Optionen, 7 July 1978.

25. For a good summary of the issues see Strobe Talbott, *Deadly Gambits: The Reagan Administration and the Stalemate in Arms Control* (New York, 1985), 28–33.

26. *AAPD 1978/I*, doc. 144, 699–700.

27. PAAA, B150 1978, Telko Nr. 2387, Schmidt's letter to Carter, 17 May 1978.

28. Ibid.

29. *AAPD 1978/I*, doc. 172, 861–4. Cf. *AAPD 1978/II*, 1523, note 9. For Schmidt's evolving ideas regarding SALT III and LRTNF, see also analyses of German government thinking in TNA, FCO 46/1822 Non-Central Nuclear Delivery Systems ('Grey Area' Systems) 1.1.–31.12.1978 [Part C], especially the documents, Letter from the Private Secretary, 10 Downing Street (Bryan Cartledge) to George G. H. Walden (FCO) on 'Prime Minister's discussion with chancellor Schmidt in Bonn 18/19 October: Grey Area Systems, 20 October 1978; and Note from Wilberforce to Peter Jay (Washington) on 'Grey Area Systems' incl. 'pretty full summary' of 'Prime Minister's discussion with chancellor Schmidt in Bonn 18/19 October: Grey Area Systems'.

30. PAAA, B150 1978, Abt. 2 to Bundesminister, Betr.: SALT—hier: Grauzonen + Brief Genscher to Apel u. Anlage, 12 June 1978; Leiter des Planungsstabes to Minister, Vorschlag: Einführung der anliegenden Aufzeichnung in die Gespräche mit dem Bundeskanzleramt und dem BMVg, Betr.: Grauzone, 20 June 1978; Dg22 to D2, Betr.: SALT, 21 June 1978.

31. PAAA, B150 1978, Fernschreiben Nr. 807, Pauls, Bruessel NATO to Bonn AA, 19 July 1978, 1978.

32. Euromissiles Crisis CWIHP Document Reader, Response to PRM-38: Long-Range Theater Nuclear forces, 19 August 1978, 3–4, <http://www.wilsoncenter.org/publication/the-euromissiles-crisis-reader>.

33. JCL, NLC 31-127-6-4-7, Special Coordinating Committee Summary of Conclusions, August 23, 1978, 2; Brzezinski, *Power and Principle*, 307–8; Raymond L. Garthoff, *Détente and Confrontation: American–Soviet Relations from Nixon to Reagan* (Washington, DC, 1985), 862.

34. The National Security Archive (henceforth NSA-GWU), Thirtieth Anniversary of NATO's Dual-Track Decision, The Nuclear Vault website, <http://www.nsarchive.gwu.edu/nukevault/ebb301/index.htm>, Richard A. Ericson and George S. Vest to the

Secretary of State, briefing memo 'SCC Meeting on PRM-38, August 23', 16 August 1978, <http://www.gwu.edu/~nsarchiv/nukevault/ebb301/doc02.pdf>. See also Brzezinski, *Power and Principle*, 307–8.

35. TNA, FCO 46/1827 Theatre Nuclear Force (TNF) Modernisation: Long Term Defence Planning 1.1.–31.12.1978 [Part C], Note by Tebbit on 'Points made by Dr Lynn Davis (US Deputy Assistant Secretary [ISA/OSD])' in Quinlan's office on 15 Sept. 1978, 15 September 1978. NSA-GWU, Nuclear Vault, State Department cable 258185 to U.S. Embassy London, 'TNF Bilateral with UK', 11 October 1978, <http://www.gwu.edu/~nsarchiv/nukevault/ebb301/doc03.pdf>.

36. TNA, FCO 46/1827, Letter from Killick to Quinlan on 'TNF etc', 26 September 1978. In the same file, see also, Letter from J. L. Bullard (Minister, UK embassy, Bonn) to Quinlan on 'TNF: HLG', 29 September 1978. Cf. *AAPD 1978/II*, doc. 308, 1516–21.

37. TNA, FCO 46/1827, Record of a meeting held on 16 Oct. 1978 in the German delegation to NATO to discuss the work of the High Level Group on TNF Modernisation, 25 October 1978.

38. Ibid.; TNA, FCO 46/1828 Theatre Nuclear Force (TNF) Modernisation—Long Term Defence Planning (1978—Part Annex), UK record of October High Level Group meeting held in Brussels—16–17 October 1978, 10 November 1978. See also the Norwegian summary of results of the October HLG meeting in Brussels included in: FD-NOR, FD 200.18 HLG/TNF 1978, 'NPG – High Level Group on TNF modernization – hovedpunktene fra gruppens 5. møte, Brussel 30 november–1 desember 1978', no date, December 1978.

39. TNA, FCO 46/1827, Note by Tebbit on 'NPG Meeting 18/19 October 1978' incl. brief of 17 October 1978 'Agenda item IIIb long term improvements (discussion of the work of the High Level group)', 23 October 1978. See also, PAAA, B150 1978, Abt. 2 to Bundesminister, 3 November 1978.

40. On the shift in policy within Germany away from *Schichtenparitäten* (component parity), cf. NSA-GWU, Nuclear Vault, State Department cable 261791 to US Embassy Bonn, 'Bilateral with the FRG on TNF Issues (11 October 1978)', 16 October 1978, <http://www.gwu.edu/~nsarchiv/nukevault/ebb301/doc04.pdf>. *AAPD 1978/II*, doc. 307, 1513–16; *AAPD 1978/II*, doc. 309, 1521–5. TNA, FCO 46/1822, telegram (no 786) by Sir J. O. Wright (UK ambassador, Bonn)—Subject: telno 754, Grey Areas—FRG Views, 13 September 1978. See also, PAAA, B150 1978, Abt. 2 to Bundesminister, Betr.: SALT, 7 July 1978. PAAA, B150 1978, Betr.: Dt.-frz. Direktorenkonsultationen am 25.10.1978 in Paris, 30 October 1978 (quoting *Schichtenparität* on p. 4).

41. TNA, FCO 46/1827, Note by Tebbit on 'NPG High Level Group – TNF Modernisation' incl. 'UK record of High Level Group meeting in Brussels on 30 November and 1 December 1978', 19 December 1978.

42. JCL, Agency File, NATO 10/78-2/79, Memorandum, National Security Council—Information: Robert Hunter to Zbigniew Brzezinski; Subject: North Atlantic Council, 12 December 1978.

43. See PAAA, B150 1978, Abt. 2 to Bundesminister, Betr.: TNF Modernisierung, 1 December 1978.

44. *AAPD 1978/II*, doc. 308, 1516–21.

45. *AAPD 1978/II*, doc. 293, 1462, note 47. See also BA, B136/16777, AL 2 an BK, Betr.: Vierertreffen—UnterVerschluβ!, 8 November 1978; TNA, FCO 46/1822, Private Secretary to Walden on 'The Prime Minister's Conversation with Dr. Brzezinski on 4 October 1978: Grey Area Systems', 5 October 1989; Brzezinski, *Power and Principle*,

295. On the summit idea originating from Schmidt in late 1977, see also US Declassified Documents References System (henceforth US DDRS), reference CK3100099284, Memo to President Carter from Z. Brzezinski relates contents of NSC weekly report no. 36, 11 November 1977; and JCL, Agency File, NATO 6–9/78, Memorandum, National Security Council—Information: Gregory F. Treverton and Robert Hunter to David Aaron; Subject: Consultations with NATO Allies, 27 July 1978. Cf. Secret correspondence on preparations for Guadeloupe in late 1978 can be found in the files TNA, FCO 46/1822 and FCO 46/1823 Non-Central Nuclear Delivery Systems ('Grey Area' Systems) 1.1.–31.12.1978 [Part D]. See also Valéry Giscard d'Estaing, *Le pouvoir et la vie*, vol. 2 (Paris, 1991), 363 who claims that the summit was his idea.

46. Archiv der sozialen Demokratie, Bonn (henceforth AdsD), Depositum Egon Bahr (henceforth DEB), Box 413, Letter from Schmidt to Bahr, 15 December 1978.

47. AdsD, DEB, Box 413, Letter from Bahr to Schmidt, 21 December 1978; and Letter from Bahr to Schmidt, 27 January 1979. The latter was an addendum ('Ergänzung') to the former.

48. AdsD, DEB, Box 413, Letter from Bahr to Schmidt, 21 December 1978.

49. HSPA, HS privat, EA 2.8–7.10.1979, Nr. 21, Bulletin des Presse- und Informationsamtes der Bundesregierung, Nr. 118, 1093, 5.10.1979, Sicherung des Friedens als zentrale politische Aufgabe—Bundeskanzler an neue akkredidierte Botschafter in Bonn am 25.9.1979.

50. *AAPD 1978/II*, doc. 293, 1457 and 1462 note 47. It is noteworthy too that, contrary to British thinking, Brzezinski met with Schmidt the day before he consulted with Callaghan in Blackpool on 4 October 1978. See Callaghan, James, *Time and Chance* (London, 1987), 542. It was indeed Schmidt who raised the summit talks issue with Brzezinski first; and then also with Carter in a telephone conversation on 5 October. See also PAAA, B150 1978, Telefongespräch des Bundeskanzlers Schmidt mit Präsident Carter—Betr.: SALT/Grauzone, Strategie der NATO, Nahostkonflikt und Konferenz von Camp David, Währungsfragen, GATT, 5 October 1978. Cf. Brzezinksi, *Power and Principle*, 294–5; Klaus Wiegrefe, *Das Zerwürfnis: Helmut Schmidt, Jimmy Carter und die Krise der deutsch–amerikanischen Beziehungen* (Berlin, 2005), 261–2. Even in his own memoirs Schmidt keeps himself in the background and points to Carter's initiative! Schmidt, *Menschen und Mächte*, 231.

51. Callaghan, *Time and Chance*, 544; Giscard, *Le pouvoir*, II, 369–2; Jürgen Ruhfus, *Aufwärts: Erlebnisse und Erinnerungen eines diplomatischen Zeitzeugen 1955 bis 1992* (Sankt Ottilien, 2006), 216. See also Flora Lewis, 'Britain will Sell Fighters to China, Callaghan Says at Summit Meeting', *New York Times*, 6 January 1979, 1. For a fuller discussion of the material in this section, see Kristina Spohr, 'Helmut Schmidt and the Shaping of Western Security in the Late 1970s: The Guadeloupe Summit of 1979', *International History Review* 37, no. 1 (2015), 167–92.

52. Giscard, *Le pouvoir*, II, 372, 381–2; Callaghan, *Time and Chance*, 544; Ruhfus, *Aufwärts*, 216. See also, JCL, NLC-128-4-12-3-9, Personal, brief notes by Jimmy Carter, 7, 16, 18; BA, B136/16777, Ref. 212 to BK, Guadeloupe—hier: Ablauf- und Themenübersicht, 28 December 1978.

53. James Reston, 'Swimming Pool Summit', *New York Times*, 29 December 1978, A23.

54. Giscard, *Le pouvoir*, II, 375.

55. TNA, PREM 16/1984 DEFENCE. 'Grey Area' Medium Range Nuclear Weapon Systems: Arms Control and Deployment 4.10.1978–4.4.1979, Extract from Four-Power Discussions in Guadeloupe 5/6 January 1979: Second Session, 3.

56. Giscard, *Le pouvoir*, II, 375; Brzezinski, *Power and Principle*, 295; TNA, PREM 16/1984, Extract from Four-Power Discussions in Guadeloupe 5/6 January 1979: Second Session, 3. Jimmy Carter, *Keeping Faith: Memoirs of a President* (New York, 1982), 235; see also JCL, NLC-128-4-12-3-9, Personal, brief notes by Jimmy Carter, 8–9 (emphasis added).

57. *AAPD 1979/I*, doc. 3, 17.

58. TNA, PREM 16/1984, Extract from Four-Power Discussions in Guadeloupe 5–6 January 1979: Second Session, 4; cf. Callaghan, *Time and Chance*, 549–50; Giscard, *Le pouvoir*, II, 379–80.

59. TNA, PREM 16/1984, Extract from Four-Power Discussions in Guadeloupe 5/6 January 1979: Third Session, 1.

60. 'Carter at Summit talks: A Gain in Stature', *New York Times*, 8 January 1979, A3. Cf. Giscard, *Le pouvoir*, II, 383; Edward Walsh, 'Summit Ends in Harmony', *Washington Post*, 7 January 1979, A1; Robert Held, 'Die Sicherheit verstärken und Spannungen abbauen – Iran, China und der Abschluß des SALT-II-Abkommens die Hauptthemen der Gespräche von Guadeloupe', *Frankfurter Allgemeine Zeitung*, 8 January 1979, 1.

61. 'West is Considering Missile for Europe Able to Hit Soviet: A Reply to Moscow's Buildup – Weapons Discussed at Guadeloupe Parley, Seen as response to SS-20 and New Bomber', *New York Times*, 20 January 1979, 1. See also Heinz Stadlmann, 'Westeuropa muß seinen Standpunkt zu "Salt III" erst erarbeiten – Washington befürchtet Schwierigkeiten bei den Verbündeten', *Frankfurter Allgemeine Zeitung*, 19 January 1979, 5.

62. John Vinocur, 'Schmidt says Bonn assumes growing global role: U.S. aide arrives for talks', *New York Times*, 13 January 1979, 6; 'Aus Guadeloupe zurück', *Süddeutsche Zeitung*, 13–14 January 1979; Robert Held, 'Die "grossen westlichen Vier" mit einer langen Themenliste', *Frankfurter Allgemeine Zeitung*, 6 January 1979, 1.

63. BA, B136/16777, Emb. Rome to AA, FSNr. 1523, Betr.: Vierertreffem in Guadeloupe, 19 December 1978; AL 2 to BK, Guadeloupe—hier: ital. Reaktion auf Nichtbeteiligung, 21 December 1978; and, Vermerk—STS van Well and amb. Orlandi-Contucci, 19.12.1978, 21 December 1978.

64. Brzezinski, *Power and Principle*, 295; JCL, NLC-128-4-12-3-9, Personal, brief notes by Jimmy Carter, 10; *AAPD 1979/I*, doc. 31, 137–45.

65. PAAA, B150 1979, Leitlinien für die Lösung des Grauzonenproblems, 31 Jan. 1979—Betr.: Besuch des Stellv. Vorsitzenden des Nationalen Sicherheitsrates der Vereinigten Staaten, Mr David Aaron, in Bonn am 6.2.1979, 5 February 1979.

66. TNA, PREM 16/1984, Extract from Four-Power Discussions in Guadeloupe 5/6 January 1979: Third Session, 1–2; *AAPD 1979/I*, doc. 5, 22; PAAA, B150 1979, Aaron-Besuch in Bonn, 6 February 1979; Vermerk—Betr.: Gespräch von Dg22 mit Mr Goodby am 20.2.1979, 20 February 1979. *AAPD 1979/I*, doc. 45, 200–2; *AAPD 1979/I*, doc. 65, 291–2.

67. PAAA, B150 1979, Telko Nr. 1315, Grauzonen-Rüstungskontrollaspekte der TNF Modernisierung, Anlage 2, 13 March 1979.

68. Cf. James A. Thomson, 'The LRTNF Decision: Evolution of U.S. Theater Nuclear Policy, 1975–9', *International Affairs (RIIA)* 60, no. 4 (October 1984), 601–14, here 609; Helga Haftendorn, 'Das doppelte Mißverständnis: Die Vorgeschichte des NATO-Doppelbeschlusses von 1979', *Vierteljahrshefte für Zeitgeschichte* 33, no. 2 (1985), 244–87, here 274–5. US DDRS, reference CK3100543617, Memorandum to President Jimmy Carter from [David Aaron thru] Zbigniew Brzezinski regarding plans for the deployment of long-range theatre nuclear forces (LRTNF) in West European countries, 13 February 1979.

69. FD-NOR, FD 200.18, NPG I 1-12000 1979, Cover note by Vidar Wikberg, Det Kgl. Utenrikensdepartement, plus 'Referat fra første møte (19.–20.4.1979) i NATO's *Special Group on Arms Control and Related Matters* i forbindelse med Theater Nuclear Weapons (TNF)', 4 May 1979; Cover note by Vidar Wikberg, Det Kgl. Utenrikensdepartement, plus 'Referat fra annet møte (4. mai. 1979) i NATO's *Special Group on Arms Control and Related Matters* i forbindelse med Theater Nuclear Weapons (TNF)', 22 May 1979.

70. Ibid.; NSA-GWU, Nuclear Vault, SCC Meeting, 12 April 1979, White House Situation Room, <http://www.gwu.edu/~nsarchiv/nukevault/ebb301/doc07.pdf> (emphasis in quote added).

71. FD-NOR, FD 200.18, NPG I 1-12000 1979, Cover note by Vidar Wikberg, Det Kgl. Utenrikensdepartement, plus 'Referat fra første møte (19.–20.4.1979) i NATO's *Special Group on Arms Control and Related Matters* i forbindelse med Theater Nuclear Weapons (TNF)', 4 May 1979; Indeed, 'to arm to disarm' could imply foregoing LRTNF deployments altogether, i.e. a zero option, which the USA certainly did not have in mind.

72. FD-NOR, FD 200.18, NPG I 1-12000 1979, Cover note by Vidar Wikberg, Det Kgl. Utenrikensdepartement, plus 'Referat fra annet møte (4. mai. 1979) i NATO's *Special Group on Arms Control and Related Matters* i forbindelse med Theater Nuclear Weapons (TNF)', 22 May 1979.

73. FD-NOR, FD 200.18, NPG I 1-12000 1979, Cover note by Vidar Wikberg, Det Kgl. Utenrikensdepartement, plus 'Referat fra annet møte (4. mai. 1979) i NATO's *Special Group on Arms Control and Related Matters* i forbindelse med Theater Nuclear Weapons (TNF)', 22 May 1979. Cf. Raymond L. Garthoff, 'The NATO Decision on Theater Nuclear Forces', *Political Science Quarterly* 98, no. 2 (1983), 197–214, here 204.

74. *AAPD 1979/I*, doc. 113, 498–505. Cf. PAAA, B150 1979, Kaempf to Genschel, Betr.: Gespräch BM Dr. Apel mit dem Bundeskanzler am 20.4.1979 zu den Problemen der kommenden NPG-Sitzung in Homestead/USA, 7 May 1979.

75. *AAPD 1979/I*, doc. 113, 503.

76. *AAPD 1979/I*, doc. 114, 505–9. The Americans tended to believe that the German government—due to intra-SPD differences, hostile public opinion, and potential Soviet pressure ('Soviet Finlandisation efforts')—would be unable to lead or certainly would procrastinate over what to do. See US DDRS, reference CK3100543617, Memorandum to President Jimmy Carter from [David Aaron thru] Zbigniew Brzezinski regarding plans for the deployment of long-range theatre nuclear forces (LRTNF) in West European countries, 13 February 1979; US DDRS, reference CK3100108810, Memo to President Jimmy Carter from Secretary of State Cyrus Vance and Secretary of State Harold Brown on US diplomacy regarding the deployment of long-range nuclear systems on the European continent to counteract the Soviet nuclear modernization efforts, 9 May 1979.

77. *AAPD 1979/I*, doc. 114, 507–9; PAAA, B150 1979, Abt. 2 to Bundesminister, Betr.: Kabinettssitzung am 2. Mai 1979, 30 April 1979.

78. AdsD, HSA, Box 006524, Bundeskanzler vor der Bundestagsfraktion, 6 February 1979. HSPA, HS privat, EA 1.1.–6.2.1979, Nr. 22, Helmut Schmidt vor der Bundestagsfraktion, February 1979. See also, 'Annäherung zwischen Koalition und Union in der Abrüstungs-Debatte', *Frankfurter Allgemeine Zeitung*, 12 February 1979; and BA, B136/17739, AA to BMVG, FSNr. 38 from emb. in Den Haag, incl. article: 'Herbert Wehner en de bewapening in Duitsland', *NRC Handelsblad*, 3 February 1979.

79. See *AAPD 1979/I*, doc. 87, 386, note 7; *AAPD 1979/I*, doc. 147, 685–90. See also JCL, Zbigniew Brzezinski Collection, Subject File, Alpha Channel (Misc.)—5/79–8/79, Box 20, Memorandum—Action: Zbigniew Brzezinski to the President; Subject: Vance/Brown

Memo on TNF (c), 17 May 1979; HSPA, HS privat, EA 15.5.–3.6.1979, Nr. 5, Rede von Bundeskanzler Helmut Schmidt auf der Sicherheitspolitischen Informationstagung der SPD am 19.5.1979 in Bremen. See also, Stenographische Berichte, Deutscher Bundestag—8. Wahlperiode—141. Sitzung, 8.3.1979, 11119 ff.; Stenographische Berichte, Deutscher Bundestag—8. Wahlperiode—142. Sitzung, 8.3.1979, 111235 ff.

80. AdsD DEB, Box 356, Letter from Bahr to Schmidt, 2 June 1979.

81. This text in English comes from PAAA, B 150 1979, Unterabt. 2 to BM, Betr.: Bundessicherheitsratssitzung am 20.9.1979, 19 September 1979. For the original speech see Stenographische Berichte, Deutscher Bundestag—8. Wahlperiode—167. Sitzung, 4.7.1979, 13317–8.

82. Egon Bahr, *Zu meiner Zeit* (Munich, 1996), 509–10. In an interview with *Der Spiegel* in October Bahr was careful to stick to the government line: 'Bahr: In der Katastrophe sind wir vereint', *Der Spiegel*, no. 42/1979, 15 October 1979, 30–4.

83. John Vinocur, 'Schmidt says Bonn assumes growing global role: U.S. aide arrives for talks', *New York Times*, 13 January 1979, 6. HSPA, HS privat, EA 5.6–20.7.1979, Nr. 5, An Interview with Helmut Schmidt: 'Wars may become possible for the single reason of competition for oil', *Time*, 11 June 1979, 39–40 (quote on 40).

84. *AAPD 1979/I*, doc. 113, 498–505. PAAA, B150 1979, Abt. 2 to Staatssekretär + Anlage, 10 May 1979.

85. *AAPD 1979/I*, doc. 138, 647–50, and esp. 650, note 15.

86. *AAPD 1979/I*, doc. 156, 736–44; *AAPD 1979/I*, doc. 160, 773.

87. *AAPD 1979/I*, doc. 156, 737.

88. PAAA, B 150, Abt. 2 to Bundesminister, Betr.: Grauzonenproblem—plus draft letter Schmidt to Carter, 15 May 1979; Telko Nr. 580, Letter + memo (in English), 19 May 1979. Cf. PAAA, B150 1979, Unterabteilung 22 to Bundesminister, Betr.: Unsere künftige Haltung zur TNF-Modernisierung und zur parallelen Präsentation einer rüstungskontrollpolitischen Initiative, 28 May 1979; Washington embassy to AA, Fernschreiben Nr. 2035, Betr.: TNF Modernisierung, 31 May 1979; Hofmann to Ref 220, Betr.: TNF-Modernisierung/Rüstungskontrolle, 1 June 1979.

89. PAAA, B150 1979, Plurez 3.6.1979, Betr.: Schreiben Carter-Schmidt vom 1.6.1979, 3 June 1979; Hofmann to D2, encl. Analyse des Briefes von Präsident Carter an Herrn Bundeskanzler vom 2.6.1979, 3 June 1979.

90. PAAA, B150 1979, Plurez 3.6.1979, Betr.: Schreiben Carter-Schmidt vom 1.6.1979, 3 June 1979; Hofmann to D2, encl. Analyse des Briefes von Präsident Carter an Herrn Bundeskanzler vom 2.6.1979, 3 June 1979. See also, Abt. 2 to BM, Betr.: Reise des Herrn Bundeskanzler in die USA, 5 June 1979; Abt. 2 to Bundesminister, Betr.: Richtlinien für die weitere Arbeit der Delegation der Bundesrepublik Deutschland bei der SG, 7 June 1979.

91. *AAPD 1979/I*, doc. 132, 601–8.

92. HSPA, HS privat, EA 5.6–20.7.1979, Nr. 5, An Interview with Helmut Schmidt: 'Wars may become possible for the single reason of competition for oil', *Time*, 11 June 1979, 39–40 (quote on 39).

93. Brian J. Auten, *Carter's Conversion: The Hardening of American Defense Policy* (Columbia, MO, 2008), 270.

94. U.S. DDRS, reference CK3100108807-11, Memorandum to Carter from Vance and Brown, 9 May 1979. The memo's attachments are in JCL, Subject File, Alpha Channel (Misc.)—5/79–8/79, Box 20, 'TNF Decision / Consultation Track' (attached document 7D) and 'Illustrative Deployment Programme' (attached document 7E). Cf. Auten, *Carter's Conversion*, 269–71.

95. *AAPD 1979/I*, doc. 143, 673; *AAPD 1979/I*, doc. 139, 651–3. See also the documents related to Schmidt's correspondence with Carter (in the second half of May) and Schmidt's visit to Washington in early June 1979: *AAPD 1979/I*, doc. 147, 685–90; *AAPD 1979/I*, doc. 163, 786–9; *AAPD 1979/I*, doc. 175, 843–6. JCL, Subject File, Alpha Channel (Misc.)—5/79–8/79, Box 20, Memorandum from Zbigniew Brzezinski for the Secretary of State and the Secretary of Defense, Subject: TNF Modernisation (c), 18 May 1979; Memorandum—Action: Zbigniew Brzezinski to the President, Subject: Vance/Brown Memo on TNF (c), 17 May 1979. US DDRS, reference CK3100473881, Memorandum to President Jimmy Carter from Zbigniew Brzezinski regarding correspondence between Carter and West German Chancellor Helmut Schmidt concerning arms control issues, 31 May 1979; US DDRS, reference CK 3100148248, Letter from President Jimmy Carter to West German Chancellor Helmut Schmidt regarding the need for long-range nuclear systems in Europe capable of reaching Soviet territory, 1 June 1979.

96. PAAA, ZA 116887 Modernisierung der NATO TNF—LRTNF (1979), Vermerk, Betr.: Heutige Direktorenbesprechung—hier: Ausführungen von StS van Well zum Zeitplan für TNF-Modernisierung, gez. Gorenflos, 13 June 1979. See also, *AAPD 1979/I*, doc. 175, 845; *AAPD 1979/I*, doc. 163, 787; *AAPD 1979/I*, doc. 147, 690–1, note 16.

97. PAAA, B150 1979, Ref. 201, Betr.: Modernisierung der Mittelstreckenwaffen der NATO in Europa, 11 June 1979; *AAPD 1979/I*, doc. 163, 786–90; *AAPD 1979/I*, doc. 175, 844.

98. *AAPD 1979/I*, docs 142 + 144.

99. *AAPD 1979/II*, doc. 210, 1023–8.

100. *AAPD 1979/II*, doc. 219, 1056. On Italy's resentment see this chapter, fn. 63.

101. *AAPD 1979/II*, doc. 274, 1345–8; *AAPD 1979/II*, doc. 278, 1357. PAAA, B150 1979, Vermerk: Betr.: TNF Modernisierungsentscheidung—hier: Gespräch zwischen Herrn Minister und dem italienischen Außenminister 18.9.1979, 4 October 1979. Cf. Report of the conversation between Italian Presidente del Consiglio Cossiga and Dutch Prime Minister van Agt, 6 December 1979, <http://www.digitalarchive. wilsoncenter.org/document/111279>.

102. PAAA, B150 1979, Ref. 201, Sachstand und Bewertung (abgestimmt mit BMVg), Betr.: TNF Modernisierung, 26 July 1979; Ref. 201, Gesprächsvorschlag (abgestimmt mit BMVg), Betr.: LRTNF Modernisierung, 26 July 1979; Telko Nr. 857, Betr.: LRTNF-Modernisierung, 9 August 1979.

103. *AAPD 1979/II*, doc. 211, 1028–33. See also PAAA, B150 1979, FSNr. 2335, Washington to Bonn AA, 22 June 1979. For the SALT II treaty and protocol, see BA 136/17749, Betr.: SALT II—hier: Inhalt des Vertrages und der Begleiturkunden, 19 June 1979.

104. *AAPD 1979/I*, docs 188 and 193, 905–18 and 937; cf. PAAA, B150 1979, Bundeskanzleramt an Wallau, Ministerbüro AA, Vermerk über das Gespräch des BK mit PM Nordli am 12.7.1979, 13 July 1979.

105. JCL, NLC31-13-3-11-8, CIA National Foreign Assessment Center, Assessment on Likely Soviet Responses to a NATO TNF Modernization Decision, 29 June 1979, A-1.

106. *AAPD 1979/II*, doc. 227, 1085–6. PAAA, B150 1979, D2 to Bundesminister, Gespräch des Bundesministers mit Herrn Bundeskanzler am 3.9.79 ds. Js., 31 August 1979.

107. See PAAA, B150 1979, Telko Nr. 3321, 2 July 1979; Leiter Planungsstab an Staatssekretär, Betr.: TNF-Modernisierung und Grauzonen-Rüstungskontrollvorschlag—

hier: Beschluss des BSR vom 18.6.1979—Richtlinien für HLG und Special Group, 4 July 1979.

108. *AAPD 1979/II*, doc. 282, 1383–8; TNA, FCO 28/3695 NATO Theatre Nuclear Force (TNF) Modernization (1979—part B), Letter from D. H. Gillmore (Defence Department, FCO) to Head of Chancery on 'Theatre Nuclear Force Modernisation', 12 October 1979. See also, PAAA, B150 1979, FSNr. 3277, Washington to Bonn AA, Betr.: TNF Modernisierung, 17 September 1979; Abt. 2 to Bundesminister, Betr.: LRTNF Modernisierung, 19 September 1979; FSNr. 3314, Washington to Bonn, 19 September 1979; FSNr. 950, Bruessel NATO to Bonn AA, 26 September 1979.

109. PAAA, B150 1979, Abt. 2 to BM, Betr.: Zusammenhang LRTNF Modernisierung/Rüstungskontrollvorschlag, 31 August 1979. See also PAAA, B150 1979, Abt. 2 to Bundesminister, Betr.: LRTNF Modernisierung, Bezug: Anforderung des Entwurfs eines 'non-papers' durch den Herrn Bundeskanzler zum 22. Aug. 1979, 17 August 1979; D2 to Bundesminister, Betr.: TNF Modernisierung/Rüstungskontrollangebot, 21 August 1979.

110. PAAA, B150 1979, Abt. 2 to Bundesminister, Betr.: Sechsergespräch am 13.9.1979, 10 September 1979; Telko Nr. 4132, Betr.: Special Group Bericht zu 'Arms Control Involving TNF', 14 September 1979; Blech to Bundesminister, Betr.: Bundessicherheitsratssitzung am 20.9.1979, 19 September 1979.

111. PAAA, B150 1979, Telko Nr. 1038, 19 September 1979. See also PAAA, B150 1979, FSNr. 957, Bruessel NATO to Bonn AA, 27 September 1979.

112. PAAA, B150 1979, FSNr. 3308, Washington an Bonn AA, 19 September 1979, Fernschreiben Nr. 3318, Washington an Bonn AA, 20 September 1979.

113. *AAPD 1979/II*, doc. 268, esp. 1324, note 8. See also, PAAA, B150 1979, Unterabt. 2 to Bundesminister, Betr.: Bundessicherheitsratssitzung am 20.9.1979, 19 September 1979.

114. *AAPD 1979/II*, doc. 282, 1383–8. PAAA, B150 1979, FSNr. 958 und Nr. 963, Bruessel NATO to Bonn AA, 28 September 1979.

115. Cf. U.S. DDRS, reference CK3100518247, Memorandum from Cyrus Vance to President Carter, 29 September 1979. See also, PAAA, B150 1979, Abt. 2 to Bundesminister, Betr.: Äußerungen Breschnews gegenüber dem Abrüstungsausschuß der Sozialistischen Internationale, 4 October 1979; FSNr. 973, Bruessel NATO to Bonn AA, Betr.: TNF-Modernisierung—hier: Entgegnung auf sowj. Propagandaoffensive, 3 October 1979.

116. PAAA, B150 1979, Telko Nr. 4982, Betr.: Sitzung des Abrüstungsausschusses der SI mit Breschnew am 1.10.79, 4 October 1979.

117. PAAA, B150 1979, Moskau to Bonn AA, FSNr. 3847, 6 October 1979; Abt. 2 to Bundesminister, Betr.: Äusserungen Breschnews gegenüber dem Abrüstungsausschuß der Sozialistischen Internationale, 4 October 1979.

118. TNA, FCO 28/3694 NATO Theatre Nuclear Forces Modernisation (1979—part A), telegram (no. 66) from Edwin Bolland (UK delegation in Vienna [MBFR talks]) to FCO, MOD etc. incl. his comments on 'Brezhnev's speech of 6 October 1979/MBFR', 7 October 1979. PAAA ZA 120237 LRTNF (Dezember 1979), Sachstand: LRTNF-Modernisiserung; sowjetische Kampagne gegen die geplante Modernisierung [no author], 4 December 1979. PAAA, ZA 120235 LRTNF (1.9.–31.10.1979), Botschafter Ruth to Genscher; Betr.: Rede Breschnews am 6.10.1979, 6 October 1979; telegram (Nr. 3585) from Washington embassy to AA, 8 October 1979; BMVg Paper [FÜ S III 5] Betr.: Erste Überlegungen zur Reaktion auf die Breschnew-Rede vom 6. Oktober in Ost-Berlin, 8 October1979; Vermerk—Betr.: LRTNF

Modernisierung, 10 October 1979. On British views of Brezhnev's speech and the subsequent Soviet anti-LRTNF or 'peace-' campaign, see four big files in the TNA, FCO 28/3694–28/3697 NATO TNF Modernisation (1979—parts A–D); for the West German perspective, see three fat files in PAAA, ZA 120235–37. Cf. Library of Congress, Washington, W. Averell Harriman papers, Box 1050, Subject File L. Brezhnev 1975–82, Specific points and comments on Brezhnev's 6 October speech.

119. *AAPD 1979/II*, doc. 259, 1284–8; doc. 295, 1471–4. Cf. PAAA, B150 1979, To Ref. 202, Betr.: Dt.-frz. Konsultationen der Staats- und Regierungschefs am 1./2. Oktober 1979 in Bonn, 2 Anlagen zu SALT II/III, LRTNF, Rüstungskontrollangebot, SG, 27 September 1979.

120. Cf. PAAA, B150 1979, FSNr. 3330, Washington to Bonn AA, 19 September 1979.

121. 'German Fears "Real Crisis" If Arms Pact Not Ratified', *Los Angeles Times*, 3 October 1979, A2.

122. PAAA, B150 1979, Telko Nr. 1116, 8 October 1979.

123. HSPA, HS privat, EA 13.11.–2.12.1979, Nr. 10, Tagesdienst, infos der SPD Fraktion—27.11.1979, 28 November 1979. 'Gromyko Besuch – Alles offen', *Der Spiegel*, no. 48/1979, 26 November 1979, 21–3.

124. HSPA, HS privat, EA 13.11.–2.12.1979, Nr. 10, Schlußbemerkungen, HS vor der Fraktion, 27 November 1979—not published (*Macher*). See also HSPA, HS privat, EA 4.12.1979–15.1.1980, Nr. 1 Referat des Bundeskanzler Helmut Schmidt auf dem Bundesparteitag der SPD in Berlin am 4.12.1979.

125. See PAAA, ZA 120237, telegram no. 498 from Den Haag embassy to AA, 5 December 1979; telegram no. 407 from Oslo embassy to AA, 6 December 1979; Personal message from Danish Foreign Minister Kjeld Olesen to Genscher, 23 November 1979; telegram no. 412 from Oslo embassy to AA, 7 December 1979. On Dutch–American diplomacy between October and December, see Cold War International History Project, e-collection: Euromissiles, <http://www.digitalarchive.wilsoncenter.org/collection/38/euromissiles-crisis>. See also US DDRS, reference CK3100573316, Letter from Carter to Schmidt, 1 November 1979.

126. TNA, FCO 28/3697 NATO TNF Modernisation (1979—part D), telegrams (nos 329 and 330) by Sir Clive Rose (Head of UK delegation to NATO) to FCO on 'Joint Ministerial Meeting: TNF Modernisation and Arms Control', 12 December 1979.

127. See Special Meeting of Foreign and Defence Ministers in Brussels, Chairman: Mr J. Luns, <http://www.nato.int/cps/en/natohq/official_texts_27040.htm?selectedLocale=en>.

128. PAAA, ZA 120238 LRTNF, NATO Doppelbeschluss (1.1.–28.2.1980), Note from Wagner to Referat 013, AA, Betr.: SALT—hier: Gründung der 'Special Consultative Group' der NATO am 24.1.1980, undated, possibly 25 January 1980.

129. On last-minute German liaising with the Norwegians, see AdsD, HSA, Box 006603, letter by Dietrich Genschel (Oberst im Generalstab und Leiter der Gruppe 23 im Bundeskanzleramt) to Bundekanzler, 6 December 1979; Vermerk über Bundekanzler Gespräch mit Stoltenberg, 4 December 1979. On earlier Dutch pressure for the 'zero option', see NSA-GWU, Nuclear Vault, US Mission to NATO cable 07693 to State Department, 'TNF: Permreps 6 November Discussion of Integrated Decision Document—Detailed Report', 7 November 1979, <http://www.gwu.edu/~nsarchiv/nukevault/ebb301/doc10.pdf>. On Schmidt's rallying of the SPD see, HSPA, HS privat, EA 13.11–2.12.1979, Nr. 10, Tagesdienst—Informationen der sozialdemokratischen Bundestagsfraktion, 27.11 1979 (28 Nov. 1979), and actual speech: Schlußbemerkungen Helmut Schmidts vor der Fraktion (nicht veröffentlicht), 27 November 1979; Nr. 15, Sitzung Parteirat, Berlin, 2 December 1979.

130. HSPA, HS privat, EA 13.11.–2.12.1979, Nr. 15, Sitzung Parteirat, Berlin, 2 December + Schlußwort; Nr. 10, Tagesdienst—Informationen der sozialdemokratischen Bundestagsfraktion, 27.11 1979 (28 Nov. 1979) and actual speech: Schlußbemerkungen Helmut Schmidts vor der Fraktion (nicht veröffentlicht), 27 November 1979.
131. Talbott, *Deadly Gambits*, 40.
132. Johannes Gross, 'Gehen die Lichter aus?', *Frankfurter Allgemeine Zeitung*, 31 December 1979, 1.

5. THE DOUBLE INTERPRETER

1. Helmut Schmidt Privatarchiv, Hamburg (henceforth HSPA), HS privat, Presse-Echo, 6.12.1979–5.1.1980, Heinz P. Dietrich, 'Bei Kanzlers fehlt der Tannenbaum', *Stuttgarter Nachrichten*, 24 December 1979; 'Schmidt 61! Nachts spielte der Kanzler Klavier...', *Bild*, 24 December 1979.
2. HSPA, HS privat, Presse-Echo, 6.12.1979–5.1.1980, 'Beunruhigt über das Vorgehen der Sowjetunion in Asien', *Die Welt*, 2 January 1980; 'Die Welt ist in Unruhe', *Frankfurter Rundschau*, 2 January 1980; Hartmut Palmer, 'Schmidt ändert seine Neujahrsrede: Passage über Entspannungswillen Moskaus durch Invasion in Afghanistan überholt', *Süddeutsche Zeitung*, 31 December 1979.
3. Jimmy Carter, *Keeping Faith: Memoirs of a President* (New York, 1982), 472; cf. Raymond L. Garthoff, *Détente and Confrontation: American–Soviet Relations from Nixon to Reagan* (Washington, DC, 1985), 944–65.
4. Jimmy Carter, Address to the Nation on the Soviet Invasion of Afghanistan, 4 January 1980, The American Presidency Project (henceforth APP) website, <http://www.presidency.ucsb.edu/ws/index.php?pid=32911&st=&st1=>.
5. Carter—'Meet the Press' interview, 20 January 1980, APP website, <http://www.presidency.ucsb.edu/ws/index.php?pid=33060&st=&st1=>; cf. Ernest R. May, *'Lessons' of the Past: The Use and Misuse of History in American Foreign Policy* (Oxford, 1973), ch. 2.
6. Letter to President of the US Olympic Committee, 20 January 1980 (APP), <http://www.presidency.ucsb.edu/ws/index.php?pid=33059&st=&st1=>.
7. Carter—'Meet the Press' interview, 20 January 1980, APP website, <http://www.presidency.ucsb.edu/ws/index.php?pid=33060&st=&st1=>.
8. Horst Möller et al., eds, *Akten zur Auswärtigen Politik der Bundesrepublik Deutschland 1980, Band I: 1. Januar bis 30. Juni 1978* (Munich, 2011) (henceforth *AAPD 1980/I*), docs 10 and 17; 'Bonn: Draht nach Moskau gestört?', *Der Spiegel*, no. 5/1980, 28 January 1980, 19–22, here 21; US Declassified Documents Reference System (henceforth US DDRS), reference CK3100097002, Memorandum of Schmidt–Vance conversation in Bonn, 25 February 1980; Raymond L. Garthoff, *Détente and Confrontation: American–Soviet Relations from Nixon to Reagan* (Washington, DC, 1985), 978.
9. Jimmy Carter Library, Atlanta, Georgia (henceforth JCL), Plains, Box 1, personnel, Memo of phone conversation between Carter and Schmidt, 1:30–1:42, 24 January 1980; 'Bonn: Draht nach Moskau gestört?', *Der Spiegel*, no. 5/1980, 28 January 1980, 21.
10. Wellington Long, 'Schmidt gives Carter a sweet and sour apple', *Christian Science Monitor*, 4 March 1980, 7; 'Mit den Amerikanern nicht in den Tod', *Der Spiegel*,

no. 18/1980, 28 April 1980, 18. HSPA, HS privat, Presse-Echo, 16.3.–20.4.1980, Wehners 'Signale', *Rheinische Post*, 17 March 1980; 'Battle of Wits, Not a Confrontation', *The Guardian*, 17 March 1980; John Vinocur, 'Re-Election Chances Harmed: Schmidt Faces Attack from his Party's Left', *Herald Tribune*, 31 March 1980.

11. Joint Carter–Schmidt press statement, 5 March 1980, APP website, <http://www.presidency.ucsb.edu/ws/index.php?pid=33109&st=&st1=>; Long, 'Schmidt gives Carter a sweet and sour apple', 7; 'For Schmidt, a Modest Success', *Los Angeles Times*, 9 March 1980, F4. 'Dynamic Duo on the Road: Schmidt visits the US; Giscard woos the Gulf', *Time*, 17 March 1980, 22–3; Paul Martin, 'The Reluctant Powerhouse', *Newsweek*, 17 March 1980, 7–9. Cf. HSPA, HS privat, Presse-Echo, 16.3.–20.4.1980, 'Endgültig aus: Deutsche nicht zur Moskau Olympiade', *Welt am Sonntag*, 16 March 1980.

12. For Brezhnev's 4 March letter, see *AAPD 1980/I*, doc 78, 440–50. For the backchannel communications, see, HSPA HS privat, Pz, UDSSR 1979–1980, Bd. 5, Nr. 15 Selbmann about his talks in Moscow on 1.4.1980—Nur für den Bundeskanzler—streng vertraulich!!!, 31.3.1980; Nr. 18 Vermerk für Bundeskanzler: Gespräch mit L., 9.4.1980 and Bahr to Schmidt (analysis of L talks), 10.4.1980.

13. As news over the backchannel opening leaked to the press, there was speculation whether Wehner, Bahr, and Selbmann (of the SPD) were effectively conducting a Moscow-friendly *Nebenaussenpolitik* (in parallel to the government foreign policy), HSPA, HS privat, Presse-Echo, 16.3.–20.4.1980, Heinz Schweden, 'Zum Tage: Tabu-Mann Wehner?', *Rheinische Post*, 14 April 1980.

14. HSPA, HS privat, EA 4.12.1979–15.1.1980, Nr. 14, Stern Interview—'Auch Demokraten brauchen Führung', 3 January 1980; EA 28.2.–11.4. 1980, Nr. 3, Bulletin der Bundesregierung Nr. 29, 18.3.1980, 237, Besuch des Bundeskanzlers in den Vereinigten Staaten vom 4.–6.3.1980; see also HSPA, HS privat, Presse-Echo, 16.3.–20.4.1980, 'Ich habe klare Zusagen des Präsidenten die Entspannungspolitik fortzusetzen', *Münchener Merkur*, 5 April 1980.

15. SPD Pressemitteilung, 15 April 1980, no. 228/80, text of Essen speech, digitzed, <http://www.library.fes.de/cgi-bin/digibert.pl?id=002415&dok=26/002415>; cf. SPD Pressemitteilung, 13 April 1980, no. 224/80, extracts of Hamburg speech, digitized, <http://www.library.fes.de/cgi-bin/digibert.pl?id=002414&dok=26/002414>. HSPA, HS privat, Presse-Echo, 16.3.–20.4.1980, Kanzler Schmidt befürchtet jetzt eine neuen Weltkrieg, *Welt am Sonntag*, 13 April 1980; 'Die Weltkrise 1980 erinnert Schmidt an das Jahr 1914', *Frankfurter Allgemeine Zeitung*, 14 April 1980.

16. HSPA, HS privat, Pz, UDSSR 1979–1980, Bd. 5, Nr. 17, Schmidt to Brandt, 2 April 1980.

17. 'Angst, daß die Sicherungen durchbrennen', *Der Spiegel*, no. 17/1980, 21 April 1980, 21–8. According to the magazine (p. 25) Schmidt's interest in 1914 had been stimulated by the writings of physicist and philosopher Carl Friedrich von Weizsäcker and by an essay of the American scholar Miles Kahler, 'Rumors of War: The 1914 Analogy', *Foreign Affairs* 58, no. 2 (Winter 1979), 374–96.

18. HSPA, HS privat, EA 12.4.–4.6 1980, Nr. 1, Stellvertretender SPD Vorsitzender Bundeskanzler Helmut Schmidt führte auf der Wahlveranstaltung in Essen am 12.4.1980 aus; Nr. 4, Landespressekonferenz, Düsseldorf, 17.4.1980 Helmut Schmidt und Johannes Rau (endgültige unkorrigierte Fassung). *AAPD 1980/I*, doc. 111, 606–7, notes 3 and 4, and doc. 126, 665–6.

19. *AAPD 1980/I*, doc. 126, 665, note 4.

20. HSPA, HS privat, Presse-Echo 21.4–16.5.1980 'Wink mit Raketen', *General-Anzeiger*, 16 April 1980; Hans Jörg Sottorf, 'SPD- Sicherheitskongress: Der Kanzler stellt klar',

21 April 1980. See also HSPA, HS privat Pz, Innenpolitik, M–Z, 1980, Bd. 15, 'S', Sprechzettel für Lage-Überblick, Helmut Schmidt im SPD-Spitzengespräch, Bungalow, 13.4.1980.

21. *AAPD 1978/I*, doc. 110, 606, note 26.

22. HSPA, HS privat, Presse-Echo, 16.3.–20.4.1980, '"Der Kanzler machte eine konstruktive Geste": Regierungssprecher Bölling verweist auf Werben Schmidts für Abrüstungsgespräche mit Moskau', *Frankfurter Rundschau*, 15 April 1980. Here Schmidt's spokesman Klaus Bölling stated that the chancellor had sought with a 'constructive gesture' to make the first step towards the Soviets:

> um die Gespräche über Rüstungsbegrenzungen 'wieder flottzukriegen'. Der BK habe bedauert, daß diese Initiative den Nachrichtenagenturen, die über seine Reden in Hamburg und Essen am Wochenende berichtet hatten, entgangen sei, sagte Bölling. 'Neu' sei an dem Vorschlag des Kanzlers, daß er der sowjetischen Regierung vorgeschlagen habe, 'zumindest einen Dislozierungsstopp' für Ihre Mittelstreckenraketen SS20 zu beschließen.

See also HSPA, HS privat, Presse-Echo, 16.3.–20.4.1980, Schmidt auf Extratour, *Die Welt*, 16 April 1980; 'Schmidt Consuslts Allies on Brezhnev Invitation', *Financial Times*, 17 April 1980.; Kurt Becker, 'Bevor der Kanzler nach Moskau reist', *Die Zeit*, 25 April 1980; Heinz-Peter Finke, 'Moskauer Zuckerbrot', *Rheinische Post*, 17 April 1980. HSPA, HS privat, Presse-Echo 21.4.–16.5.1980, Hans O. Staub, 'Kremlreise', *Die Weltwoche (Zürich)*, 23.4.1980; Eghard Mörbitz (Bonn), 'Moskau steht vor der Wahl', *Frankfurter Rundeschau*, 23 April 1980.

23. JCL, Brzezinski Material, Presidential Correspondence with Foreign Leaders file, Box 7, Germany—Chancellor Helmut Schmidt 3–8/80, Draft Cable from the President to Chancellor Schmidt, 24 April 1980.

24. JCL, Plains file, Box 1, personnel, Carter–Schmidt telephone conversation, 15 May 1980; Schmidt–Carter conversation, 6:46–6:58pm, 14 May 1980. On the politics of the Olympic boycott, see Rolf Pfeiffer, *Sport und Politik: Die Boykottdiskussionen um die Olympischne Spiele von Mexico City 1968 bis Los Angeles 1984* (Frankfurt a.M., 1987), 303–427.

25. HSPA, HS privat, EA 9.6.–10.6 1980, Nr. 1, Wahlparteitag Essen, Grugahalle 9./10.6.1980, 'Sicherheit für Deutschland'—Referat des stellvertretenden Vorsitzenden Bundeskanzler Helmut Schmidt.

26. John Vinocur, 'Key Bonn Aide, Backer of US, Changing Tone: Says Soviet Has Legitimate Security Interests, Too – Schmidt Urges Missile Freeze', *New York Times*, 10 June 1980, A3.

27. JCL, Brzezinski Material, Presidential Correspondence with Foreign Leaders file, Box 7, Germany—Chancellor Helmut Schmidt 3–8/80, Carter letter to Schmidt (two drafts), 12 June 1980 and notes on presidential approval of letters of 6 and 11 June 1980. *AAPD 1980/I*, doc. 170, 889–91, and esp. note 4; Brzezinski, Zbigniew, *Power and Principle: Memoirs of the National Security Adviser, 1977–1981* (London, 1983), 462–3.

28. *AAPD 1980/I*, doc. 182, 949; Don Cook, 'Venice, American Leadership Is on the Line', *Los Angeles Times*, 22 June 1980, G1.

29. 'Die Stimmung ist unterkühlt bis eisig', *Der Spiegel*, no. 26/1980, 23 June 1980, 19–20; Michael Getler, 'U.S. Diplomats Term Carter Letter to Schmidt An Unnecessary Insult', *Washington Post*, 21 June 1980, A8.

30. Carter, *Keeping Faith*, 536–7; Jimmy Carter, *White House Diary* (New York, 2010), 439–40. JCL, Plains file, Box 1, personnel, Conversation with HS during Venice Economic Summit, Sat. evening, 21 June 1981, and formal memo of conversation

approved by Carter; Brzezinski, *Power and Principle*, 310; *AAPD 1980/I*, doc. 182, 956; Helmut Schmidt, *Menschen und Mächte* (Berlin, 1987), 254–64.

31. Presidential Press Conference, 21 June 1980, American Presidency Project <http://www.presidency.ucsb.edu/ws/index.php?pid=44639&st=&st1=>. Cf. 'Carter, Schmidt Express Agreement on Deployment of Missiles', *Washington Post*, 22 June 1980, A1; 'Carter–Schmidt Clash Fogs Summit', *Chicago Tribune*, 22 June 1980, 2.

32. Elizabeth Pond, 'Chinese Visit Upstaged', *Christian Science Monitor*, 23 June 1980, 10. HSPA, HS privat, EA 11.6.–15.8.1980, Nr. 4, An Bundeskanzler von Bundespresseamt, 13.6.1980—Einzige Ausfertigung: Transcript—Discussion with Chancellor Helmut Schmidt at the European–American Workshop on Current Security Issues, Friday, 13 June 1980, FES, Bonn-Bad Godesberg.

33. Venice Economic Summit Conference—(Carter) Interview with Reporters Following the Conclusion of the Conference, 23 June 1980, APP website, <http://www.presidency.ucsb.edu/ws/index.php?pid=44648&st=&st1=>.

34. Dan Fisher, 'Schmidt Meets Brezhnev, Urges Afghan Pullout', *Los Angeles Times*, 1 July 1980, B1; *AAPD 1980/I*, doc. 192, esp. 1030. Details of the Moscow trip, as referred in the two paragraphs in the main text, can be found in HSPA, HS privat, Pz, UDSSR 1980–2, Bd. 6, Nr. 1 Privataufzeichnung – Berndt von Staden 30.6.–1 July 1980.

35. 'Das lief in Moskau – Zucker', *Der Spiegel* no. 28/1980, 7 July 1980, 19.

36. *AAPD 1980/II*, doc. 193, 1040.

37. Ibid., 1043.

38. *AAPD 1980/II*, doc. 194, 1050–63; 'Das lief in Moskau – Zucker!', *Der Spiegel* no. 28/1980, 7 July 1980, 21. Note: The 'continental dagger' was a polemical term used in the 18th and 19th centuries to describe Britain's harnessing of Prussia for its own security objectives. It was first used in the context of British subsidies for Frederick the Great during the Seven Years War and later, by extension, for any situation in which Prussia or Germany appeared to serve as an instrument for British policy. In the context of Schmidt's chancellorship, the metaphor was reoriented to critique the subordination of West German security interests to those of the United States.

39. *AAPD 1980/I*, doc. 97, 541 Angela Stent, *From Embargo to Ostpolitik: The Political Economy of West German–Soviet Relations, 1955–80* (Cambridge, 1981), 238–9. See also David K. Willis, 'Schmidt and Brezhnev Talk At – and Past – Each Other', *Christian Science Monitor*, 2 July 1980, 5; Jim Gallagher, 'Schmidt Leaves Moscow with Little Gained', *Chicago Tribune*, 3 July 1980, B6; 'Bonn's line to Moscow doesn't run through the White House', *Daily Telegraph*, 27 June 1980.

40. Willis, 'Schmidt and Brezhnev Talk At – and Past – Each Other', 5; Gallagher, 'Schmidt Leaves Moscow with Little Gained', B6; *AAPD 1980/I*, doc. 97, 541; Stent, *From Embargo to Ostpolitik*, 238–9.

41. 'Hans Ulrich Kempski berichtet aus Moskau: Krieg und Frieden im Katharinen-Saal', *Süddeutsche Zeitung*, 2 July 1980, 3. HSPA, HS privat, Presse-Echo, 1.–31.7.1980, Uwe Engelbrecht, 'Verwirrung und Verschnupftheit in der Zwischenphase: In Moskau lief nicht alles nach Wunsch – Kurzfristig flimmerte die Vision eines Scherbenhaufens auf', *General-Anzeiger*, 2 July 1980.

42. Willis, 'Schmidt and Brezhnev Talk At – and Past – Each Other', 5; Gallagher, 'Schmidt Leaves Moscow with Little Gained', B6.

43. HSPA, HS privat, Presse-Echo, 1.–31.7.1980, Hilde Purwin, 'Helmut Schmidt kam vom Kreml in den Kessenicher Hof—Gromyko zum Kanzler: "Bei uns wären Sie eigentlich noch ein Komsomolze"', *Neue Rhein-Ruhr Zeitung*, 3 July 1980; Almut Hauenschild, 'Vom Kreml direkt zu den "Kanälern"', *Die Welt*, 3 July 1980.

44. See 'Das lief in Moskau – Zucker!', *Der Spiegel* no. 28/1980, 7 July 1980,19–24. See also HSPA, HS privat, Presse-Echo, 1.–31.7.1980, 'Schmidt hält sich zurück mit Einzelheiten zu seinem vorsichtigen Raketen-Optimismus', *Frankfurter Allgemeine Zeitung*, 3 July 1980; Hilde Purwin, 'Helmut Schmidt kam vom Kreml in den Kessenicher Hof – Gromyko zum Kanzler: "Bei uns wären Sie eigentlich noch ein Komsomolze"', *Neue Rhein-Ruhr Zeitung*, 3 July 1980; Almut Hauenschild, 'Vom Kreml direkt zu den "Kanalern"', *Die Welt*, 3 July 1980; Evi Keil, 'Eine Unterrichtung der Opposition fand nicht statt – Vergeblich auf den Text der Kanzlerrede gewartet', *Bonner Rundschau*, 4 July 1980.

45. *AAPD 1980/II*, docs 196 and 198; John M. Goshko, 'Soviets Said To Modify Arms Stance: Muskie Sees Hint of a Softening on Missiles in Europe; Soviet Arms Stance Said Modified', *Washington Post*, 3 July 1980, A1.

46. On Schmidt's first conversation with president-elect Ronald Reagan on 20 November 1980 in Washington and their good 'chemistry', see Georgetown University Library Special Collections, Washington, DC, Walter John Stoessel, Jr, Papers, Box 10, Confidential Memorandum for the Record of conversation between Schmidt and Reagan, 20 November 1980.

47. Mark Kramer, 'Poland 1980–81: Soviet Policy during the "Polish Crisis"', *Cold War International History Project Bulletin*, 5 (1995), quoting on 137.

48. HSPA, HS privat, EA 7.10.–18.12.1980, Nr. 30, *Vertrauliches* Informationsgespräch des Bundeskanzlers mit den Chefredakteuren am 8.12.1980 im Bundeskanzleramt.

49. Ronald Reagan—The President's News Conference, 29 January 1981, APP website, <http://www.presidency.ucsb.edu/ws/index.php?pid=44101&st=&st1=>.

50. HSPA, HS privat, EA 7.10.–18.12.1980, Nr. 26, Gespräch Bundeskanzler Helmut Schmidt mit Bonner Korrespondenten am 9.12.1980—off the record. Elizabeth Pond, 'Sparks Fly on Both Sides of Atlantic over Schmidt–Reagan Meeting', *Christian Science Monitor*, 3 December 1980, 7.

51. Schmidt, *Menschen und Mächte*, 290.

52. HSPA, HS privat, EA 19.12.1980–28.2.1981, Nr. 30 Fraktionssitzung, Do., 19.2.1981, Bundeskanzler Helmut Schmidt. HSPA, HS privat, EA 1.5.–26.6.1981, Nr. 18, SPD Konferenz im SPD Bezirk westl. Westfalen am 16.5.1981 in Recklinghausen; Nr. 19, Rede von Bundeskanzler Helmut Schmidt auf dem 30. Landesparteitag der Bayrischen SPD in Wolfratshausen, 17.5.1981. Cf. HSPA, HS privat, EA 1.5.–26.6.1981, Nr. 10, DFS, 20:15 'Die Nachrüstung'—statements by H. Schmidt, E. Eppler (SPD), Dr Geissler (CDU), H. Sonnenfeldt (ehem Mitarbeiter Kissingers). HSPA, HS privat, politische Korrespondenz, 1981, L–Z, Bd. 24, Carl-Friedrich von Weizsäcker to Schmidt, 22 June 1981 and CFvW Diskussionsbemerkungen at FES on 20 June 1981; 'Helmut Schmidt: Hamburgs Polizeisenator macht "Nägel mit Köpfen"', *Christ und Welt*, 23 March 1962. Cf. Helmut Schmidt, *Was ich noch sagen wollte* (Munich, 2015), 167–9.

53. Ronald Reagan Presidential Library, Simi Valley, California, Executive Secretariat, NSC Records, Country File, Europe and Soviet Union: Germany, FRG (1/20–6/30/81), Box 14, Memcon – Schmidt-Reagan meeting, 10:30-12:00 (noon), Oval Office, 21 May 1981.

54. Reagan, Joint Statement Following Discussions With Chancellor Helmut Schmidt of the Federal Republic of Germany, 22 May 1981, APP website, <http://www.presidency.ucsb.edu/ws/index.php?pid=43852&st=&st1=>; Strobe Talbott, *Deadly Gambits: The Reagan Administration and the Stalemate in Nuclear Arms Control* (New York, 1985), 47–50.

55. 'Versetzen Sie sich mal in unsere Lage…', *Der Spiegel*, 2 November 1981, 39, 42, 58; see also HSPA, HS privat, Presse-Echo, 11.11.–4.12.1981, 'Moscow's Aim: Split NATO', *Time*, 16 November 1981; HSPA, HS privat, EA 26.2.–1.4.1982, Nr. 21,

Hintergrundgespräch, Donnerstag, 17:25–20:40 im Bundeskanzleramt—vertraulich, 25 March 1982. On the Bonn peace protest, see Holger Nehring and Benjamin Ziemann, 'Do All Paths Lead to Moscow? The NATO Dual-Track Decision and the Peace Movement – A Critique', *Cold War History* 12, no. 1 (2012), 6. On the political atmosphere in Bonn, see US DDRS, reference CK3100548074, Cable, State Department—Update on political atmosphere in Bonn—issues uppermost on Schmidt's and Genscher's minds ahead of US Secretary of State Haig's visit, 10 September 1981.

56. Reagan, Remarks to Members of the National Press Club on Arms Reduction and Nuclear Weapons, 18 November 1981, APP website, <http://www.presidency.ucsb. edu/ws/index.php?pid=43264&st=&st1=>; John Vinocur, 'Bonn and London Pleased', *New York Times*, 19 November 1981, A1; see also Talbott, *Deadly Gambits*, chs 3–4; Richard Aldous, *Reagan and Thatcher: The Difficult Relationship* (London, 2012), 60–3 . See also Oskar Fehrenbach, 'Friedenstaube aus Washington', *Stuttgarter Zeitung*, 20 November 1981:

> Wer jedoch die Sicherheitsdiskussion aufmerksam verfolgt hat, der weiß, daß die Europäer, daß die NATO in Brüssel und daß vor allem Bundeskanzler Helmut Schmidt die Null-Lösung bereits seit geraumer Zeit als verbindliche Verhandlungslinie des Westens empfehlen. Reagan hat also nur auf den Druck der Verbündeten reagiert und das europäische Konzept mit bravourösem Geschick als seinen eigenen Geniestreich verkauft.

57. HSPA, HS privat, EA 28.10.–27.11.81, Nr. 5, Informationsgespräch (off the record), Bundeskanzler Helmut Schmidt mit 18 amerikanischen Journalisten, die auf Einladung der KAS sich fünf Tage in Bonn und Berlin aufhalten, Do., 16:05–17:55 im großen Kabinettssaal des Bundeskanzleramts, 29 October 1981; Nr. 26, Mitteilung an die SPD Fraktions-Pressestelle: Schmidt in der heutigen Sitzung der SPD Bundestagsfraktion über den Breschnew Besuch, 26 November 1981; Nr. 27, DFS, Die Fernsehdiskussion, 20:15, 'Bonn nach dem Breschnew Besuch', 26 November 1981. John Vinocur, 'Opening Gambit: Brezhnev Trip to Bonn Sets the State for Missile Talks', *New York Times*, 22 November 1981; Flora Lewis, *New York Times*, 27 November 1981, A27. See also Rosemary Callman, 'Der Kanzler als Dolmetscher: Breschnews dritte Visite am Rhein', *Westfälische Rundschau*, 23 November 1981. Cf. Avril Pittman, *From Ostpolitik to Reunification: West German–Soviet Political Relations since 1974* (Cambridge, 1992), 101–8.

58. 'Auch die Sowjets wollen den Kompromiß', *Der Spiegel*, no. 49/1981, 30 November 1981, 17–20. HSPA, HS privat, Presse-Echo, 11.11.–4.12.1981, John Morrison, 'Brezhnev Turns Down Reagan's offer to Drop Deployment of Missiles', *The Herald Tribune*, 24 November 1981.On Geneva, see HSPA, HS privat, Presse-Echo, 11.11.–4.12.1981, John Vinocur, 'Schmidt Says U.S., Soviet Stances at Geneva Cannot lead to Accord', *International Herald Tribune*, 27 November 1981; 'Letzte deutsch-amerikanische Konsultationen vor Genf: Cheunterhändler Paul Nitze am Wochenende bei Genscher und Schmidt', *General-Anzeiger*, 28 November 1981; 'The Talking Starts', *The Times* (London), 30 November 1981; 'The Chancellor Stakes Political Future on Neo-Détente', *International Herald Tribune*, 26 November 1981; Hella Pick, 'Fervent Handshake Seals Bonn Summit Success', *The Guardian*, 26 November 1981.

59. Elizabeth Pond, 'West Germans Sign Huge Pipeline Deal', *Christian Science Monitor*, 23 November 1981. HSPA, HS privat, EA 28.10.–27.11.1981, Nr. 19, transcript of interview with Patricia Clough, *The Times* (London), 13 November 1981. See generally

Anthony J. Blinken, *Ally versus Ally: America, Europe and the Siberian Pipeline Crisis* (New York, 1987), esp. chs 1–5; Claudia Wörmann, *Osthandel als Problem der Atlantischen Allianz* (Bonn, 1986), esp. ch. D.

60. HSPA, HS privat, EA 29.6.–10.9.1981, Nr. 47, *Vorwärts*-Gespräch mit Bundeskanzler Helmut Schmidt, 'Wir fahren einen mittleren Weg', 10 September 1981; EA 11.09.–27.10.81, Nr. 1, Hintergrundsgspräch Bundeskanzler Helmut Schmidt mit Chefredakteuren—off the record. 11 September 1981.

61. John Vinocur, 'Crisis Does Not Affect Schmidt Trip', *New York Times*, 14 December 1981, A20; Blinken, *Ally versus Ally*, 96–7. On Schmidt's cautious stability-oriented Poland policy, see Dominik Pick, *Brücken nach Osten: Helmut Schmidt und Polen* (Bremen, 2011), 102–16.

62. John Vinocur, 'On This Visit, Schmidt Does Not Seem Relaxed', *New York Times*, 6 January 1982, A16.

63. See *Der Spiegel* issue no. 43/1981, which was entitled 'Der herzkranke Kanzler', and included several stories about his heart disease and pacemakers, for example, 'Das ist ein dummes Gefühl' and '"Dann rumpelt es in der Brust..."': Die Krankengeschichte des Patienten Helmut Schmidt', *Der Spiegel*, no. 43/1981, 19 October 1981, 17–24 and 25–30.

64. HSPA, HS privat, EA 16.4.–10.5.1982, Nr. 4, ZDF, heute journal, 21:00—Bundeskanzler Helmut Schmidt zur SPD Diskussion über den sicherheitspolitischen Redeausschnitt aus dem SPD Parteitag, 22 April 1982.

65. Reagan, Address before the Bundestag in Bonn, 9 June 1982, APP website, <http://www.presidency.ucsb.edu/ws/index.php?pid=42618&st=&st1=>; Steven R. Weisman, 'Reagan, in Berlin, Bids Soviet Work for a Safe Europe', *New York Times*, 12 June 1982, 1; John Tagliabue, 'Thousands of Anti-Reagan Protestors Clash with the Police in West Berlin', *New York Times*, 12 June 1982, 8.

66. Talbott, *Deadly Gambits*, 136. Memcon of Paul Nitze's 'Walk in the woods', 16 July 1982, <http://www.thereaganfiles.com/nitze-walk-in-the-wood.pdf>.

67. HSPA, HS privat, EA 9.9.–6.10.1982, Nr. 4, Deutscher Bundestag—Fr., 17.9.1982, 115. Sitzung, Plenarprotokoll (0/115), 7072; cf. Dennis L. Bark and David R. Gress, *A History of West Germany*, 2 vols, (2nd edn, Oxford, 1993), vol. 1, 376–9.

68. HSPA, HS privat, Presse-Echo 17.9–28.9.1982, 'Die Abrechnung', *Frankfurter Allgemeine Zeitung*, 17 September 1982.

69. Sten Martenson, 'Sekt wurde nicht gereicht', *Stuttgarter Zeitung*, 30 September 1982, 3; Anselm Beugeser, 'Nur mühsam konnte Schmidt die Tränen zurückhalten', *Hamburger Abendblatt*, 2/3 October 1982, 25.

70. Klaus Bölling, *Die letzten 30 Tage des Kanzlers Helmut Schmidt: Ein Tagebuch* (Hamburg, 1983), 110, 162–73. HSPA, HS privat, Presse-Echo 17.–28.9.1982, Stefan Vogel, 'Abschied von der Macht – Schmidt hängt schon die Bilder ab', *Bild*, 20 September 1982.

71. Bölling, *Die letzten 30 Tage des Kanzlers Helmut Schmidt*, 114.

72. Bölling, *Die letzten 30 Tage des Kanzlers Helmut Schmidt*, 115–16.

CONCLUSION

1. 'Dreizehn Jahre geliehene Macht (II)', *Der Spiegel*, no. 40/1982, 4 October 1982, esp. 50, 55.

2. Hartmut Soell, *Helmut Schmidt, 1918–1969: Vernunft und Leidenschaft, vol. 1* (Berlin, 2003); *Helmut Schmidt, 1969 bis heute: Macht und Verantwortung, vol. 2* (Berlin,

2008); Hans-Joachim Noack, *Helmut Schmidt: Die Biographie* (Berlin, 2010); Martin Rupps, *Helmut Schmidt: Eine politische Biographie* (Stuttgart/Leipzig, 2002). Cf. Journalistic accounts on Schmidt's life, such as Michael Schwelien, *Helmut Schmidt: Ein Leben für den Frieden* (Hamburg, 2003); Theo Sommer, *Unser Schmidt: Der Staatsmann und der Publizist* (Munich, 2011); Gunter Hofmann, *Helmut Schmidt: Soldat, Kanzler, Ikone* (Munich, 2015).

3. Henry Kissinger, *White House Years* (London, 1979), 54–5, 1474.

4. Henry Kissinger, *Years of Renewal* (London, 1999), 610–11. Similarly, Archie Brown writes that, despite his commanding presence, 'Schmidt's historical significance, however, hardly matched that of Brandt'. Archie Brown, *The Myth of the Strong Leader: Political Leadership in the Modern Age* (London, 2014), 136.

5. Cf. on this debate about the 1970s, Daniel Sargent, 'The Cold War and the International Political Economy in the 1970s', *Cold War History* 13, no. 3 (2013), 393–425.

6. Author interview with Helmut Schmidt, Hamburg, 15 October 2015.

7. Harold James, *International Monetary Cooperation since Bretton Woods* (New York, 1996), 175–6, 263–5.

8. John Vinocur, 'The Schmidt Factor', *New York Times*, 21 September 1980.

9. Henry Kissinger, *White House Years* (London, 1979), 54.

10. Quotations from Jeremi Suri, 'Henry Kissinger and Geopolitics of Globalization', in Niall Ferguson et al, eds, *The Shock of the Global: The 1970s in Perspective* (Cambridge, MA, 2010), 175; Niall Ferguson, *Kissinger, 1923–1968: The Idealist* (London, 2015), 2.

11. This was for Kissinger's joint role in bringing about a ceasefire in Vietnam. The award of the Peace Prize has, of course, also been vehemently criticized, given Kissinger's involvement in bombing Cambodia and toppling Salvador Allende in Chile. For a useful discussion, see Jussi Hanhimäki, *The Flawed Architect: Henry Kissinger and American Foreign Policy* (New York, 2004), xiii–xix, xx–xxii. No accusations of 'war crimes' have ever been levelled at Helmut Schmidt.

12. Quotations from Ferguson, *Kissinger*, 242; Suri, 'Henry Kissinger', 173, 187. Schmidt quoted from Horst Möller et al., eds, *Akten zur Auswärtigen Politik der Bundesrepublik Deutschland 1975, Band I: 1. Januar bis 30. Juni 1975* (Munich, 2006), doc. 173, 809. Helmut Schmidt, *A Grand Strategy for the West: The Anachronism of National Strategies in an Interdependent World* (New Haven, CT, 1985).

13. Kissinger, *Years of Renewal*, 611.

14. Helmut Schmidt Privatarchiv, Hamburg (henceforth HSPA), HS privat, Eigene Arbeiten (henceforth EA) 5.6.–20.7.1979, Nr. 1, Schmidt, Speech at Harvard Commencement, 7 June 1979.

15. Helmut Schmidt, 'Glanz und Elend der Gipfeldiplomatie – und ihre Notwendigkeit', in Helmut Schmidt and Walter Hesselbach, eds, *Kämpfer ohne Pathos: Festschrift für Hans Matthöfer zum 60. Geburtstag am 25. September 1985* (Bonn, 1985), 237–9; Helmut Schmidt, *Weggefährten: Erinnerungen und Reflexionen* (Berlin, 1996), 264, 304, 306.

16. Schmidt, 'Glanz und Elend', 236, 238.

17. HSPA, HS privat, EA 29.6.–10.9.1981, Nr. 8, Background discussion with Flora Lewis and John Vinocur of the *New York Times*, 7 July 1981.

18. HSPA, HS privat, EA 28.10.–27.11.1981, Nr. 27, DFS TV discussion, 'Bonn nach dem Breschnew Besuch, 20:15', 26 November 1981; Schmidt, 'Glanz und Elend', 237–9.

19. John Vinocur, 'The Schmidt Factor', *New York Times*, 21 September 1980.

Bibliography

PRIMARY SOURCES

Archives

Archiv der sozialen Demokratie, Friedrich-Ebert-Stiftung, Bonn
    Depositum Egon Bahr
    Helmut Schmidt Archiv

Bundesarchiv, Koblenz
    B136 (Bundeskanzleramt)

Carter, Jimmy, Presidential Library, Atlanta, Georgia
    Brzezinski, Zbigniew, Collection
    Carter, Jimmy, Presidential Papers
    Chief of Staff Butler
    Chief of Staff Jordan
    National Security Affairs
    Mondale, Walter F., Papers
    Plains File
    RAC (Remote Archives Capture)/CREST (CIA Records Search Tool):
        digitized and declassified secret files
    Solomon Collection
    Vertical File
    White House Central File

Det kgl. Forsvarsdepartementet, Oslo
    FD 200.18, MNW 1978
    FD 200.18, HLG/TNF 1978
    FD 200.18, NPG I 1–12000 1979

Ford, Gerald R., Presidential Library, Ann Arbor, Michigan
    Online archive: <http://www.fordlibrarymuseum.gov/library/docs.asp>

Georgetown University Library Special Collections, Washington, DC
    Stoessel, Walter John, Jr, Papers

Library of Congress, Washington, DC
    Harriman, W. Averell, Papers

National Archives and Records Administration, College Park, Maryland
    RG 59, State Department
        Office of the Counselor, Helmut Sonnenfeldt

Office of the Secretary of State,
  Transcripts of the Secretary of State Henry Kissinger's Staff meetings, 1973–77
  Records of Henry Kissinger, 1973–77
  Policy and Planning Staff
  Office of the Director, Records of Anthony Lake, 1977–81

Politisches Archiv des Auswärtigen Amts, Berlin
  B1 (Ministerbüro)
  B2 (Büro Staatssekretäre)
  B3 (Büro Parlamentarischer Staatssekretär)
  B4 (Parlaments- und Kabinettsreferat)
  B9 (Planungsstab)
  B14 (Atlantisches Bündnis und Verteidigung, Ref. 201)
  B24 (Frankreich, Ref. 202)
  B28 (Ost-West Beziehungen/KSZE, Ref. 212)
  B32 (USA/Großbritannien, Ref. 204)
  B38 (Außenpolitische Fragen, die Berlin und Deutschland als Ganzes betreffen, Ref. 210)
  B41 (UdSSR, Ref. 213)
  B43 (Sicherheit in Europa, Abrüstung und Rüstungskontrolle, Ref. 220, 221)
  B80 (Völkerrecht und Staatsverträge, Ref. 500)
  B83 (Strafrecht, Ref. 511)
  B150 (Dokumente für die Edition 'Akten zur Auswärtigen Politik der Bundesrepublik
  Deutschland')

Reagan, Ronald, Presidential Library, Simi Valley, California
  Executive Secretariat, NSC Records
    Country File, Europe and Soviet Union: Germany, FRG

Schmidt, Helmut, Privatarchiv, Hamburg
  HS privat, Eigene Arbeiten
  HS privat, Presse-Echo
  HS privat, Buchmanuskript—Verteidigung oder Vergeltung 1961
  HS privat, Schriftwechsel—Verteidigung oder Vergeltung, engl. Ausgabe 1961—Allgemeiner
  Schriftwechsel
  HS privat, Buchmanuskript—Strategie des Gleichgewichts 1969
  HS privat, Schriftwechsel—Strategie des Gleichgewichts 1969
  HS privat, Fritz Erler 14.7.1913–22.2.1967—Unterlagen/Korrespondenz 1950–1992
  HS privat, Fritz Erler—Reden 1949–67 (Bundestag)
  HS privat, politische Korrespondenz, L–Z, 1981
  HS privat, Tg 1980/I
  HS privat, Pz, öknomisches Papier 1974 mit Unterlagen
  HS privat, Pz, Helsinki Gespräche, 29.7.–1.8.1975
  HS privat, Pz, UdSSR 1977–1978 (Bd. III)
  HS privat, Pz, UdSSR 1978–1979 (Bd. IV)
  HS privat, Pz, UdSSR 1979–1980 (Bd. V)
  HS privat, Pz, UdSSR 1980–1982 (Bd. VI)
  HS privat, Pz, UdSSR 1980–1982—Unterlagen BK zu Kontakten mit sowj. Politikern
  (Bd. II)
  HS privat, Pz, Innenpolitik, A–L, 1980
  HS privat, Pz, Innenpolitik, M–Z, 1980
  HS privat, Pz, Dokumentation Weißbuch 1970
  Korrespondenz privat politisch, 1959–1961, A–Z

Korrespondenz privat politisch, 1952–1965, A–Z
Korrespondenz HS privat, 2008, K–L
Material Flutkatastrophe Febr. 1962, Kopien—EA, Korrespondenz, Presse-Echo
Wehner Briefe

Thatcher, Margaret, Foundation
  Online archive: <http://www.margaretthatcher.org/archive/default.asp>

The National Archives, Kew, London
  Cabinet Office
    CAB 128
  Foreign and Commonwealth Office
    FCO 28
    FCO 33
    FCO 41
    FCO 46
    FCO 49
    FCO 93
    FCO 96
    FCO 99
  Ministry of Defence
    DEFE 11
    DEFE 13
    DEFE 19
    DEFE 23
    DEFE 24
    DEFE 25
    DEFE 31
    DEFE 68
    DEFE 70
  Prime Minister's Office
    PREM 16
    PREM 19

Printed and Digitized Official Documents
Bundesministerium des Inneren und Bundesarchiv, eds, *Dokumente zur Deutschlandpolitik, VI. Reihe, Band 4: 1.1.1975–31.12.1976* (Munich, 2007)
Bundesministerium der innerdeutschen Beziehungen, ed., *Zur Lage der Nation* 1975 (Coburg, 1975)
Bundesminister der Verteidigung, ed., *Weißbuch 1969 zur Verteidigungspolitik der Bundesregierung* (Bonn, 1969)
Bundesminister der Verteidigung, ed., *Weißbuch 1970: Zur Sicherheit der Bundesrepublik Deutschland und zur Lage der Bundeswehr* (Bonn, 1970)
Bundesminister der Verteidigung, ed., *Weißbuch 1971/1972: Zur Sicherheit der Bundesrepublik und zur Entwicklung der Bundeswehr* (Bonn, 1972)
Bundesminister der Verteidigung, ed., *Weißbuch 1973/1974: Zur Sicherheit der Bundesrepublik und zur Entwicklung der Bundeswehr* (Bonn, 1974)
Bundespresseamt, *Bulletin* (Bonn, 1974–82)
Bundestag, *Protokolle des Deutschen Bundestages* (Bonn, 1974–82)
Cold War International History Project (CWIHP), The Euromissiles Crisis and the end of the Cold War, 1977–1987—A Document Reader, <http://www.wilsoncenter.org/publication/the-euromissiles-crisis-and-the-end-the-cold-war-1977–1987>

Independent Commission on International Economic Development, *North/South: A Programme for Survival* (London, 1980)

Möller, Horst, et al., eds, *Akten zur Auswärtigen Politik der Bundesrepublik Deutschland 1975–1982, 17 vols* (Munich, 2006–13)

Public Papers of the Presidents of the United States, The American Presidency *Project*, <http://www.presidency.ucsb.edu/ws/>

Saltoun-Ebin, Jason, and Chiampan, Andrea, 'The Reagan Files: The Euromissiles Crisis to the Intermediate Range Nuclear Forces Treaty, 1979–1987', <http://www.thereaganfiles.com/inf-treaty.html>

Schwarz, Hans-Peter, et al., eds, *Akten zur Auswärtigen Politik der Bundesrepublik Deutschland 1974, 2 vols* (Munich, 2005)

The National Security Archive, The Nuclear Vault, 'Thirtieth Anniversary of the Dual Track Decision – The Road to the Euromissile Crisis and the end of the Cold War', <http://www.nsarchive.gwu.edu/nukevault/ebb301/index.htm>

US Declassified Documents Research Database (1945–)

US State Department, *Foreign Relations of the United States*, Washington, DC, 1969–76, <https://history.state.gov/historicaldocuments>

US State Department, *Foreign Relations of the United States*, Washington, DC, 1977–80, <https://history.state.gov/historicaldocuments>

Contemporaneous Books, Speeches, and Essays

Brandt, Willy, and Helmut Schmidt, *Partner und Rivalen: Der Briefwechsel (1958–1992)* (edited and introduced by Meik Woyke) (Bonn, 2015)

Davis, Lynn E., 'NATO's Requirements and Policy for LRTNF, in Robert L. Rinne, ed., *The History of NATO TNF Policy: The Role of Studies, Analysis and Exercises—Conference Proceedings, Vol. 2: Papers and Presentation* (Albuquerque, NM/Livermore, CA, 1994), 169–94

Kissinger, Henry, 'The Industrial Democracies and the Future', speech at Pittsburgh, 11 Nov. 1975, 1–12, Gerald R. Ford Presidential Library, White House Press Releases, box 17—digitized

Kissinger, Henry, *Nuclear Weapons and Foreign Policy* (New York, 1957)

Kissinger, Henry, *The Necessity for Choice: Prospects of American Foreign Policy* (New York, 1960)

Schmidt, Helmut, *Verteidigung oder Vergeltung: Ein deutscher Beitrag zum strategischen Problem der NATO* (Stuttgart, 1961)

Schmidt, Helmut, *Defense or Retaliation: A German View* (New York, 1962)

Schmidt, Helmut, *Beiträge* (Stuttgart, 1967)

Schmidt, Helmut, *Strategie des Gleichgewichts: Deutsche Friedenspolitik und die Westmächte* (Stuttgart, 1969)

Schmidt, Helmut, *The Balance of Power: Germany's Peace Policy and the Super Powers* (Foreword by Denis Healey) (London, 1971)

Schmidt, Helmut, *Kontinuität und Konzentration* (2nd edn, Bonn–Bad Godesberg, 1976)

Schmidt, Helmut, *Der Kurs heißt Frieden* (Düsseldorf, 1979)

Schmidt, Helmut, *Pflicht zur Menschlichkeit: Beiträge zu Politik, Wirtschaft und Kultur* (Düsseldorf, 1981)

Schmidt, Helmut, *Freiheit verantworten* (Düsseldorf, 1983)

Schmidt, Helmut, *A Grand Strategy for the West: The Anachronism of National Strategies in an Interdependent World* (New Haven, CT, 1985)

Schmidt, Helmut, 'Probleme der militärischen Strategie', *Die Neue Gesellschaft* 21 (1965), 616–28

Schmidt, Helmut, 'Deutschland und das europäische Sicherheitssystem der Zukunft', *Wehrkunde* 16, no. 3 (1967), 118–24

Schmidt, Helmut, 'Germany in the Era of Negotiations', *Foreign Affairs* 49, no. 1 (October 1970), 40–50

Schmidt, Helmut, 'The Struggle for the World Product: Politics between Power and Morals', *Foreign Affairs* 52, no. 3 (April 1974), 437–51

Schmidt, Helmut, 'Private Memorandum on International Concertation of Economic Action, 30 July 1975', in Hartmut Soell, *Helmut Schmidt—Pioneer of International Economic and Financial Cooperation* (Heidelberg, 2014), 73–5

Schmidt, Helmut, 'Die internationale Verantwortung der Bundesrepublik Deutschland', *Die Neue Gesellschaft* 5 (1976), 396–403

Schmidt, Helmut, 'The 1977 Alastair Buchan Memorial Lecture', *Survival* 20, no. 1 (1978), 2–10

Schmidt, Helmut, 'The Case for More Intra-European Monetary Cooperation: Summary of Comments Made in Copenhagen, 7 April 1978 (Personal)', in Hartmut Soell, *Helmut Schmidt—Pioneer of International Economic and Financial Cooperation* (Heidelberg, 2014), 83–7

Schmidt, Helmut, 'A Policy of Reliable Partnership', *Foreign Affairs* 59, no. 4 (Spring 1981), 743–55

Schmidt, Helmut, 'The Zero Solution: In the German Interest', *Atlantic Community Quarterly* 25 (1987), 244–52

Thomson, James A., 'The LRTNF Decision: Evolution of US Theater Nuclear Policy, 1975–9', *International Affairs* 60, no. 4 (October 1984), 601–14

Memoirs

Apel, Hans, *Der Abstieg: Politisches Tagebuch 1978–1988* (Stuttgart, 1990)

Bahr, Egon, *Zu meiner Zeit* (Munich, 1996)

Brandt, Willy, *People and Politics* (Boston, 1978)

Brandt, Willy, *Erinnerungen* (Zurich, 1989)

Brandt, Willy, *My Life in Politics* (New York, 1992)

Brzezinski, Zbigniew, *Power and Principle: Memoirs of the National Security Adviser, 1977–1981* (London, 1983)

Callaghan, James, *Time and Chance* (London, 1987)

Carter, Jimmy, *Keeping Faith: Memoirs of a President* (New York, 1982)

Carter, Jimmy, *White House Diary* (New York, 2010)

Dobrynin, Anatoly, *In Confidence: Moscow's Ambassador to America's Six Cold War Presidents, 1962–1986* (New York, 1995)

Ford, Gerald R., *A Time to Heal* (London, 1979)

Genscher, Hans-Dietrich, *Erinnerungen* (Berlin, 1995)

Giscard d'Estaing, Valéry, *Le pouvoir et la vie: vol. 1—La recontre* (Paris, 1988)

Giscard d'Estaing, Valéry, *Le pouvoir et la vie: vol. 2—L'affrontement* (Paris, 1991)

Healey, Denis, *The Time of My Life* (New York, 1990)

Kissinger, Henry, *White House Years* (London, 1979)

Kissinger, Henry, *Years of Upheaval* (London, 1982)

Kissinger, Henry, *Years of Renewal* (London, 1999)

Kohl, Helmut, *Erinnerungen, 1930–1982* (Munich, 2004)

Keworkow Wjatscheslaw, *Der geheime Kanal: Moskau, der KGB und die Bonner Ostpolitik* (Berlin, 1995)

Leber, Georg, *Vom Frieden* (Munich, 1980)

Ruhfus, Jürgen, *Aufwärts: Erlebnisse und Erinnerungen eines diplomatischen Zeitzeugen 1955 bis 1992* (Sankt Ottilien, 2006)

Schmidt, Helmut, *Weggefährten: Erinnerungen und Reflexionen* (Berlin, 1983)

Schmidt, Helmut, *Menschen und Mächte* (Berlin, 1987)

Schmidt, Helmut, *Men and Power: A Politcal Retrospective* (Introduction by Henry A. Kissinger) (London, 1990)

Schmidt, Helmut, *Menschen und Mächte, 2: Die Deutschen und ihre Nachbarn* (Berlin, 1990)

Schmidt, Helmut, 'Politischer Rückblick auf eine unpolitische Jugend', in Helmut Schmidt and Loki Schmidt, eds, *Kindheit und Jugend unter Hitler* (Berlin, 1992), 213–54

Schmidt, Helmut, *Außer Dienst: Eine Bilanz* (Berlin, 2008)

Schmidt, Helmut, *Ein letzter Besuch: Begegnungen mit der Weltmacht China* (Berlin, 2013)

Schmidt, Helmut, *Was ich noch sagen wollte* (Munich, 2015)

Schmückle, Gerd, *Ohne Pauken und Trompeten: Erinnerungen an Krieg und Frieden* (Stuttgart, 1982)

Shultz, George P., *Turmoil and Triumph: My Years as Secretary of State* (New York, 1993)

Strauß, Franz J., *Die Erinnerungen* (Berlin, 1989)

Vance, Cyrus, *Hard Choices: Critical Years in American Foreign Policy* (New York, 1983)

Newspapers and Weeklies

Badische Zeitung
Bergedorfer Zeitung
Bild
Chicago Tribune
Christian Science Monitor
Christ und Welt
Daily Telegraph
Das Handelsblatt
Der Spiegel
Die Andere Zeitung
Die Welt
Die Zeit
Frankfurter Allgemeine Zeitung
General-Anzeiger
Hamburger Abendblatt
International Herald Tribune
Los Angeles Times
Münchener Merkur
Neue Rhein-Ruhr Zeitung
Neue Züricher Zeitung
Newsweek
New York Times
Rheinische Post
Stern
Stuttgarter Zeitung
Süddeutsche Zeitung
The Economist
The Guardian
The Observer
The Spectator
The Times (London)

Time
Unsere Zeit
Vorwärts
Wall Street Journal
Washington Post
Welt am Sonntag
Westdeutsche Zeitung

Interviews
Helmut Schmidt, Hamburg, 16 October 2013
Helmut Schmidt, Hamburg, 15 October 2015

Unpublished PhD Theses
Albers, Martin, 'The Policies of Britain, France and West Germany towards the People's Republic of China, 1969–1982', unpublished PhD dissertation, Cambridge University, 2014
Benning, Elizabeth J., 'Economic Power and Political Leadership: The Federal Republic, the West and the Re-Shaping of the International Economic System, 1972–1976', unpublished PhD dissertation, London School of Economics and Political Science, 2011
Häussler, Matthias, 'Helmut Schmidt and Anglo-German Relations, 1974–1982', unpublished PhD dissertation, Cambridge University, 2015
Lutsch, Andreas, 'Westbindung oder Gleichgewicht? Die nukleare Sicherheitspolitik der Bundesrepublik Deutschland zwischen Atomwaffensperrvertrag und NATO Doppelbeschluss (1961–1979)', Johannes-Gutenberg-Universität, Mainz, 2015

SECONDARY SOURCES

Books
Abelshauser, Werner, *Deutsche Wirtschaftsgeschichte seit 1945* (Munich, 2004)
Adomeit, Hannes, *Imperial Overstretch: Germany in Soviet Policy from Stalin to Gorbachev: An Analysis based on New Archival Evidence, Memoirs, and Interviews* (Baden-Baden, 1998)
Albrecht, Henning, *'Pragmatisches Handeln zu sittlichen Zwecken': Helmut Schmidt und die Philosophie* (Bremen, 2008)
Aldous, Richard, *Reagan and Thatcher: The Difficult Relationship* (London, 2012)
Altrichter, Helmut, and Hermann Wentker, eds, *Der KSZE-Prozess: Vom Kalten Krieg zu einem neuen Europa 1975 bis 1990* (Munich, 2011)
Auger, Vincent A., *The Dynamics of Foreign Policy Analysis: The Carter Administration and the Neutron Bomb* (London, 1996)
Aust, Stefan, *Der Baader Meinhof Komplex* (Hamburg, 1985)
Auten, Brian J., *Carter's Conversion: The Hardening of American Defense Policy* (Columbia, MO, 2008)
Bald, Detlef, *Die Bundeswehr: Eine kritische Geschichte 1955–2005* (Munich, 2005)
Bald, Detlef, *Hiroshima, 6. August 1945: Die nukleare Bedrohung* (Munich, 1999)
Bald, Detlef, *Politik der Verantwortung: Das Beispiel Helmut Schmid—Der Primat des Politischen über das Militärische 1965–1975. Mit einem Vorwort von Helmut Schmidt* (Berlin, 2008)
Beer, A. K., *Eine Schule, die hungrig machte: Der Einfluss der Lichtwarkschule auf Helmut und Loki Schmidt* (Bremen, 2007)
Berghahn, Volker R., and Simone Lässig, eds, *Biography between Structure and Agency: Central European Lives in International Historiography* (New York and Oxford, 2008)

Betts, Richard K., ed., *Cruise Missiles: Technology, Strategy, Politics* (Washington, DC, 1981)

Birkner, Thomas, *Mann des gedruckten Wortes: Helmut Schmidt und die Medien* (Bremen, 2014)

Birkner, Thomas, *Comrades for Europe?: Die 'Europarede' Helmut Schmidts 1974* (Bremen, 2005)

Blanning, T. C., and David Cannadine, eds, *History and Biography* (Cambridge, 1996)

Bluth, Christoph, *Britain, Germany, and Western Nuclear Strategy* (Oxford, 1995)

Bluth, Christoph, *Germany and the Future of European Security* (New York, 2000)

Bluth, Christoph, *The Two Germanies and Military Security in Europe* (New York, 2002)

Bödeker, H. E., ed., *Biographie Schreiben* (Göttingen, 2003)

Böhm, Enrico, *Die Sicherheit des Westens: Entstehung und Funktion der G7-Gipfel (1975–1981)* (Munich, 2014)

Booz, Rüdger M., *'Hallsteinzeit': Deutsche Außenpolitik 1955–1972* (Bonn, 1995)

Bormann, Patrick, Thomas Freiberger, and Judith Michel, eds, *Angst in den Internationalen Beziehungen* (Göttingen, 2010)

Borstelmann, Thomas, *1970s: A New Global History from Civil Rights to Economic Inequality* (Princeton, 2011)

Boutwell, Jeffrey D., Paul Doty, and Gregory F. Treverton, eds, *The Nuclear Confrontation in Europe* (London, 1985)

Bresselau von Bressendorf, Agnes, *Frieden durch Kommunikation: Das System Genscher und die Entspannungspolitik im Zweiten Kalten Krieg 1979–1982/83* (Berlin, 2015)

Brown, Archie, *The Myth of the Strong Leader: Political Leadership in the Modern Age* (London, 2014)

Buteux, Paul, *Strategy, Doctrine, and the Politics of Alliance: Theater Nuclear Force Modernization in NATO* (Boulder, CO, 1983)

Campbell, John, *Roy Jenkins: A Well-Rounded Life* (London, 2014)

Carr, Jonathan, *Helmut Schmidt: Helmsman of Germany* (London, 1985)

Cohen, Raymond, *Negotiating across Cultures: International Communication in an Interdependent World* (2nd revsd edn, Washington, DC, 1999)

Conze, Eckart, *Die Suche nach Sicherheit: Eine Geschichte der Bundesrepublik Deutschland von 1949 bis in die Gegenwart* (Munich, 2009)

Conze, Eckart, ed., *Geschichte der internationalen Beziehungen: Erneuerung und Erweiterung einer historischen Disziplin* (Cologne, 2004)

Creuzberger, Stefan, *Westintegration und Neue Ostpolitik: Die Außenpolitik der Bonner Republik* (Berlin, 2009)

Daalder, Ivo H., *The Nature and Practice of Flexible Response: NATO Strategy and Theater Nuclear Forces since 1967* (New York, 1991)

Dallek, Robert, *Nixon and Kissinger: Partners in Power* (New York, 2007)

Dewey, P. J., *Callaghan's Journey to Downing Street* (Basingstoke, 2010)

Dietl, Ralph, *Equal Security: Europe and the SALT Process, 1969–1976* (Stuttgart, 2013)

Dittgen, Herbert, *Deutsch-amerikanische Sicherheitsbeziehungen in der Ära Helmut Schmidt: Vorgeschichte und Folgen des NATO-Doppelbeschlusses* (Munich, 1991)

Doering-Manteuffel, Anselm, and Lutz Raphael, *Nach dem Boom: Perspektiven auf die Zeitgeschichte seit 1970* (Göttingen, 2008)

Dönhoff, Marion Gräfin, *Hart am Wind: Helmut Schmidts politische Laufbahn* (Hamburg, 1978)

Dönhoff, Marion Gräfin, *Foe into Friend: The Makers of the New Germany from Konrad Adenauer to Helmut Schmidt* (New York, 1982)

Duffield, John S., *World Power Forsaken: Political Culture, International Institutions, and German Security Policy after Unification* (Stanford, CA, 1998)

Dunn, David H., ed., *Diplomacy at the Highest Level: The Evolution of International Summitry* (London, 1996)

Eibl, Franz, *Politik der Bewegung: Gerhard Schröder als Außenminister 1961–1966* (Munich, 2001)

Eichhorn, Joachim S., *Durch alle Klippen hindurch zum Erfolg: Die Regierungspraxis der ersten Großen Koalition, 1966–1969* (Munich, 2009)

Enders, Thomas, *Die SPD und die äußere Sicherheit: Zum Wandel der sicherheitspolitischen Konzeption der Partei in der Zeit der Regierungsverantwortung, 1966–1982* (Melle, 1987)

Enders, Thomas, *Franz Josef Strauß: Helmut Schmidt und die Doktrin der Abschreckung* (Koblenz, 1984)

Enskat, Sebastian, and Carlo Masala, eds, *Internationale Sicherheit: Eine Einführung* (Wiesbaden, 2014)

Erickson, Paul et al., *How Reason Almost Lost Its Mind: The Strange Career of Cold War Rationality* (Chicago, 2013)

Evans, Peter B., Harold K. Jacobson, and Robert D. Putnam, *Double-Edged Diplomacy: International Bargaining and Domestic Politics* (Berkeley, CA, 1993)

Faulenbach, Bernd, *Das sozialdemokratische Jahrzehnt: Von der Reformeuphorie zur Neuen Unübersichtlichkeit. Die SPD 1969–1982* (Bonn, 2011)

Ferguson, Niall, *Kissinger: 1923–1968—The Idealist* (London, 2015)

Ferguson, Niall, et al., eds, *The Shock of the Global: The 1970s in Perspective* (Cambridge, MA, 2010)

Finney, Patrick, ed., *Palgrave Advances in International History* (Basingstoke, 2005)

Freedman, Lawrence, *The Evolution of Nuclear Strategy* (New York, 2003)

Gaddis, John L., *Strategies of Containment: A Critical Appraisal of American National Security Policy during the Cold War* (expanded edn, New York, 2005)

Gaddis, John L., *The United States and the Origins of the Cold War, 1941–47* (New York, 1972)

Gaddis, John L., *We Now Know: Rethinking Cold War History* (New York, 1997)

Garthoff, Raymond L., *Détente and Confrontation: American–Soviet Relations from Nixon to Reagan* (Washington, DC, 1985)

Garton Ash, Timothy, *In Europe's Name: Germany and the Divided Continent* (London, 1993)

Gassert, Philipp, Tim Geiger, and Hermann Wentker, eds, *Zweiter Kalter Krieg und Friedensbewegung: Der NATO-Doppelbeschluss in deutsch-deutscher und Internationaler Perspektive* (Munich, 2011)

Gavin, Francis J., *Nuclear Statecraft: History and Strategy in America's Atomic Age* (Ithaca, NY, 2012)

Geier, Stephan, *Schwellenmacht: Bonns heimliche Atomdiplomatie von Adenauer bis Schmidt* (Paderborn, 2013)

Geiger, Tim, *Atlantiker gegen Gaullisten: Außenpolitischer Konflikt und innerparteilicher Machtkampf in der CDU/CSU 1958–1969* (Munich, 2008)

Gfeller, Aurélie Elisa, *Building a European Identity: France, the United States, and the Oil Shock, 1973–1974* (New York, 2012)

Gienow-Hecht, Jessica C. E., and Frank Schumacher, eds, *Culture and International History* (Oxford, 2003)

Gildea, Robert, *France since 1945* (Oxford, 2002)

Glad, Betty, *An Outsider in the White House: Jimmy Carter, His Advisors, and the Making of American Foreign Policy* (Ithaca, NY, 2009)

Glad, Thomas C., *Theater Nuclear Force Modernization as an Issue in West German Politics, 1977–1980* (Monterey, CA, 1980)

Goldblat, Josef, *Arms Control: The New Guide to Negotiations and Agreements* (2nd edn, London, 2009)

Görtemaker, Manfred, *Die unheilige Allianz: Die Geschichte der Entspannungspolitik 1943–1979* (Munich, 1979)

Görtemaker, Manfred, *Geschichte der Bundesrepublik Deutschland: Von der Gründung bis zur Gegenwart* (Munich, 1999)

Görtemaker, Manfred, *Kleine Geschichte der Bundesrepublik Deutschland* (Bonn, 2003)

Gray, Colin S., *The Second Nuclear Age* (London, 1999)

Gray, Colin S., *War, Peace and International Relations: An Introduction to Strategic History* (New York, 2007)

Greiner, Bernd, Christian Th. Müller, and Claudia Weber, eds, *Ökonomie im Kalten Krieg* (Bonn, 2010)

Hacke, Christian, *Die Außenpolitik der Bundesrepublik Deutschland: Von Konrad Adenauer bis Gerhard Schröder* (Berlin, 2004)

Haftendorn, Helga, *Abrüstungs- und Entspannungspolitik zwischen Sicherheitsbefriedigung und Friedenssicherung: Zur Außenpolitik der BRD 1955–1973* (Düsseldorf, 1974)

Haftendorn, Helga, *Sicherheit und Entspannung: Zur Außenpolitik der Bundesrepublik Deutschland 1955–1982* (Baden-Baden, 1983)

Haftendorn, Helga, *Sicherheit und Stabilität: Außenbeziehungen der Bundesrepublik zwischen Ölkrise und NATO-Doppelbeschluss* (Munich 1986)

Haftendorn, Helga, *Kernwaffen und die Glaubwürdigkeit der Allianz: Die NATO-Krise von 1966/67* (Baden-Baden, 1994)

Haftendorn, Helga, *Deutsche Außenpolitik zwischen Selbstbeschränkung und Selbstbehauptung 1945–2000* (Stuttgart, 2001)

Haftendorn, Helga, *Coming of Age: German Foreign Policy since 1945* (Lanham, MD, 2006)

Halliday, Fred, *The Making of the Second Cold War* (London, 1983)

Halverson, Thomas E., *The Last Great Nuclear Debate: NATO and Short-Range Nuclear Weapons in the 1980s* (Houndmills, 1995)

Hammerich, Helmut, *Das Heer 1950 bis 1970: Konzeption, Organisation, Aufstellung* (München, 2006)

Hanhimäki, Jussi M., *The Flawed Architect: Henry Kissinger and American Foreign Policy* (New York, 2004)

Hanhimäki, Jussi, Georges-Henri Soutou, and Basil Germond, eds, *The Routledge History of Transatlantic Security* (London, 2010)

Hanhimäki, Jussi M., Benedikt Schoenborn, and Barbara Zanchetta, *Transatlantic Relations since 1945: An Introduction* (New York, 2012)

Hanhimäki, Jussi M., *The Rise and Fall of Détente: American Foreign Policy and the Transformation of the Cold War* (Washington, DC, 2013)

Hanrieder, Wolfram F., *Helmut Schmidt: Perspectives on Politics* (Boulder, CO, 1982)

Hanrieder, Wolfram F., *Germany, America, Europe: Forty Years of German Foreign Policy* (New Haven, CT, 1989)

Hanshew, Karrin, *Terror and Democracy in West Germany* (Cambridge, 2012)

Haslam, Jonathan, *The Soviet Union and the Politics of Nuclear Weapons in Europe, 1969–1987: The Problem of the SS-20* (Basingstoke, 1989)

Heep, Barbara D., *Helmut Schmidt und Amerika: Eine schwierige Partnerschaft* (Bonn, 1990)

Hennessy, Peter, *Cabinets and the Bomb* (Oxford, 2007)

Herf, Jeffrey, *War by Other Means: Soviet Power, West German Resistance, and the Battle of the Euromissiles* (New York, 1991)

Herz, John H., *Staatenwelt und Weltpolitik: Aufsätze zur internationalen Politik im Nuklearzeitalter* (Hamburg, 1974)

Herz, John H., *Weltpolitik im Atomzeitalter* (Stuttgart, 1961)

Heumann, H. D., *Hans-Dietrich Genscher: Die Biographie* (Paderborn, 2012)

Heuser, Beatrice, *NATO, Britain, France and the FRG: Nuclear Strategies and Forces for Europe, 1949–2000* (Basingstoke, 1997)

Heuser, Beatrice, *Nuclear Mentalities? Strategies and Beliefs in Britain, France and the FRG* (Basingstoke, 1998)

Heuser, Beatrice, *The Bomb: Nuclear Weapons in their Historical, Strategic and Ethical Context* (New York, 2000)

Heuser, Beatrice, *Den Krieg denken: Die Entwicklung der Strategie seit der Antike* (Paderborn, 2010)

Hickson, Kevin, *The IMF Crisis of 1976 and British Politics* (London, 2005)

Hildebrand, Klaus, *Integration und Souveränität: Die Außenpolitik der Bundesrepublik Deutschland 1949–1982* (Bonn, 1991)

Hildebrand, Klaus, *Von Erhard zur Großen Koalition 1963–1969* (Wiesbaden, 1984)

Hillgruber, Andreas, *Deutsche Geschichte 1945–1986: Die 'deutsche Frage' in der Weltpolitik* (6th edn, Stuttgart, 1987)

Hinrichsen, Hans-Peter E., *Der Ratgeber: Kurt Birrenbach und die Außenpolitik der Bundesrepublik Deutschland* (Berlin, 2002)

Hofmann, Gunter, *Willy Brandt und Helmut Schmidt: Geschichte einer schwierigen Freundschaft* (3rd edn, Munich, 2013)

Hofmann, Gunter, *Helmut Schmidt: Soldat, Kanzler, Ikone* (Munich, 2015)

Holloway, David, *The Soviet Union and the Arms Race* (New Haven, 1983)

Holm, Hans-Henrik, and Nikolaj Petersen, eds, *The European Missiles Crisis: Nuclear Weapons and Security Policy* (London, 1983)

Huth, Paul K., *Extended Deterrence and the Prevention of War* (New Haven, 1988)

Hymans, Jacques E. C., *The Psychology of Nuclear Proliferation: Identity, Emotions, and Foreign Policy* (Cambridge, 2006)

Ischinger, Wolfgang, ed., *Towards Mutual Security: Fifty Years of Munich Security Conference* (Göttingen, 2014)

Jackson, Ben, and Robert Saunders, eds, *Making Thatcher's Britain* (Cambridge, 2012)

Jäger, Thomas, et al., eds, *Deutsche Außenpolitik: Sicherheit, Wohlfahrt, Institutionen und Normen* (Wiesbaden, 2007)

Jäger, Wolfgang, and Werner Link, *Republik im Wandel 1974–1982: Die Ära Schmidt, Vol. 5/II* (Geschichte der Bundesrepublik Deutschland) (Stuttgart, 1994)

James, Harold, *International Monetary Cooperation since Bretton Woods* (Oxford, 1996)

James, Harold, *Rambouillet, 15. November 1975: Die Globalisierung der Wirtschaft* (Munich, 1997)

Jarausch, Konrad H., ed., *Das Ende der Zuversicht? Die siebziger Jahre als Geschichte* (Göttingen, 2008)

Jonas, Rainer, and Manfred Tietzel, *Die Neuordnung der Weltwirtschaft* (Bonn–Bad Godesberg, 1976)

Judt, Tony, *Postwar: A History of Europe since 1945* (London, 2005)

Kaiser, Karl, and John Roper, eds, *Die stille Allianz: Deutsch-britische Sicherheitskooperation* (Bonn, 1987)

Kaldor, Mary, *The Imaginary War: Understanding the East–West Conflict* (Oxford, 1990)

Kaplan, Fred, *The Wizards of Armageddon* (New York, 1984)

Kaplan, Lawrence S., *NATO and the United States: The Enduring Alliance* (Boston, MA, 1988)

Kaplan, Lawrence S., *The Long Entanglement: NATO's First Fifty Years* (Westport, CT, 1999)

Kielmansegg, Peter Graf, *Nach der Katastrophe: Eine Geschichte des geteilten Deutschland* (Berlin, 2000)

Knipping, Franz, and Matthias Schönwald, eds, *Aufbruch zum Europa der zweiten Generation: Die europäische Einigung 1969–1984* (Trier, 2006)

König, Mareike, and Matthias Schulz, eds, *Die Bundesrepublik Deutschland und die europäische Einigung 1949–2000: Politische Akteure, gesellschaftliche Kräfte und internationale Erfahrungen* (Stuttgart, 2004)

Krotz, Ulrich, and Joachim Schild, *Shaping Europe: France, Germany, and Embedded Bilateralism from the Elysée Treaty to Twenty-First Century Politics* (Oxford, 2013)

Lappenküper, Ulrich, *Die Außenpolitik der Bundesrepublik Deutschland 1949 bis 1990* (Munich, 2008)

Leffler, Melvyn P., and Odd Arne Westad, eds, *The Cambridge History of the Cold War*, three vols (Cambridge, 2010)

Lehberger, Reiner, *Die Lichtwarkschule in Hamburg: Das pädagogische Profil einer Reformschule des höheren Schulwesens in der Weimarer Republik. Darstellung und Quellen* (Hamburg, 1996)

Liddell Hart, B. H., *Deterrent or Defence* (London/New York, 1960)

Lippert, Werner D., *The Economic Diplomacy of Ostpolitik: Origins of NATO's Energy Dilemma* (New York, 2011)

Little, Richard, *The Balance of Power in International Relations: Metaphors, Myths and Models* (Cambridge, 2007)

Loth, Wilfried, ed., *La gouvernance supranationale dans la construction européenne* (Bruxelles, 2005)

Lucas, Hans-Dieter, ed., *Genscher, Deutschland und Europa* (Baden-Baden, 2002)

Ludlow, Peter, *The Making of the European Monetary System: A Case Study of the Politics of the European Community* (London, 1982)

Ludlow, N. Piers, ed., *European Integration and the Cold War: Ostpolitik–Westpolitik, 1965–1973* (Abingdon, 2007)

Merseburger, Peter, *Der schwierige Deutsche: Kurt Schumacher* (Stuttgart, 1995)

Mey, Holger, *NATO Strategie vor der Wende: Die Entwicklung des Verständnisses nuklearer Macht im Bündnis zwischen 1967 und 1990* (Baden-Baden, 1992)

Miard-Delacroix, Hélène, *Partenaires de choix? Le chancelier Helmut Schmidt et la France, 1974–82* (Frankfurt a. M., 1993)

Morgan, Kenneth O., *Callaghan: A Life* (Oxford, 1997)

Mourlon-Druol, Emmanuel, *A Europe Made of Money: The Emergence of the European Monetary System* (Ithaca, NY, 2012)

Mourlon-Druol, Emmanuel, and Federico Romero, eds, *International Summitry and Global Governance: The Rise of the G7 and the European Council, 1974–1991* (London, 2014)

Njølstad, Olav, *Peacekeeper and Troublemaker: Jimmy Carter's Containment Policy, 1977–1978* (Oslo, 1994)

Njølstad, Olav, ed., *The Last Decade of the Cold War: From Conflict Escalation to Conflict Transformation* (London, 2004)

Noack, Hans-Joachim, *Helmut Schmidt: Die Biographie* (Berlin, 2010)

Nuti, Leopoldo, ed., *The Crisis of Détente in Europe: From Helsinki to Gorbachev, 1975–1985* (London, 2008)

Nuti, Leopoldo et al., eds, *Euromissile Crises and the End of the Cold War* (Stanford, CA, 2015)

Osgood, Robert, *Limited War: The Challenge to American Strategy* (Chicago, 1957)

Osgood, Robert, *NATO: Problems of Strategy and Independence* (New York, 1959)

Paes, Thomas, *Die Carter-Administration und die Regierung Schmidt: Konsens und Dissens über die Sowjetunion-Politik 1977–81* (Rheinfelden, 1991)

Pamperrien, Sabine, *Helmut Schmidt und der Scheißkrieg: Die Biografie 1918 bis 1945* (Munich, 2014)

Patel, Kiran Klaus, and Kenneth Weisbrode, eds, *European Integration and the Atlantic Community in the 1980s* (Cambridge, 2014)

Peters, Butz, *Tödlicher Irrtum: Die Geschichte der RAF* (Berlin, 2004)

Peters, Susanne, *The Germans and the INF Missiles: Getting Their Way in NATO's Strategy of Flexible Response* (Baden-Baden, 1990)

Pick, Dominik, *Brücken nach Osten: Helmut Schmidt und Polen* (Bremen, 2012)

Pierre, Andrew J., ed., *Nuclear Weapons in Europe* (New York, 1984)

Pittman, Avril, *From Ostpolitik to Reunification: West German–Soviet Political Relations since 1974* (Cambridge, 1992)

Ploetz, Michael, *Wie die Sowjetunion den Kalten Krieg verlor: Von der Nachrüstung zum Mauerfall* (Berlin, 2000)

Ploetz, Michael, and Hans-Peter Müller, *Ferngelenkte Friedensbewegung? DDR und UdSSR im Kampf gegen den NATO-Doppelbeschluss* (Münster, 2004)

Prittie, Terence, *The Velvet Chancellors: A History of Post-war Germany* (London, 1979)

Putnam, Robert D., and Nicholas Bayne, *Hanging Together: Cooperation and Conflict in the Seven-Power Summits* (2nd edn, London, 1987)

Quinlan, Michael, *Thinking about Nuclear Weapons: Principles, Problems, Prospects* (New York, 2009)

Raithel, Thomas et al., eds, *Auf dem Weg in eine neue Moderne? Die Bundesrepublik Deutschland in den siebziger und achtziger Jahren* (München, 2009)

Raphael, Lutz, and Anselm Doering-Manteuffel, *Nach dem Boom: Perspektiven auf die Zeitgeschichte seit 1970* (Göttingen, 2008)

Reynolds, David, *Summits: Six Meetings that Shaped the Twentieth Century* (London, 2007)

Risse-Kappen, Thomas, *Die Krise der Sicherheitspolitik: Neuorientierungen und Entscheidungsprozesse im politischen System der Bundesrepublik Deutschland 1977–1984* (Munich, 1988)

Risse-Kappen, Thomas, *Null-Lösung: Entscheidungsprozesse zu den Mittelstreckenwaffen 1970–1987* (Frankfurt a. M., 1988)

Rödder, Andreas, *Die Bundesrepublik Deutschland 1969–1990* (Munich, 2004)

Rödder, Andreas, *Deutschland einig Vaterland: Die Geschichte der Wiedervereinigung* (Munich, 2009)

Romano, Angela, *From Détente in Europe to European Détente: How the West Shaped the Helsinki CSCE* (Brussels, 2009)

Rother, Bernd, *Willy Brandts Aussenpolitik* (Wiesbaden, 2014)

Rueckert, George L., *Global Double Zero: The INF Treaty from Its Origins to Implementation* (Westport, CT, 1993)

Rühl, Lothar, *Mittelstreckenwaffen in Europa: Ihre Bedeutung in Strategie, Rüstungskontrolle und Bündnispolitik* (Baden-Baden, 1987)

Rupps, Martin, *Helmut Schmidt: Politikverständnis und geistige Grundlagen* (Bonn, 1997)

Rupps, Martin, *Helmut Schmidt: Eine politische Biographie* (Stuttgart/Leipzig, 2002)

Rupps, Martin, *Troika wider Willen: Wie Brandt, Wehner und Schmidt die Republik regierten* (Berlin, 2005)

Sargent, Daniel J., *A Superpower Transformed: The Remaking of American Foreign Relations in the 1970s* (New York, 2015)

Schneider, Andrea H., *Die Kunst des Kompromisses: Helmut Schmidt und die Große Koalition 1966–1969* (Paderborn 1999)

Schöllgen, Gregor, *Angst vor der Macht: Die Deutschen und ihre Außenpolitik* (Frankfurt a. M., 1993)

Schöllgen, Gregor, *Deutsche Außenpolitik: Von den Anfängen bis zur Gegenwart* (3rd and expanded edn, Munich, 2004)

Schöllgen, Gregor, *Jenseits von Hitler: Die Deutschen in der Weltpolitik von Bismarck bis heute* (Berlin, 2005)

Schulz, Mathias, and Thomas A. Schwartz, eds, *The Strained Alliance: U.S.–European Relations from Nixon to Carter* (Cambridge, 2009)

Schwelien, Michael, *Helmut Schmidt: Ein Leben für den Frieden* (Hamburg, 2003)

Seelow, Gunnar, *Strategische Rüstungskontrolle und deutsche Außenpolitik in der Ära Helmut Schmidt* (Baden-Baden, 2013)

Simonian, Haig, *The Privileged Partnership: Franco-German Relations in the European Community, 1969–1984* (Oxford, 1985)

Sodaro, Michael, *Moscow, Germany and the West from Khrushchev to Gorbachev* (Ithaca, NY, 1993)

Soell, Hartmut, *Helmut Schmidt: 1969 bis heute—Macht und Verantwortung* (Munich, 2008)

Soell, Hartmut, *Helmut Schmidt: 1918–1969—Vernunft und Leidenschaft* (Munich, 2003)

Soell, Hartmut, ed., *Helmut Schmidt—Pioneer of International Economic and Financial Cooperation* (Heidelberg, 2014)

Sommer, Theo, *Unser Schmidt: Der Staatsmann und der Publizist* (Munich, 2011)

Spanier, John L., *Games Nations Play: Analyzing International Politics* (New York, 1972)

Stent, Angela, *Wandel durch Handel? Die politisch-wirtschaftlichen Beziehungen zwischen der Bundesrepublik Deutschland und der Sowjetunion* (Köln, 1983)

Stöver, Bernd, *Der Kalte Krieg 1947–1991: Geschichte eines radikalen Zeitalters* (Munich, 2007)

Suri, Jeremi, *Henry Kissinger and the American Century* (Cambridge, MA, 2007)

Talbott, Strobe, *Deadly Gambits: The Reagan Administration and the Stalemate in Arms Control* (New York, 1985)

Vogtmeier, Andreas, *Egon Bahr und die deutsche Frage: Zur Entwicklung der sozialdemokratischen Ost- und Deutschlandpolitik vom Kriegsende bis zur Vereinigung* (Bonn, 1996)

von Karczewski, Johannes, *'Weltwirtschaft ist unser Schicksal': Helmut Schmidt und die Schaffung der Weltwirtschaftsgipfel* (Bonn, 2008)

von Nayhauß, Mainhardt Graf, *Helmut Schmidt: Mensch und Macher* (Bergisch-Gladbach, 1988)

Waechter, Matthias, *Helmut Schmidt und Valéry Giscard d'Estaing: Auf der Suche nach Stabilität in der Krise der 70er Jahre* (Bremen, 2011)

Waltz, Kenneth N., *Man, the State and War: A Theoretical Analysis* (New York, 1959)

Wasserman, Sherri L., *The Neutron Bomb Controversy* (New York, 1983)

Weinachter, Michèle, *Valéry Giscard d'Estaing et l'Allemagne: Le double rêve inachevé* (Paris, 2004)

Westad, Odd Arne, *The Global Cold War* (Cambridge, 2005)

Wiegrefe, Klaus, *Das Zerwürfnis: Helmut Schmidt, Jimmy Carter und die Krise der deutsch–amerikanischen Beziehungen* (Berlin, 2005)

Zipfel, Astrid, *Der Macher und die Medien: Helmut Schmidts politische Öffentlichkeitsarbeit* (Tübingen/Stuttgart/Heidelberg, 2005)

Zubok, Vladislav M., *A Failed Empire: The Soviet Union in the Cold War from Stalin to Gorbachev* (Chapel Hill, NC, 2007)

Articles and Chapters

Ahonen, Pertti, 'Franz Josef Strauß and the German Nuclear Question, 1956–1962', *Journal of Strategic Studies* 18, no. 2 (1995), 25–51

Benning, Elizabeth, 'The Road to Rambouillet and the Creation of the Group of Five', in Emmanuel Mourlon-Druol and Federico Romero, eds, *International Summitry and Global Governance: The Rise of the G7 and the European Council, 1974–1991* (London, 2014)

Bingen, Dieter, 'Realistische Entspannungspolitik: Der mühsame Dialog mit dem Osten— Die Bundesrepublik und ihre östlichen Nachbarn' (1974–1982), in Hans-Dieter Lucas, ed., *Genscher, Deutschland und Europa* (Baden-Baden, 2002), 155–84

Bluth, Christoph, 'Reconciling the Irreconcilable: Alliance Politics and the Paradox of Extended Deterrence in the 1960s', *Cold War History* 1, no. 2 (2001), 73–102

Böckenförde, Stephan, 'Die Veränderung des Sicherheitsverständnisses', in Sven B. Gareis, ed., *Deutsche Sicherheitspolitik: Herausforderungen, Akteure und Prozesse* (Opladen, 2009), 11–44

Boutwell, Jeffrey D., 'NATO Theatre Nuclear Forces: The Third Phase 1977–85', in Jeffrey D. Boutwell et al., eds, *The Nuclear Confrontation in Europe* (Dover MA, 1985), 67–86

Burr, William, and David Alan Rosenberg, 'Nuclear competition in an era of stalemate, 1963–1975', in Melvyn P. Leffler and Odd Arne Westad, eds, *The Cambridge History of the Cold War, Vol. II: Crises and Détente* (Cambridge, 2010), 88–111

Chiampan, Andrea, '"Those European Chicken Littles": Reagan, NATO, and the Polish Crisis, 1981–2', *The International History Review* 37, no. 4 (2015), 682–99

Conze, Eckart, 'Griff nach der Bombe? Die militärischen Pläne des Franz-Josef Strauß', in Martin Doerry and Hauke Janssen, eds, *Die SPIEGEL-Affäre: Ein Skandal und seine Folgen* (München 2013), 69–85

Conze, Eckart, 'Konfrontation und Détente: Überlegungen zu einer historischen Analyse des Ost-West-Konflikts', *Vierteljahrshefte für Zeitgeschichte* 46, no. 2 (April, 1998), 269–82

Conze, Eckart, 'Sicherheit als Kultur: Überlegungen zu einer "modernen Politikgeschichte" der Bundesrepublik Deutschland', *Vierteljahrshefte für Zeitgeschichte* 53, no. 3 (Juli 2005), 357–80

Conze, Eckart, 'Modernitätsskepsis und die Utopie der Sicherheit: NATO-Nachrüstung und Friedensbewegung in der Geschichte der Bundesrepublik', *Zeithistorische Forschungen/Studies in Contemporary History*, Online-Ausgabe 7, no. 2 (2010) <http://www.zeithistorische-forschungen.de/16126041-Conze-2-2010>

Corthorn, Paul, 'The Cold War and British Debates over the Boycott of the 1980 Moscow Olympics', *Cold War History* 13, no. 1 (2013), 43–66

Creswell, Michael H., and Dieter H. Kollmer, 'Power, Preferences, or Ideas? Explaining West Germany's Armaments Strategy, 1955–1972', *Journal of Cold War Studies* 15, no. 4 (2013), 55–103

Demidova, Ksenia, 'The Deal of the Century: The Reagan Administration and the Soviet Pipeline', in Kiran Klaus Patel and Kenneth Weisbrode, eds, *European Integration and the Atlantic Community in the 1980s* (Cambridge, 2014), 59–82

Dietl, Ralph, 'Introduction: On Nuclear Order', *Historische Mitteilungen* 24 (2011), 6–10

Dietl, Ralph, 'European Nuclear Decision Making? The United States, Nuclear Non-Proliferation and the "European Option", 1967–1972', *Historische Mitteilungen* 24 (2011), 43–89

Dietl, Ralph, '"Wir müssen sie produzieren": Adenauer und die deutsch-französische Nuklearkooperation, 1956–1963', in Klaus Schwabe, ed., *Konrad Adenauer und Frankreich 1949–1963: Stand und Perspektiven der Forschung zu den deutsch-französischen Beziehungen in Politik, Wirtschaft und Kultur* (Bonn 2005), 40–64

Domber, Gregory F., 'Transatlantic Relations, Human Rights, and Power Politics', in Poul Villaume and Odd Arne Westad, eds, *Perforating the Iron Curtain: European Détente, Transatlantic Relations, and the Cold War, 1965–1985* (Copenhagen, 2010), 195–214

Doty, Paul, and Robert Metzger, 'Arms Control Enters the Gray Area', *International Security* 3, no. 3 (Winter 1978–1979), 17–52

Eckart, Michael, 'Die Anfänge der Atompolitik in der Bundesrepublik Deutschland', *Vierteljahrshefte für Zeitgeschichte* 37, no. 1 (Januar 1989), 115–43

Eibl, Franz, 'Die deutsch-französischen Konsultationen vom 3./4. Juli 1964 und de Gaulles "Angebot" einer nuklearen Zusammenarbeit', in Karl G. Kick et al., eds, *Wandel durch Beständigkeit: Studien zur deutschen und internationalen Politik: Jens Hacker zum 65. Geburtstag* (Berlin 1998), 389–408

Elli, Mauro, 'Callaghan, the British Government and the N-Bomb Controversy', *Cold War History* 15, no. 3 (2015), 321–39

Freedman, Stefanie, 'The Making of an Accidental Crisis: The United States and the NATO Dual-Track Decision of 1979', *Diplomacy & Statecraft* 25, no. 2 (2014), 331–55

Friedrich-Ebert-Stiftung, ed., 'Die Siebzigerjahre: Gesellschaftliche Entwicklungen in Deutschland', *Archiv für Sozialgeschichte* 44 (2004)

Gaffney, Henry H., 'Euromissiles as the Ultimate Evolution of Theater Nuclear Forces', *Journal of Cold War Studies* 16, no. 1 (2014), 180–99

Gala, Marilena, 'NATO Modernization at a Time of Détente: A Test of European Coming of Age?', *Historische Mitteilungen* 24 (2011), 90–120

Gassert, Philipp, 'Did Transatlantic Drift Help European Integration? The Euromissiles Crisis, the Strategic Defense Initiative, and the Quest for Political Cooperation', in Kiran Klaus Patel and Kennneth Weisbrode, eds, *European Integration and the Atlantic Community in the 1980s* (Cambridge, 2014), 154–76

Gavin, Francis J., 'Nuclear Nixon: Ironies, Puzzles, and the Triumph of Realpolitik', in Frederik Logevall and Andrew Preston, eds, *Nixon in the World: American Foreign Relations, 1969–1977* (Oxford, 2008), 126–45

Geiger, Tim, 'Die "Landshut" in Mogadischu: Das außenpolitische Krisenmanagement der Bundesregierung angesichts der terroristischen Herausforderung 1977', *Vierteljahrshefte für Zeitgeschichte* 57, no. 3 (Juli 2009), 413–56

Gray, William G., 'Floating the System: Germany, the United States, and the Breakdown of Bretton Woods, 1969–1973', *Diplomatic History* 31, no. 2 (2007), 295–323

Gray, William G., 'Abstinence and Ostpolitik: Brandt's Government and the Nuclear Question', in Carole Fink and Bernd Schäfer, eds, *Ostpolitik, 1969–1974: European and Global Responses* (New York, 2009), 244–68

Gray, William G., 'Toward a "Community of Stability"? The Deutsche Mark between European and Atlantic Priorities, 1968–1973', in Matthias Schulz and Thomas A. Schwartz, eds, *The Strained Alliance: U.S.–European Relations from Nixon to Carter* (Cambridge, 2010), 145–68

Hacke, Christian, 'Die Bedeutung des nationalen Interesses für die Außenpolitik der Bundesrepublik', in Gottfried Niedhart, et al., eds, *Deutschland in Europa: Nationale Interessen und internationale Ordnung im 20. Jahrhundert* (Mannheim, 1997), 18–35

Hacke, Christian, 'Die Sicherheitspolitik der Bundesrepublik Deutschland', in Klaus J. Bremm et al., eds, *Entschieden für Frieden: 50 Jahre Bundeswehr 1955–2005* (Freiburg i. B., 2005), 269–82

Häckel, Erwin, 'Die nuklearpolitische Interessenlage Deutschlands', *Internationale Politik* 51, no. 10 (1996), 3–8

Haftendorn, Helga, 'Das doppelte Mißverständnis: Zur Vorgeschichte des NATO-Doppelbeschlusses von 1979', *Vierteljahrshefte für Zeitgeschichte* 33, no. 2 (April 1985), 244–87

Haftendorn, Helga, 'Das Projekt einer multilateralen NATO-Atomstreitmacht (MLF): Vademecum für die Glaubwürdigkeit der nuklearen Strategie?', *Militärgeschichtliche Mitteilungen* 54 (1995), 417–50

Haftendorn, Helga, 'The Harmel Report and its Impact on German Ostpolitik', in Wilfried Loth and Georges-H. Soutou, ed., *The Making of Détente: Eastern and Western Europe during the Cold War 1965–1975* (London, 2008), 103–16

Hanhimäki, Jussi M., '"Dr. Kissinger" or "Mr. Henry"? Kissingerology, Thirty Years and Counting', *Diplomatic History* 27, no. 5 (2003), 637–76

Hanhimäki, Jussi M., 'Searching for a Balance: The American Perspective', in N. Piers Ludlow, ed., *European Integration and the Cold War: Ostpolitik–Westpolitik, 1965–1973* (Abingdon, 2007), 152–73

Hattersley, Roy, 'Callaghan, Leonard James [Jim], Baron Callaghan of Cardiff (1912–2005)', *Oxford Dictionary of National Biography*, Oxford University Press, Jan 2009; online edn, <http://www.oxforddnb.com/view/article/94837>

Häussler, Mathias, 'A Cold War European? Helmut Schmidt and European integration, 1945–82', *Cold War History*, 15, no. 4 (2015), 427–47

Hemmerle, Oliver B., 'Explaining NATO to the West Germans: Helmut Schmidt as a Military Affairs Writer in the 1960s', in Christian Nünlist and Anna Locher, eds, *Transatlantic Relations at Stake: Aspects of NATO, 1956–1972* (Zürich, 2006), 215–34

Hershberg, Jim G., 'The Cuban Missile Crisis', in Melvyn P. Leffler and Odd Arne Westad, eds, *The Cambridge History of the Cold War, Vol. II: Crises and Détente* (Cambridge, 2010), 65–87

Heuser, Beatrice, 'Britain and the Federal Republic of Germany in NATO, 1955–1990', in Jeremy Noakes et al., eds, *Britain and Germany in Europe, 1949–1990* (Oxford, 2002), 141–62

Heuser, Beatrice, 'Die Strategie der NATO während des Kalten Krieges', in Klaus J. Bremm et al., eds, *Entschieden für Frieden: 50 Jahre Bundeswehr 1955–2005* (Freiburg i. B., 2005), 51–62

Heuser, Beatrice, 'Alliance of Democracies and Nuclear Deterrence', in Vojtech Mastny et al., eds, *War Plans and Alliances in the Cold War: Threat Perceptions in the East and West* (New York, 2006), 193–217

Heuser, Beatrice, 'Partners in NATO: Britain, Germany and the "Nuclear Issue"', in Manfred Görtemaker, ed., *Britain and Germany in the Twentieth Century* (Oxford, 2006), 145–83

Heuser, Beatrice, and Kristan Stoddart, 'Großbritannien zwischen Doppelbeschluss und Anti-Kernwaffen-Protestbewegungen,' in Philipp Gassert et al., eds, *Zweiter Kalter Krieg und Friedensbewegung: Der NATO-Doppelbeschluss in deutsch-deutscher und internationaler Perspektive* (Munich, 2011), 305–25

Hiepel, Claudia, 'Introduction', in Claudia Hiepel, ed., *Europe in a Globalising World: Global Challenges and European Responses in the 'Long' 1970s* (Baden-Baden, 2014), 9–26

Hiepel, Claudia, 'Willy Brandt, Georges Pompidou und Europa: Das deutsch–französische Tandem in den Jahren 1969–1974', in Franz Knipping and Matthias Schönwald, eds, *Aufbruch zum Europa der zweiten Generation: Die europäische Einigung 1969–1984* (Trier, 2006), 28–46

Hilfich, Fabian, 'West Germany's Long Year of Europe: Bonn between Europe and the United States', in Matthias Schulz and Thomas A. Schwartz, eds, *The Strained Alliance: U.S.–European Relations from Nixon to Carter* (Cambridge 2009), 237–57

Iriye, Akira, 'Culture and International History', in Michael J. Hogan and Thomas G. Paterson, eds, *Explaining the History of American Foreign Relations* (Cambridge, 1991), 214–25

Irving, R. E. M., and W. E. Paterson, 'The West German General Election of 1976', *Parliamentary Affairs* 30, no. 2 (1977), 209–25

Jarausch, Konrad H., et al., 'Die 1970er-Jahre – Inventur einer Umbruchzeit', *Zeithistorische Forschungen/Studies in Contemporary History* 3, no. 3 (2006)

Kaiser, Karl, 'Kernwaffen als Faktor der internationalen Politik', in Hans-Peter Schwarz, ed., *Weltpolitik: Strukturen—Akteure—Perspektive* (Bonn, 1985), 102–18

Kaltefleiter, Werner, 'Nukleare Waffen: Abschreckung und Friedenssicherung', in Michael Salewski, ed., *Das nukleare Jahrhundert. Eine Zwischenbilanz* (Stuttgart, 1998), 252–7

Krieger, Wolfgang, 'Verteidigung durch Entspannung? Die deutsch-amerikanischen Sicherheitsbeziehungen 1968–1990', in Detlef Junker et al., eds, *Die USA und Deutschland im Zeitalter des Kalten Krieges 1945–1990: Ein Handbuch, Vol. 2—1968–1990* (Stuttgart/Munich, 2001), 177–99

Krieger, Wolfgang, 'Zur politischen Geschichte der Kernwaffen: Vollständige Abrüstung oder Abschreckung kombiniert mit Rüstungsbegrenzung?', in Wolfgang Bender and Wolfgang Liebert, eds, *Wege zu einer nuklearwaffenfreien Welt* (Münster, 2001), 19–31

Lahey, Daniel J., 'The Thatcher Government's Response to the Soviet Invasion of Afghanistan, 1979–1980', *Cold War History* 13, no. 1 (2013), 21–42

Lehmkuhl, U., 'Diplomatiegeschichte als internationale Kulturgeschichte: Theoretische Ansätze und empirische Forschung zwischen Historischer Kulturwissenschaft und Soziologischem Institutionalismus', *Geschichte und Gesellschaft* 27, no. 3 (2001), 394–423

Loth, Wilfried, 'Deutsche Europapolitik von Helmut Schmidt bis Helmut Kohl', in Franz Knipping and Matthias Schönwald, eds, *Aufbruch zum Europa der zweiten Generation: Die europäische Einigung 1969–1984* (Trier, 2006), 474–88

Loth, Wilfried, 'Angst und Vertrauensbildung', in Jost Dülffer and Wilfried Loth, eds, *Dimensionen Internationaler Geschichte* (Berlin, 2012), 29–46

Ludlow, N. Piers, 'The Real Years of Europe? U.S.–West European Relations during the Ford Administration', *Journal of Cold War Studies* 15, no. 3 (2013), 136–61

Lutsch, Andreas, 'Souveränität im Atomzeitalter? Die nukleare Sicherheitspolitik der Bundesrepublik Deutschland zwischen Atomwaffensperrvertrag und NATO-Doppelbeschluss', *Newsletter des Arbeitskreises für Militärgeschichte* 16 (2011), 4–7

Mergel, Thomas, 'Überlegungen zu einer Kulturgeschichte der Politik', *Geschichte und Gesellschaft* 28 (2002), 574–606

Miard-Delacroix, Hélène, 'Ungebrochene Kontinuität: François Mitterrand und die deutschen Kanzler Helmut Schmidt und Helmut Kohl, 1981–1984', *Vierteljahrshefte für Zeitgeschichte* 47, no. 4 (Oktober 1999), 539–58

Mourlon-Druol, Emmanuel, '"Managing from the Top": Globalisation and the Rise of Regular Summitry', *Diplomacy & Statecraft* 23, no. 4 (2012), 679–703

Müller, Christian Th., 'Der Erdgas-Röhren Konflikt 1981/82', in Bernd, Greiner Christian Th. Müller, and Claudia Weber, eds, *Ökonomie im Kalten Krieg* (Bonn, 2010), 501–20

Nehring, Holger, and Benjamin Ziemann, 'Do All Paths Lead to Moscow? The NATO Dual-Track Decision and the Peace Movement–A Critique', *Cold War History* 12, no. 1 (2012), 1–24

Niedhart, Gottfried, 'Der alte Freund und der neue Partner: Die Bundesrepublik und die Supermächte', in Detlef Junker et al., eds, *Die USA und Deutschland im Zeitalter des Kalten Krieges 1945–1990: Ein Handbuch, Vol. 2—1968–1990* (Stuttgart/Munich, 2001), 46–55

Niedhart, Gottfried, 'Frieden als Norm und Erfahrung in der Außenpolitik der Bundesrepublik Deutschland', Thomas Kühne, ed., *Von der Kriegskultur zur Friedenskultur? Zum Mentalitätswandel in Deutschland seit 1945* (Hamburg, 2000), 182–201

Niedhart, Gottfried, and Oliver Bange, 'Die "Relikte der Nachkriegszeit" beseitigen: Ostpolitik in der zweiten außenpolitischen Formationsphase der Bundesrepublik Deutschland und ihre internationalen Rahmenbedingungen 1969–1971', *Archiv für Sozialgeschichte* 44 (2004), 415–48

Njølstad, Olav, 'The Collapse of Superpower Détente, 1975–1980', in Melvyn P. Leffler and Odd Arne Westad, eds, *The Cambridge History of the Cold War, Vol. III: Endings* (Cambridge, 2010), 135–55

Nuti, Leopoldo, 'The Origins of the 1979 Dual Track Decision – A Survey', in Leopoldo Nuti, ed., *The Crisis of Détente in Europe: From Helsinki to Gorbachev, 1975–1985* (London, 2008), 57–71

Nuti, Leopoldo, 'Italy and the Battle of the Euromissiles: The Deployment of the US BGM-109 G "Gryphon", 1979–83', in Olav Njølstad, ed., *The Last Decade of the Cold War: From Conflict Escalation to Conflict Transformation* (London, 2004), 98–115

Otte, Thomas G., 'Diplomacy and Decision-making', in Patrick Finney, ed., *Palgrave Advances in International History* (Basingstoke, 2005), 36–57

Peterson, Christian Philip, 'The Carter Administration and the Promotion of Human Rights in the Soviet Union, 1977–1981', *Diplomatic History* 38, no. 3 (2014), 628–56

Pridham, Geoffrey, 'Ecologists in Politics: The West German Case', *Parliamentary Affairs* 31, no. 4 (1978), 436–44

Quinlan, Michael, 'Deterrence and Deterrability', *Contemporary Security Policy* 25, no.1 (2004), 11–17

Rebentisch, Dieter, 'Gipfeldiplomatie und Weltökonomie: Weltwirtschaftliches Krisenmanagement während der Kanzlerschaft Helmut Schmidts, 1974–1982', *Archiv für Sozialgeschichte* 28 (1988), 307–32

Reynolds, David, 'Summitry as Intercultural Communication', *International Affairs*, 85, no. 1 (2009), 115–27

Romero, Federico, 'Cold War Historiography at the Crossroads', *Cold War History* 14, no. 4 (2014), 685–703

Romero, Federico, ed., 'The International History of European Integration in the Long 1970s: A Roundtable Discussion on Research Issues, Methodologies, and Directions', *Journal of European Integration History* 17, no. 2 (2011), 331–60

Schlarp, Karl-Heinz, 'Die ökonomische Untermauerung der Entspannungspolitik: Visionen und Realitäten einer deutsch-sowjetischen Wirtschaftskooperation im Zeichen der neuen Ostpolitik', *Archiv für Sozialgeschichte* 45 (2005), 77–100

Schoenborn, Benedikt, 'NATO Forever? Willy Brandt's Heretical Thoughts on an Alternative Future', in Jussi Hanhimäki, Georges-Henri Soutou, and Basil Germond, eds, *The Routledge History of Transatlantic Security* (London, 2010), 74–88

Scholtyseck, Joachim, 'The United States, Europe, and the Dual Track Decision', in Mathias Schulz and Thomas A. Schwartz, eds, *The Strained Alliance: U.S.–European Relations from Nixon to Carter* (New York, 2010), 101–23

Schulz, Matthias, 'Review of "The Atlantic Community Unravelling? States, Protest Movements, and the Transformation of US–European Relations, 1969–1983"', *H-Soz-u-Kult, H-Net Reviews*, November 2004 <http://www.h-net.org/reviews/showrev.php?id=28225>

Schulz, Matthias, 'Vom "Atlantiker" zum "Europäer"? Helmut Schmidt, deutsche Interessen und die europäische Einigung', in Mareike König and Matthias Schulz, eds, *Die Bundesrepublik Deutschland und die europäische Einigung 1949–2000: Politische Akteure, gesellschaftliche Kräfte und internationale Erfahrungen* (Stuttgart, 2004), 185–220

Soell, Hartmut, 'Zwischen reaktivem und konzeptionellem Handeln', in Konrad H. Jarausch, ed., *Das Ende der Zuversicht? Die siebziger Jahre als Geschichte* (Göttingen, 2008), 279–95

Soutou, Georges-Henri, 'The Linkage between European Integration and Détente: The Contrasting Approaches of de Gaulle and Pompidou, 1965 to 1974', in N. Piers Ludlow, ed., *European Integration and the Cold War: Ostpolitik–Westpolitik, 1965–1973* (Abingdon, 2007), 11–36

Soutou, Georges-Henri, 'Mitläufer der Allianz? Frankreich und der NATO-Doppelbeschluss', in Philipp Gassert et al., eds, *Zweiter Kalter Krieg und Friedensbewegung: Der NATO-Doppelbeschluss in deutsch-deutscher und internationaler Perspektive* (Munich, 2011), 363–76

Spohr, Kristina, 'Germany and the Politics of the Neutron Bomb, 1975–1979', *Diplomacy & Statecraft* 21, no. 2 (2010), 259–85

Spohr, Kristina, 'Conflict and Cooperation in Intra-Alliance Nuclear Politics: Western Europe, the United States, and the Genesis of NATO's Dual-Track Decision, 1977–1979', *Journal of Cold War Studies* 13, no. 2 (2011), 39–89

Spohr, Kristina, 'Helmut Schmidt and the Shaping of Western Security in the Late 1970s: The Guadeloupe Summit of 1979', *The International History Review* 37, no. 1 (2015), 167–92

Suri, Jeremi 'Henry Kissinger and the Geopolitics of Globalization', in Niall Ferguson et al., eds, *The Shock of the Global: The 1970s in Perspective* (Cambridge, MA, 2010), 173–88

Thiemeyer, Guido, 'Helmut Schmidt und die Gründung des Europäischen Währungssystems 1973–1979', in Franz Knipping and Matthias Schönwald, eds, *Aufbruch zum Europa der zweiten Generation: Die europäische Einigung 1969–1984* (Trier, 2004), 245–68

Treverton, Gregory F., 'Nuclear Weapons and the "Gray Area"', *Foreign Affairs* 57, no. 5 (Summer 1979), 1075–89

van Dijk, Ruud, '"A Mass Psychosis": The Netherlands and NATO's Dual-Track Decision, 1978–1979', *Cold War History* 12, no. 3 (2012), 381–405

Weinachter, Michèle, 'Le tandem Valéry Giscard d'Estaing–Helmut Schmidt et la gouvernance européenne', in Wilfried Loth, ed., *La gouvernance supranationale dans la construction européenne* (Bruxelles, 2005), 205–38

Weinachter, Michèle, 'Franco-German Relations in the Giscard–Schmidt Era, 1974–81', in Carine Germond and Henning Türk, *A History of Franco-German Relations in Europe: From 'Hereditary Enemies' to Partners* (Basingstoke, 2008), 223–33

Wettig, Gerhard, 'Die Sowjetunion in der Auseinandersetzung über den NATO-Doppelbeschluss 1979–1983', *Vierteljahrshefte für Zeitgeschichte* 57, no. 2 (April 2009), 217–59

Wettig, Gerhard, 'Entspannung: Sicherheit und Ideologie in der sowjetischen Politik 1969 bis 1979–Zur Vorgeschichte des NATO-Doppelbeschlusses', *Militärgeschichtliche Zeitschrift* 68, no. 1 (2009), 75–116

Wettig, Gerhard, 'Sowjetische Euroraketenrüstung und Auseinandersetzung mit den Reaktionen des Westens: Motivationen und Entscheidungen', in Philipp Gassert et al., eds, *Zweiter Kalter Krieg und Friedensbewegung: Der NATO-Doppelbeschluss in deutsch-deutscher und internationaler Perspektive* (Munich, 2011), 49–64

Young, John W., 'Western Europe and the end of the Cold War, 1979–1989', in Melvyn P. Leffler and Odd Arne Westad, eds, *The Cambridge History of the Cold War, Vol. III: Endings* (Cambridge, 2010), 289–310

Zubok, Vladislav M., 'Soviet Foreign Policy from Détente to Gorbachev, 1975–1985', in Melvyn P. Leffler and Odd Arne Westad, eds, *The Cambridge History of the Cold War, Vol. III: Endings* (Cambridge 2010), 89–111

Index